# Industrial Digital Transformation

Accelerate digital transformation with business optimization, AI, and Industry 4.0

**Shyam Varan Nath**

**Ann Dunkin**

**Mahesh Chowdhary**

**Nital Patel**

BIRMINGHAM—MUMBAI

*"The most comprehensive and insightful book on industrial digital transformation. A decade of real-world experience to help guide the C-suite to compete in a changing world."*

– William Ruh, CEO, LendLease Digital

*"In the 21st century, new technology emerges at an ever-faster pace and government agencies struggle to keep up. In Industrial Digital Transformation, Ann Dunkin, Shyam Varan Nath, Mahesh Chowdhary, and Nital Patel describe this struggle and show the reader how to put the pedal to the metal and begin to catch up."*

– Rob Klopp, Former CIO, US Social Security Administration

*"There's a reason digital transformation is an industrial trend today; it's not just a buzzword phrase! Companies that do not consider how digital technology can streamline their processes are at a significant productivity disadvantage. This book explains why and outlines how to get there."*

– Dr. Richard Soley, Chairman and CEO of OMG®, Executive Director Industrial Internet Consortium (IIC), Digital Twin Consortium (DTC), and Cloud Standards Customer Council

*"The industrial digital transformation journey cannot be just a set of trials and errors. This book is a must-read for business and technology leaders trying to get their company ahead of the game in the industry. The authors have shared their own lessons on industrial transformation in an easy-to-follow way."*

– Dr. Ashutosh Misra, Chief Technology Officer – Electronics; Senior Fellow, Air Liquide

*"Industrial Digital Transformation is written by authors who are experts in their respective fields. They bring years of experience and have provided a lesson in the history and current status of cutting-edge technologies that the reader can use as a guide on their own journey. I highly recommend this book to anyone interested in learning about the risks and benefits of digital transformation and how the latest research in big data and machine learning can be beneficially leveraged."*

– Dr Diego Klabjan, Northwestern University; Professor, Industrial Engineering and Management Sciences; Director, Master of Science in Analytics; Director, Center for Deep Learning

*"Industrial Digital Transformation is an excellent read. Not only does it provide a good overview of important developments that are making a difference, but it also deep-dives into topics that add business value. It broadened my field of view to help me appreciate the essential adjacencies one needs to be concerned about."*

– Devadas Pillai, Intel Senior Fellow, Logic Technology Development, Intel Corporation

*"Industrial Digital Transformation is a must-read book for any business and technology professional leading their company toward digital transformation".*

– Diwakar Kasibhotla, VP Engineering, GE Digital

*"You can't afford an expensive failure in your industrial digital transformation. This book captures the essence of lessons learned from the transformation journey globally."*

– Sabina Zafar, Architecture Leader at GE Digital, Grid Software Solutions and Vice-Mayor at the City of San Ramon

*"A must-read book describing emerging technologies in digital transformation that connect the dots between AI, ML, and automation."*

– Dr Jessica Lin, Associate Professor, George Mason University

"Discussions about the topic of digital transformation are very popular these days among business leaders, technologists, technology vendors, and related services companies. This book focuses on providing a grounding in the history, technologies used, cultural shifts needed, and economic impact of such projects. If you are new to this topic in an industrial setting, you will find value in this book."

– Robert Stackowiak, Independent Consultant, Instructor, and Author, Coauthor of the Book Architecting the Industrial Internet.

"Industrial Digital Transformation isn't a competitive advantage; it's a way of life and it's critical to survival. The authors provide a common-sense approach to start the journey of digital transformation. The authors provide both fundamental and nuanced guidance in the practical pursuit of industrial digital transformation."

– Jim Kohli, DTM Principal Cybersecurity Architect at GE Healthcare and Past International Director at Toastmasters International

"Shyam has a wealth of knowledge on the digital transformation space. We are lucky he and the coauthors are sharing their knowledge with us."

– Bett Bollhoefer, Instagram, Technical Product Manager, and Author

"Industrial digital transformation is the next wave of the technological revolution that will dramatically transform manufacturing, energy, healthcare, transportation, and other industrial sectors. This transformation will require new technologies that will connect data centers, industrial control systems, industrial machines, and humans. The connectivity and interoperability of heterogeneous systems are the foundations of industrial digital transformation and major prerequisites to realize its full potential. It will be critical to build systems that can automate data collection, cleansing, and aggregation."

– Dr. Alisher Maksumov, VP Engineering and Architecture, Hitachi Vantara

# Industrial Digital Transformation

Copyright © 2020 Packt Publishing

All rights reserved. No part of this book may be reproduced, stored in a retrieval system, or transmitted in any form or by any means, without the prior written permission of the publisher, except in the case of brief quotations embedded in critical articles or reviews.

Every effort has been made in the preparation of this book to ensure the accuracy of the information presented. However, the information contained in this book is sold without warranty, either express or implied. Neither the author, nor Packt Publishing or its dealers and distributors, will be held liable for any damages caused or alleged to have been caused directly or indirectly by this book.

Packt Publishing has endeavored to provide trademark information about all of the companies and products mentioned in this book by the appropriate use of capitals. However, Packt Publishing cannot guarantee the accuracy of this information.

**Commissioning Editor**: Vijin Boricha

**Acquisition Editor**: Preet Ahuja

**Senior Editor**: Rahul Dsouza

**Content Development Editor**: Nihar Kapadia

**Technical Editor**: Sarvesh Jaywant

**Copy Editor**: Safis Editing

**Project Coordinator**: Neil D'mello

**Proofreader**: Safis Editing

**Indexer**: Rekha Nair

**Production Designer**: Prashant Ghare

First published: November 2020

Production reference: 1271020

Published by Packt Publishing Ltd.

Livery Place

35 Livery Street

Birmingham

B3 2PB, UK.

ISBN 978-1-80020-767-7

www.packt.com

Packt.com

Subscribe to our online digital library for full access to over 7,000 books and videos, as well as industry leading tools to help you plan your personal development and advance your career. For more information, please visit our website.

## Why subscribe?

- Spend less time learning and more time coding with practical eBooks and Videos from over 4,000 industry professionals

- Improve your learning with Skill Plans built especially for you

- Get a free eBook or video every month

- Fully searchable for easy access to vital information

- Copy and paste, print, and bookmark content

Did you know that Packt offers eBook versions of every book published, with PDF and ePub files available? You can upgrade to the eBook version at packt.com and as a print book customer, you are entitled to a discount on the eBook copy. Get in touch with us at customercare@packtpub.com for more details.

At www.packt.com, you can also read a collection of free technical articles, sign up for a range of free newsletters, and receive exclusive discounts and offers on Packt books and eBooks.

# Contributors

## About the authors

**Shyam Varan Nath** is the author of a book on the **Industrial Internet of Things** (**IIoT**) titled *Architecting the Industrial Internet*. Shyam has worked for large companies, including Oracle, GE, IBM, Deloitte, and Halliburton. His areas of expertise include IIoT, cloud computing, AI/ML, and databases. He has worked on driving digital transformation at several large companies. Shyam has also earned **Distinguished Toastmaster** (**DTM**) status with Toastmasters International. He has an undergraduate degree from IIT Kanpur, India, and an MS (Computer Science) and an MBA from FAU, Boca Raton, FL. Shyam is part of the Program Committee of IoTSWC. He is active on Twitter at @ShyamVaran. You can contact Shyam at shyamvaran@gmail.com

> *I would like to thank my professional colleagues at Oracle and GE, as well as others who I interact with regularly in the industry. I would like to acknowledge the key experiences acquired through my participation at the* **Industrial Internet Consortium** *(IIC) and as a result of attending the IoTSWC events in Barcelona over the years. Finally, a big thanks to my co-authors of this book.*

**Ann Dunkin**, P.E., is Chief Strategy and Innovation Officer at Dell Technologies. She has over a decade of experience as a **Chief Information Officer** (**CIO**), including as CIO of the US EPA in the Obama Administration. She has led digital transformations in large organizations and has written and spoken extensively on the topics of technology modernization, organizational transformation, and digital services. She serves on several non-profit and for-profit boards and has received numerous awards for her contributions to government digital transformation. She holds a Master of Science and a Bachelor of Industrial Engineering degree, both from the Georgia Institute of Technology. She is a licensed professional engineer in the states of California and Washington. You can contact Ann at ann.dunkin@gmail.com

*A big thank you to the IT teams I led at the US EPA, Santa Clara County, Palo Alto Unified School District, and Hewlett-Packard. I learned everything I know about technology leadership and digital transformation from the people I've worked with. Thank you to all my co-authors, especially Shyam, who invited me to collaborate. And thanks to Kathleen, who always believed in me.*

**Mahesh Chowdhary**, Ph.D., is a Fellow and the Director of Strategic Platforms and the IoT Excellence Center at STMicroelectronics, based in Santa Clara, CA. He leads the effort on the development of solutions and reference designs for mobile phones, consumer electronic devices, automotive and industrial applications that utilize MEMS sensors, and computing and connectivity products. His areas of expertise include AI/ML, MEMS sensors, IoT, digital transformation, and location technologies. He has been awarded 24 patents. He has spoken extensively internationally about ML, smart sensors, and IoT. Mahesh received his Ph.D. in applied science (particle accelerators) from the College of William and Mary in Virginia. He is also an adjunct professor at IIT, Delhi. You can contact Mahesh at mahesh.chowdhary@st.com

*I would like to thank my management at STMicroelectronics, along with the customers, professional colleagues, faculty, and students at universities from whom I have gained a lot of insight into IoT and digital transformation. I would also like to thank my co-authors. It was a pleasure working with them to develop our ideas on digital transformation into a book.*

**Nital Patel**, Ph.D., is a Principal Engineer responsible for advanced manufacturing systems research and development at Intel Corporation. He has spent his career contributing to digital transformation activities and projects across the manufacturing spectrum, as well as in the sphere of enabling agility in the enterprise supply chain by leveraging data fusion, ML, and AI. He is the lead inventor on 11 patents, has published over 50 papers, and serves on the editorial board of the peer-reviewed academic journal, *IEEE Transactions on Semiconductor Manufacturing*. He was an adjunct professor at Arizona State University and has been awarded the Mahboob Khan Award from the Semiconductor Research Corporation for mentoring Ph.D. student research. You can contact Nital at nital.s.patel@intel.com

*I would like to thank my colleagues and management at Intel Corporation for encouraging informed risk-taking on our digitization and smart manufacturing journey. With many ups and downs, it has been an incredible ride. Lastly, a special thanks to my co-authors for the effort and dedication they applied to put this book together.*

# About the reviewers

**Dr. Hakim Laghmouchi** is a senior expert in Industry 4.0 with over 13 years of experience in information technology and smart products. His domain expertise lies mainly in process, condition, and production systems monitoring, data analytics, and Industry 4.0 applications. He worked for over 7 years at the Fraunhofer Institute for Production Systems and Design Technology (IPK), a leading Industry 4.0 application-oriented institute in Germany, before moving to Accenture Industry X.0. He holds a Diploma (*dipl.- ing.*) and Ph.D. (*dr.-ing.*) in computational engineering sciences from the Technical University Berlin and an MA in sustainability and quality management from Berlin School of Economics and Law.

> *I would like to thank Packt Publishing for the opportunity to review this wonderful book. Moreover, I would also like to thank my parents, siblings, relatives, and friends for their continued support and encouragement for everything that I do.*

**Bill Maile** served for sixteen years in the executive and legislative branches of the California State Government, including the Governor's Office, Attorney General's Office, the California Senate, and the California Technology Agency. While serving in Governor Schwarzenegger's Administration, he was part of an executive team that established the Office of the State Chief Information Officer, a statewide office created in 2006 to oversee major IT projects and set state technology policy across more than 130 departments. He also spent five years as the editor of Techwire, a technology trade magazine he founded in 2011. Currently, Bill runs a boutique media firm, Maile Media, that specializes in government technology communications.

**Gopa Periyadan**, an engineer/MBA turned entrepreneur with decades of experience, was co-founder of Mobiveil Inc. (and is currently its COO) and GDA Technologies Inc (serving as the VP of Business development for Product Engineering Business Unit). GDA was later acquired by L&T Intech. Prior to GDA, Gopa worked at OPTi, the leading PC chipset provider at that time, and also with VeriFone, working on the I/O subsystems of the Gemstone series of electronic cash registers. He started his career as a hardware engineer with HCL Ltd., in India, driving the implementation of high-performance SCSI I/O subsystems in multiprocessor systems. Gopa also serves on the Board of Albeado Inc., and as a member of the advisory board of nCorium Inc.

*I strongly believe that maintaining the scientific temper and intellectual curiosity in society is critical to improving living standards, promoting social justice, and reversing climate change to address the many deep issues affecting our planet Earth. Books like this will go a long in promoting that cause by spreading the light of knowledge. I thank the authors of this book, Shyam V. Nath, Ann Dunkin, Mahesh Chowdhary, and Nital Patel, the publishers at Packt, and Neil D'mello, who managed this review process with precision.*

## Packt is searching for authors like you

If you're interested in becoming an author for Packt, please visit `authors.packtpub.com` and apply today. We have worked with thousands of developers and tech professionals, just like you, to help them share their insight with the global tech community. You can make a general application, apply for a specific hot topic that we are recruiting an author for, or submit your own idea.

# Table of Contents

## Preface

## Section 1: The "Why" of Digital Transformation

# 1
## Introducing Digital Transformation

| | |
|---|---|
| Exploring industrial digital transformation | 16 |
| Identifying the business drivers for industrial digital transformation | 18 |
| Business drivers in the commercial sector | 19 |
| Business drivers in the public sector | 21 |
| Technology drivers for transformation | 24 |
| The evolution of industrial transformation | 30 |
| What do crises teach us in terms of transformation opportunities? | 32 |
| The first industrial revolution | 36 |
| The second industrial revolution | 39 |
| The third industrial revolution | 40 |
| The fourth industrial revolution – Industry 4.0 | 40 |
| The impact of industrial digital transformation on business | 42 |
| Quantifying business outcomes and shareholder value | 44 |
| New digital revenues | 44 |
| Productivity gains | 45 |
| Social responsibility | 45 |
| The phases of the digital transformation journey | 45 |
| Summary | 49 |
| Questions | 49 |

# 2
## Transforming the Culture in an Organization

| | |
|---|---|
| Technical requirements | 52 |
| Cultural pre-requisites of digital transformation | 52 |
| The concept of agile development as a | |

foundation for digital transformation 53
Lean Startup 57
Beyond agile development and Lean Startup 59
Disruptive innovation 65
Design thinking 66
Digital transformation is a team sport 71

## The emergence of the CDO and the digital competency 72

The rise of the CDO 72
CIO versus CDO – roles and responsibilities 73
The CDO role in the public sector 75
The CIO as the leader of the digital transformation 75
Independent digital services office 76
Chief innovation officer 76

## Reorganization versus strategic transformation 76

Top-down versus bottom-up digital transformation 77
Sustaining the transformation 78
Digital talent 78
Sustaining digital transformation 81
Introducing reverse-mentoring programs 81

## Skills and capabilities for digital transformation 82

Leadership principles for digital transformation 83
Soft skills for delivering digital transformation 85
Technical skills for delivering digital transformation 89

Summary 91
Questions 91
Further reading 92

# 3
# Emerging Technologies to Accelerate Digital Transformation

## The need for new digital capabilities 94

Digital transformation in manufacturing 95
Digital transformation in consumer products 95
Digital transformation in the public sector 96
Identifying emerging technologies 97

## Industry landscape of the emerging technologies 98

Internet of Things 98
AI 109
Big data 111
Robotics 112
AR and VR landscape 116

3D printing 118
Digital twins 119
Different types of maintenance 120
The digital thread and the supply chain 122
Digital platforms 123

## Transformation case studies from consumer industries 125

Peloton 126
Ridesharing 127
Nest 129

Summary 130
Questions 131

# 4
## Business Drivers for Industrial Digital Transformation

| | |
|---|---|
| **Business process** | **134** |
| Transformation by business process improvement | 135 |
| Data-driven process improvement | 137 |
| **Business model** | **141** |
| Reinventing the business model | 145 |
| To cannibalize or not to cannibalize | 148 |
| **The state of the industrial sector** | **154** |
| Oil and gas industry | 155 |
| Semiconductor industry | 156 |
| **Major challenges in industrial companies** | **157** |
| Lack of expertise | 157 |
| Funding | 157 |
| Legacy business model | 157 |
| Organizational structure | 158 |
| Lack of an overall digitization strategy | 158 |
| Employee pushback | 158 |
| Outdated processes | 159 |
| Lack of automation | 159 |
| **Overcoming the challenges** | **160** |
| Business model change by Tesla | 160 |
| Overcoming challenges using digital technology | 161 |
| Overcoming challenges by partnership | 162 |
| **Summary** | **164** |
| **Questions** | **165** |

# Section 2:
# The "How" of Digital Transformation

# 5
## Transforming One Industry at a Time

| | |
|---|---|
| **Transforming the chemical industry** | **170** |
| Digitization of process control | 170 |
| Digitization for inspection and maintenance | 173 |
| Monitoring for demand predictability and optimized delivery | 175 |
| **Transforming the semiconductor industry** | **177** |
| Digitization and lights-out manufacturing | 178 |
| Digitization for process monitoring and control | 183 |
| Big data and digitization for yield management | 192 |
| **Disrupting industrial manufacturing** | **198** |
| Flexible manufacturing | 198 |
| Design prototyping of mechanical parts | 200 |
| Techniques for preventing downtime | 201 |
| Value beyond the product | 202 |

## Transforming buildings and complexes — 205
Facility monitoring — 205
Smart buildings — 206

## Transforming the manufacturing ecosystem — 207
Concerns in supply chain management — 207
Role of digitization — 208

## Promoting industrial worker safety — 210

## Summary — 215

## Questions — 216

# 6
# Transforming the Public Sector

## Unique challenges of industrial digital transformation in the public sector — 218
Access to new technology — 218
Government culture — 222
Hiring challenges – process and pay and skill gaps — 225
Budgets and technical debt — 228
The digital divide — 229

## Transforming the citizen experience — 230
The role of government services — 231
What citizens expect from the government today — 231
Transformation across the government — 231
Smart cities – Lake Nona, Florida — 252

## Transformation on a national and global scale — 255
Airports as the first line of health defense — 256
Digital India — 258

## Summary — 263
## Questions — 264

# 7
# The Transformation Ecosystem

## Moving the needle in industrial digital transformation projects — 266
Shipping industry — 267
Farm to folk — 268
Autonomous vehicles — 269

## Partnerships for transformation — 270
What are public-private partnerships? — 271
Partner programs — 277
Consortiums — 279

## Partnerships and alliances in digital transformation — 283
International Electrotechnical Commission — 283
Jedec — 284
SEMI — 284
Edge AI and Vision Alliance — 285

## Semiconductor company ecosystems — 285
STMicroelectronics ecosystem — 286

| Nucleo ecosystem | 287 | Summary | 291 |
| STM32Cube ecosystem | 288 | Questions | 291 |
| Partner programs | 289 | | |

# 8
# Artificial Intelligence in Digital Transformation

| The difference between AI, machine learning, and deep learning | 294 | AI for the dynamic optimization of warehouse operations | 307 |
| --- | --- | --- | --- |
| Artificial intelligence | 294 | Monetization of data assets for high-value business scenarios | 308 |
| Machine learning | 294 | ML at the edge | 310 |
| Deep learning | 294 | AI in the public sector | 314 |
| Choices in ML algorithms | 295 | **Organizational change influenced by AI** | **318** |
| **Applications of AI in industry** | **300** | | |
| AI in factories | 300 | Security considerations for industrial digital transformation | 322 |
| AI for predictive maintenance | 300 | The rise of DevSecOps | 323 |
| AI in quality assurance and inspection | 303 | AI for cybersecurity | 325 |
| AI in image recognition for quality of inspection | 304 | **Summary** | **326** |
| AI in medical domain image recognition | 305 | **Questions** | **326** |

# 9
# Pitfalls to Avoid in the Digital Transformation Journey

| Indicators of failure | 328 | Three causes of failure | 339 |
| --- | --- | --- | --- |
| Lack of an industrial digital transformation strategy | 328 | Cybersecurity challenges | 348 |
| Other indicators | 329 | **Summary** | **349** |
| Digital transformation failures | 331 | **Questions** | **349** |
| **Failed transformations** | **336** | | |
| Public sector failures | 336 | | |
| Private sector failures | 339 | | |

# 10
# Measuring the Value of Transformation

| | | | |
|---|---|---|---|
| Developing the business case for transformation | 352 | Digital revenue | 361 |
| Defining the problem | 353 | Electricity value chain | 361 |
| Defining the expected benefits | 355 | Digital airports | 363 |
| Estimating the cost of the project | 355 | Airbnb Experiences | 364 |
| Identifying and assessing risks | 356 | **Social good** | **365** |
| Recommending a solution | 356 | The United Nations | 366 |
| Describing the implementation approach | 357 | Kenya | 366 |
| Calculating the ROI | 357 | Microsoft – technology for social impact | 367 |
| | | COVID-19 response | 368 |
| **Productivity and efficiency gains** | **358** | **Summary** | **369** |
| The airline industry | 358 | **Questions** | **369** |

# 11
# The Blueprint for Success

| | | | |
|---|---|---|---|
| How to ensure success in digital transformation | 372 | Business model canvas | 380 |
| Know what you are trying to accomplish | 372 | Digital transformations to embrace new opportunities | 381 |
| Complete the right proof of concept | 373 | Innovation model applied to the public sector | 383 |
| Obtain organizational support and resources | 373 | Moonshot digital transformations | 385 |
| Select initial teams and projects wisely | 373 | Exploratory (moonshot) project template | 385 |
| Align your culture and hone your team's skills | 374 | Innovation process steps for a moonshot project | 388 |
| Do what you said you would | 374 | Some lessons from X Development for moonshot projects | 390 |
| Measure your progress | 375 | | |
| Scale cautiously | 375 | | |
| **The transformation playbook** | **375** | **Sustaining the pace of transformation** | **391** |
| Transforming products and processes using existing technologies | 376 | Delivery of a single product or process | 391 |

| | | | |
|---|---|---|---|
| Creation of a digital center of excellence | 391 | Summary | 398 |
| Transformation of the entire enterprise | 392 | Questions | 398 |
| Digital transformation at home | 395 | | |

## Other Books You May Enjoy

## Index

# Preface

Industrial digital transformation requires both an understanding of opportunities and the ability to identify and apply the right business model, technology, and organizational and cultural changes to be able to benefit from that opportunity. This book will help readers understand all these aspects of the transformation process. This book provides a rich set of industry use cases and case studies, as well as processes and methodologies that business and technology professionals can easily relate to and apply in their own settings. This book is a comprehensive resource that delivers all this relevant information in one place. This book provides a way for business and IT leaders in industry to share a common language with the mid-career professionals who are crucial to any transformation journey.

## Who this book is for

The audience for this book will be a mix of IT leaders, **line of business** (**LOB**) leaders looking for digital transformation opportunities within their organizations, and professional services and management consulting professionals. Mid-career-level IT and LOB professionals will use this book to find transformation approaches that can be applied to a variety of sectors including industrial manufacturing, the automotive sector, distribution, and government.

## What this book covers

*Chapter 1*, *Introducing Digital Transformation*, describes the concept of industrial digital transformation across different industry sectors and explains the importance of transformation to different internal and external stakeholders. It will help develop the reader's understanding of the economic and productivity gains that can be achieved through digital transformation.

*Chapter 2*, *Transforming the Culture in an Organization*, covers the importance of the *culture of change* as a company positions itself organizationally for the transformation.

*Chapter 3*, *Emerging Technologies to Accelerate Digital Transformation*, explains the current and emerging digital technologies that facilitate and accelerate industrial digital transformation.

*Chapter 4*, *Business Drivers for Industrial Digital Transformation*, describes the changes to business processes and business models that are required for a successful digital transformation, as well as the right set of digital technologies.

*Chapter 5*, *Transforming One Industry at a Time*, looks at a selection of industrial digital transformation case studies, including the chemical, semiconductor, manufacturing, and construction industries.

*Chapter 6*, *Transforming the Public Sector*, examines case studies from different levels of the public sector, including federal, state, and local governments. These transformation scenarios are rarely driven by profitability but instead focus on the citizen experience and social good.

*Chapter 7*, *The Transformation Ecosystem*, describes the complete ecosystem that is needed to make a large-scale impact on an entire industry or sector.

*Chapter 8*, *Artificial Intelligence in Digital Transformation*, considers the different paradigms of learning, including artificial intelligence, machine learning, and deep learning, and how these are being applied to accelerate the process of digital transformation.

*Chapter 9*, *Pitfalls to Avoid in the Digital Transformation Journey*, describes how digital transformation projects can go wrong, and how a lack of transformation may impact the long-term success of an enterprise. The chapter will help readers learn how to avoid such shortcomings.

*Chapter 10*, *Measuring the Value of Transformation*, showcases how to develop a business case, quantify the business outcomes, and develop the ROI of a transformation initiative.

*Chapter 11*, *The Blueprint for Success*, teaches the reader how to ensure the success of their digital transformation project and sustain it in the long term. This chapter provides tools and templates for developing detailed plans for transformation in different settings.

# To get the most out of this book

Readers will get the most out of this book if they start identifying opportunities for digital transformation in their own work or other settings where they can be a change agent. As they read the book, they will be able to apply the principles and technologies discussed within to create their own blueprints for transformation. The industry case studies will help them refine their blueprints and their overall approach to transforming their own organizations.

## Download the example code files

The supplementary material for the book is also hosted on GitHub at `https://github.com/PacktPublishing/Industrial-Digital-Transformation`. Relevant content will be updated on the existing GitHub repository.

We also have other code bundles from our rich catalog of books and videos available at `https://github.com/PacktPublishing/`. Check them out!

## Download the color images

We also provide a PDF file that has color images of the screenshots/diagrams used in this book. You can download it here: `http://www.packtpub.com/sites/default/files/downloads/9781800207677_ColorImages.pdf`.

## Conventions used

The following text convention is used throughout this book:

> **Tips or important notes**
> Appear like this.

## Get in touch

Feedback from our readers is always welcome.

**General feedback**: If you have questions about any aspect of this book, mention the book title in the subject of your message and email us at `customercare@packtpub.com`.

**Errata**: Although we have taken every care to ensure the accuracy of our content, mistakes do happen. If you have found a mistake in this book, we would be grateful if you would report this to us. Please visit `www.packtpub.com/support/errata`, selecting your book, clicking on the Errata Submission Form link, and entering the details.

**Piracy**: If you come across any illegal copies of our works in any form on the Internet, we would be grateful if you would provide us with the location address or website name. Please contact us at `copyright@packt.com` with a link to the material.

**If you are interested in becoming an author**: If there is a topic that you have expertise in and you are interested in either writing or contributing to a book, please visit `authors.packtpub.com`.

## Reviews

Please leave a review. Once you have read and used this book, why not leave a review on the site that you purchased it from? Potential readers can then see and use your unbiased opinion to make purchase decisions, we at Packt can understand what you think about our products, and our authors can see your feedback on their book. Thank you!

For more information about Packt, please visit `packt.com`.

# Section 1: The "Why" of Digital Transformation

You will learn why digital transformation is an important trend in the industry and why every company needs to understand it.

This part of the book comprises the following chapters:

- *Chapter 1, Introducing Digital Transformation*
- *Chapter 2, Transforming the Culture in an Organization*
- *Chapter 3, Accelerating Digital Transformation with Emerging Technologies*
- *Chapter 4, Industrial Digital Transformation*

# 1
# Introducing Digital Transformation

Industrial digital transformation is the journey that organizations undertake where they integrate business model change, process improvement, and cultural shift, often leveraging a number of digital and emerging technologies. We will refer to industrial digital transformation often in the context of companies from the commercial or public sector that deal with physical assets, factories, and field operations, generally dealing with business-to-business scenarios, and the transformation involves improvements in these products, equipment, and operations. On the other hand, when the transformation involves software or business enhancements for asset-light or pure tertiary services companies, including business-to-consumer scenarios, then we will refer to it as digital transformation. To include both, we will refer to it simply as transformation. Likewise, our use of the term *industrial* includes both the commercial and public sectors, in the same way as industrial revolutions have used this term.

On the one hand, this book will be a guide for business leaders, **Line of Business** (**LoB**) managers, C-suite executives, including the **Chief Information Officer** (**CIO**) and **Chief Technology Officer** (**CTO**), and digital leaders to help identify opportunities for transformation. On the other hand, this book will provide mid-career professionals in **Information Technology** (**IT**) and business with recipes for success in the transformation journey, both in terms of digital technology selection and implementation, to help achieve the associated business outcomes. This book will prepare technology professionals to influence business decision makers toward industrial digital transformation. In this process, mid-career professionals will achieve significant professional advancement.

In this chapter, we'll be exploring the following topics:

- Exploring industrial digital transformation
- Identifying the business drivers for industrial digital transformation
- The evolution of industrial transformation
- The impact of industrial digital transformation on business
- Quantifying business outcomes and shareholder value
- The phases of the digital transformation journey

## Exploring industrial digital transformation

Industrial digital transformation may often bring a radical rethinking to the use of technology, culture, people, and processes in an enterprise. This can lead to a fundamental change in business performance and outcomes, as well as how the customers perceive the company. *Figure 1.1* provides an easy way to look at the transformation. It shows that culture and technology changes go hand in hand with the business process and business model changes. Several books have been written on the broad topic of digital transformation, and some of these will be referenced here. George Westerman and Didier Bonnet wrote a book entitled *Leading Digital: Turning Technology into Business Transformation, George Westerman, Didier Bonnet, Andrew McAfee, Harvard Business Review Press*, published in 2014:

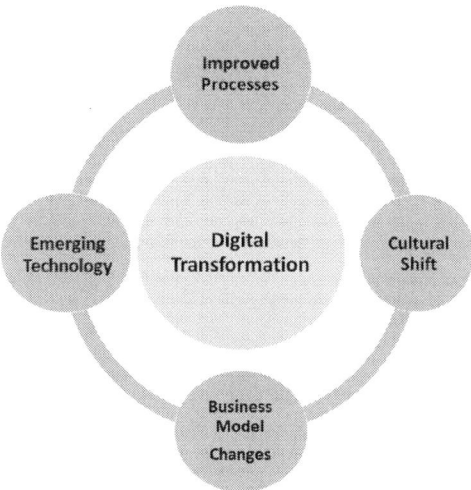

Figure 1.1 – Digital transformation

The technologies used to help drive an industrial digital transformation may include one or more from the **Internet of Things (IoT)**, cloud and edge computing, **Artificial Intelligence (AI)**, big data and analytics, blockchain, robotics, drones, 3D printing, **Augmented Reality (AR)** and **Virtual Reality (VR)**, **Robotic Process Automation (RPA)**, and mobile technologies. New technologies continue to emerge, so this list is not meant to be an exhaustive one. The main goal of these transformations is to gain a competitive advantage, drive new revenues, improve productivity and efficiency, as well as enhance customer and stakeholder engagement. The term *technology*, or *digital technology*, in the context of industrial digital transformation is not limited to software or IT only. It may include physical, chemical, or biological/life sciences-related technologies as well. For example, in the context of autonomous vehicles, it can be **Light Detection and Ranging (LIDAR)** or a more efficient car battery. In an industrial safety context, it can be a sensor or a system for fall detection or a thermal scanning camera for infectious disease detection or prevention. These emerging technologies that often accelerate industrial digital transformation will be covered in detail in *Chapter 3, Emerging Technologies to Accelerate Digital Transformation*.

According to the Customer Insights & Analysis group of the **International Data Corporation (IDC)**, the worldwide investment in industrial digital transformation-related initiatives is expected to exceed $6 trillion over the next 4 years (2020–2024): see (`https://www.businesswire.com/news/home/20190424005113/en/Businesses-Spend-1.2-Trillion-Digital-Transformation-Year`). Smart manufacturing will account for a large part of this spending. Other sectors, such as finance, retail and logistics management, and transportation, will also undergo a large-scale industrial digital transformation.

In April 2020, while delivering the quarterly earnings of Microsoft, their CEO, Satya Nadella, said *We've seen 2 years' worth of digital transformation in 2 months*. Interestingly, this book has been written around the same time frame and has captured many recent transformative initiatives. In the next section, we will learn about the business drivers for industrial digital transformation.

# Identifying the business drivers for industrial digital transformation

The power of transformation applies to some or every aspect of an organization. It can generate business value, agility, and resilience. The importance of resilience is shown at the time of local or global crises. This book will focus on driving transformation in industries – in both commercial and public sectors – to accelerate business outcomes, by deploying the digital technologies in combination with transformative planning and shifts in the culture.

The different forces that help to shape the industrial digital transformation in an organization are shown in *Figure 1.2*. The industrial digital transformation often entails a series of big bets or bold steps, to achieve large-scale benefits or competitive advantage. This differentiates transformation from regular generational changes, which are often linear or a series of small and gradual steps. Humans climbed mountains through the historic ages and eventually climbed Mount Everest. However, the same series of incremental improvements could not land a human on the moon. This is probably an extreme example of scaling *new heights* in the history of humanity. But so is a level 5 autonomous car (see `https://www.nhtsa.gov/technology-innovation/automated-vehicles-safety#topic-road-self-driving`) compared to the first car with an internal combustion engine built in 1885 [Germany Patent DRP No. 37435]:

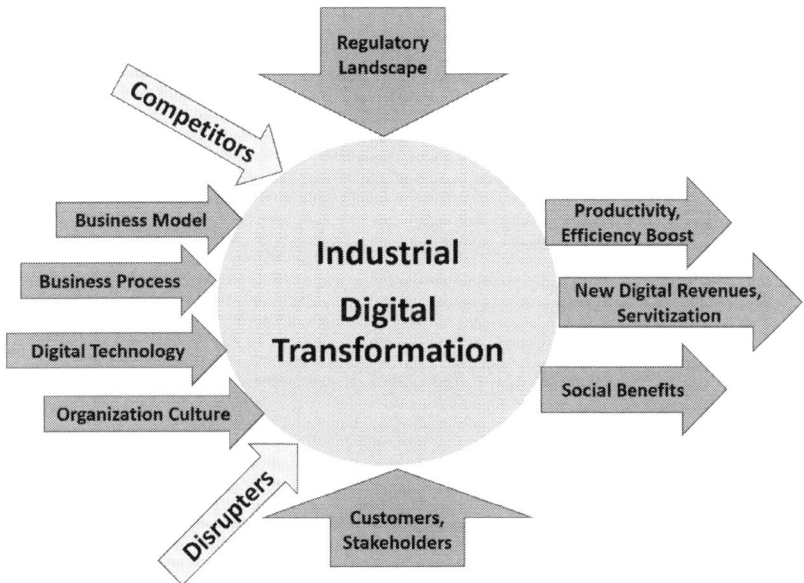

Figure 1.2 – Industrial digital transformation forces

*Figure 1.2* shows the change agents on the left-hand side, such as the business process and model changes, with support from technological and cultural shifts. This is often forced by traditional competitors or disrupters. The regulatory changes and the expectations of the customers as well as the shareholders change over time. Transformation helps to ensure that productivity, profitability, and social responsibility improve and align with the stakeholders.

## Business drivers in the commercial sector

In the commercial sector, often, the need for industrial digital transformation is driven by two kinds of strategy:

- Defensive strategy
- Offensive strategy

The defensive strategy of transformation refers to protecting the business from competitors and disrupters. Most car manufacturers started manufacturing electric vehicles as a defensive strategy. According to Moody's, traditional US car manufacturers lose $7,000 to $10,000 per electric vehicle. The major reason why car manufacturers continue to invest in electric vehicles is that this market is expected to grow by almost 20% in the next decade. With breakthrough innovations expected in battery and related technologies, the cost of production is expected to go down.

While most automobile manufacturers pursued a defensive strategy, Tesla is an example of using an offensive strategy, where it is trying to disrupt the rest of the industry. A large part of both outlook and forecasts in the automobile industry today has been driven by Tesla, which was founded in 2003 and is newer than most US and global auto giants. Today, it reduces some of its losses by charging a price premium by differentiating itself based on becoming a status symbol and offering driver-assisted technologies. Tesla is not a profitable company as of early 2020, but is aggressively reducing losses because of lifestyle status and innovation that enables them to charge a price premium. Tesla is a good example of industrial digital transformation at work in the automotive industry. The Tesla Semi is targeted to disrupt the trucking industry next.

Tesla's approach is to futureproof their cars with the necessary hardware that will make the cars increasingly autonomous in the near future with **Over-the-Air** (**OTA**) updates. This will increase Tesla's market valuation as well as the value of Tesla cars for the current owners. While Tesla, being a newer company, is free of cumbersome legacy processes, there are areas where Tesla can transform internally. The reliability score of Tesla, especially Model X, has been poor, mainly due to challenges in the design of the door. Tesla has the paradox of high emotional attachment as it is a fun car to drive, but has not-so-great quality scores (see `https://www.forbes.com/sites/petercohan/2020/07/25/the-tesla-paradox-highest-emotional-attachment-lowest-quality-says-jd-power/#3bd0e5a97594`).

The transformation at Tesla is effectively implemented across its entire value chain, with the integration of its products, services, and operations. Tesla is an example of a connected car that allows the creation of the digital twin of a car. The digital twin is a virtual representation of a physical object or a system that can be used to improve the performance and efficiency of the physical counterpart. Tesla uses the digital twin of the car to provide new services with OTA updates to the software. We will learn more about the role of the digital twin and the somewhat related concept of the digital thread in *Chapter 3, Emerging Technologies to Accelerate Digital Transformation*. A digital thread is often used in the industrial manufacturing sector to improve the product quality and the throughput across the entire life cycle of the product.

In the next section, we will look at the drivers for transformation in the public sector, where the concept of profitability is often different than in the private sector.

## Business drivers in the public sector

Government Digital Service leaped into public consciousness in 2013 during the implementation of the **Affordable Care Act (ACA)**, also known as Obamacare. For a variety of reasons, the development of the federal healthcare exchange – that is, the frontend websites and the backend databases and processes known as `HealthCare.gov`, started late and development failed miserably. See `https://www.gao.gov/assets/670/668834.pdf`.

**Health and Human Services (HHS)** had used the same process that the government has used for many years to develop and deliver solutions and had achieved roughly the same results that government technology projects had achieved for decades. A team within an agency within HHS developed a set of requirements, published a **Request for Proposal (RFP)**, accepted bids, selected a vendor, and then waited for delivery of a product, which turned out not to meet the requirements, and, in fact, failed to deliver the required capabilities for a successful launch of the new healthcare marketplace.

Faced with the failure of the administration's signature legislation, the Obama administration did something different than past administrations and project leaders: they put out a call to the private sector for help. A group of engineers led by Mikey Dickerson worked around the clock for months to repair and modernize `HealthCare.gov`. In a moment of clarity that comes all too infrequently, members of the team and others within the government recognized that `HealthCare.gov` was but one example of a larger problem with the way that the public sector builds and buys technology solutions. See `https://money.cnn.com/2017/01/17/technology/us-digital-service-mikey-dickerson/index.html`.

Many of the leaders of the `HealthCare.gov` rescue effort, including Dickerson, became the core of the **United States Digital Service (USDS)**, part of the executive office of the president reporting to the then US CTO, Todd Park, the USDS, 18F at GSA, and other digital services teams were created due to a general recognition within the federal government that technology projects took too long, cost too much, failed too often, and, even when considered successful, rarely met the needs of the public that they were designed to serve.

The US government spent close to $75.6 billion on various IT projects in 2014 (see `https://www.brookings.edu/blog/techtank/2015/08/25/doomed-challenges-and-solutions-to-government-it-projects/`) across all federal agencies, including the department of defense, large cabinet-level departments, such as the departments of labor, transportation, and agriculture, medium-sized agencies, such as the environmental protection agency, and small agencies, including the small business administration and the nuclear regulatory commission. In addition, according to the Standish Group, of the over 3,000 IT projects with labor costs that exceeded $10 million that the government executed between 2003 and 2012, only 6.4% of projects were considered successful and over 41% were complete failures – that is, they had to be scrapped and restarted. This problem was not limited to the federal government or the development of new solutions; it plagued state and local governments as well.

Government inefficiencies are often blamed for these failures, but the true cause is both more complex and more understandable. It is simply impossible to specify all the functionality of a large software system and anticipate all the complexities before the development process has begun. Nor is it reasonable to expect that in a time when the technology life cycle is frequently less than 2 years that the technical design and needs of users can be fully specified years in advance. Simply put, it was clear after decades of large-scale failures that the longstanding practice of spending years gathering requirements, months or years selecting a vendor, and then years waiting for a big-bang delivery of a solution that had been developed in seclusion, wasn't working and possibly had never worked.

In addition to the fact that the traditional government project development process didn't deliver consistently working software that met the requirements initially specified by the project team, the traditional model rarely delivered software that met the needs of end users. Government software was frequently developed with a small number of stakeholders in mind. Stakeholders in the government are generally the individuals who sponsor or fund a solution, but they rarely represent the bulk of users of a system. For example, if the design of a new timecard system is stakeholder-centered, it would be designed to streamline the process for the handful of individuals in accounting who manage the back-office processes. In contrast, a user-centered design would focus on the needs of the large majority of users who interact with the system.

Another example of the power of user-centered design is the **US Environmental Protection Agency (EPA)**'s eManifest system. This is a voluntary fee-based system successfully deployed by the EPA in 2018, but it didn't always seem certain that the project would be successful. In 2015, as the project was floundering and under increasing scrutiny, the EPA's new CTO, Greg Godbout, led a relaunch of the program. One of the first things he learned was that the project team had never talked to a single end user. He arranged for the team to go on a listening tour. During this tour, the project team learned that the solution they were proposing to develop wasn't what the users needed. They were trying to solve the wrong problem. Talking to users before writing code allowed the project team to reset early when the costs were low, rather than after the project had been completed when the cost of changing course would have been a complete reboot costing millions of dollars. The key idea of user-centered design means that the transition to digital services moves the government closer to the public, allowing the government to develop solutions that more closely match the needs of its constituents.

As mentioned earlier in this chapter, traditional development processes don't just hamper the delivery of new capabilities to the public; they also put existing service delivery at risk. The COVID-19 crisis has exposed this vulnerability to millions of out-of-work Americans who were unable to file for unemployment benefits in a timely manner as states were unable to scale up the systems that process unemployment claims due to antiquated architectures and reliance on obsolete hardware. During the early days of state lockdowns, individuals attempting to file claims reported system crashes, unavailable websites, and hours-long hold times or busy signals as many state systems required individuals call to complete their claims that had been started online. Many of these systems reside on mainframes and are written in obsolete languages such as **COBOL** and do not follow the best practices used in coding today, as messy *spaghetti* code was written to preserve then-precious processing power and comments were non-existent.

> **Important note**
> The outbreak of COVID-19 tested the limits of many older government IT systems and highlighted the need for modernization of legacy systems. Many of these legacy systems were written in COBOL, a language that hasn't been taught at most universities since the 1970s. You can read about how keeping these systems running has created a need for COBOL programmers, much like the Y2K bug did in the late 1990s: `https://nymag.com/intelligencer/2020/04/what-is-cobol-what-does-it-have-to-do-with-the-coronavirus.html`

In addition to the need to be able to implement technology to support government policy, to deliver new capabilities to the public, and to ensure the reliability of existing services, crises such as 9/11, the COVID-19 pandemic, hurricanes, earthquakes, and wildfires all demonstrate the need for the government to be fast and nimble. COVID-19 required a combination of fixed sensors and contact tracing applications to control the spread. Governments must be able to expand the capabilities of existing systems and deploy new, previously unanticipated solutions in order to respond to crises. Ironically, these same crises demonstrate that the government can be nimble. With a state of emergency declared with the outbreak of COVID-19 and procurement rules suspended, one federal agency hired contractors and redeployed a government loan program application over a weekend, while a state agency engaged a firm to provide call center software, a ticketing system, and agents to augment their unemployment system over another weekend. With a sense of urgency and without the constraints of a highly regimented procurement system, governments can move fast and serve constituents better.

As the case became clear and heroic successes such as `HealthCare.gov` were demonstrated, individuals and teams at all levels of government around the world began to explore institutionalizing digital services across government. In *Chapter 6, Transforming the Public Sector*, we will discuss the government digital services journey in greater detail, how the movement has developed, where it is now, and what's next.

In the next section, we look at how the emerging technologies are becoming an integral part of the transformation journey.

# Technology drivers for transformation

In this book, we will be exposed to a variety of technologies related to such industrial-scale transformation. No specific technology is a solution for all areas of Industry 4.0, but must be paired with an appropriate problem statement, along with an understanding of its limitations. In addition, there are several technologies that are in what may be considered the *hype* phase of their maturity cycle and it remains to be seen whether these will be viable in the future. A practitioner is well-served by taking an objective stance to these technologies versus climbing onto the hype bandwagon.

A specific example relevant today is that of blockchain. Blockchain was conceived as a solution for anonymous, untrusting parties to transact with each other and avoid the double spending problem (see Satoshi Nakamoto, *Bitcoin: A Peer-to-Peer Electronic Cash System*, 2008, available at www.bitcoin.org). Blockchain can be viewed as a solution looking to solve a problem in the industrial setting. In order to be seen as a viable solution, the problem must satisfy the core premise underlying Bitcoin – namely, transactions across anonymous untrusting parties. In addition, a large number of industrial use cases involve rates of transactions that are much more suited to traditional databases versus a distributed ledger. We will cover one viable case where blockchains make sense across the supply chain in later chapters.

*Hype Cycle for Blockchain Technologies* (July 2019) from Gartner shows a 5 to 10-year timeframe before blockchain becomes mainstream and has a transformational impact across the industries (see https://www.gartner.com/en/newsroom/press-releases/2019-09-12-gartner-2019-hype-cycle-for-blockchain-business-shows). We advise that you vet the blockchain application closely to ensure it is the best fit for your unique scenarios. In the hype cycle, from an industrial perspective, most of the top contenders, such as the use of blockchain in transportation and logistics, blockchain in supply chain and smart contracts, and blockchain in insurance, highlight the likelihood of blockchain-led transformation in the supply chain and distribution space within the next decade. However, the use case of a company called Colu based around the digital currencies for cities, to encourage citizens to spend their money locally, has not been as successful as they might have hoped (see https://www.wired.com/story/whats-blockchain-good-for-not-much/ for more details).

Having reviewed one example of an upcoming technology, you should consider other technologies that will be covered later in this book. Some of these are much more mature than blockchain. *Figure 1.3* gives a preview of what will be covered next:

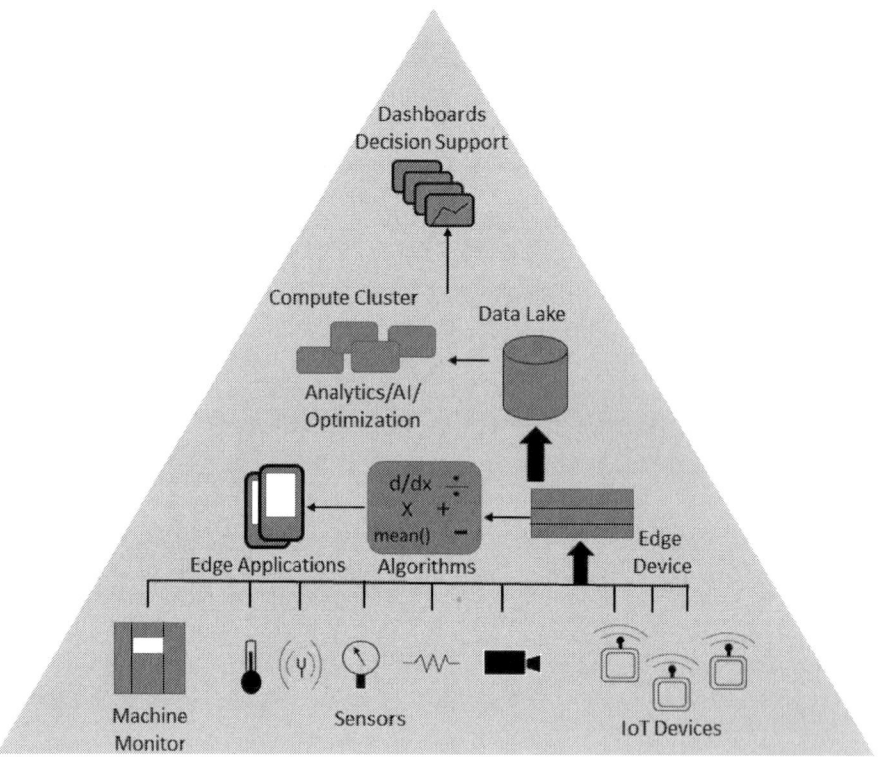

Figure 1.3 – Key technical components for digital transformation. The pyramid denotes distilling information and increasing data intelligence as we move from the bottom toward the top

We will now walk through some of the components illustrated in the diagram:

- **Sensing**: Before we can talk about digitization, it is imperative to ensure that you have a solid foundation for sensing and collecting data across the enterprise. Data collection can scale from sensors in the process flow – potentially augmented by IoT devices at the edge, which collect and aggregate data, to external factors related to logistics and demand sensing. Another aspect of sensing is machine vision systems and their associated algorithms, which analyze the image data via edge computing and send summarized data to the data aggregation systems. Such sensor data has to be analyzed in the broader context of the enterprise data, which may originate in **enterprise resource planning** (**ERP**) and other manufacturing or maintenance systems.

- **Data aggregation**: Rather than keeping this data in silos, we must aggregate it in a common location – which can range from an internal data lake hosted on-premises to **Storage as a Service** (**STaaS**) hosted by an off-premises cloud services provider. Typically, the latter also offers additional services to entice customers to move to their platforms. Data aggregation is critical to enable everyone involved in the enterprise to get a single version of the truth. Connectivity and integration across various segments of the enterprise are key to enable this capability.

- **Analytics**: This comprises a suite of methodologies to operate on the aggregated data.

- **Statistical analysis**: This is fundamental for all smart manufacturing efforts. Initial use cases revolved around **statistical process control** (**SPC**), first proposed by Walter Shewhart in 1924 with the invention of the control chart (see Walter Shewhart, *Economic Control of Quality of Manufactured Product*, American Society for Quality Control, 1931), which found widespread use during World War II – leading to the six sigma methodology. Shewhart greatly influenced W. E. Deming, who created the now-famous funnel experiment resulting in a greater reliance on statistical process control that initially hindered the application of modern control systems methodologies to industrial problems. In 1951, Box and Wilson introduced response surface methodology, which led to the development of the design of experiments. This was the first attempt to systematically develop input-output models of industrial processes in order to drive the process to the optimal operating point. In addition, statistical analysis is widely used in inventory management across the industrial supply chain.

- **AI**: This is a broad field covering traditional rule-based systems, statistical machine learning, and recently deep learning. This topic is covered in a *Chapter 8, Artificial Intelligence in Digital Transformation* and for now, we will refer you to *Figure 1.4*, which shows the relationships between these various methods:

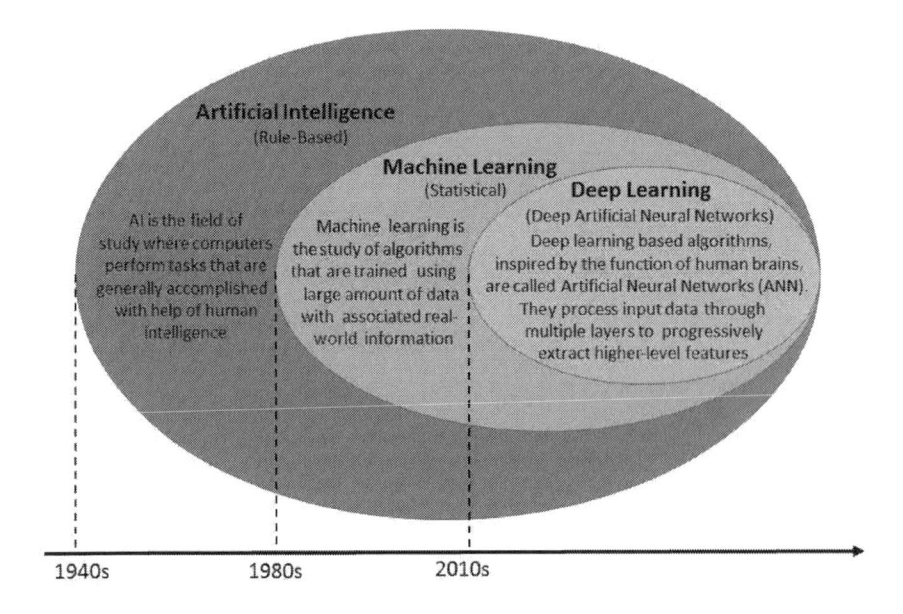

Figure 1.4 – Different fields under AI and the approximate timeframe they gained in popularity

- Some examples of specific techniques that have been popularized across these fields are as follows. **Traditional AI**: rule-based systems and fuzzy logic inferencing (Zadeh, L.A. (1965), *Fuzzy Sets, Information and Control*. 8 (3): 338–353); **Statistical machine learning**: tree-based classifiers, such as random forests (Breiman L (2001), *Random Forests, Machine Learning*, 45 (1): 5–32), and support vector machines (Cortes, C. and Vapnik, V. N. (1995), Support-vector networks, *Machine Learning*. 20 (3): 273–297); **Deep Learning**: convolutional neural networks for image processing (Lecun, Y., Bottou, L., Bengio, Y. and Haffner, P. (1998), *Gradient-based learning applied to document recognition, Proceedings of the IEEE*, 86 (11): 2278-2324); and deep reinforcement learning (Arulkumaran, K., Deisenroth, M. P., Brundage, M. and Bharath, A. A. (2017), *Deep Reinforcement Learning: A Brief Survey, IEEE Signal Processing Magazine*, 34 (6): 26–38).

You must take care to select the correct methodology for the task – as is often the case, the simplest methodology leads to the most robust and sustainable solution. Later chapters in the book will provide some examples of what is applicable in specific scenarios.

- **Optimization and simulation**: Optimization and simulation are critical tools for implementing any kind of decision system. Such systems can function either in an automated mode – for example, scheduling systems – or can be used to guide a human to make decisions by simulating and optimizing various scenarios (that is, the user asks *what if xyz were to occur* and the system will simulate that condition and optimize system performance to give the answer).

- **Visualization and dashboards**: As data moves through the analytic engines, there is still a need to visualize it from time to time. In order for a person to make sense of the data, there is a need for the analytics to distill the raw information across all sources to a few key metrics that will be meaningful to the user.

As AI applications proliferate, the user would need to get less and less involved in mundane decision making and would only need to respond in situations where the autonomous decision system is unable to make a decision or to course correct an erroneous decision. As such, the metrics should reflect not only the overall health of the industrial system (be it a manufacturing plant, or the entire supply chain), but also relevant metrics to track the robustness of the AI models.

You will also hear the term *big data* associated with machine learning. There is definitely an intersection between the two – however, big data focuses more on the data storage infrastructure, the platform for executing analysis of this data in an efficient manner, and computationally scalable algorithms for feature extraction (or dimensionality reduction) in order to make this large volume of data amenable to machine learning algorithms.

One of the most successful big data platforms is Hadoop, with its distributed filesystem and the capability to efficiently implement MapReduce algorithms that provide the highly scalable processing of large volumes of data (see Dean, J. and Ghemawat, S. (2004), *MapReduce: Simplified Data Processing on Large Clusters, Communications of the ACM*, 51(01): 137-150).

While these digital technologies are adopted, it is important to keep the security and safety of people and property in mind. As the physical world gets connected to the network due to IoT, the cybersecurity considerations become of paramount importance. As the digital twins are created and stored, they could be targets of security breaches, to get access to restricted data or operating details that are otherwise not public information. The hijackers for the 9/11 aircraft had reportedly trained on flight simulators and software games (see `https://publicintegrity.org/national-security/authorities-question-criteria-for-access-to-flight-simulators/`). It is important to ensure that the digital twins of power plants or nuclear plants and other critical infrastructure do not fall into the wrong hands. This book will cover the cybersecurity, data security, privacy, and regulatory considerations in *Chapter 8, Artificial Intelligence in Digital Transformation*, and *Chapter 9, Pitfalls to Avoid in the Digital Transformation Journey*.

In the next section, we will learn about the historical evolution of large-scale industrial transformations and how it leads to industrial digital transformation.

# The evolution of industrial transformation

Changes in the global landscape seen during the healthcare and economic crisis in the first half of 2020 due to COVID-19 (`https://www.cdph.ca.gov/Programs/CID/DCDC/Pages/Immunization/ncov2019.aspx`) have highlighted the need to develop a deeper understanding and preparedness for transformation, not only for the government at different levels (federal, state, and local), but the commercial sector as well, across the board, be it a family-run business or a global enterprise. This book will cover some of the major crises the world has experienced in the last several decades and the lessons learned from each of them. This would allow us to see concrete examples where the industry has successfully identified an opportunity for transformation.

Let's look at some examples of past crises and the lessons learned in the following table:

| Serial Number | Crisis | Scope | Time Period | Lesson(s) Learned | Technology Contributing to Transformation |
|---|---|---|---|---|---|
| 1 | COVID-19 pandemic | Global | 2020 (H1) | Remote working capability, the importance of basic industries such as healthcare, retail stores for food and essential supplies, and distribution systems | Cloud computing, Video conferencing, 3D printing, open source and collaborative manufacturing, and contact tracing |
| 2 | Financial crisis | US | 2008–09 | Changes in regulations, Dodd-Frank | Tools for governance, risk management, and compliance (GRC) |
| 3 | September 11 | US | 2001 | Aviation safety | Screening technologies at airports |
| 4 | AIDS, SARS, swine flu, bird flu, and so on | Global | | Healthcare awareness | Thermal cameras and the rapid development of vaccines and new drugs |
| 5 | The Gulf war | Middle-East, Asia | 1991 | Oil crisis | Renewable energy sources to reduce dependency on oil and battery banks to store energy |

| Serial Number | Crisis | Scope | Time Period | Lesson(s) Learned | Technology Contributing to Transformation |
|---|---|---|---|---|---|
| 6 | The Great Depression | US, global | 1929–33 | Preserving food and use of canned food | Mechanization of farming |
| 7 | World war, famine, natural disasters, and so on | Global | 1900s | Alliances between countries are powerful | World War II – mechanized code breaking (essentially the first computers)<br><br>World War I – the beginnings of modern warfare with the use of planes |

Progressive companies take the approach that no crisis should go to waste. As a result, looking at major crises is important to study their impact on the industrial landscape over time. This provides valuable insights into how to identify future opportunities for industrial digital transformation. We will look at several examples of such innovations and transformations.

## What do crises teach us in terms of transformation opportunities?

Let's look at all the innovations seen in the short term due to the COVID-19 crisis. *Figure 1.5* describes the voluntary use of smartphone location technology to track the risk of infecting others. Smartphone data has been utilized to track adherence to social distancing guidelines (see `https://www.washingtonpost.com/technology/2020/03/24/social-distancing-maps-cellphone-location/`):

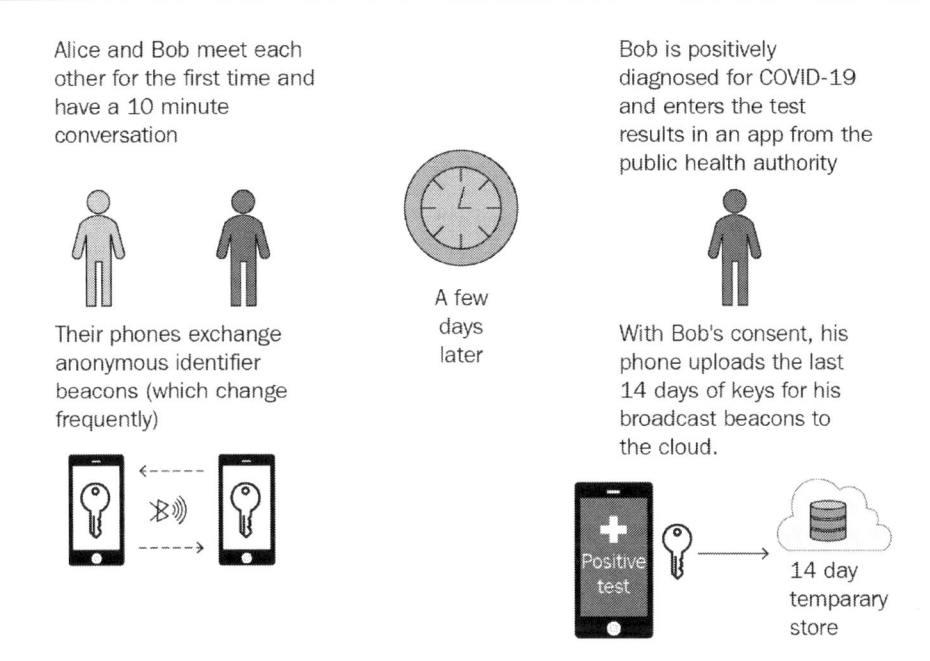

Figure 1.5 – Using smartphones to track the spread of COVID-19

Another is the 3D printing of masks and ventilators to speed up the production of critically required materials and equipment. In the same vein, the medical devices manufacturing company Medtronic and Intel are working together to add IoT features, such as remote management capability for PB980 ventilators (see `http://newsroom.medtronic.com/news-releases/news-release-details/medtronic-provides-ventilator-progress-update`). This allows the clinicians to control and adjust the settings of the ventilator remotely. As a result, they do not have to go to the **Intensive Care Unit (ICU)**, thus staying away from patients. This reduces the healthcare worker and clinician's exposure to patients recovering from COVID-19.

In this context, Medtronic has also open sourced its ventilator design (see `https://www.medtronic.com/us-en/e/open-files.html?cmpid=vanity_url_medtronic_com_openventilator_Corp_US_Covid19_FY20`) to allow others to collaborate and speed up the manufacturing and contribute improvements to this critical device. The use of blockchain technology for tracking the integrity of the ventilators is another such use of emerging technology (see `https://www.industryweek.com/technology-and-iiot/article/21127623/getting-ventilators-to-the-people-is-a-problem-built-for-blockchain`). **General Electric (GE)** healthcare has also deployed IoT-based, remote patient data monitoring technology that allows the clinicians to fight the battle against the critical COVID-19.

This solution would allow the monitoring of critical patients across the health system (see `https://www.businesswire.com/news/home/20200415005370/en/GE-Healthcare-Deploys-Remote-Patient-Data-Monitoring`). These are great examples of industrial digital transformation driven by a crisis, where industrial companies acted fast. However, many of these innovations will continue after the crisis and drive transformations in other areas. Other examples include the use of drones for spraying virus disinfectants and the delivery of medicines to rural areas.

The 9/11 crisis in the US led to several transformations in the aviation industry. Many new technologies emerged to make airports and passenger screening much stricter. The regulatory landscape changed as well. The **Travel Security Administration** (**TSA**) was created in the US on November 19, 2001 (see `https://www.tsa.gov/about/tsa-mission`).

Companies such as Clear started in 2004 and transformed the airport experience for frequent airport passengers by using biometrics for identification. Clear saw this opportunity and was much ahead of the TSA PreCheck system that started in October 2011. These are good examples to show that national and global crises often accelerate emerging technology and create industrial digital transformation opportunities for companies or government agencies that capitalize on them.

Can the proactive readiness of the company avert a crisis or help them overcome the crisis quickly? In recent times, the Boeing 737 MAX aircraft (see `https://boeing.mediaroom.com/2019-04-05-Statement-from-Boeing-CEO-Dennis-Muilenburg-We-Own-Safety-737-MAX-Software-Production-and-Process-Update`) has been a subject of much controversy. This crisis led to the loss of lives in aircraft crashes. Unfortunately, Boeing has also been impacted by the ripple effect of the airlines, which saw over a 90% reduction in travel in the US after the COVID-19 crisis. This book will discuss how large enterprises have to be on the lookout for disruptive forces, whether internal or external to the company. The ability to transform rapidly in light of a crisis or threat of disruption is critical in this age.

Is industrial digital transformation only about survival in the industry? Interestingly, the book titled *Digital Transformation: Survive and Thrive in an Era of Mass Extinction*, *Tom Siebel*, *RosettaBooks*, ties it to the concept of *mass extinction*. We have seen not only civilizations that have perished due to a *crisis*, but also large global companies. One example is Lehman Brothers, which collapsed in 2008 soon after the financial crisis. Can digital transformation help with risk management to prevent the reoccurrence of the fall of large companies? On the other hand, the example of the rise of Netflix and the fall of Blockbuster shows that Netflix disrupted the industry, leveraging the technology of video streaming.

In recent times, many companies have looked for opportunities to disrupt themselves before the competition does. As a result, companies have invested resources to stay ahead of the curve:

- **Need for disruption from within**: Utility companies such as Exelon moving toward renewable sources (solar and wind) is an example of disruption from within. Probably, Intuit is a good example of going digital using cloud technology. They acquired the company Turbo Tax for $7.1 billion, to get a good share of the tax market in the case of individuals as well as the small and medium company sector. Hence, transformation initiatives may include both organic changes as well as **Mergers and Acquisitions (M&As)**.

- **Fear of getting disrupted**: An example is **General Electric (GE)**, where IBM and other technology companies were trying to offer **predictive maintenance** services to industrial customers, such as to goods train operators. GE Transportation sold locomotives to these companies along with the highly profitable service contracts.

We will look at the historical evolution of large-scale transformations. The industrial revolution can be defined as the process of change from the current state of society and economy to the next advanced state, powered by technology. These revolutions have created monumental changes to humans in the last few hundred years. That is why it is important to understand these revolutions, before discussing any kind of transformation going forward. The world changed for the better after each of these revolutions, as we will see in the following sections. There were massive disruptions in each phase. Each phase also introduced some challenges that can be seen as opportunities to solve in the future, such as the high density of populations in cities and additional constraints on natural resources. The four waves are as follows:

- **The first industrial revolution**: The first industrial revolution originated in the 18th century in Britain and then spread to the other parts of the world.

- **The second industrial revolution**: Following the first industrial revolution, almost a century later, the world went through the second industrial revolution.

- **The third industrial revolution**: The third industrial revolution laid the foundation of the internet and many technologies that are mainstream today.

- **The fourth industrial revolution, or Industry 4.0**: The fourth industrial revolution started in the early 2010s and we are still experiencing it, as this book is being written. Industrial digital transformation is one of the biggest opportunities for the 2020s. This book has been written to help companies capitalize on the transformations in their respective industry sectors (see `https://trailhead.salesforce.com/en/content/learn/modules/learn-about-the-fourth-industrial-revolution/meet-the-three-industrial-revolutions`):

```
┌─────────────────────────────────────────────┐
│         Fourth industrial revolution        │
│            Cyber physical systems           │
└─────────────────────────────────────────────┘

┌─────────────────────────────────────────────┐
│         Third industrial revolution         │
│     Electronics and IT systems, automation  │
└─────────────────────────────────────────────┘

┌─────────────────────────────────────────────┐
│         Second industrial revolution        │
│       Mass production and electricity       │
└─────────────────────────────────────────────┘

┌─────────────────────────────────────────────┐
│          First industrial revolution        │
│    Mechanization, steam, and water power    │
└─────────────────────────────────────────────┘
```

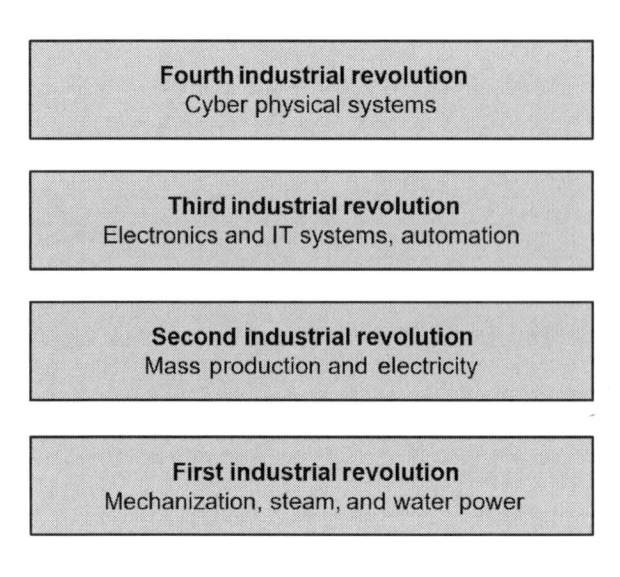

Figure 1.6 – The history of industrial revolutions

*Figure 1.6* represents the history of industrial revolutions. Next, we will look at the details.

## The first industrial revolution

The first industrial revolution had many features – namely, technological, socioeconomic, and cultural. Its origin is tied to the rapid mechanization in the textile industry in Britain at the time (see `https://www.economist.com/leaders/2012/04/21/the-third-industrial-revolution`). The final outcome of this revolution was the mass production of manufactured goods. There were 27 inventions, as shown in the following table, that were made during this period that are considered as breakthroughs or *transformations* that moved the world forward:

| Number | Invention | Time Period |
|---|---|---|
| 1 | Flying shuttle made weaving easy. | 1733 |
| 2 | The spinning jenny increased wool mills' productivity. | 1764 |
| 3 | The Watt steam engine: the engine that changed the world. | 1775 |
| 4 | The cotton gin: the engine that made cotton production boom. | 1794 |
| 5 | Telegraph communications, a pillar of the industrial revolution. | 1800 |
| 6 | Portland Cement and the invention of concrete. | 1824 |
| 7 | The modern roads designed by John McAdam. | 1800s |
| 8 | The Bessemer process that changed steel. | 1856 |
| 9 | The first modern battery by Volta. | 1800s |
| 10 | The locomotive revolution. | 1804 |
| 11 | The first factory opened by Lombe. | 1721 |
| 12 | The power loom, taking over all UK factories. | 1784 |
| 13 | Arkwright's water frame spinning machine. | 1769 |
| 14 | The spinning mule: the yarn game-changer. | 1775 |
| 15 | Henry Cort's puddling process. | 1783 |
| 16 | Gaslighting lighting the streets of the modern world. | 1804 |
| 17 | 2,000 cells to create the first arc lamp. | 1807 |
| 18 | The tin can, jumping to new production heights. | 1810 |
| 19 | The hydrogen fuel cell spectrometer (how we studied glowing objects). | 1814 |
| 20 | Camera obscura: the first photograph. | 1814 |
| 21 | The first electromagnet findings. | 1832 |
| 22 | The Mackintosh raincoat | 1823 |
| 23 | Modern friction matches made possible with wood. | 1826 |
| 24 | Every great writer's companion: the typewriter. | 1829 |
| 25 | The dynamo, powered by the Faraday principle. | 1830s |
| 26 | Blueprints from Herschel and Poitevin. | 1839 |
| 27 | The hydrogen fuel cell | 1838 |

(See https://interestingengineering.com/27-inventions-of-the-industrial-revolution-that-changed-the-world).

The technological advancements during this period consisted of the following:

- Iron and steel as the basic raw materials for manufacturing
- Energy sources, such as coal and petroleum, and motive power, such as the steam engine, internal combustion engine, and electricity
- Machines such as the power loom and the spinning jenny, which helped to amplify human energy, resulting in large-scale production
- Organizations such as the factory system that advocated the division of labor and the specialization of roles
- Transportation and communication means, such as the steam engine, steam ships, the automobile, telegraph, and the radio
- Science applied to the industrial sector

The following illustration dates back to the first industrial revolution:

Figure 1.7 – The first industrial revolution (Source: `http://brewminate.com/the-market-revolution-in-early-america/`, License: CC BY-SA-NC)

The preceding description of the first wave of the industrial revolution highlights that it consists of a series of transformations that together propelled society and the economy forward over a period of time. *Figure 1.7* depicts the industrial and societal landscape in that period, which is important to help us understand how this series of industrial revolutions accelerate the change to lead us to our current landscape. This book will explore and highlight how well-orchestrated industrial digital transformation opportunities lead the world forward.

## The second industrial revolution

The second industrial revolution (1870–1914) saw large-scale electrification and the buildout of railroad infrastructure. The use of electricity dramatically changed the lifestyle and profession of people. In the 1870s, the first commercial electric generators were used. Great Britain built the first power station around 1881. In the early 1900s, these power stations started powering whole towns or parts of larger cities.

Alexander Graham Bell invented the telephone in 1876. Soon after, in 1879, Thomas Edison and Joseph Swan designed the light bulb for home use. This period also saw the creation of the first electric railroad in Germany, as well as electric streetcars replacing horse-drawn carriages in major European cities. The first radio waves were sent across the Atlantic Ocean in 1901 and were credited to Guglielmo Marconi. The Wright brothers invented the first airplane in 1903. The motion picture, which is the foundation of the modern film industry, also started at this time:

Figure 1.8 – The second industrial revolution (Source: `https://en.wikipedia.org/wiki/File:Ford_assembly_line_-_1913.jpg`, License: CC BY-SA)

Large-scale socio-economic changes took place around this time in North America as well. By 1913, the US overtook Great Britain, France, and Germany combined in industrial productivity. The US accounted for one-third of the world's production. This helped to improve the economic status of the middle class, leading to increased purchasing power. This led to rapid urbanization and about 11 million Americans moved from rural and agricultural professions to city-based living between 1870 and 1920. By the end of this period, there were more city dwellers than those living on farms. This period also saw large-scale immigration to the Americas.

Overall, it shows that the second industrial revolution changed society from agrarian to primarily urban. This period saw the rise of technical skills and laid the foundation for the *pursuit of prosperity* based on an individual's capabilities. *Figure 1.8* shows the concept of the assembly line in the factories. Even current day manufacturing uses assembly lines, after a few generations of automation added to them. This highlights that transformation is not just about rip-and-replace, but rather perfecting concepts that work well.

## The third industrial revolution

The third industrial revolution, or the computing and digital revolution, started in the 1950s. The key invention was the transistor. The transistor emerged at the Bell Laboratories in Murray Hill, New Jersey, which was the research arm of **American Telephone and Telegraph** (**AT&T**). The invention of the transistor was accredited to three scientists, namely, William Shockley, John Bardeen, and Walter Brattain. The third industrial revolution saw the large-scale transition from analog to digital technologies. The semiconductor industry paved the way to mainframe and personal computing and eventually to the internet. This was the beginning of the information age. Electronic appliances and gadgets invaded households in this period.

## The fourth industrial revolution – Industry 4.0

The fourth industrial revolution started around the 2010s. The term Industry 4.0 was coined in 2011 by the German government. In this phase, the focus of companies shifts from pure manufacturing to the delivery of services and outcomes around the product. *Servitization* is the key feature and point of differentiation. This term was first used by Sandr Vandermerwe and Juan Rada in 1988 when they wrote the article *Servitization of Business: Adding Value by Adding Services,* in the European Management Journal (see `https://www.sciencedirect.com/journal/european-management-journal/vol/6/issue/4`). Servitization helps to transform a company from having a focus on product manufacturing and sales to the delivery of results to the customer.

According to the company Salesforce, *The Fourth Industrial Revolution is a way of describing the blurring of boundaries between the physical, digital, and biological worlds.* As a result, the advances in AI, robotics, IoT, 3D printing, quantum computing, genetic engineering, **Global Positioning System** (**GPS**) and related technologies fused together to achieve outcomes unseen in the past.

Today, voice-activated systems facilitate the conversation between a human and car navigation system to recommend the optimal route when traveling (see `https://www.salesforce.com/blog/2018/12/what-is-the-fourth-industrial-revolution-4IR.html?`).

What is the relationship between the four industrial waves or the revolutions and this book, *Industrial Digital Transformation*? We are in the second decade of the fourth wave of the industrial revolution. The authors of this book strongly believe that the year 2020 will help to shape this decade in the form of industrial digital transformations across the board – the public and the commercial sector. Hence, industrial digital transformation will help to unleash the real power of the fourth industrial revolution to the world at large.

Despite the large-scale development of our civilization in the last 300 years, the benefits have not reached the 7 billion people of the earth in an equitable manner. As a result, the United Nations has set 17 **Sustainability Development Goals** (**SDGs**) to help transform the world by 2030 (see `https://www.un.org/development/desa/disabilities/envision2030.html`):

| Number | Description | Digital Transformation Opportunity |
|---|---|---|
| Goal 1 | No poverty | Micro-lending and peer-to-peer lending |
| Goal 2 | Zero hunger | Smart farming, newer techniques to conserve resources, and vertical farming |
| Goal 3 | Good health and well-being | Digital twin of humans |
| Goal 4 | Quality education | Remote delivery of education |
| Goal 5 | Gender equality | Better tracking of equality in the public and private sector |
| Goal 6 | Clean water and sanitation | Smart water management |
| Goal 7 | Affordable and clean energy | Smart micro grids |

| Number | Description | Digital Transformation Opportunity |
| --- | --- | --- |
| Goal 8 | Decent work and economic growth | |
| Goal 9 | Industry, innovation, and infrastructure | IIoT testbeds |
| Goal 10 | Reduced inequality | |
| Goal 11 | Sustainable cities and communities | Smart cities |
| Goal 12 | Responsible consumption and production | |
| Goal 13 | Climate action | |
| Goal 14 | Life below water | DARPA Ocean of Things |
| Goal 15 | Life on land | |
| Goal 16 | Peace and justice; strong institutions. | |
| Goal 17 | Partnerships to achieve the goals | Consortiums and public-private partnerships |

For more details on DARPA Ocean of Things, see `https://gcn.com/articles/2020/01/03/darpa-ocean-of-things.aspx`.

The preceding list of UN goals showcases some fundamental challenges to solve using industrial digital transformation, which will have a profound impact on the world. When a private sector company creates a complete solution or part of the technology toward a solution, then it is very likely to be deployed and adopted. This helps to build the business case for the transformation and reduces the investment risk. The revenue for such transformative solutions may come from the governmental agencies or the end consumers and the beneficiaries. Very often, such transformational initiatives will drive successful public-private partnerships.

# The impact of industrial digital transformation on business

The internet, web applications, and the easy availability and low cost of massive amounts of computing power and storage have revolutionized the way that businesses operate and, in the process, have reset the competitive landscape. In some cases, industrial digital transformation is a competitive advantage, but in other cases, it is simply the minimum effort required to stay in business. For many organizations, digital transformation is a do-or-die proposition.

Industrial digital transformation can serve one or more of three purposes for business:

- Improve internal processes, thereby reducing costs and increasing competitiveness.
- Streamline the delivery of existing solutions within an existing business model to reduce costs or improve customer service.
- Transform a business completely, resulting in new products and business models.

A true digital transformation is a disruptive innovation that fundamentally changes the user experience. This new experience, if delivered properly, will delight the customer and provide the business with insights into how to better serve that customer in the future. It can also enhance the customer support processes, leading to lower support costs and new insights about customers.

Industrial digital transformation is not simply the automation of existing processes using new technology, but rather the re-engineering of existing processes and products to deliver fundamentally different solutions. A simple example of internal process improvement is the routing of a document for review. When that document is routed on paper, it would move to each individual reviewer in sequence. Once that document is digitized, it could continue to route to each reviewer sequentially. However, if the process were redesigned, it might be routed to all the reviewers except the final approver, concurrently shaving days or weeks off the review process.

At the product level, industrial digital transformation allows the creation of entirely new products that could not exist before digital solutions existed, disrupting entire markets. For example, the ridesharing applications Lyft and Uber would not exist if not for the digital disruption of business models. Before the advent of the smartphone and sophisticated algorithms that can rapidly match riders and drivers and manage pricing to keep supply and demand evenly matched, these car-sharing services could not have existed. They have disrupted both the taxi and car rental markets.

Digital transformation matters to businesses because virtually all businesses are being disrupted. New entrants are arriving with lower costs and new approaches to the existing business or with new business models that cannibalize their business. Incumbents must transform their culture, processes, and technologies to compete and thrive in this changing landscape.

# Quantifying business outcomes and shareholder value

The decision process in large public or private organizations is often driven by strategic goals or value of investments to its stakeholders while making the organization stronger and sustainable. As a result, any new initiatives beyond the incremental efforts to preserve the business goes through a business case of **Return on Investment** (**ROI**) analysis. As a result, it is important to understand the key benefits of the industrial digital transformation to the business. The desired outcomes of digital transformations are often as follows:

- New digital revenues
- Productivity gains
- Corporate social responsibility

In *Chapter 10, Measuring the Value of Transformation*, we will look in-depth into how to quantify these outcomes. Let's understand these outcomes qualitatively here.

## New digital revenues

In this scenario, transformation is used to drive new lines of business or new digital revenues for an existing business. A good example is the servitization of a product. In this model, the company tries to wrap the physical product with services that bring recurring revenues – for example, buying the scheduled maintenance service when buying a car. This prevents the service revenue from going to the after-market parts and third-party service providers. More complex examples include a jet engine provider selling *thrust* by the hour for an aircraft or the *power by the hour* model. To build the business case for this type of outcome of industrial digital transformation, the proposed investment is weighed against the possible new revenues (see `https://knowledge.wharton.upenn.edu/article/power-by-the-hour-can-paying-only-for-performance-redefine-how-products-are-sold-and-serviced/`).

## Productivity gains

In this scenario, the primary goal of industrial digital transformation is to improve the bottom line and drive efficiency. Let's take the example of a wind turbine owner or the operator. The cost of servicing a certain type of wind turbine that includes an oil change and servicing the bearings of the wind turbine is about $8,000 per event. In order to prevent overly frequent servicing, which would result in higher routine maintenance costs and not servicing when it is due, leading to expensive damages to the wind turbine, the company decides to go to **Condition-Based Maintenance** (**CBM**). They add sensors to monitor the viscosity and particulate levels in the oil. This allows the company to come up with the optimal frequency of servicing by monitoring wind turbine remotely. This is a good case study for productivity gains through the use of industrial digital transformation.

## Social responsibility

Often, both private and public sector companies look at transformative ways to fulfill their corporate citizenship goals. The business case for these may consist of tangible and intangible benefits. For instance, an airline may set stringent goals for carbon offset and look for transformative changes to accomplish that.

In the next section, we will look at the different phases of the industrial digital transformation journey.

# The phases of the digital transformation journey

Let's look at an example of a phased approach to digital transformation using the example of the automotive industry. In recent decades, we have experienced phases such as going from gas to electric cars to the use of driver-assisted technologies on its way to the different levels of autonomous driving. This journey continues and next, we may witness unmanned taxis and possibly flying taxis in the future.

In this example of autonomous cars, it is important to think through the breadth of the impact. As autonomous cars become mainstream, it has an impact on how roads, traffic signs, and even cities and airports are designed. Likewise, it may have a profound economic impact not only on the automotive industry, but also on the utility providers, due to electric vehicles, and finally, on employment via the automobile and the trucking industry.

Finally, auto insurance and the department of motor vehicles would have to adapt to this change as well. Hence, a technology-led digital transformation of the automobile has a profound socio-economic and political impact. The change management and phased approach applies not only to the *technical* aspect of the transformation, but also to the change of the business landscape as well as the societal impact.

Future chapters will revisit the presented methodologies along with specific examples of where they have been applied and a discussion on the approach and methodology to ensure success in the transformation activity.

Although this book will cover several examples of what an industrial digital transformation looks like, we will give you some ideas into how to discover the correct opportunity. A lot can be gained by examining the normal business cycle that an industry goes through in order to manufacture goods or provide a service. We will specifically look at an example where a company is going through a new product introduction. The stages typically involved are illustrated in *Figure 1.9*:

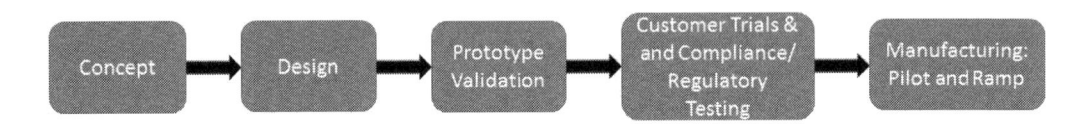

Concept → Design → Prototype Validation → Customer Trials & and Compliance/Regulatory Testing → Manufacturing: Pilot and Ramp

Figure 1.9 – Generic steps involved in a new product introduction

Industrial digitization can play a crucial role in each of these stages. We will briefly look at some examples here:

- **Concept**: This is the initial ideation stage that helps define the requirements for a new product. Digitization can help here by providing machine learning solutions that combine unstructured data to look for key customer trends. Several suppliers offer platforms – for example, analyzing social media messages to gauge positive or negative sentiments related to features in existing products.

    In addition, given the lead times to move from concept to production ramp, it is in the company's interest to forecast product feature sets that will be of interest when the product is in general availability, as well as the expected sales volumes. Machine learning and data mining can provide significant benefits in this area.

- **Design**: Digitization can help in the design process by allowing greater collaboration between designers. Collaborative tools that allow designers across the globe to work together on a common platform – in fact, even being able to share and edit drawings concurrently – goes a long way in speeding up the design process. In addition, digitization provides the means to reuse components already in use by a company and limits later headaches on raw material SKU management, as well as adds to the economies of scale to keep costs down.

- **Prototype and validation**: Rapid prototyping is key to evaluating the design for fitness and functionality, and to make any final revisions before the product is released to manufacturing. Additive manufacturing can play a key role in the rapid prototyping of mechanical parts. For electronics, there are special companies that specialize in small-batch orders with a quick turnaround to get samples back to the customer quickly. These companies leverage computer-integrated manufacturing to quickly reconfigure tooling between customer orders.

- **Customer trials, compliance and regulatory testing**: By being able to send prototype samples to customers, the manufacturer can get rapid feedback on new product features. As Steve Jobs once said, "*People do not know what they want until you show it to them*" (see *Isaacson, W. Steve Jobs: The Exclusive Biography*. New York: Simon & Schuster, 2011). Rapid prototyping provides such an avenue. Customer trials using prototypes can be sped up by employing technologies such as digital twins. These can be employed to conduct tests under extreme environmental conditions, which would help guide the design to meet regulatory requirements.

- **Manufacturing**: Although this is called out as a single item here (to be expanded into more detail in a later chapter), this encompasses several areas, each with its own sets of challenges and opportunities for digitization. Manufacturing comprises not just the factory or network of factories, but the entire supply chain network. This area alone is teeming with digitization opportunities, some of which we will cover later in the book.

You can find several publications and videos related to the use of augmented reality, control rooms, machine learning/AI, detailed real-time simulation models (see, for example, demonstrations from GE on their models of aircraft engines – also referred to as a *digital twin*), and autonomous planning and scheduling.

This is perhaps because manufacturing and the processes involved are relatively well understood and you can control the sensors and metrologies around these versus, for example, by applying natural language processing and sentiment analysis to unstructured data to determine new features that may entice customers during the concept phase. The connected products and operations provide opportunities to improve customer support operations and drive efficiencies.

Lastly, you should keep in mind that the aim of digital transformation is to enable the following: faster time to market with a cheaper cost per unit; managing and reducing the environmental footprint; and reducing risk to production by enabling digitization of the supply chain and the workforce. The aim of a commercial enterprise is to maximize profit, revenue, and market share and digitization technologies implemented correctly provide opportunities for visibility, efficiency, and agility.

How will industrial digital transformation impact the future of work? This will be a key driver from the perspectives of those who will be responsible for driving the strategy, as well as the execution of the transformation. The growth of automation and the use of ubiquitous AI will profoundly change how we work. The *lights out* data center is one good example of that. Likewise, *cobots,* or collaborative robots, where humans work alongside robots in factory settings, are another indicator of the future of work.

The explosion in the use of remote conferencing working technologies, such as Zoom and Webex, in the first quarter of 2020 during the COVID-19 crisis is another example of the changing nature of work that is possible in extreme scenarios. Telemedicine grew as well in this period and the regulatory landscape was relaxed (see `https://www.hhs.gov/hipaa/for-professionals/special-topics/emergency-preparedness/notification-enforcement-discretion-telehealth/index.html`).

The *gig economy,* or shared economy, has been possible due to transformations in related industries. As we move to autonomous vehicles, such as autonomous trucks, will it disrupt the profession of truck drivers? Interestingly, during the first half of 2020, long-haul truck drivers have been in very high demand for the distribution of food and grocery to the retail industry. On a related note, over the last decade, we have seen atlas maps move to apps. Apps powered by maps and geolocation information have really transformed the transportation industry. Truck drivers can look for the fastest route and avoid restrictions for commercial vechicles, such as a bridge with weight restrictions or a highway overpass with vehicle height restrictions, via such apps.

One of the focuses of this book is to help with the professional development of those who are part of the transformation journey. The authors of this book have been part of different industrial digital transformations at large companies. This book captures their first-hand professional experiences in their journeys.

# Summary

In this chapter, we learned about the importance of the cultural, technological, and business drivers for industrial digital transformation. We learned about the history of such large-scale industrial transformations to understand how to identify and select transformation initiatives going forward. Part one of this book will go further into the details of these topics and part two will show detailed examples of industrial digital transformations at work.

In the next chapter, we will explore the capabilities necessary to enable successful digital transformations. A digital transformation simply cannot be accomplished with existing staff with existing skills in the existing culture. We will discuss how to create the right culture for transformation as well as the skills required. We will discuss the rise of the chief digital officer and their role in implementing a digital transformation.

# Questions

Here are some questions to test your understanding of the chapter:

1. What are the main drivers of industrial digital transformation?
2. Are there major differences in the commercial sector compared to the public sector for transformation objectives?
3. What is the role of digital technology in driving transformation?
4. What are the benefits of industrial digital transformation to an organization?
5. Why is it important to understand the history of the industrial revolutions in order to understand industrial digital transformation?

# 2
# Transforming the Culture in an Organization

In the previous chapter, we learned about the importance of industrial digital transformation in the commercial and public sectors. The digital technology and business drivers enabling transformation were introduced. The historical evolution of the industrial revolutions leading to the current phase was also covered. Finally, we learned how global and local crises can often accelerate the pace of transformation.

In the first part of this chapter, we will learn that successful digital transformations are reliant on cultural changes that enable transformation. We will learn about the cultural environment that organizations must establish to achieve a successful digital transformation. Next, we will learn about the new roles that are required to complete a successful digital transformation and how we can develop those new skills. We'll also learn about the emergence of the **Chief Digital Officer** (**CDO**) and why the CDO is an important enabler of digital transformation. Finally, the chapter will wrap up with a review of the skills that people and organizations need to successfully execute a digital transformation and how organizations can develop those skills in their individual staff members and teams. In summary, we will learn about the following:

- Cultural pre-requisites for digital transformation
- The emergence of the CDO and digital competency
- Reorganization versus strategic transformation
- Skills and capabilities for digital transformation

# Cultural pre-requisites of digital transformation

Digital transformations require technology teams to develop a deeper understanding of the business needs to ensure that the product that is delivered meets the needs of the end users. In addition, digital transformation involves the use of new technologies to deliver these products. However, a successful digital transformation is not accomplished just by changing the technologies used to deliver capabilities. It also involves changing the way that organizations work. In fact, changing the way organizations work – organizational culture – is one of the critical parts of digital transformations and critical to their success.

## The concept of agile development as a foundation for digital transformation

While digital transformation is most frequently discussed in the context of how the products, services, and often entire business models delivered are different from traditional products and services, digital transformation starts with the way that those products, services, and business models are created. The fundamental concept underpinning all digital transformations is the idea of agile development.

While many products of digital transformation are ultimately reliant on hardware or transformation of business models and processes, software underlies all digital transformation and a firm understanding of modern development practices is necessary to understand the way that digital transformation happens. Furthermore, the core ideas embodied in agile practices – such as experimentation, solving the most difficult problems first, and identifying minimum viable products – apply to process, product, and business development as well and are closely linked with Lean practices, which will be discussed later in this chapter. In addition, some hardware-focused development teams practice Rapid Learning Cycles, a hardware product-optimized version of agile (see https://www.leanfrontiers.com/wp-content/uploads/2016/10/Katherine-Radeka-LPD.pdf for more information about this methodology). This methodology has been adopted by a diverse range of companies, including Volvo, SunPower, Hyster-Yale, Phillips, Johnson & Johnson, and Novo Nordisk, according to Rapid Learning Cycles founder Katherine Radeka.

Companies across diverse industries have embraced the agile methodology as a foundation for the digital transformation efforts of their products, processes, and business models. Notable examples include IBM, CISCO, Microsoft, 3M, and AT&T, as well as less obvious organizations, including CafePress, Schlumberger, LEGO Digital Solutions, and Principal Financial Group, an insurance and retirement planning firm.

Agile development was first recognized as a practice after the agile manifesto, which can be found at www.agilemanifesto.org, was written at the Snowbird meeting in 2001. However, agile is rooted in the frustrations with the frequent failure of waterfall development practices dating back to the 1980s. These frustrations led to the development of iterative development, new programming techniques such as eXtreme programming, and, ultimately, agile development.

Both the waterfall and iterative development methodologies are beyond the scope of this book. For more information on waterfall, see https://www.toolsqa.com/software-testing/waterfall-model/ and to learn more about iterative development see: https://airbrake.io/blog/sdlc/iterative-model.

While agile is a development methodology, it is very different from the historical methodologies that we have discussed in that, as described in the agile manifesto, it is really an approach to development based on *a set of shared values*, rather than a set of rules and processes. These values are applied using a variety of development practices and tools that are compatible with agile – most commonly, Scrum and eXtreme programming.

Since they serve as the foundation of the agile methodology, it is important to understand the four values that comprise the agile manifesto:

- Individuals and interactions over processes and tools
- Working software over comprehensive documentation
- Customer collaboration over contract negotiation
- Responding to change over following a plan

The authors of the agile manifesto stated the following:

> *"While there is value in the items on the right, we value the items on the left more."*

That means they value individuals and interactions more than processes and tools; working software more than comprehensive documentation; customer collaboration more than contract negotiation; and responding to change more than following a plan. These values reflect the desire to balance the highly structured development processes of the past with the need to deliver working products that meet the needs of the customer. These values inform the practices and culture described throughout this book.

Agile development projects can be broken down into three phases: discovery, development, and continuous improvement, as shown in *Figure 2.1*:

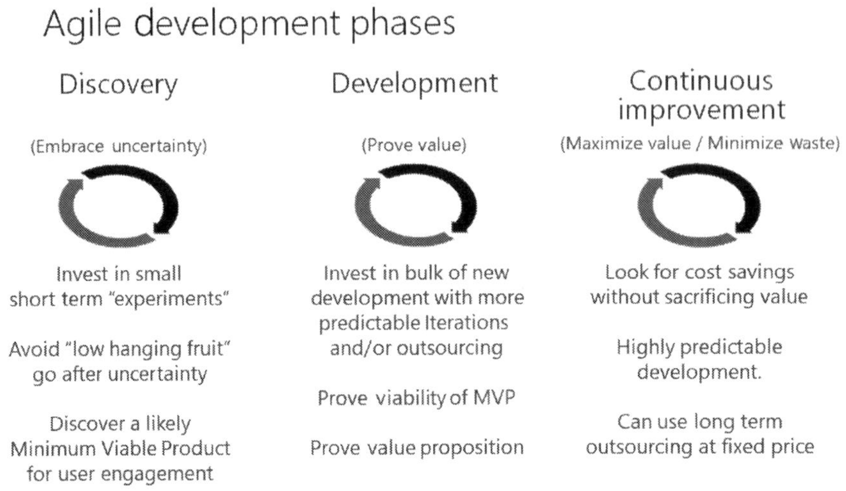

## Agile development phases

### Discovery
(Embrace uncertainty)

Invest in small short term "experiments"

Avoid "low hanging fruit" go after uncertainty

Discover a likely Minimum Viable Product for user engagement

### Development
(Prove value)

Invest in bulk of new development with more predictable Iterations and/or outsourcing

Prove viability of MVP

Prove value proposition

### Continuous improvement
(Maximize value / Minimize waste)

Look for cost savings without sacrificing value

Highly predictable development.

Can use long term outsourcing at fixed price

Figure 2.1 – Agile development phases

Let's discuss these phases in detail:

- **The discovery phase**: During the discovery phase, the goal is to identify the most complex problems to be solved. The most complex problems are those that will ultimately determine whether a viable product can be delivered. While it is often tempting to deliver the simplest functionality or an attractive user interface or industrial design during this phase of development, that approach must be avoided, because it does not achieve the goal of the first phase, solving the critical problems that will enable solution delivery. The result of the discovery phase should be the understanding of a potential **Minimum Viable Product** (**MVP**) that can be shared with end users or the understanding that the product will not be successful. If it is determined that the product cannot be successfully developed, the project will be abandoned. Failure is a frequent and appropriate outcome at this point in the life cycle, as it allows low-cost experimentation.

- **The development phase**: During the development phase, the bulk of the product is developed. Since the hardest problems have been solved, progress is more predictable during the development phase. The development phase will involve frequent user interaction as new capabilities are developed in each iteration. These require user feedback to be incorporated into the MVP and to validate that the product has user value.

- **The continuous improvement phase**: During the continuous improvement phase, new features are added to the product to provide a more robust user experience. In the continuous improvement phase, development tends to be more predictable. However, teams should not lose sight of the basic principles of agile development or of the need to stay in close contact with their customers to ensure they are continuing to provide features that meet user needs.

While the discovery phase demonstrated that a product could be built, the development phase demonstrates that the product can meet customer needs, and the continuous improvement phase fleshes out the product with a complete set of features. While the general requirements for each phase are broadly understood, it is important that organizations also determine specific criteria for moving between phases for each individual project. The MVP will be discussed further in the section on Lean Startup.

## Agile development compared to traditional development

One of the challenges with the traditional waterfall or iterative development processes is that many organizations either outsource development or set internal development schedules based on a set of requirements that were developed before the project was started. These set contracts and development programs are the primary cause of the failure of waterfall or iterative development projects. Whether building hardware, software, or a new business model, product development teams have generally treated requirements as fixed throughout the development process, disregarding new information gained during the development process that might change requirements, as the development process was not equipped to accommodate changes.

Agile acknowledges the reality that the requirements of business models, software and hardware projects, and new technologies are fluid, changing as the developers and target users of the product start to see it develop. It is simply impossible to accurately predict all of the requirements for a software, hardware, or new technology project or how long it will take to deliver those requirements before the project starts. This is where the value of the discovery phase of agile development becomes clear.

The cone of uncertainty is the term that is used to describe the lack of understanding of the full requirements of a product, as well as the lack of understanding of the difficulty of the hardest problems that must be solved. As shown in *Figure 2.2*, the cone of uncertainty is extremely wide at the beginning of the project and becomes smaller over the course of the project:

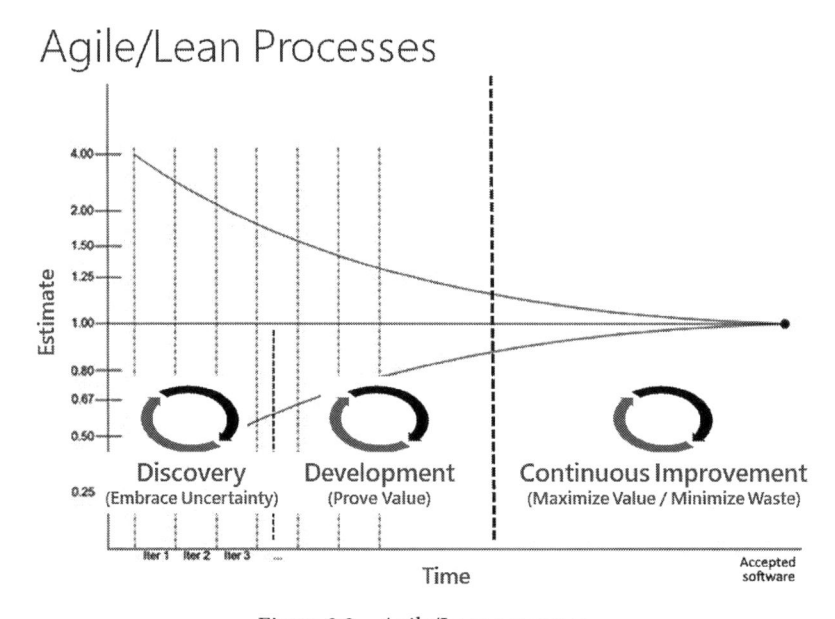

Figure 2.2 – Agile/Lean processes

When projects employ the traditional waterfall or iterative development methodologies, the requirements must be fixed at the beginning of the project when the cone of uncertainty is at its widest. This results in vendors quoting very high prices and developers and engineers proposing long schedules to account for the great uncertainty in the schedule. The use of the discovery phase in agile reduces the cone of uncertainty, allowing increasingly predictable schedules and deliveries over the course of product development.

Now that we understand the basic concepts of agile development, we will discuss a specific implementation of the agile methodology that is frequently used to develop new products: Lean Startup.

## Lean Startup

The industrial giant Honeywell started making N95 masks at their Smithfield Rhode Island plant around April 2020 to provide protection against COVID-19. The company stated the following:

> *"The setup usually takes about nine months but was completed in five weeks to meet the urgent need of frontline workers during the coronavirus outbreak."*

Honeywell used its aerospace facility in Phoenix, AZ to manufacture the masks in May 2020. Together, these two facilities produced more than 20 million masks per month and created more than 1,000 jobs in the US. This is a good example of industrial digital transformation at work at the time of a crisis. A company as large as Honeywell with over 100,000 employees and that is over 100 years old could act like a Lean Startup at the time of a crisis.

Companies like Honeywell are transforming the beliefs that govern their business models and their employee and customer interactions. At the same time, they have to build more resilient supply chains while encouraging data sharing with privacy and compliance in mind. According to McKinsey & Company, one of the modern dilemmas is best expressed as *how will you bring out digital products in days or weeks, as your competitors are trying to do?*

The challenges posed to the industrial giants by a crisis such as COVID-19 are summarized as follows:

- Overnight digital transformation
- Making the most of data
- Virtual customer engagement

Let's look at the methodologies and practices that the industrial giants can use to help them be nimble when faced with a crisis or disruptive competition. The Lean Startup methodology was proposed by Eric Ries in 2008. Eric Ries is the author of the book titled *The Lean Startup: How Today's Entrepreneurs Use Continuous Innovation to Create Radically Successful Business*, published by *Crown*, in 2011. The best way to define it is the Lean Startup method teaches you how to drive a startup – how to steer, when to turn, and when to persevere and grow a business with maximum acceleration. The concept of **MVP** is often associated with Lean Startup. In this context, this *startup* can be within a large industrial company, such as Honeywell, **General Electric** (**GE**), or Intel, or a new emerging company out of the garage of Silicon Valley founders:

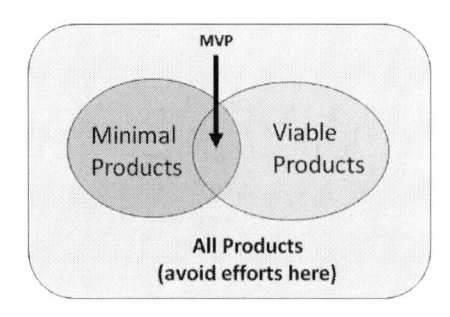

Figure 2.3 – MVP

MVP advocates iterative learning in the new product or service development. Eric Ries defined an MVP as the form of the offering that can be released to the customer, under certain constraints. Yet, MVP allows the product or the service development team to collect valuable usage and feedback information from real users, which can accelerate the development life cycle and reduce the risk. In addition, it allows customers to be part of the development and feel empowered to steer the direction and speed of improvements. The following figure shows the traditional approach to build a product:

Figure 2.4 – Traditional approach to build a product [Source: Henrik Kniberg]

*Figure 2.4* and *Figure 2.5* explain the concept of the development of products using the MVP approach. The key concept is that each MVP is usable and testable by the user community. *Figure 2.4* shows the evolution of the car from wheel to axle to body to the whole car. The user cannot use the axle or the body of the car to provide interim feedback. However, in *Figure 2.5*, the user can drive the two-wheeler and the three-wheeler for transportation and provide more meaningful product feedback:

Figure 2.5 – MVP approach to build a product with lower risk [Source: Henrik Kniberg]

Let's move beyond agile now.

# Beyond agile development and Lean Startup

Up to this point, this chapter has primarily been focused on the principles of agile as described by the agile manifesto and Lean Startup. However, a true digital transformation requires a fully evolved version of agile and encompasses a number of capabilities beyond agile. This section will examine the additional capabilities required to deliver modern digital services and the evolution of organizations adopting those capabilities. These capabilities are summarized in the following table:

| Values | Evolving | Mature |
| --- | --- | --- |
| Agile | Disciplined agile methodology. | Cross-functional team (including users) participating regularly. |
| User-Centered Design | Engaged with users on regular basis and integrated into the development cycle. | User engagement occurs in a production state. |
| Shared Services | Integrating some shared services per digital service consultants' recommendations. | Integrating all shared services per digital service consultants' recommendations. |
| API-First Development | APIs are integral to the architecture. | APIs are using an approved API gateway. |
| Cloud | Clear strategy to integrate IaaS, PaaS, or SaaS in an elastic and scalable cloud. | Integrated IaaS, PaaS, or SaaS, in an elastic and scalable cloud. |

| Values | Evolving | Mature |
|---|---|---|
| DevOps | Integration of automated testing. | Integration of automated and continuous deployment tools as well as security to evolve to DevSecOps and cyber-physical security. |
| Adoption of Open Source Code and Tools | Limited use of open source code and tools. | Significant use of open source code and tools. |
| Open Source Code Repository | Working in private but deploying code in an open repository in stages. | Working in an open repository. |
| Lean Practices | Align system development with business/mission process changes. | Align system development with business/mission value metric (not a self-reported metric). |

We will now discuss each capability in detail.

## Agile

The first step in adopting agile is for development teams to adopt and follow the agile methodology with discipline, using a practice such as Scrum to structure their development activities. Mature organizations not only follow a disciplined and regular process but also ensure that a cross-functional team, including end users, participates in the development process on a regular basis.

## User-centered design

As discussed in *Chapter 1*, *Introducing Digital Transformation*, historically, many products were designed without input from the individuals who would actually use the system. Often, large investments were made in products that failed in the market due to a lack of interest or an inappropriate set of features. User-centered design addresses that problem by engaging the intended product users throughout the process. An organization that is evolving their use of user-centered design may consult with users on a regular basis throughout the design process, presenting concepts and completed software for review. An organization that has fully implemented user-centered design will have users embedded in the product team participating in team meetings and design reviews, as well as evaluating releases at the end of each iteration. In these organizations, the end users are as much a part of the product team as the developers.

## Shared services

Shared services are a wide array of technical specialties that are not part of a traditional development team but that are critical to the success of a development team. Specialties that are considered shared services can include the following (list from `https://www.scaledagileframework.com/shared-services/`):

- Agile and software/systems engineering coaches
- Application/web portal management
- Configuration management
- Data modeling, data engineering, and database support
- Desktop support
- End user training
- Enterprise architecture
- Information architecture
- Infrastructure and tools management
- Internationalization and localization support
- **IT Service Management (ITSM)** and deployment operations
- Security specialists (InfoSec)
- Regulatory and compliance
- System QA and exploratory testing
- Technical writers

In an organization that is evolving its digital services practice, a few of these individuals, most notably coaches, will be embedded in the team as engaged resources. As organizations evolve the maturity of their digital services, more of these resources will be embedded in the product team until most or all of the specialties are engaged with the team on an ongoing basis.

## API-first development

API-first development is a practice that defines the API structures for a product first and uses APIs to mediate all interactions within the products. APIs allow developers to logically separate components of a product, delivering microservices rather than monolithic products. The implementation of APIs and microservices allows flexibility in the development process. Multiple services can be delivered in parallel and individual product components can be modified and upgraded independently, ensuring a better user experience. All digital services require that APIs be integrated into the product architecture. As organizations evolve their digital services maturity, teams move toward the use of API gateways to manage and orchestrate the routings of API requests throughout the product.

McKinsey defines APIs as the *connective tissue* to link the ecosystems of markets, technologies, and organizations. In *Chapter 7, The Transformation Ecosystem*, these ecosystems will be discussed in depth. APIs allow businesses to monetize their operations, products, and services via the data and insights. APIs are key parts of the digital platforms that can be used to forge profitable partnerships and open new pathways for innovation and growth. Digital platforms will be discussed in *Chapter 3, Emerging Technologies to Accelerate Digital Transformation*.

## Cloud

One of the fundamental concepts of digital services is that they are developed to be *cloud-ready* and are deployed in the cloud. This means that applications are able to take advantage of the benefits of portability and scalability offered by the cloud regardless of whether the implementation is in a private, public, or hybrid cloud. For an architecture to be cloud-ready, it generally must meet the following five requirements:

- The application is a collection of microservices.
- The data layer is decoupled from the application layer.
- Communications are API-based.
- The application is designed for scalability.
- Security is part of the application architecture, not an afterthought.

Mature digital services are not just designed for the cloud, they are fully implemented in the cloud in an infrastructure-as-a-service, platform-as-a-service, or software-as-a-service model, depending on the application.

## DevOps, DevSecOps, and cyber-physical security

The concept of DevOps or DevSecOps resolves one of the biggest challenges that confronts modern development: the *release train*. The release train has historically been a long process that involved testing by a variety of groups before the product could be queued for and released to production. Release trains historically took anywhere from 6 weeks to 6 months, a process that is untenable in an environment where the objective is to release code to production as frequently as every week. DevOps streamlines the release train by automating test and release processes and, in the case of DevSecOps, includes automation of security reviews as well. DevOps requires both robust test automation and the inclusion of shared services. If the test, security, and operations teams are not embedded in the development team, the release process cannot be automated. Early DevOps processes might simply automate testing, a process that is traditionally fully controlled by the development team. A fully mature DevSecOps process will automate every stage of the process with new code deployed to production at the touch of a button on a frequent basis.

As more and more physical devices, such as cameras, sensors, and industrial and household automation products, are integrated with software systems, communicating over private and public networks, the importance of DevSecOps and cyber-physical system security is increasing. Development teams must ensure not only that the software and hardware they develop is secure but also that the security of the third-party components that are integrated into those systems, as well as the supply chain that provides the physical devices and firmware. Development teams must work closely with security subject matter experts to ensure that security is designed into the product architecture and that solutions are designed for rapid updating and remediation when a vulnerability is identified. There are also reusable architecture patterns that can be leveraged as good coding principles.

## Adoption of open source code and tools

The use of open source tools for modern digital services is probably the least obvious of all the best practices of modern digital services development. It might seem that the modern practices that have been defined so far in this book could be delivered using any product, and it is certainly true that development teams do use agile practices when developing products and services using proprietary software languages and tools. However, the vast majority of digital services are delivered using open source tools. There are many reasons that modern development communities have embraced open source tools. According to `OpenSource.com`, a few of the most important ones are as follows:

- It allows developers to focus on higher-value work, as other developers have solved the easy problems, such as content management or operating system features.
- It delivers a lower total cost of ownership through the elimination of licensing costs.
- The quality of open source software and tools tends to be higher since many more developers have reviewed the code than would be the case with proprietary products.
- Open source products also follow the modern development practices enumerated here, resulting in more rapid development cycles, more functionality, and faster bug fixes.
- Patching schedules can be set by the development team, not forced by a vendor.

As organizations develop more mature modern development practices, their toolset naturally evolves from limited use of open source code and tools to significant or complete use of open source code and tools as the value of those tools becomes increasingly apparent to the team.

## Open source code repository

In most traditional development environments, each developer will store their code on their local machine or private repository until it is time to check it into the main code base. Most digital services efforts start with the developers working in this manner. Over time, as development efforts mature, teams move toward working directly in the open source repository, ensuring that all code is shared and accessible to all developers at all times. Depending on the project, the repository may be private and only visible to the team, or it may be public and open to others outside the organization.

## Lean practices

As discussed earlier in this chapter, Lean principles are an important part of modern development practices. Rather than writing code that replicates current, obsolete business processes or products, modern development projects start with optimizing or reinventing business processes and products. In modern digital services, all products are aligned with, support, and sometimes lead changes in the business and mission. As digital services mature, product teams become more aware of the business drivers and focus on ensuring that products are developed that align with the business value metrics reported by the business, rather than internal performance metrics developed by the product team.

## Disruptive innovation

As discussed in *Chapter 1, Introducing Digital Transformation*, digital transformation can serve three major purposes: to improve internal business processes, to improve the efficiency and effectiveness of existing business models, and to create new business models. While it is obvious that creating a new business model is a disruptive innovation, it is also possible for innovations that support internal business processes or existing business models to be disruptive as well. This happens when innovations fundamentally change the way that people and systems work to create transformative rather than incremental innovations.

While not exhaustive, *Figure 2.6* lists some of the conditions that lead to the delivery of disruptive innovation and true digital transformation:

### Innovation

| Sustaining Innovation | Disruptive Innovation |
|---|---|
| Existing Busines/Operating Model<br>Existing Culture | New Business/Operating Model<br>New Culture |
| Agile/Lean<br>Modular Development<br>Modular Contracting<br>IaaS<br>PaaS<br>Virtualization<br>Cost/Process Optimization | User-Centered<br>Open Innovation<br>DevOps<br>Agile Security<br>Elastic/Scalable Cloud<br>SaaS<br>Mission Enablement |

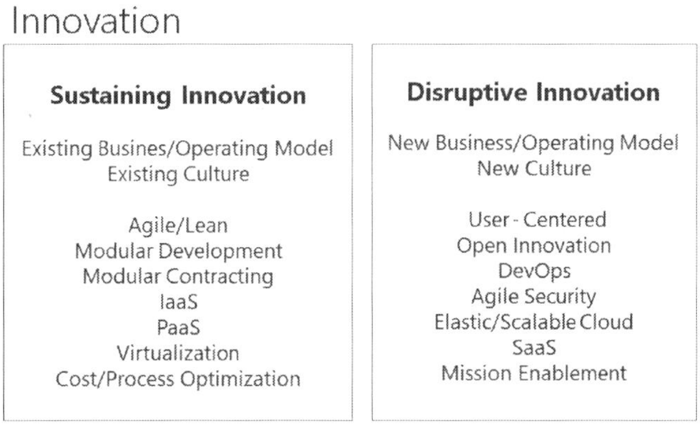

Figure 2.6 – Innovation continuum

This is not a case where one set of conditions represents things that are bad and the other represents things that are good, but rather, the factors that support sustaining innovation are frequently necessary for disruptive innovation as well. Therefore, if you find your organization primarily engaging in activities described as part of sustaining innovation, you should not despair. It is an indication that you are on track toward disruptive innovation.

## Design thinking

The term *design thinking* was coined by Tim Brown of IDEO. Design thinking is *largely a set of heuristics for guiding team-based collaboration*. It helps to explain how design contributes toward the products and services in the modern world. IDEO claims the following:

> *"Across numerous fields, advanced practitioners are fostering design thinking by encouraging its use and adapting it to specific domains and applications."*

The authors of this book have firsthand experience of applying design thinking in the context of industrial digital transformation.

Forbes discussed the five steps to leverage the design thinking principles to accelerate digital transformation. The five main steps of design thinking are as follows:

- Empathize
- Define
- Ideate
- Prototype
- Test

In the book *Crossing the Chasm: Marketing and Selling Disruptive Products to Mainstream Customers*, by *Geoffrey A. Moore*, published by *Harper Business*, the author discusses the technology adoption life cycle. Innovations can create large-scale changes that require significant adaptation for the stakeholders. When traditional IT shops adopt agile methodologies, they may experience a similar chasm among their stakeholders. The largest gap is the one observed between the early adopters and the early majority. The term **Chasm** refers to this gap, which is like a pitfall, as shown in *Figure 2.7*:

## Technology Adoption Life Cycle

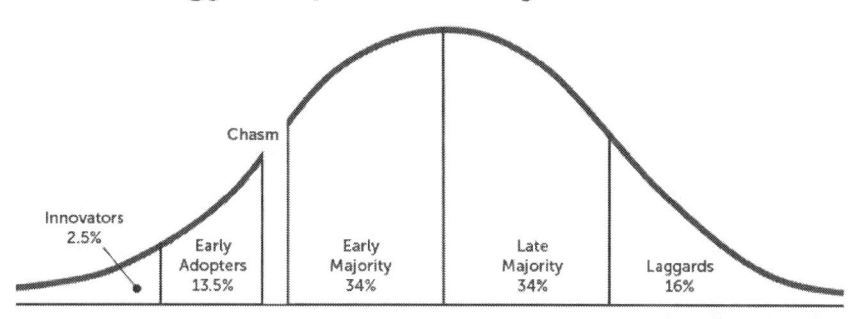

Figure 2.7 – Crossing the chasm

The design thinking frameworks (*Figure 2.8*) can be effectively employed to help overcome these chasms in an organization. Its goal is to help find user-centric solutions in a team-oriented working process and to foster a culture of continuous innovation. Design thinking starts with identifying a problem area and asking questions openly to turn it into a design opportunity. Design thinking places a stronger focus on the people and teams who are tasked to drive innovation.

Often, one of the salient features of digital transformation is to provide an excellent customer experience. To do that, design thinking can guide the product or the service team to empathize with the customer and get insights into their requirements, motivations, and pain points earlier in the product life cycle:

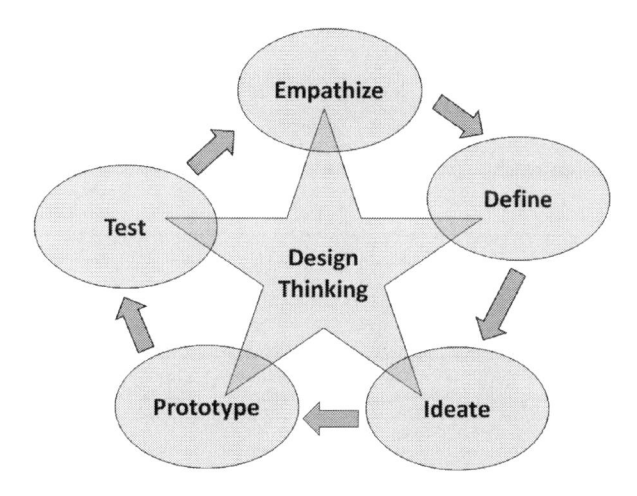

Figure 2.8 – The five steps of design thinking

Why is such a structured process needed for innovation? After all, legend has it that Newton came up with his theory of gravity after he saw an apple falling from a tree. The design thinking philosophy is that a *problem* is almost half-solved if it is very *well-stated*. It is like viewing problems with the right lenses. However, design thinking helps create an ongoing culture of developing a rich understanding of the complex problems at hand to solve. This leads to a sustainable culture of innovation and digital transformation. Design thinking promotes a human-centered approach to transformation. You do not have to be a *designer* to think like one. Design thinking helps industrial companies minimize the uncertainty that rapid innovation often brings:

> "When businesses are confronted by diverse challenges with multiple possible solutions, design thinking can be immensely helpful. It can define the right problem to solve, and offer a wider range of potential solutions that meet user needs and encourage adoption."
>
> – David Glenn, Director at KPMG

In the previous section of this chapter, we learned about the role of design thinking and the Lean Startup methodology in the industrial digital transformation journey. These approaches may not be mainstream for a **Chief Information Officer** (**CIO**)-led traditional IT organization. As a result, we have seen new roles and organization structures emerge, to accelerate the digital transformation. The `cio.com` article quoted in this chapter also made a bold observation: *The need for innovation requires radical organizational change.* A company-wide buy-in to put customers first is required for successful innovation and digital transformation. Interestingly, Jack Welch, the former CEO of GE from 1981 to 2001, said that the relentless pursuit of maximizing only the shareholder value was the "*dumbest idea in the world.*" When companies focus only on maximizing the shareholder value, they tend to be run by generalists with quarter-over-quarter or short-term vision. Successful innovation and transformation will only work when businesses have a company-wide buy-in on putting users first.

The book *Leading Digital: Turning Technology into Business Transformation*, by *George Westerman*, *Didier Bonnet*, and *Andrew McAfee*, published by *Harvard Business*, talks about operational paradoxes (*Figure 2.9*) that traditional industrial companies may face. These paradoxes are created by the six levers of operational improvements. The goal of industrial digital transformation is to use these levers to break free from the traditional operating modes that often make companies prone to disruption from non-traditional competitors. The package delivery company **United Parcel Service** (**UPS**) is known for the standardization of its delivery processes. By using emerging digital technologies such as IoT and AI, it came up with **On-Road Integrated Optimization Navigation** (**ORION**) routing software. UPS saved about $50 million per year with each of its over 100,000 drivers driving 1 mile less per day. The savings come from about a total of 100 million miles less driven per year, leading to a reduction in fuel of about 10 million gallons. This led to 100,000 metric tons less of greenhouse gas emissions annually. Let us see the six levels of operational improvements visually:

Standardizing ↔ Empowering

Controlling ↔ Innovating

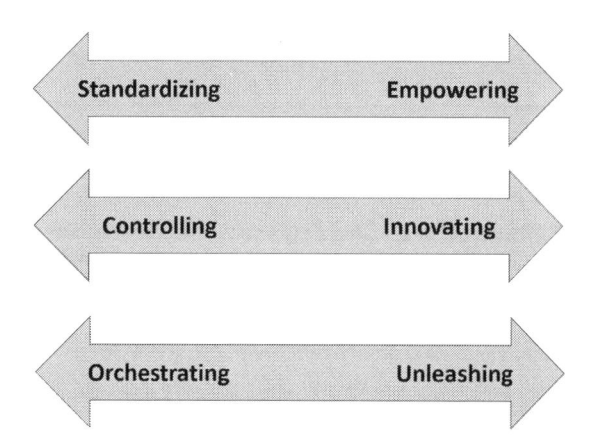

Orchestrating ↔ Unleashing

Figure 2.9 – The paradoxes (Source: Leading Digital)

To get the full benefits of transformative technology, often the current business models and processes have to be tweaked as well. Jack Levies, the senior director of process management at UPS, said "*With technologies that are transformational—like ORION—you have to be willing to let go of your existing business paradigms. You have to start with an open mind about how the technology can change the business*" (see `https://www.bsr.org/en/our-insights/case-study-view/center-for-technology-and-sustainability-orion-technology-ups`). UPS also tried out a truck-launched drone for residential delivery starting in 2017. In late 2019, the **Federal Aviation Administration** (**FAA**) allowed UPS to use drones for the delivery of medication.

Since 2018, UPS had collaborated with the FAA and the WakeMed campus in Raleigh, NC on the drone delivery of medical packages. It tested the delivery of packages containing blood samples and tissue to the different buildings on the WakeMed campus, according to Scott Price, the chief strategy and transformation officer at UPS. This year-long drone delivery trial flew over 1,000 flights across the campus. UPS is working on other initiatives, such as **Enhanced Dynamic Global Execution (EDGE)**, with a target of over $200 million in productivity boosts annually. These series of examples show that UPS has a culture of innovation and truly embodies the design thinking principles. *Figure 2.10* is a good conceptual representation of how UPS has put an MVP-based approach into practice:

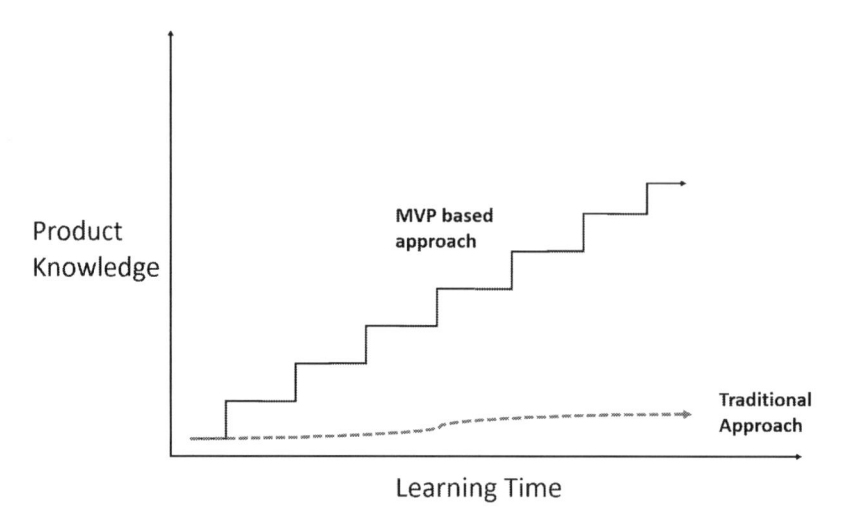

Figure 2.10 – The accelerating innovation using MVPs

This spirit of *Figure 2.10* to accelerate the knowledge discovery about a company's own business to allow rapid innovation is best captured here. A company such as UPS has been in the business of moving packages from one location to another for over a century. UPS has approached this with a series of ever-evolving innovations. Each step in *Figure 2.10* represents a bold step. Not all of these bold steps will get into the mainstream. The company will have to decide, whether to pivot or persevere, at each critical juncture. For example, UPS experimented with the cargo e-bike for delivery in the Seattle area in 2018. It will be interesting to see the future of this initiative and how other courier companies react to it.

## Digital transformation is a team sport

The first part of this chapter has described the principles and practices that create the cultural foundation for digital transformation. Throughout the discussion of these practices, the development team, the end users, and other players throughout the organization have been mentioned as critical to innovation. Each individual plays their part by performing their role on the team, whether they are a developer, user, Scrum Master, or one of dozens of specialists who comprise the shared services teams. Each individual must also be a change agent. Each member of the digital transformation team must act as an evangelist for the cultural change that enables digital transformation to stick and scale.

When one of the authors of this book, Ann Dunkin, was serving as the CIO at the United States Environmental Protection Agency, her **Chief Technology Officer (CTO)**, Greg Godbout, put forward the concept of a *policy and governance echo chamber*. Digital transformation advocates were cultivated in every part of the organization so that when individuals attempted to take a different path, one that did not reflect the values and behaviors of the agency's digital transformation, they would receive feedback that would redirect them toward the behaviors appropriate for supporting the agency's digital transformation. This policy and governance echo chamber concept is illustrated in *Figure 2.11*:

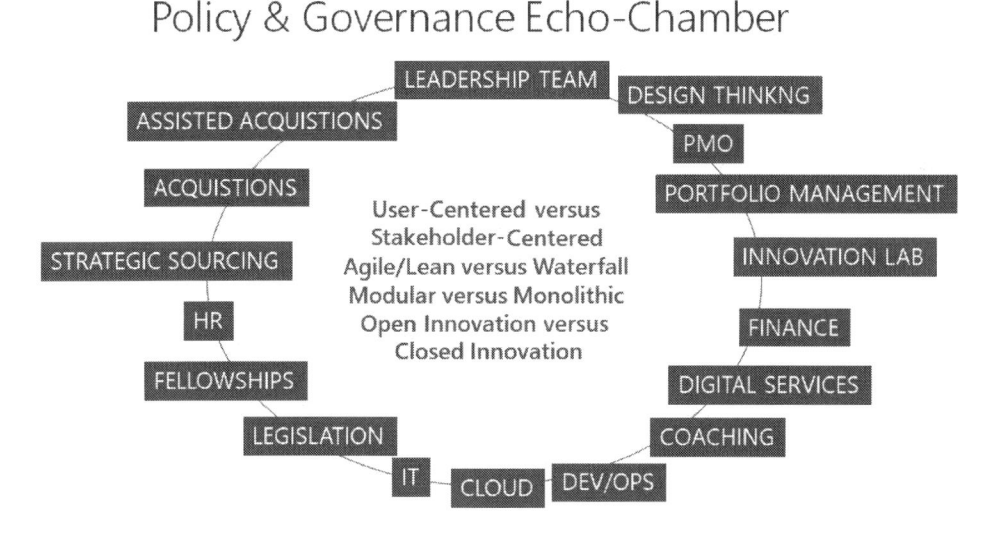

Figure 2.11 – The policy and governance echo chamber

Now that we are aware of the cultural prerequisites for digital transformation, let's see what role a CDO plays in this digital transformation.

# The emergence of the CDO and the digital competency

The later part of the last decade (2015 to 2019) saw several commercial and public sector organizations start a digital competency. This often resided outside the traditional **Information Technology** (**IT**) group and consisted of people with cross-functional knowledge. In the following sections, we will look at the roles and charters of this new group.

## The rise of the CDO

According to a study by Deloitte, large companies typically spend between 3% and 5% of their total revenue on IT (*Figure 2.12*):

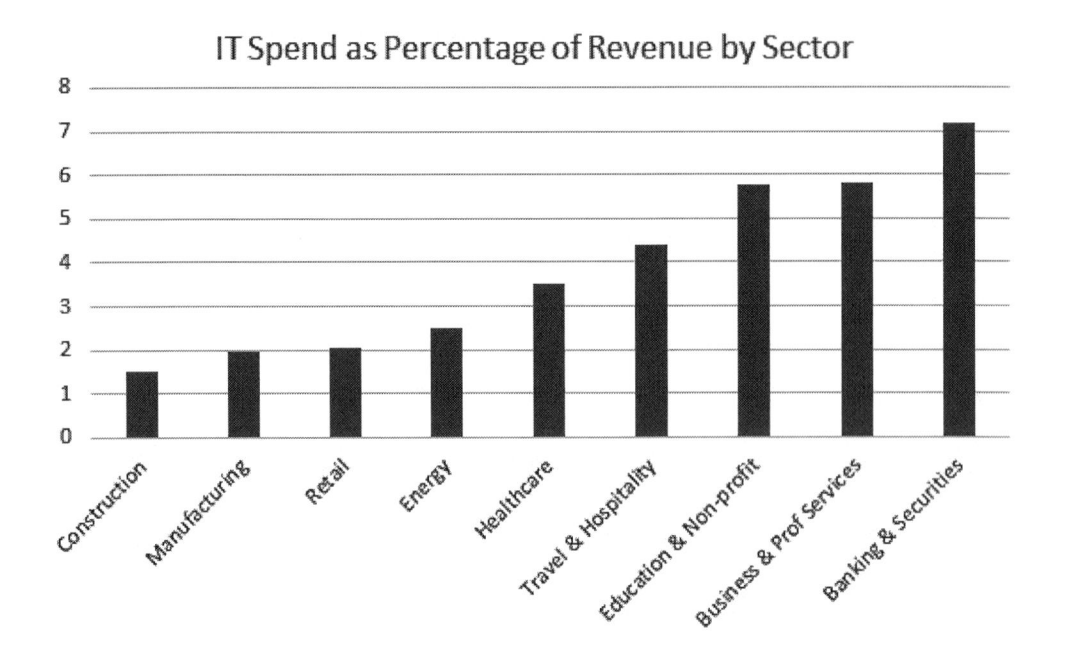

Figure 2.12 – IT budget as percentage of revenue

This often corresponds to the budget of the CIO. To simplify the math, let's say for every $100 of the company's revenue, $5 is spent on IT. Now, if the CIO makes the IT organization 20% more efficient and cuts the expenses by the same amount, then the top line of the company does not change but the bottom line or the profitability improves by 1%. On the other hand, if this 20% saving is invested in other transformative initiatives and produces 200% benefits – that is, $2 for every $1 invested – then it drives the top-line revenue by $2, keeping the bottom line the same. In a nutshell, for the CIO organization, a reinvestment of 20% saving with 200% returns on those new initiatives can only drive 2% incremental revenue for the company, in this simplified example.

This would be an example of incremental *transformation*. More often, such incremental efforts have only led to incremental improvements. When similar changes are part of another C-suite leader's organization, who owns a larger part of the company's budget or revenue, a large-scale transformation is possible. However, the risks are higher too.

## CIO versus CDO – roles and responsibilities

CIOs have become good at the operational responsibilities *to keep the lights on* for Enterprise IT. In their role, they deploy and maintain the technology to support different business operations. CDOs are often brought in with the goal of creating business value using current business assets or newly acquired capabilities. CDOs often have **Profit & Loss (P&L)** responsibilities. They are often seen as the new value creators for enterprises. It is expected that the CDO thinks about the new markets and new channels to operate and develops new business models. In some enterprises, the CDO organization is not allowed to intervene with the existing business unless it is seen as disruptive or transformative in nature. As a result sometimes, the CDO has to deal with new ideas that may *compete* with some of the existing lines of business – for example, providing value-added services for competitors' products, along with services for the physical products of their own company.

A CDO is expected to have a multi-disciplinary background, including business, operations, and technology. Sometimes, the CDO reports directly to the CEO or the president of the **Line of Business (LOB)**. As a result of this background, the CDO is often comfortable with talking to different departments within the company, as well as in peer industry forums externally. The CDO is expected to transform the digital anarchy into a digital symphony at an organization. This leaves a lot of room for digital creativity in problem-solving associated with the CDO role. In a blog article about the important traits of CDOs, Stephanie Overby from Adobe mentioned that CDOs are very creative problem-solvers and skillful storytellers. We have personally observed that in our interactions with GE's CDO Bill Ruh. Interestingly, Guido Jouret, who has been ABB's CDO since 2016, also noted: "*I like to refer to chief digital officers as a company's chief storyteller.*"

Debra Logan, distinguished analyst and a fellow at Gartner, said that digital leaders such as CDOs are not meant to be a replacement for IT leadership roles, such as CIOs or CTOs. CIOs are generally not responsible for outcomes that CDOs are expected to drive. The CDO's role is evolving to business leadership in the context of digital-led transformation. CIOs and CDOs will continue to demonstrate and lead different competencies that are required for transformation in this digital era. The CDO's role would be expected to help the company assess its current level and create a vision to progress the company along the digital maturity model, as described by the **International Data Corporation (IDC)**.

IDC has defined a digital maturity model with five levels:

- Digital resistor
- Digital explorer
- Digital player
- Digital transformer
- Digital disruptor

The last decade, 2010–19, has seen a number of CDOs being appointed. A few are listed here:

- Jason Goldman in 2015 as the CDO of the Obama administration, the US Federal Government
- Bill Ruh in 2015 at GE
- Atif Rafiq in 2013 at McDonald's
- Guido Jouret in 2016 at ABB
- Rachel Haot in 2011, for the City of New York, and then at New York State
- Rochet Lubomira in 2014 at L'Oréal

The preceding list of CDOs is meant to be a representative list across the commercial and public sectors. How successful each of these CDOs has been in their industrial digital transformation journey is not specifically discussed here. As we look into case studies of transformation, in later chapters, this will be further discussed. Tony Saldanha, former Procter and Gamble IT executive and author of *Why Digital Transformations Fail*, published by *Berrett-Koehler*, states that CEOs created the CDO role because they believed that the CIO role lacked sufficient business acumen to drive industrial digital transformation. Likewise, the CEO believed that the LOB leaders lacked the necessary technical and digital skills to conceive the art of the possible, via transformation.

Saldanha cautions that adding additional layers of leadership, such as a CDO and CIO, can bring its own problems. For instance, the digital systems required to drive and support the transformation may be under the CIO. In future chapters, we will look in more depth at CDOs' accomplishments, or lack of, with a few examples. In cases such as GE and ABB, the CDO role came to an end eventually. Likewise, it remains to be seen whether the whole digital organization under a CDO should exist for a limited time frame to get the industrial digital transformation jump-started and then hand it back to LOBs, or whether CDOs will evolve to be a permanent part of organizations.

There are different ways to look at the CDO role, and each one comes with different expectations.

## The CDO role in the public sector

Many, if not most, private sector organizations have handed CDOs the customer-facing business transformation mandate and focus CIOs on internal operations and process improvement. In the public sector, only a handful of CDOs have been hired and few have demonstrated notable success. In many cases, after the initial CDO left, they were not replaced. Rather, the three most common paths that public sector organizations have taken when assigning leadership for digital transformation are to include it in the CIO's role, to add an independent digital services office, and to hire a **CIO**.

## The CIO as the leader of the digital transformation

In most public sector organizations, responsibility for digital transformation is aligned with the CIO. Because most public sector organizations do not deliver revenue-generating technology products to the public, the vast majority of an agency's technology portfolio is managed by the CIO. In addition, in many cases, public sector organization leadership is not interested in technology other than as a mission enabler and, even then, likely will exhibit an interest in technology only when it breaks. This attitude is most readily exemplified by the frequently heard statement from agency heads to CIOs that *your job is to make sure I don't have to think about technology*. Under these circumstances, while the implementation of a transformation may be delegated to a chief technology or innovation officer within the CIO's organization, the CIO is generally the initiator, leader, and executive sponsor of any digital transformation efforts.

## Independent digital services office

In recent years, starting with the Obama administration's US Digital Services, a number of federal, state, and local agencies have set up digital services offices that operate independently of the agency's CIO. These groups are given a great deal of autonomy to work with mission leaders throughout the agency they support, to identify opportunities to create new digital services and modernize legacy systems. However, unlike many industry CDOs, the digital services office rarely owns the portfolio that it works on, an arrangement that can generate conflict with the CIO and their team.

## Chief innovation officer

In the past few years, several agencies have hired a chief innovation officer who reports outside of IT, usually to a senior appointed or elected official. Chief innovation officers generally have a small staff or no staff at all and are tasked with identifying new opportunities for their organization to deliver digital services to their community. Innovation officers tend to find themselves in conflict with the CIO less frequently than digital services teams, as they are rarely tasked with taking on projects within the CIO's existing technology portfolio.

# Reorganization versus strategic transformation

Very often, companies have a reorganization at the beginning of the fiscal year, which moves people around. Some companies may undergo similar business restructuring in response to financial headwinds. Such changes are usually reactive and usually do not contribute significantly toward industrial digital transformation. On the other hand, strategic transformation is required to develop a culture of innovation and make it a part of the DNA of the company.

According to Innosight, the acid test for strategic transformation is the ability of the organization to do the following:

- Sustain the transformation and culture of innovation over a period of time
- Significantly improve the customer and stakeholder experience
- Attract and retain digital talent
- Influence the industry in a positive manner

Next, let's compare top-down and bottom-up digital transformation.

## Top-down versus bottom-up digital transformation

The book *Leading Digital* states that in order to succeed in industrial digital transformation, you should start from the top. There are no good success stories of a bottom-up approach creating a true digital transformation in a large company. The bottom-up approach can, at best, help to transform a department in a large company. However, Douglas Squirrel and Jeffrey Fredrick argue that we should lead our digital transformation from the bottom up (see: `https://techbeacon.com/enterprise-it/why-you-should-lead-your-digital-transformation-bottom`). They suggest building trust in the teams and empowering them with the agile and Scrum tools required to succeed.

While it is true that it is impossible to transform a company without high-level sponsorship, it is also true that it is impossible to transform an organization without the engagement of front-line staff. If the development and operations teams do not understand the purpose and value of a digital transformation, the effort will not be successful. In addition, grassroots efforts to transform can become models for the organization at large if the power of the employee-led change is recognized and celebrated by senior leaders.

There can be a blended approach to digital transformation as well. The importance of the *frontline* cannot be ignored. A feasible approach is where the corporate (top-down) and frontline (bottom-up) can converge into a powerful blended team to identify the opportunities and drive the transformation together.

By its very nature, digital transformation can feel disempowering to middle management. Some leaders may question their role in the organization, and many will struggle to support the effort. This is because digital transformations are often the vision of an inspirational leader who reaches out to the entire organization, bypassing the typical organizational model that cascades guidance one layer at a time. Large transformation efforts tend to involve a great deal of organization-wide communication and encouragement for staff to practice new behaviors.

To compound this message, the new behaviors often take the form of largely self-directed work performed by self-organizing teams. Middle managers must shift from directing work to coaching and developing employees and clearing roadblocks for the team. As the teams are inspired to take charge of their work, managers may start to question their role in the organization. In the worst case, managers will actively undermine the transformation effort. It is important for executives leading digital transformation efforts to ensure that all levels of the organization, especially middle managers, understand their role in the organization and the value they bring to the transformation.

## Sustaining the transformation

In a 2017 MIT Sloan School of Business survey, 80% of those responding said that their companies drive digital transformation by cultivating a strong digital business culture. This culture fosters collaboration, agility, risk-taking, and continuous learning. Mahatma Gandhi said *we must live the changes we want to see in the world*. That seems very relevant in this context:

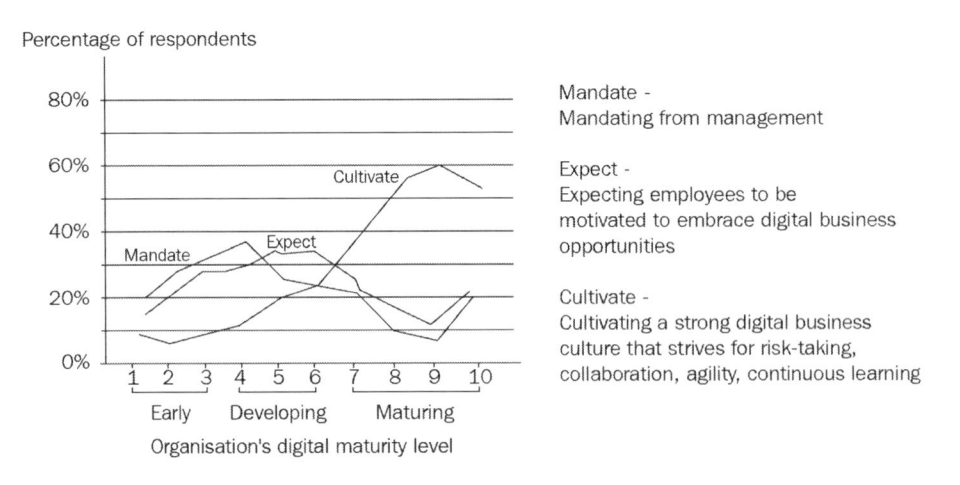

Figure 2.13 – Driving business adoption

*Figure 2.13* shows how different organizations drive the adoption of digital transformation as they go through the different levels of digital maturity. While it may start with a top-down mandate in the early stages, mature organizations rely heavily on the right culture.

## Digital talent

To succeed in industrial digital transformation, a company needs to craft a vision for the transformation and invest in building their strategy around it. The vision and the strategy must clearly articulate how the transformed state will look and communicate it to its employee and stakeholders. Next, the company needs to engage its digital talent, as it embarks on the journey to make the industrial digital transformation vision a reality. According to a Capgemini study, 77% of companies consider the lack of digital skills as the key hurdle to their digital transformation journey. The traditional human resources department has not been actively involved in digital skills development. The training and digital strategy are rarely aligned. The following figure shows how to build and enhance digital talent in an organization:

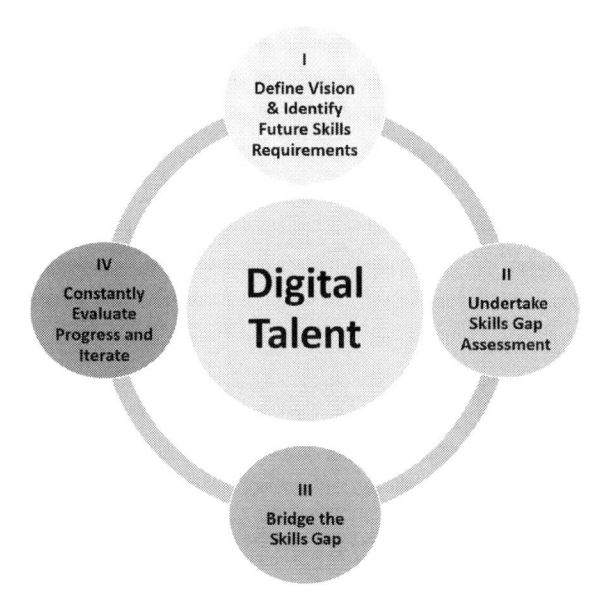

Figure 2.14 – The cycle of digital talent development

Gartner defined the essential digital skills in their publication *A Roadmap to Discover Digital Talent*. However, the definition of digital talent, from the author's viewpoint, is broader than just digital skills. Digital talent should include all the key skills needed by the organization to help build the digital transformation strategy and plan and its execution and sustenance. Digital transformation thrives on the ability to undertake changes to processes and thinking. The right digital talent can help drive these changes that span the internal organizational silos. As a result, the delineation between digital technical skills and leadership skills is no longer black and white. Sometimes, these are referred to as hybrid digital skills. These can be technology folks who are trying to become business savvy and, likewise, functional folks trying to become more technology savvy.

Digital talent should not equate to coders only, but to business and soft skills as well. Can you go to school for learning digital transformation, just like data scientists can be hired out of school? A lot of industrial companies from different parts of the world visit Silicon Valley to see this culture and digital talent at work in the pursuit of digital transformation. The authors of this book (Nath and Chowdhary) have been involved in hosting some large companies such as Samsung, LG Electronics, Air Liquide, and Boeing during their executive team tour of Silicon Valley. A common question asked on such trips is *How do you develop and retain digital talent? Figure 2.14* shows the cycle of digital talent, and successful management of this cycle is key to the transformation initiatives.

Crowd-sourcing and hackathons are another way of developing digital talent. Cross-functional teams compete in these hackathons. Hackathons enable new ways of involving, grooming, and motivating the digital talent within a company or in the ecosystem, via gamification. You may be familiar with the origin of the company FedEx. Its founder, Frederick Smith, expressed the core concept for FedEx's system of efficiently routing packages through a central hub in his college term paper. Likewise, via hackathons, pairing IT and business employees with academicians can create fertile ground for innovative ideas. These initiatives can help nurture and retain digital talent, without relying on compensation alone.

## The capabilities model and scorecard for digital talent have to evolve

Companies such as GE and Intel have championed cross-industry initiatives such as the IoT Talent Consortium, which has the tagline *Enabling Business Transformation* to help develop the next generation of digital talent.

The book *Leading Digital* quotes Kurt De Ruwe on various ways of grooming digital talent internally. Kurt was the CIO at Bayer MaterialScience between 2007 and 2013. He focused on engaging digital talent via micro-blogging to drive and enable open information and knowledge management. De Ruwe believed that once the digital talent finds its voice and the right platform for expression, then the magic happens. This drives cultural transformation inside a company.

Let's look at a similar example from Intel on the importance of learning from failures in cultivating digital initiatives. Kim Stevenson, the CIO of Intel, highlights the importance of learning from failed experiments and, in subsequent attempts, leverage the knowledge gained. At Intel, Stevenson promoted an initiative to encourage informed calculated risk-taking. Intel designed cards for its employees that stated *I took a risk, it failed, and I learned something and applied it*. Through these cards, Intel encouraged its digital talent to learn from failures and not be risk-averse. The idea was to use this experience as a learning opportunity from the failed attempts. This is one way that Intel encourages its digital talent to embark on its innovation journey. This culture of internal inclusion and crowd-sourcing sends a strong top-down message that everyone has a chance to help shape the industrial digital transformation initiative.

Like Intel, a retailer, Sainsbury's, from the United Kingdom, engages over 2,000 employees on a monthly basis on important management decisions. It is important for companies to leverage the right social platform to continuously engage its digital talent and foster a culture of inclusion and diversity to gather insights on new digital business avenues, improved productivity, and customer collaborations.

The previous section looked at the internal activities and investments to cultivate digital talent. In the industry today, many CIOs and IT staff have college degrees related to computer science, computer engineering or related engineering degrees. Many business leaders have an MBA. Many data scientists have a PhD or Masters in related fields. Hence, it is obvious to ask whether digital transformation can be taught at schools and universities. We looked at the following Masters-level programs that are related to digital transformation in early 2020:

- Master of Global Management in global digital transformation at Arizona State University
- Executive master in digital transformation leadership at Barcelona Technology School
- Executive master in digital transformation and innovation leadership at IE School of Human Sciences and Technology
- MSc in digital transformation management and leadership at the ESCP Business School, London

This list of university programs for formally learning digital transformation is not meant to be an exhaustive list, but a good indicator that schools are stepping up to augment and fast-track digital talent to help drive industrial digital transformation.

## Sustaining digital transformation

Sustaining the momentum of industrial digital transformation is always tricky. In this context, Joe Gross of Allianz Group, a large insurance company, expressed concerns over its ability to sustain and drive the initial momentum for the transformation. The ability to accelerate the transformation and continue the quest for new digital opportunities is key. Otherwise, the company can get complacent and resort to traditional ways of business and practices and stay in its comfort zone.

## Introducing reverse-mentoring programs

Jack Welch, CEO of GE between 1981 and 2001, pioneered the concept of reverse mentoring. Jack believed this was a powerful technique to pair the digital-savvy talent with executives in a non-hierarchical way. This concept of pairing up people across the different levels of an organization in an unorthodox mentor-mentee relationship can spark new levels of realizations and a deeper understanding of the industrial digital transformation.

In the next section, we will look at the organization skills and capabilities required to drive the transformation successfully.

# Skills and capabilities for digital transformation

The earlier parts of this chapter discussed the new practices that organizations must embrace to be successful, as well as new roles that exist in organizations that are delivering digital transformations. To be able to work in new ways and deliver transformative products, staff must learn new skills as well. While it is obvious that staff must learn new technical skills, it may be less obvious that they also need to learn new ways of working. The CEO and CDO have to add empowerment from the top to accelerate the pace of innovation while realizing that the culture of the organization is hard to change overnight.

GE has been known to run leadership programs to groom the next generation of leaders. Historically, these leadership programs have been the perfect foundation for accelerating learning and development in particular areas from commercial to operations, from human resources to information technology, and from finance to communications.

Tisoczki and Bevier described this as *a personalized rotation program to develop future leaders* in their book titled *Experience-Driven Leadership Program*, published by *Wiley*. One of the authors of this book (Nath) joined the **Experienced Architecture Leadership Program** (**EALP**) in 2013, at GE's Center of Excellence in San Ramon, California. This location later became the headquarters for GE Digital. The EALP morphed into a breeding ground for digital leaders. The first EALP batch of 2013 had 20 participants and about two thirds came from outside GE. They came from companies such as Apple, Cisco, IBM, Microsoft, Oracle, and SAS, as well as companies such as Pacific Gas & Electric, Wells Fargo, and Nationwide. At that stage, GE had realized that to turn into a digital industrial company, GE needed digital talent both from inside and outside and to put them together through the cultural evolution. The growth of GE Digital under the then CDO of GE, Bill Ruh, was aimed to align the digital talent with the organizational structure to foster industrial digital transformation.

# Leadership principles for digital transformation

Every organization must select those values and principles that they want to instill in their teams to make them more effective in delivering value. While each organization will, therefore, have a different set of principles, the following four principles are critical for any organization that is taking on a digital transformation, and leaders should incorporate these ideas into their principles:

- Informed risk-taking
- Learning organization
- Customer focus
- Partnering

To ensure a successful digital transformation, leaders must take responsibility for modeling these principles and instilling them in the organization as part of the transformation effort.

## Informed risk-taking

The basic premise of digital transformation is that it delivers innovations that fundamentally change the way that people work and how products and services are delivered. Change, especially large, disruptive change, does not happen without risk. Furthermore, early development cycles in an agile development process are focused on experimentation, determining what solutions will work and what solutions will not work, naturally amplifying the risk of failure.

Robert F. Kennedy said the following:

> *"Only those who dare to fail greatly can achieve greatly."*

However, it is not the natural state of individuals to embrace failure or of organizations to reward failure. Therefore, organizations that want to transform must make it clear to employees that risk-taking and early, low-cost failures are expected and will be rewarded, not punished. Senior executives must model this by embracing their own failures and recognizing the failures of others in the organization as experiments that demonstrate what won't work, rather than as problems that need to be fixed.

## Learning organization

Hand-in-hand with embracing risk-taking, organizations that want to transform must become learning organizations. According to David Garvin, a learning organization is the following:

> *"An organization skilled at creating, acquiring, and transferring knowledge, and at modifying its behavior to reflect new knowledge and insights."*

He further describes the five characteristics of a learning organization as follows:

- Systematic problem solving
- Experimentation
- Learning from past experiences
- Learning from others
- Transferring knowledge

Looking at this list, it quickly becomes clear why being a learning organization is important to digital transformation. The basic principles that establish a learning organization are key to the ability of a product development team to experiment and learn and to develop and deliver new products. Without the skills present in a learning organization, innovation would be stifled and digital transformation would be impossible.

## Customer focus

User-centered design has been discussed extensively in this chapter as it is an important tenet of digital transformation. In addition, in *Chapter 1, Introducing Digital Transformation*, we described a case where the development team was designing their product for their stakeholders, rather than the customers. It is not enough to engage some users in the development process. Teams must engage the right users in the design and development process. These are the final customers of the product, whether those are other employees in the development team's organization, customers who are buying the product, or members of the public using a government service.

Product development teams must listen to feedback intently and ask probing questions to understand the users' needs. They must have a desire to develop a product that will delight the customer and maintain that focus as their North Star throughout the development process.

## Partnering

When development teams worked in a waterfall model, they would often receive a set of requirements from a group of business analysts and independently develop a product without any interaction with the analysts or the end users. They might not even know what the customer thought of the product until enhancement requests begin to arrive in the ticketing system or from sales and marketing.

The development process was equally disjointed, with hardware and code handed off to testing, security, and the deployment or manufacturing team with little feedback other than defects reported in the defect tracking system. In this environment, there was no need to partner with anyone. Every discipline was an island. In an agile environment, however, that is completely different. All the technical disciplines needed to define, develop, deliver, and receive user feedback are part of the product team. To deliver a successful product in this environment, the development team must partner with the shared service providers and the customer throughout the product life cycle.

# Soft skills for delivering digital transformation

Every organization that is contemplating a digital transformation will need to develop a different set of soft skills in their staff depending on both the current state of the organization and the future state objectives for the organization. Organizations will need to formally assess the skills of their workforce and develop a transformation plan. Workforce analysis is beyond the scope of this book. However, because a digital transformation relies so much on effective interactions between members of the development team and between the development team and partners and users, it is important to highlight the skills that are necessary for any organization that undertakes a digital transformation to enable a successful team collaboration.

Organizations can effectively deliver the skills identified in this section through formal training courses. However, informal activities led by training staff and the leadership team to reinforce these skills are necessary to ensure that learning is reinforced and applied rather than lost. Any training program developed to deliver these skills should include follow-up activities to ensure practice and retention. In this section, we will briefly discuss each skill and its importance. The specific skills that we will be discussing in this section include the following:

- Emotional intelligence
- Personal accountability
- Meeting management
- Effective feedback

- Integrity and trust
- Diversity, equity, and inclusion
- Coaching and employee development
- Personality and work skills

Let's look at them one by one.

## Emotional intelligence

Emotional intelligence is defined as follows:

> *"The ability to monitor one's own and other people's emotions, to discriminate between different emotions and label them appropriately, and to use emotional information to guide thinking and behavior."*
>
> – Peter Salovey and John D. Mayer, Emotional Intelligence, 1990

While members of digital transformation teams spend time on engineering and development tasks, they also spend a great deal of time meeting with their colleagues on the development team, their partners in shared services, and end users. This differs from the stereotype of engineers and developers as loners who write code or design hardware all day and lack social skills. The ability of individuals to understand their own behavior and its impact on others is a crucial capability for members of digital transformation teams, who must work closely together to achieve results.

In addition to helping team members enhance their working relationships, emotional intelligence enables a growth mindset, a concept introduced by Carol Dweck in her book *Mindset: The New Psychology of Success, Carol S. Dweck, Ballantine Books*. A growth mindset, as opposed to a fixed mindset, is the idea that new skills and capabilities can be learned and that an individual is open to feedback and embraces new ideas. It is also the mindset that orients individuals toward accepting risk, rather than avoiding risk.
A growth mindset is critical to the success of a learning organization. Clearly, emotional intelligence is a critical capability for staff participating in digital transformations.

## Personal accountability

In organizations that have historically used traditional development methodologies, team members may be accustomed to developing hardware and writing code independently with weeks or months between deliverables. When organizations transform, developers and engineers suddenly must participate in daily meetings and contribute designs, code, and other artifacts on a frequent basis. Some organizations utilize practices such as pair programming that require team members to spend most of their work week collaborating. These working environments require staff to demonstrate personal accountability to support the overall objectives of their team. Concepts such as above and below the line behaviors support personal accountability to the team. Above and below the line behaviors, an idea first popularized by Carolyn Taylor in her book *Walking the Talk*, by *Carolyn Taylor*, published by *Cornerstone*, provide a framework for discussing behaviors that are helpful to the team's performance and those that are detrimental to performance. This framework provides a model for positive accountability and can be useful in helping team members adapt to this way of working.

## Meeting management

Digital transformation teams are primarily self-organizing, assigning tasks, reaching out to customers and partners, and managing backlogs as a group. These new ways of working that are a part of a digital transformation require more meetings to keep teams aligned and they require team members to be more actively engaged in those meetings than they might have been in the past work environment. Tools such as meeting agendas, action item tracking, and team norms are critical to the success of digital transformation teams.

## Effective feedback

Digital transformation requires substantially more communication between team members and across the organization than the old ways of working. In the past, team members worked on their own code and hardware subsystems and discussed interfaces. Managers communicated between teams and with partners. In a digital product development environment, where team members, partners, and customers are in constant communication, feedback is critical. Individuals must have the tools and ability to give and receive effective feedback on requirements, outcomes, and behaviors. Organizations should train team members on a variety of techniques for giving and receiving feedback so that members of the team can select tools that are comfortable for their style and the given situation.

## Integrity and trust

Teams working on digital transformation projects must work closely together to design solutions and develop and deliver products. These activities can generate strong opinions and disagreements. While emotional intelligence and effective feedback skills will help teams navigate these discussions, team members also need to act with integrity and develop an environment of trust to facilitate open and honest discussion and decision making. Trust stems from a shared set of organizational values and individual actions that align with those values. Teams should adopt a set of shared values and create accountability within the team to adhere to those values.

## Diversity, equity, and inclusion

As the global workforce continues to become more diverse, the diversity of agile teams naturally increases as well. While it is important to embrace the diversity of race, religion, gender, sexual orientation, and gender identity on the digital teams, it is equally important to understand and embrace the differences in work styles that diversity brings. Team members need to be aware of their implicit biases, that is, those that we are unaware of but that still impact our behavior, when interacting with each other and create a safe space where all team members can be effective. Only when all team members feel safe and included can the digital transformation reach its full potential.

## Coaching and employee development

Because digital transformation teams tend to be self-managed, it is easy for managers to neglect coaching and employee development. However, in the fast-paced and dynamic environment of digital transformation teams, managers need to master the ability to coach and develop their employees, rather than directing their work as in the past. Team members also need to learn coaching skills to enhance the effectiveness of the feedback that they provide each other as they work together. Staff must also learn to effectively advocate for themselves and chart their career paths through the transforming organization.

## Personality and work styles

Many organizations find that having the entire team complete a personality or work styles assessment helps team members understand each others' strengths and interests better and work more effectively together. Assessments also provide a common language for discussing work styles. Commonly used assessments include the Myers-Briggs Type Indicator, DISC, Hexaco, and Enneagram. A different type of assessment is the Strengths Finder assessment (recently rebranded as CliftonStrengths), which identifies team members' greatest strengths, allowing them to focus on building on those strengths and helping team members know who has skills they can call on when needed.

As mentioned, there are many types of personality assessments available that you may find helpful in understanding yourself and your team. Here's where you can learn more about some of them and find out how to take the assessments:

- Myers-Brigg Type Indicator: `https://www.mbtionline.com/`
- DISC: `https://www.discprofile.com/what-is-disc/overview/`
- Hexaco: `http://hexaco.org/`
- Enneagram: `https://www.truity.com/test/enneagram-personality-test`
- CliftonStrengths: `https://www.gallup.com/cliftonstrengths/en/strengthsfinder.aspx`

Now, we will move on to technical skills.

# Technical skills for delivering digital transformation

The technical skills required for delivering digital transformation vary depending on the product to be developed and the technologies to be used. Rather than discussing the specific technical skills that teams need to learn, this section will focus on how to develop new skills in an organization.

### In-house training classes

Fundamental skills that many or all team members will need to effectively contribute to the digital transformation should be delivered in-house to intact or mixed teams. These skills will vary by organization but may include training on the use of development languages and libraries the team will use or tools such as CAD systems, code repositories, or automated test suites. In-house training should also be used to familiarize teams with methodologies and frameworks, such as Scrum and **IT Service Management (ITSM)**.

### Cross-training

One of the fastest ways to develop new skills in an organization is to hire new staff. This approach, however, is not without risks. If new staff are hired and then given lead responsibility for the digital transformation, the existing staff will be resentful and will be unlikely to contribute to the transformation. In addition, the existing staff knows how the organization works and new staff do not. Therefore, any new staff brought in for their digital skills should be partnered with existing staff with organizational knowledge so that they can train each other. In that way, long-term employees will learn fresh technical skills and new employees will understand the organization's people, products, and politics more quickly, rapidly scaling their effectiveness. The combined team will be better prepared to implement the organization's digital transformation than either group alone.

### Conferences and off-site training

The broad array of technical skills required to deliver new products means that while many skills are needed across a broad cross-section of the organization, an equally large number of skills are needed by a handful to team members with specialized responsibilities. Organizations should invest in those staff members by sending them to off-site conferences and training courses to ensure they obtain the skills and certifications they need to perform their duties effectively.

### Degree programs and other formal education

The environment in which digital transformation teams work continues to evolve rapidly and skills in the newest tools and technologies will always be at a premium. Rather than fighting to acquire these new skills on the open market, investing in existing staff who are interested in retooling makes great sense for most organizations. Depending on where an organization is located, on-campus degree programs may be available. Regardless of an organization's location, online degree programs in cutting-edge technologies such as data analytics and security are available from top colleges and universities.

In addition to two- and four-year degrees, microlearning, nano-degrees, and continuous education are gaining ground in institutions of higher learning as employers and students rethink education. The apparent success of higher education's rapid move to online learning in the spring of 2020 as a result of the COVID-19 crisis will likely accelerate the development of new models for lifelong learning.

# Summary

In this chapter, we learned about the transformation of product development culture and practices over the past two decades, including agile development, Lean Startup, and design thinking, and we saw why those new ways of working are important to achieving a successful digital transformation. We learned about the role of the CDO, how the CDO and their team have developed in the private and public sectors, and the importance of engaging all levels of an organization in the transformation. Finally, we learned about the soft skills necessary to ensure a strong digital transformation and strategies for developing new technical, leadership, and collaboration skills in an organization.

In the next chapter, we will learn about digital technology enablers for industrial digital transformation. The concepts of digital twin and digital thread will be introduced. The need and role of digital platforms will be discussed. Finally, how these digital technologies are being leveraged for the digital transformation of the consumer sector will be explained.

# Questions

Here are some questions to test your understanding of the chapter:

1. Why is the culture of an organization important for the success of industrial digital transformation?
2. What are the key phases of the agile development life cycle?
3. What are the capabilities required to deliver a modern digital service?
4. Are there major differences in digital leadership in the commercial sector as compared to the public sector?
5. What is the role of digital talent in driving transformation?
6. What are the benefits of design thinking in product innovation?
7. How is the role of CDO different from that of the CIO?

# Further reading

We recommend reading these books:

- *Leading Digital: Turning Technology into Business Transformation*, George Westerman, Didier Bonnet, Andrew McAfee, Harvard Business Review Press
- *Why Digital Transformations Fail: The Surprising Disciplines of How to Take off and Stay Ahead*, Tony Saldanha, Berrett-Koehler Publishers
- *Mindset: The New Psychology of Success*, Carol Dweck, Ballantine Books
- *Now, Discover your Strengths: How to Develop your Talents and those of the people you manage*, Marcus Buckingham, Donald Clifton, Simon & Schuster
- *High Velocity Innovation: How to Get Your Best Ideas to Market Faster*, Katherine Radeka, Career Press

# 3
# Emerging Technologies to Accelerate Digital Transformation

In *Chapter 2, Transforming the Culture in an Organization*, we learned about the key role that the culture of the organization plays in enabling industrial digital transformation. The culture of innovation and risk-taking can be a challenge for traditional organizations. The infusion of digital talent and leadership, often under the **Chief Digital Officer** (**CDO**) or its variant role, can ignite that cultural transformation and the organizational structure for a successful transformation. The culture of transformation sets the stage for the use of digital technologies and business model and process changes, which we will learn more about in this and the next chapter.

The industry landscape for major digital technologies will also be discussed in this chapter. Consumer industries and their products touch the lives of people around the world daily, unlike any other industry. A set of case studies in consumer industries will be presented in this chapter to explain how the consumer sector is leveraging these emerging technologies for its digital transformation and its impact.

In this chapter, we will be exploring the following topics:

- The role of emerging technologies as an enabler of digital transformation
- The landscape of the emerging technologies
- The role of digital twins and digital threads
- The transformation of some consumer companies by leveraging digital technologies and digital platforms

# The need for new digital capabilities

A transformation is underway where technology has started to touch every facet of our society: from communication to medicine and farming to manufacturing and more. In our daily lives, communication systems, ubiquitous sensors, and wearable devices are beginning to melt the boundary between the physical and digital worlds.

Computing power in the world has grown exponentially over the past four decades. Moore's law is still holding, with the number of transistors in a **Very Large-Scale Integration** (**VLSI**) doubling over a period of approximately 2 years. Moore's law is actually based on an observation from Gordon Moore, the co-founder of Intel (see `https://www.intel.com/content/www/us/en/history/museum-gordon-moore-law.html`). The cost of computing continues to trend lower. This is an enabler for digital transformation. Here, our focus will be on emerging technologies that are enablers of digital transformation, which is underway.

The vast majority of digital transformation efforts have been the result of new enabling technologies. In many cases, new technologies have been developed for non-commercial uses and applied by companies that saw the promise of the technology to transform their business model or operations. Others were invented to solve problems or to create new markets. This is not an unusual idea, as product manufacturers have been innovating on a schedule to facilitate their product development plans for decades. However, in recent years, these enabling technologies have been more disruptive and consequential than past efforts.

The power of digital transformation is in the combination of several new technologies to enable process and business transformation. During the dot com era, one technology, the internet, was the catalyst for the vast majority of transformations.

The hallmark of industrial digital transformation is the wide range of technologies that are advancing dramatically over a relatively short period of time. This wide range of technologies includes the **Global Positioning System (GPS)**, **Internet of Things (IoT)**, cloud computing, **Artificial Intelligence (AI)**, big data and analytics, blockchain, robotics, drones, 3D printing, **Augmented Reality (AR)** and **Virtual Reality (VR)**, **Robotic Process Automation (RPA)**, and mobile technologies, including **5G**.

New technologies have enabled and, in fact, required transformation across all enterprises, without distinction for industry type, size, or whether the enterprise is public, private, or non-profit. Those enterprises that fail to transform and adopt new technologies often risk becoming irrelevant or end up in bankruptcy.

To understand the impact on industries, let's look at examples of digital transformation in manufacturing, consumer products, and the public sector and introduce the breadth and transformative impact of these new technologies.

## Digital transformation in manufacturing

One example of the profound impact of digital transformation on manufacturing processes can be found at Airbus, one of the world's largest aircraft manufacturers.

Airbus implemented drone technology to perform a visual inspection of aircraft. Drones follow a pre-defined path within a hanger to inspect the fuselage of aircraft in their production facility. Drones maintain a safe distance from the aircraft through laser obstacle detection. High-resolution images are wirelessly transmitted to a ruggedized tablet for real-time review. Images are then transferred to a desktop inspection station, where a technician uses 3D models to compare the images to the structural model of the aircraft and detect any defects not visible to the human eye. An example of this would be micro-cracks on the surface of aircraft structures. This process will only take 3 hours to inspect an aircraft, compared to a day in a traditional visual inspection of the aircraft. For more details, see `https://www.airbus.com/newsroom/press-releases/en/2018/04/airbus-launches-advanced-indoor-inspection-drone-to-reduce-aircr.html`.

## Digital transformation in consumer products

An example of digital transformation in consumer products that is familiar to all of us is Tesla, a company whose products include many emerging technologies. To prove the feasibility of an affordable electric vehicle, Tesla had to reduce the cost and increase the range of vehicle batteries, introducing the first electric vehicle with a range of over 300 miles, and applying AI to optimize charging and maximize battery life.

Tesla has also advanced autonomous driving, using IoT capabilities, sensors, and cameras, to collect information about the environment around the car and inform driving decisions made by the vehicle's onboard computer. Tesla vehicles use wireless technology to send driving information back to the company and to receive software updates. Machine learning is used to analyze vehicle data and improve the driving performance of vehicles. Tesla vehicles can be controlled by a Bluetooth-enabled key fob or a mobile app on a smartphone. Tesla is an example of combining the technologies that enable digital transformation to deliver new experiences beyond what any one technology could provide.

# Digital transformation in the public sector

The public sector has not missed the opportunity to use emerging digital technologies to improve citizen experiences. In many cases, we are unaware that we are interacting with the government when we are using public sector digital technology. One such example is traffic management in Santa Clara County, California. Santa Clara, in the heart of Silicon Valley, is known for traffic challenges and long commutes. To reduce congestion on county-managed roads, the county's traffic engineers deployed sensors and cameras at 130 intersections. Data from the cameras is pushed to the cloud and analyzed in real time, resulting in adjustments to timing at intersections to accommodate everything from heavy traffic flows to bicycles to a slow-moving pedestrian crossing a 10-lane road. The county uses predictive analytics to forecast traffic conditions for the next 15 minutes and provides this information to county residents via their website, allowing individuals to adjust the timing and route of their commute, further reducing congestion.

## Transformations in response to public emergencies

In addition to the three examples that we have discussed so far, we can see digital transformation around us all the time. During the first months of 2020, many businesses transformed their business models – temporarily or permanently – to respond to the COVID-19 pandemic.

Companies that provided rapid prototyping services switched their 3D printers to making face shields overnight to respond to both the urgent need for personal protective equipment and the sudden evaporation of their market. At the same time, large tech companies used mobile devices, GPS, and Bluetooth to rapidly deploy proximity applications that would identify potential exposure to COVID-19. Other companies quickly developed thermal imaging technologies that could identify crowds in public spaces, such as transit, and identify both individuals who may have a fever as well as those who are not wearing masks. Governments responded by taking services, such as marriage license issuance, online and changing rules to legalize weddings to be performed over teleconference.

# Identifying emerging technologies

The rapid emergence of new products in response to the COVID-19 pandemic points to the fact that new technologies are always emerging. While it may seem like a cliché by now, change is happening faster each year, as each enabling technology opens new business opportunities and drives new experimentation. The technologies that have been identified in this chapter are relatively new technologies today, but some are already mainstream, and the rest will be common in a few years time. Therefore, it is important to be able to identify emerging technologies that we can use to improve our processes or develop new business models in the future. Those of us who are the first to identify new enabling technologies will be the first to capitalize on them.

There are a number of ways that we can identify new enabling technologies:

- **Watch global trends**. Look at new businesses that are emerging in other parts of the world and identify the new technologies that are enabling those businesses. For example, mobile payments emerged in China first before moving to the rest of the world.

- **Read technical research in the area of interest**. Every field has academic journals and conferences where scholars publish their research. Journals such as *IEEE Transactions*, where a great deal of early applied research is published, are available for subscriptions and in libraries. If you have a particular area of interest, you can attend academic conferences as well.

- **Follow basic scientific research**. There are journals, such as *Science*, that are accessible to all readers that will help you understand very early trends.

- **Watch the VC funding and angel investment trends and new alerts**. For instance, investment in autonomous vehicles and supporting technologies has been a strong trend in Silicon Valley in recent years.

- **Track corporate research**. While a great deal of research done by corporations is confidential, many companies publish research on their websites after they begin to put it in their products. This will give you a sense of technologies that are showing enough promise to be put in products. The types of patents being filed is useful information too.

- Analyst firms such as Gartner publish the hype cycles that we discussed in *Chapter 1, Introducing Digital Transformation*. This can be used as a good indicator of the level of maturity for a new trend. While innovative companies have to stay ahead of the peak to start looking at the new technology, they have to realize that both risks and rewards can be higher at this stage.

Many emerging technologies have historically taken 8 to 10 years to mature. Bitcoin and blockchain started in 2008. Amazon launched **Amazon Web Services** (**AWS**) in 2006 and the public cloud gained traction in the second half of the last decade. 5G came into being in late 2018. Hence, the CIO and the CDO have the great responsibility of discerning which digital technology is actually beneficial and what is simply hype at this stage. Next, we'll learn more about the emerging technologies that are enabling digital transformation and dive into some case studies.

# Industry landscape of the emerging technologies

The digital technologies described ahead are key to transforming multiple industries. For instance, the **IoT** is the very basis of connected products and operations and helps to launch new business models. The connected products depend on multiple ways of connecting, especially when the product is operating in the field. The sensing technologies provide the measurement of the actual physical state of the product. In the following sections, we will look into the details of the key technologies. We will look at their origin, current state, and how they can be used for specific transformative outcomes.

## Internet of Things

IoT is a powerful enabling technology for digital transformation. Three primary components are fundamental to IoT: connectivity, sensing, and computing (see *Figure 3.1*):

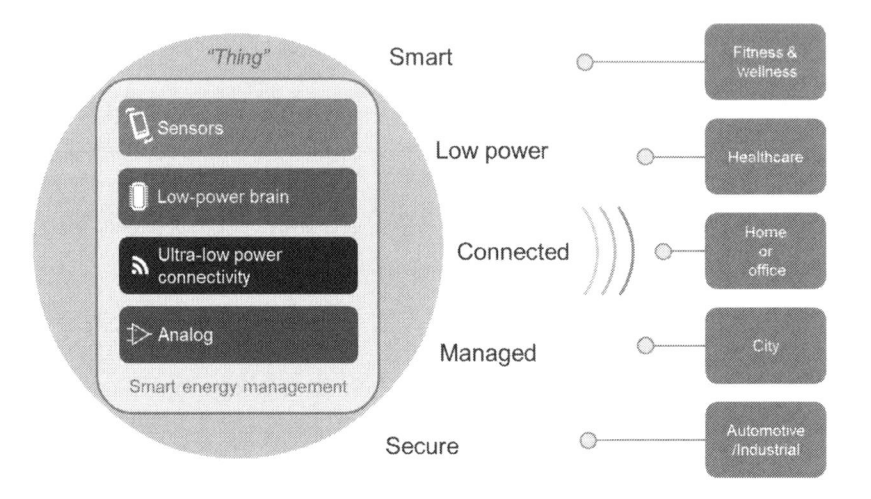

Figure 3.1 – Conceptual view

IoT enables multiple transformative outcomes, as shown on the right in *Figure 3.1*. Fitness trackers allow humans to keep track of their activities and get health advisories. Smart cities and connected cars are also enabled by IoT. Industrial assets such as IoT sensors in an aircraft body or its engines reduce its downtime via predictive maintenance. The sensors in the jet engine collect data such as temperature, pressure, and vibration that is used by the IoT systems to drive business outcomes.

Qualcomm started in 1985 with a focus on selling satellite communications systems for commercial trucks. The system was called Omnitracs for trucking fleet management. This business funded the research for **Code-Division Multiple Access** (**CDMA**) technology, which resulted in Qualcomm as we know it today.

An early example of digital transformation in this space is **Global Navigation Satellite System** (**GNSS**)-enabled cellular-based sensor gateways on a company's vehicles providing location, drivetrain condition, fuel consumption, and cargo status. This enabler can automate important tasks (the digital transformation), such as route planning and maintenance scheduling. Data analytics will help in identifying which vehicle models have the highest operating costs.

## Connectivity

A connectivity technology block is an important component to be considered with a strategic point of view before the deployment of an IoT solution. In the distributed computation architecture for an IoT solution, the connectivity solution is use case-dependent. In such an architecture, computational elements can be distributed between the sensor node, gateway device, or the cloud, and hence connection throughput, range, power budget, network topology, interoperability, and cost are important considerations. Connectivity requirements are also influenced by use cases within an industry sector.

Let's delve deeper into this topic by looking at the most common options to consider for IoT connectivity.

## Bluetooth

Bluetooth is a short-range communication technology that has evolved over the past few decades. Bluetooth Classic supports two-way point-to-point or point-to-multipoint continuous communication at a throughput of up to 2.1 Mbps in a maximum of seven associated devices. A variant, **Bluetooth Low-Energy** (**BLE**), provides communication at lower throughput (0.3 Mbps) but at 100x lower power consumption, suitable for small-scale consumer IoT applications. BLE is commonly used in consumer devices, such as smartwatches, fitness trackers, and other wearables. In such cases, smartphones connected to these devices act as a gateway for cloud applications.

The extension of this technology with Bluetooth Mesh enables a wider deployment of BLE devices. Bluetooth Mesh enables diverse applications from smart indoor lighting to control systems in smart homes. BLE beacon-based solutions are being used for indoor positioning and targeted advertising.

## Low power wide area network

**Low Power Wide Area Network (LPWAN)** technology has been developed to address IoT connectivity requirements of low power, reliable, secure, and long-range communication. There are solutions both in the licensed and unlicensed bands. NB-IoT and LTE-M are in the licensed band and LoRa, Sigfox, and MYTHINGS, are in the unlicensed band. LPWAN solutions offer long-range communication on small batteries in IoT nodes in large networks spread over industrial complexes or in commercial settings such as shopping malls. These technologies provide at least 500 meters of signal range from the gateway device to the IoT node. Coverage is the lowest in challenging deployment environments, such as urban or underground.

## Cellular

Cellular 3G/4G networks offer reliable broadband communication over a very wide coverage area. 4G networks shared about 75% of the global population coverage in 2018 and will grow to over 90% by 2025. However, cellular network connectivity options for IoT solutions have very high operating costs. The power requirements are also very high for a battery-powered IoT node. However, this option has been widely used for a long time in fleet management in transportation and logistics for supply chain visibility. Many connected cars are sold with **Advanced Driver Assistance Systems (ADAS)** and tracking services that enable applications such as real-time traffic for better route guidance and cloud service-driven infotainment. Ubiquitous high-bandwidth cellular connectivity is essential for these applications.

## Wi-Fi

This is the most commonly used solution for high-throughput data transfer in home and business environments. Wi-Fi bandwidth is higher than Bluetooth, Zigbee, and Z-Wave (we'll look at the last two a little later in this section). Wi-Fi is often not a good connectivity option when the network is massive and relies on an IoT sensor powered by a battery, because of higher power consumption. This aspect is most challenging for industrial IoT use cases.

Wi-Fi 6, released in 2019, offers many relevant features. The maximum theoretical speed increases three times to 9.6 Gbps. The new standard allows routers to communicate with many devices at once. Routers are able to send data to many devices in the same broadcast. Wi-Fi 6 allows devices to plan out communications with a router using a feature known as Target Wake Time. This allows the routers to schedule check-in times with devices. Hence, it will reduce the amount of time IoT nodes have to keep their antennas powered on, for transmission and to search for signals. This feature reduces the drainage on the batteries considerably.

## 5G technology

As 5G technology deployment rolls out, we are on track to have 200 million 5G devices in 2020. 5G offers support for high-speed mobility, as well as ultra-low latency. These features will be an enabler for a large number of diverse applications. Because of these attributes, this technology is already being used in the development of autonomous vehicles systems. Ultra-wideband and ultra-low latency offered by 5G will enhance the AR/VR experience and will enable the proliferation of use cases in business, education, and industrial applications.

## Zigbee

Zigbee is another mesh topology solution being used to extend coverage. It is done by relaying the sensor data through multiple IoT nodes. It is a short-range, low-power connectivity option that provides higher throughput compared to LPWAN. However, it is not as power-efficient as LPWAN due to its mesh configuration. Zigbee and similar mesh technologies are best-suited for medium-range IoT applications that can operate in a range of less than 100 m. Zigbee has been used in commercial building control systems.

## Sensing

Sensing technology has rapidly developed to help with the digitization of the five senses, as shown in *Figure 3.2*:

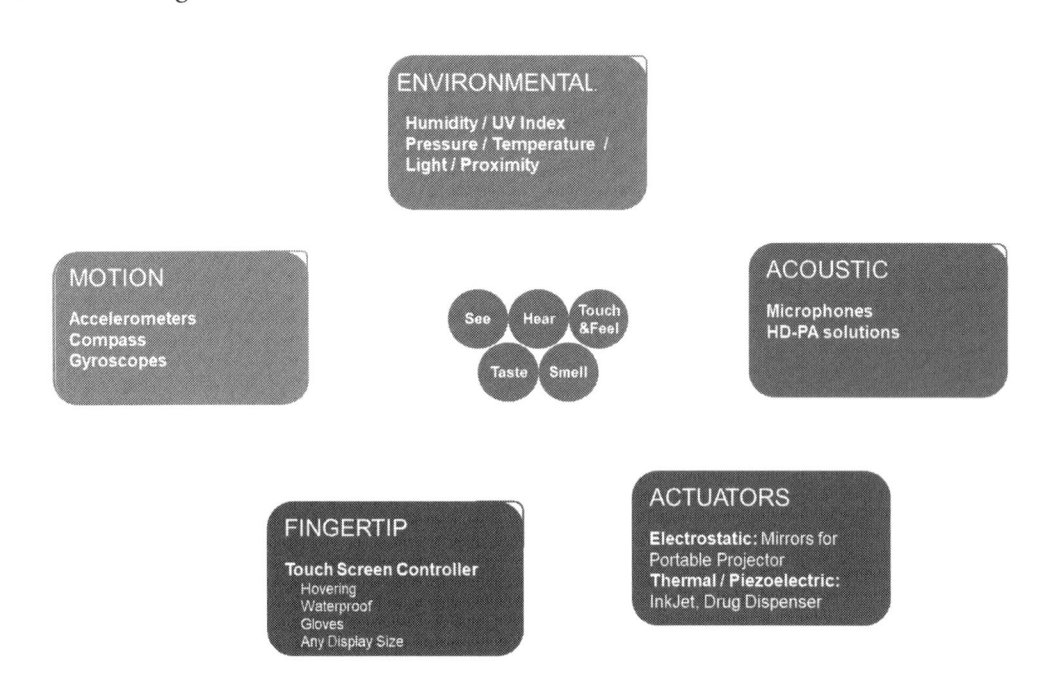

Figure 3.2 – Digitization of the five senses

Technological innovations in the development of **Micro-Electromechanical System (MEMS)** sensors has allowed high-volume production, with sensors performing within tight tolerances of the performance specification. These MEMS sensors are small enough that they fit within the height requirement of less than 1 mm and their power consumption is small enough that mobile devices such as cellphones and fitness trackers to battery-powered industrial sensor nodes contain multiple of these sensors. The latest high-end mobile phones contain more than 10 of these MEMS sensors.

MEMS accelerometers and gyroscopes have consistently improved in the past decade. Initially, MEMS accelerometers were primarily used for motion interface functions, such as automatic adjustment of portrait or landscape mode of the display on mobile phones. Since then, these sensors are now being used in a wide array of applications in consumer, automotive, and industrial applications as well.

A magnetometer senses a magnetic field. One common application of a magnetometer is to detect a compass heading relative to the earth's magnetic North pole. Magnetometers are most commonly used to determine the directional heading of mobile phone users when using digital map applications. (see: `https://www.w3.org/TR/magnetometer/`)

Audio is a very strong signal that can be used for contextual and situation awareness and the microphone is a sensor used for this purpose. Microphones produce an electrical signal by converting the air pressure variations of a sound wave. There has been a lot of development in microphones since the early days of telephone development to now. Mobile phones use more than three microphones. An array of these microphones serves as the primary sensor for voice-activated speakers, such as Amazon's Alexa or Google Assistant.

Pressure sensors enable a variety of applications. In a mobile phone, a pressure sensor measures ambient pressure to determine the floor of the building on which the user is located, for `E911` type applications. Tire pressure monitoring systems use this sensor to ensure that vehicles' tires are correctly inflated for safety and fuel efficiency.

A humidity sensor measures the amount of water vapor present in the air. In industrial environments, a rise in the humidity beyond the threshold levels can impact the performance of electronic systems. Gas sensors can measure the content of **particulate matter** (**PM2.5**), noxious gases, **Volatile Organic Compounds** (**VOCs**), and $CO_2$ in the air. Indoor or outdoor air quality monitors utilize these sensors. In industrial environments, gas sensors play a very important role in safety in detecting combustible, flammable, or toxic gases.

A proximity sensor can detect the presence of external objects and their distances without making physical contact. This sensor can be realized using multiple types of technologies, such as optical, capacitive, magnetic, or ultrasonic. A photoelectric proximity sensor contains an **Infrared** (**IR**) LED and an IR light detector. An ambient light sensor measures the amount of light present. It is commonly used in mobiles phones, notebooks, and automotive displays to increase or decrease the illumination of display based on ambient lighting conditions:

Sensing technologies (see *Figure 3.2*) are enabling and accelerating digital transformation:

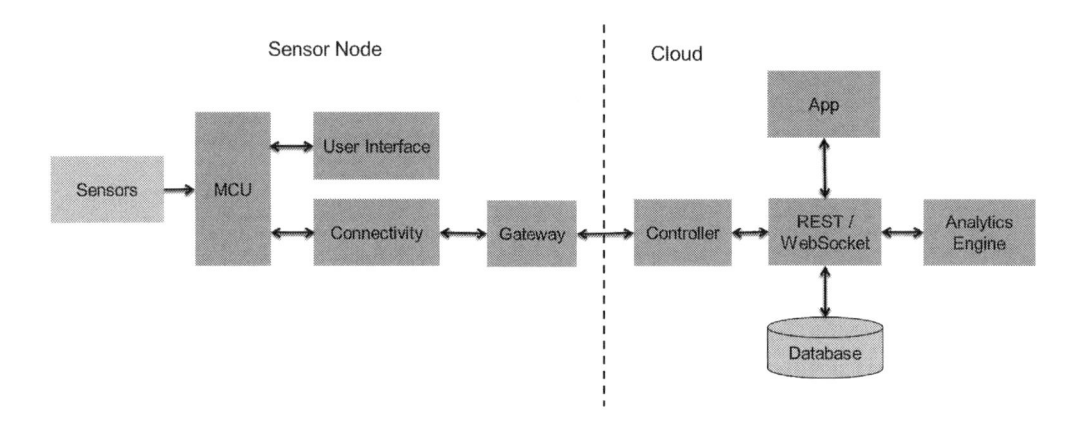

Figure 3.3 – IoT architecture concept diagram

The interaction of an IoT system with the physical world is achieved through sensing and actuation functionalities. *Figure 3.3* shows the architecture of an IoT node generating the data and the cloud piece in one implementation. Sensor data can be processed at the sensor, gateway, or cloud. Hence, different levels of computing capabilities are made available at these points based on requirements. A connectivity solution is needed to transfer sensor data from the sensor node or a gateway device to the cloud.

## Computing

Next, let's look at the different paradigms of computing. The data generated by IoT systems has to be processed and analyzed to derive business value from it. This processing may require enormous amounts of computing power when the volume of the sensor data and related attributes is very large and time-sensitive. The nature of the application determines if the computing takes place at different locations for maximum efficiency and timeliness.

## Distributed computing

Computation for IoT applications can occur in distributed architectures, including sensor nodes, gateway devices, and the cloud. Edge computations are done at or near the source of the data. IoT sensor nodes (edge devices) can run analytics and AI algorithms, and store some of the relevant sensor data or metadata. These devices can execute analytical and classification logic autonomously on ARM or x86 class processors with a small amount of memory and storage space.

A gateway provides the bridge between IoT or edge devices, such as sensor nodes in the field, the cloud, and devices such as smartphones. The IoT gateway provides a communication link between all sensors and remote connections to the cloud, applications, or users. An IoT gateway compiles data from various sensors, provides translation for protocols used by different IoT devices, and might filter or batch the data before transferring it. IoT devices may connect to a gateway using any of the connectivity technologies mentioned in the previous section. A gateway may support transmission protocols such as MQTT, CoAP, AMQP, DDS, and WebSocket.

Next, we will look at the different paradigms of cloud computing, which generally refers to the on-demand availability of shared pools of resources with fairly standardized commercial terms.

## Cloud computing

The cloud computing paradigm uses hardware and software resources, such as networking, servers, data storage, database management, and software applications including AI. These hardware and software resources can be accessed and configured by users over the internet in an automated fashion. Cloud computing resources are accessed over a platform-independent interface client platform, such as a tablet, mobile phone, or laptop. Some major cloud service providers are Microsoft Azure, **Amazon Web Services** (**AWS**), Google Cloud, Alibaba Cloud, Oracle Cloud, and IBM Cloud. Multiple users can be served using a metered pay-as-you go approach for shared cloud compute resources. End users therefore do not need to design, purchase, install, configure, and manage this infrastructure. There are different cloud providers to help meet the different implementation requirements for companies of different sizes and global presence. Cloud computing often helps to shift the financial paradigm from **CAPEX** to **OPEX** (**capital expenditure** to operating expenditure).

**Infrastructure as a Service** (**IaaS**) provides users with fundamental computational infrastructure components, such as servers, storage, and networking resources such as firewalls and routers. These resources may be accessed by users as virtual machines, which users can configure and manage. Good examples of IaaS are Amazon EC2, Oracle Cloud Infrastructure Bare Metal Instance, and Google Cloud Compute Engine.

**Platform as a Service** (**PaaS**) provides a cloud computing platform for users to develop, test, and deploy their software applications. In order to develop applications, users need a cloud service **Application Programming Interface** (**API**), associated software libraries, and development tools. The PaaS provider manages the platform software infrastructure for users. Good examples of PaaS are Amazon Elastic Beanstalk and Apache Stratos.

**Software as a Service (SaaS)** provides a complete suite of application software, including a user interface that runs in the cloud. An application enabled by SaaS is accessed over an internet connection, generally using a web browser. Any device that can run a web browser and has interconnectivity is able to access SaaS applications. This flexibility and accessibility make SaaS the most widely used form of cloud computing. Good examples of SaaS are Salesforce.com, Oracle Human Capital Management, Dropbox, and DocuSign.

There are four commonly used cloud computing models:

- **Public cloud**: In this implementation, the cloud provider offers access to cloud hardware and software services through the internet. Users, therefore, do not need to design, purchase, install, or maintain any hardware, software, or supporting networking or security infrastructure. Cloud infrastructure is owned and managed by the cloud provider, and the users are charged based on metered usage of this infrastructure. In this model, multiple customers are able to share the infrastructure of a public cloud. Public cloud service providers offer access to IaaS computing and storage resources, SaaS software applications, and PaaS for application development, testing, and deployment.

- **Private cloud**: Private cloud is an implementation of cloud infrastructure that is operated exclusively for one company. This deployment of the cloud may be managed by the company or a third party (or both) and is most often hosted primarily on a company's location. This private cloud approach allows a company to maintain greater control over different cloud resources, data security, and regulatory compliance, thus avoiding the potential impact of sharing resources with another cloud client.

- **Hybrid cloud**: Hybrid cloud integrates private and public clouds, using technology and management tools that allow workloads to move seamlessly between the two as needed for optimum performance, security, compliance, and cost-effectiveness. Hybrid cloud, for example, allows a company to store sensitive data and mission-critical legacy applications (which cannot be migrated to the cloud) at their premises. At the same time, a hybrid cloud would allow the use of the public cloud to access SaaS applications, PaaS for rapid deployment of new applications, and IaaS for additional real-time storage or computing capacity as required.

- **Multicloud**: This implementation uses infrastructure and components from different public clouds and uses services from two or more major cloud providers, or services from a major cloud provider and at least one SaaS software vendor. Businesses are increasingly adopting hybrid multicloud as the deployment model, which allows maximum flexibility while fulfilling their requirements for security and regulatory compliance as they move toward integrating their systems with legacy applications.

Today, many companies use one or more of these cloud computing models to suit their own transformation needs. In general, enterprises are reducing their own data centers and on-premises legacy applications and adopting cloud models to become more agile. Often, the cloud computing models allow rapid provisioning, a shift from CAPEX to OPEX due to subscription models, resulting in faster access to digital technologies to enable industrial digital transformation. Often, emerging technologies are either available only in the cloud or are cloud-first.

## Contextual and situational awareness applications

Mobile and wearable devices such as smartphones, tablets, smart watches, and activity trackers increasingly carry multiple sensors such as an accelerometer, gyroscope, magnetometer, barometer, and microphone that can be used either singly or jointly to detect a user's context, such as motion activities, voice activities, and spatial environment.

The following definition of context is appropriate as it accounts for interaction between an application and its user: *Context is any information that can be used to characterize the situation of an entity.* An entity is a person, place, or object that is considered relevant to the interaction between a user and an application, including the user and applications themselves (see `https://www.cc.gatech.edu/fce/ctk/pubs/PeTe5-1.pdf`).

Context-awareness information, in general, as shown in *Figure 3.4*, will be a function of input data from one sensor or several heterogeneous sensors, such as an accelerometer, barometer, gyroscope, magnetometer, microphone, GPS, camera, RF sensors, light sensor, proximity sensor, various gas sensors, and so on. The specific device being used for a particular application may have some or all of these sensors and can vary with the use case. The choice of sensor for a particular application may depend on energy constraints, the scope of the context detection task, and other specifications.

In most context detection tasks, data from one sensor only is used. The accelerometer is typically used for motion activity detection while the microphone is used for voice activity detection and spatial environment detection. The fusion of features from data obtained from three sensors – namely, an accelerometer, a microphone, and a pressure sensor – has also been used for the classification of motion activities:

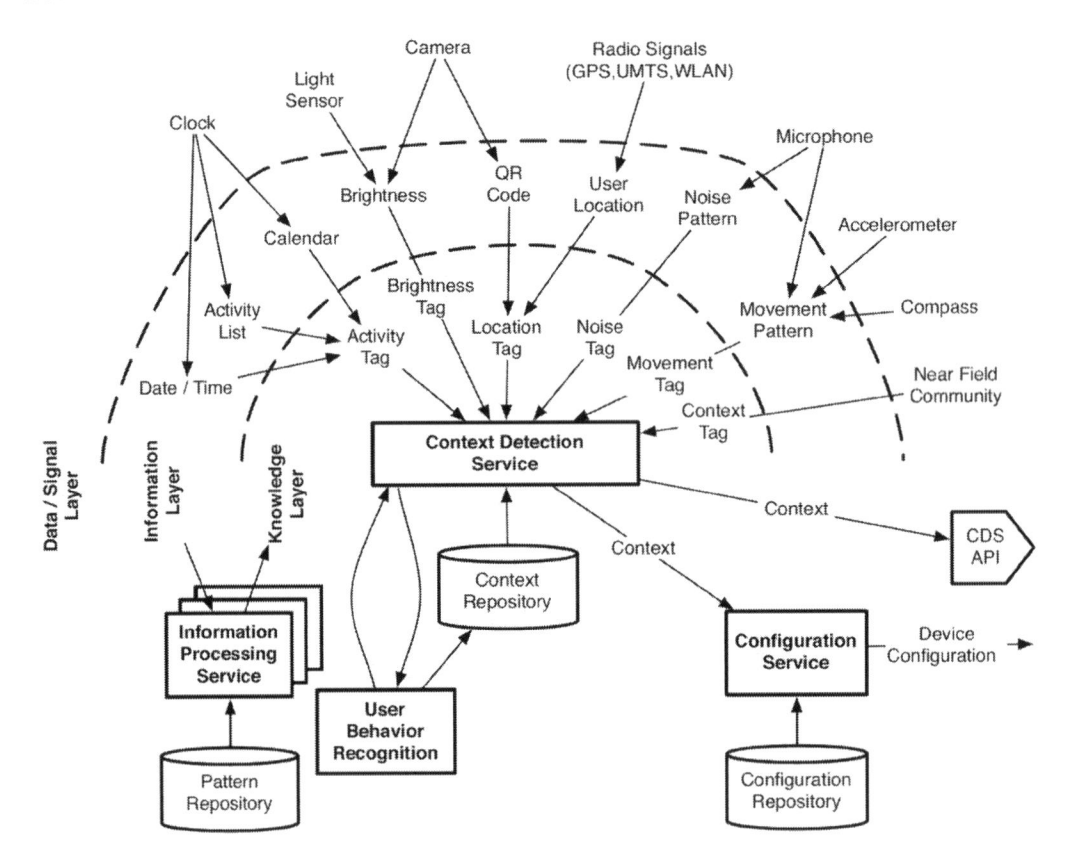

Figure 3.4 – Context awareness framework

Three layers of information granularity for context awareness applications is shown in *Figure 3.4*. The outermost layer is the data or signal layer. Here, the raw sensor data or signal is available from various sensors. This data can be processed to derive information. For example, an acceleration signal can be converted to get information about the movement pattern. The next layer is the knowledge layer, where the information from single or multiple sources is processed to derive knowledge of context. For example, movement patterns from acceleration signals and microphone data can be processed to determine the specific context of a device. This contextual information in the case of a machine can be used to raise alerts in condition-based monitoring systems.

# AI

AI and digital transformation are complementary. AI is defined as a combination of technologies that allow machines or devices to sense their environment and generate actions to successfully achieve design goals. AI uses various computational methods, such as machine learning and deep learning. Machine learning is a powerful enabler for organizations that are on path for digital transformation. AI technologies are driven primarily by relevant and large amounts of data. Hence, this key requirement of a large amount of relevant data in turn necessitates the installation of digital technologies and building blocks for generating and capturing relevant data for a successful AI transformational effort. These digital building blocks are responsible for acquisition, management, organization, processing of data, and the presentation of results. Hence, digital transformation is a prerequisite for AI transformation. The advantages of AI technologies also justify the investment for digital building blocks.

Transformation is usually required or compelled as a result of various compelling events that occur simultaneously and it fundamentally changes the business landscape. One such event is development in data-driven technologies. Among many advancements is the ability to transmit sensor data at high speed and the ability to process this large amount of data in real time to extract usable information. Edge devices, such as intelligent sensor nodes, that interact with the real-world environment have a limited amount of computing capability available for processing data and generating actionable information. Additionally, the maturing of the software processes and implementation space makes it possible to combine these blocks in the form of powerful software products and services that can be efficiently deployed and integrated into existing systems.

Next, we will learn about the machine learning platforms and why they are needed.

## Machine learning platforms

Machine learning algorithms are developed using a large amount of data. Some of this data is used for training and other parts can be set aside for testing the algorithm for its performance. These algorithms can complete tasks such as detection, classification, and predictions or make decisions. Machine learning algorithms can be classified into two broad categories: supervised learning and unsupervised learning. Supervised learning requires labeled data for the training process. Labeling indicates that training data is tagged with the best known information about the state of the system at the time of data collection. Unsupervised learning algorithms can develop patterns without any labeling or tagging information in training data. Some examples of supervised machine learning algorithms are linear regression, logistic regression, **K-Nearest Neighbors (K-NN)**, decision trees, random forest, and naïve Bayes. Some examples of unsupervised learning algorithms are clustering and dimension reduction algorithms.

Data science and machine learning platforms provide users with the tools to develop and deploy machine learning algorithms. These platforms combine machine learning decision-making algorithms with data and enable developers to create a business solution. Leading providers of these platforms are Amazon (SageMaker), Microsoft Azure ML Studio, RapidMiner, the IBM Watson machine learning platform, and MathWorks.

There are numerous examples of digital transformation enabled by AI and machine learning techniques. The AI-powered robot USTAAD is in use by Indian Railways to conduct real-time inspection on mechanical parts in railway coaches.

## Deep learning platforms

Deep learning is a subfield of machine learning concerned with algorithms, inspired by the function of the brain, called **Artificial Neural Networks** (**ANNs**). Deep learning architectures such as **Deep Neural Networks** (**DNNs**), **Recurrent Neural Networks** (**RNNs**), and **Convolutional Neural Networks** (**CNNs**) have been successfully applied in a wide variety of fields, including computer vision, speech recognition, medical image analysis, and material inspection. Some of the leading providers of deep learning platforms are the Google AI platform, TensorFlow, the Microsoft Azure Cloud AI platform, and H2O.ai.

Deep learning models such as ANNs are now used in medical imaging. There are many applications of deep learning in the entire chain of **Magnetic Resonance Imaging** (**MRI**), starting from the acquisition of images to the prediction of disease from MRI data. CNNs are used to improve the contrast of brain MRI images while reducing the dose of the contrast agent such as gadolinium. One of the major challenges in **Positron Emission Tomography/Magnetic Resonance Imaging** (**PET/MRI**) is to accurately estimate PET attenuation correction. This task is achieved by the use of a CNN.

## Virtual agents

Virtual agents use AI technologies to interact with customers and provide customer service and help with support for issues across various communication channels. A **chatbot** is typically used for a solution that can handle simple, routine queries and FAQs. **Intelligent Virtual Assistants** (**IVAs**), on the other hand, are more advanced conversational solutions that are designed with **Natural Language Understanding** (**NLU**), **Natural Language Generation** (**NLG**), and deep learning. These technologies enable them to understand and retain context and manage more productive conversations with users.

## Image recognition

Image recognition is the process of identifying and detecting an object, place, people, or features in a digital image or video. AI solutions help with pattern recognition, facial recognition, object recognition, text detection, and image analysis for achieving these objectives. Image recognition technology can also be used to verify users based on their face or license plates, diagnose diseases, and analyze clients and their behavior.

Other areas where AI technologies are making a big impact are natural language generation, speech recognition, marketing automation, robotic process automation, and biometrics. We'll look at these in more detail in *Chapter 8, Artificial Intelligence in Digital Transformation*. Next, we will look at big data.

## Big data

Big data refers to solutions that analyze and extract usable information from very large and complex datasets that cannot be managed with traditional data-processing application software. The landscape for big data has been changing over the last few years. More recently, the term big data tends to refer to the use of predictive analytics, user behavior analytics, or certain other advanced data analytics methods that extract value from data. The size of a dataset is not the most important characteristic. Data volumes continue to multiply with a proliferation of data-generating IoT devices. AI technologies enabling the analysis of such datasets can find new correlations that can lead to fruitful objectives, such as spotting business trends or even preventing diseases.

In the last decade, Hadoop was the most well-known platform for analyzing big data. However, it is running into increasing competition from cloud platforms. Hadoop was developed at a time when the cloud was not a serious option, and most data was stored on-premises. These days, cloud offerings include complete platforms for IaaS, PaaS services including streaming, data transformation, and AI. The transition from solutions such as Hadoop and Spark to the cloud is clearly accelerating with a trend of evolution toward a hybrid approach, involving a combination of public cloud, private cloud, and on-premises data storage. Cloud providers, such as AWS and Microsoft Azure, continue to grow rapidly, despite their massive scale. The recent merger of Hortonworks with Cloudera and HP's acquisition of MapR points to a changing landscape of acquisition and consolidation of pure-play providers of Hadoop.

In this new multi-cloud and hybrid cloud era, another important technology option is Kubernetes. Kubernetes is an open source solution for managing containerized workloads and services, automating application deployment, scaling, and management. It was designed by Google. Kubernetes works with a range of container tools, including Docker. Many cloud services offer a Kubernetes-based platform or infrastructure as a service (PaaS or IaaS) on which Kubernetes can be deployed as a platform-providing service. Kubernetes is also gaining momentum in the machine learning community because it provides the flexibility to choose the language, machine learning library, or framework, and train models, without involving infrastructure experts.

We will next look at robotics and how it is being used in sectors from industrial to medical.

## Robotics

The McKinsey reports (`https://www.mckinsey.com/~/media/McKinsey/Industries/Advanced%20Electronics/Our%20Insights/Growth%20dynamics%20in%20industrial%20robotics/Industrial-robotics-Insights-into-the-sectors-future-growth-dynamics.ashx`) state that deployments of robots have been growing at 19% per year for the past decade. The main drivers for growth in robotics and automation are the following:

- Reduced cost of production
- Improved quality
- Increase in productivity
- Improved capabilities of robots

These drivers will continue to drive the adoption of robotics and we will see mainstream deployments in the coming years. The growth in the adoption of robots has led to their classification by functionality. The largest growth is observed in five broad categories of robots: industrial, collaborative, mobile, medical, and exoskeleton.

### Industrial robots

The largest applications of industrial robots are in materials handling operations, welding, painting, palletizing, and assembling. Automotive **Original Equipment Manufacturers (OEMs)** and automotive suppliers make up the largest industry segment that uses these robots. Industrial robots are usually fixed, operate within safety fences without contact with human workers, and are programmed for a specific application.

Another type of industrial robots, **collaborative robots** (**cobots**), however, directly interact with human workers without safety fences and are generally designed with machine learning capabilities. These robots are used to support human workers with attributes such as precision for certain movements and strength. These robots are useful for processes that require flexibility and where the area of operation space is limited.

Mobile robots have a few variations. A couple of popular categories for industrial applications are **Autonomous Guided Vehicles (AGVs)** and **Autonomous Mobile Robots (AMRs)**. These mobile robots have navigation and route planning mechanisms either onboard (using cameras, location technologies, and scanning technologies) or external (using path-based magnetic tape, wire, or rails on the ground). Mobile robots are used for logistics and delivery operations. For example, they can be used in industrial settings for moving pieces, such as boxes, pallets, or tools, between machines, transfer points, or storage warehouses.

## Medical robots

The use of AI has led to significant advances in medical robots in the healthcare sector. Hospital robots can perform a wide variety of functions, including the distribution of medicines, laboratory specimens, and other sensitive materials, such as hospital patient data.

Aethon developed an autonomous mobile robot called the TUG, which is capable of performing all these functions. Pharmacy robots, such as the ROBOT-Rx from German healthcare firm McKesson, can automatically process, store, and restock medicines, reducing hospital costs and errors.

The most common use of robotics in surgery involves mechanical arms attached to a camera and/or surgical equipment that is controlled by a surgeon. Robot-assisted operations mean complex procedures can be completed more accurately and with greater control. Some examples of robot-assisted procedures include biopsies, cancer tumor removal, heart valve repair, and gastric bypasses. Currently, Intuitive Surgical dominates this market. Its da Vinci surgical robot system was one of the first of its kind to have been approved in 2000 by the US **Food and Drug Administration** (**FDA**). While many of these technologies are intended for use in hospitals and other healthcare centers, care robots can provide support to elderly or disabled patients in their homes. They are not yet widely deployed, but this will change significantly over the next decade, especially in countries with a shortage of caregivers, such as Japan. Care robots are mainly used nowadays to perform simple functions, such as helping patients get into and out of bed. One example is ROBEAR, a care robot developed by RIKEN and Sumitomo Riko, a Japanese research institute and manufacturing firm.

In an industrial setting, during heavy-duty or ergonomically challenging production process steps, exoskeletons can be connected to the human body for support. These types of robots are designed to boost human worker strength – for example, increasing the capacity of humans to carry heavy weight.

## Drones

Drones have been in use in defense for quite some time. Predator drones have received a lot of media coverage. Military spending on drone technology is expected to grow. A Business Insider report from September 2019 (`https://www.businessinsider.com/world-rethinks-war-as-nearly-100-countries-field-military-drones-2019-9`) states that 95 countries around the world possess some form of military drone technology.

There is a wide range of industries, public sector utilities, and other entities using drone and **Unmanned Aerial Systems** (**UASes**) in their process of digital transformation.

## Defense

Drones are becoming a more important feature of defense operations. Various technologies are leading to advancements in the capability of creating drones with the ability to fight like unmanned fighter aircraft and manned/unmanned teaming.

## Emergency response

Drones can help transform emergency response in multiple ways. Drones provide rapid situational awareness with mapping technology and 3D imagery to emergency responders. Drones are being used by firefighters to identify hot spots and assess property damage. They are being used to assess utility and infrastructure damage.

## Infrastructure inspections

Here are some examples of how drones/UASes are used for infrastructure inspections:

- **Electricity transmission and distribution lines**: Identify vegetation growth and the accumulation of wildfire fuels, leaning power poles, sagging wires, equipment wear, and vandalism.
- **Oil and natural gas pipelines**: Detect leaks and corrosion in critical equipment.
- **Vertical structures**: Inspect nuclear cooling towers, storage tanks, smokestacks, and piers for signs of wear and anomalies.
- **Dams and levees**: Identify structural defects and wear and tear that need repairs.

- **Bridges, underpasses, overpasses, and culverts**: Identify cracks and general wear-and-tear conditions.
- **Roads and freeways**: Assess cracking and maintenance needs of pavements.
- **Municipal water systems**: Aqueducts, fish ladders on older dams, reservoirs for leak detection, environmental monitoring, vegetation management, and security.
- **Railways**: Check for wear, vegetation, rocks, and security on tracks, as well as conditions of bridges, poles, and yards.
- **Utility-scale solar facilities**: For locating sub-performing arrays and repair needs.
- **On-shore and off-shore wind turbines**: Detect cracks and other maintenance needs.

Drones are used for several conservation tasks too. Let's look at them.

## Conservation

Drones are used for several conservation tasks, such as surveying wildlife, monitoring and mapping land and marine ecosystems, supporting anti-poaching and anti-wildlife trafficking efforts, and enforcing reductions in human activities in protected areas.

## Healthcare

Drones make it possible to deliver blood, vaccines, snakebite serum, and other medical supplies to rural areas and can reach victims who require immediate medical attention within minutes.

## Insurance industry

Drones can be used to gather aerial imagery data before a risk is insured and to assess damage after an event. One of the most common uses for drones by insurers is rooftop inspections. Roofs are difficult and hazardous to inspect especially after fire damage. Drones can also conduct periodic inspections of boilers and pressure vessels.

## Live entertainment

Drone are being used for light shows to create a unique collective art and music experience. They are also being used to enhance large-scale live performances, by streaming the concert on big screens for concert goers.

### Sporting events

Some professional teams in soccer, the NFL, and rugby are now using drones to further augment their training. The unique from-above-the-action vantage point and 360-degree view offered by drones help the coaching staff get a better understanding of player positioning and formations. Drones are also being used to give sports fans a better viewing experience.

## AR and VR landscape

AR is an interactive experience of a real-world environment using devices such as smart glasses, shown in *Figure 3.5*, and combines real and virtual worlds through real-time interaction while maintaining an accurate 3D representation of virtual and real objects:

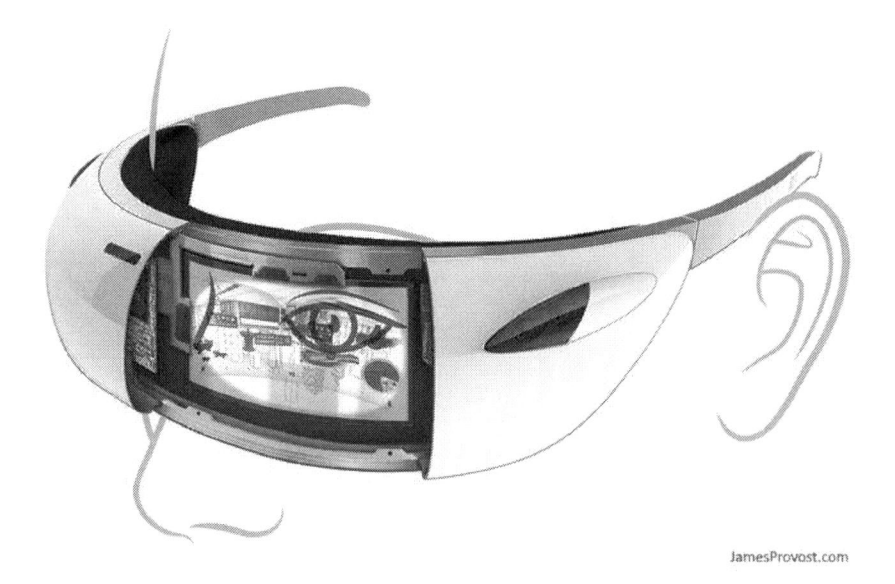

Figure 3.5 – An AR device (Source: `http://1319.virtualclassroom.org/media.html`, License: CC BY)

AR devices contain various sensors, such as a GNSS receiver to determine the location of the user and **Inertial Measurement Units** (**IMUs**) to track the motion of the wearer's head and determine where they are looking and their direction of movement. These devices may also contain tiny speakers that can provide audio cues to the wearer. These devices contain near-to-eye compact display technology, which provides images with a resolution of 720P–1,400P in a **Field of View** (**FOV**) of 40–80 degrees. The combination of these technologies allows augmenting the real world with information overlaid by the AR device to enhance interactivity with a great degree of realism.

VR devices, such as the HTC Vive, provide a simulated experience to generate realistic images, sounds, and other sensations to simulate a user's physical presence in a virtual environment.

Market growth for AR/VR lags market enthusiasm with highly optimistic forecasts. However, AR has the potential to be *the* wearable technology across markets and applications. A lot of technology developments are in progress for AR glasses that are targeted toward diverse applications in the enterprise, medical, industrial, and military markets. Let's look at some important ways in which this technology is being used in the field of medicine.

## Medical applications

Medical imaging has witnessed dramatic developments in the past few decades, with advances in ultrasonography, MRIs, ultra-fast CT scans, and so on. However, limitations in the visualization of this imaging information are still present. This is an area where VR and AR can help medical professionals. Surgeons can get pre-surgery access to this medical imaging information in form of 3D images of hearts, eyes, knee joints, and other organs. Companies such as Propio are providing AR/VR solutions that combine machine learning and AR to create ultra-precise 3D medical images. These visualization tools can help surgeons see through obstructions and collaborate with colleagues on surgery plans.

Microsoft has developed CAE VimedixAR, a commercial application for Microsoft HoloLens technology that enables immersive simulation-based training in ultrasound and anatomical education through AR.

## Applications in manufacturing

Due to the aging of the workforce, the manufacturing industry often loses the skilled workers who have long experience gained at work. AR provides a good way of providing on-the-job training and guidance to workers who are new to a manufacturing process. AR provides context-sensitive help and guidance at the workstation. Such augmentation helps to bring the new and young workers up to speed quickly and makes them productive faster. Boeing uses Skylight AR glasses for complex tasks in airplane manufacturing, such as wiring harness assembly. Focals By North (a Google company) is an interesting case study for consumer adoption of AR devices. A leading truck manufacturer in the US is using AR for the on-the-job training of its factory workers when they deal with the assembly of the newer model of the truck. In this case, the use of AR helps them reduce the time the factory workers would have to spend in a classroom setting to learn about the differences in the new models.

## 3D printing

The 3D printing process builds a 3D object using a **Computer-Aided Design** (**CAD**) software model. It is sometimes also called **Additive Manufacturing** (**AM**) because a 3D printer creates the object by adding layer upon layer of material until the modeled shape of the object is formed. 3D printing materials can include plastics, powders, filaments, and paper.

3D printing technology was first developed for rapid prototyping in manufacturing purposes. The application of 3D printing has now spread beyond prototyping to medicine, construction, robotics, automotive and industrial goods.

There are multiple technology options for 3D printing. The most used technology options are the following:

- **Fuse Deposition Modeling** (**FDM**)
- **Selective Laser Sintering** (**SLS**)
- **Stereolithography** (**SLA**)
- **MultiJet Fusion**

There is a growing demand for 3D printing solutions in aerospace, defense, healthcare, and automotive verticals. In industries such as aerospace, where highly complex components made from different parts are used, 3D printing provides an ideal solution for low-volume production. Starting from digital files, 3D printing technologies directly create parts, without the need for expensive tooling. Using techniques such as topology optimization and lattice building software, 3D printing enables creating lightweight parts, addressing an aspect unique to the aviation and aerospace industries where the lowest weight for a part is very important.

An innovative use of 3D printing is in making prosthetics. There are more than 200,000 amputations made in the US in a year. Prosthetics limbs need to be custom made for the user and the traditional process takes several weeks to produce and costs more than $5,000. Using Fuse deposition modeling 3D printing technology, prosthetic limbs can be printed in local communities for a cost of less than $200.

# Digital twins

A digital twin defines the virtual representation of an entity, including its behavior and qualities. In this context, the entity can be a physical asset, a system of assets, a process, or even a representation of a human being. In relation to IoT, a digital twin is often a digital representation that provides both the elements and the dynamics of how that *thing* or device operates through various operating conditions. The key value proposition of a digital twin is to simplify the understanding of a complex physical object. The digital twin of a human being can be used for modeling wellness, prevention, or to cure diseases. In the case of athletes, it could model their baseline for high performance and, if needed, to track their recovery after an injury. In Gartner's *Hype Cycle for Emerging Technologies* (2020), the *digital twin of a person* and the *citizen twin* are included under the innovation trigger (see: https://www.forbes.com/sites/louiscolumbus/2020/08/23/whats-new-in-gartners-hype-cycle-for-emerging-technologies-2020/).

The concept of the digital twin dates back to 2002 and is credited to Dr. Michael Grieves from the University of Michigan. The key features of digital twins are as follows:

- Physics-based model of the object: This describes how the physical object behaves in the real world – for example, metals often corrode when subjected to a high temperature for extended periods of time. The physical laws could be thermodynamics laws or, in the case of human beings, biological laws or laws of medical sciences. In the absence of a clear understanding of such physics-based models, statistical rules are derived from observed behavior and data.

- Sensor and related data collected from the object.

- Digital or software systems that can bring the data and models together to create a virtual representation and evolve it over time.

The digital twin changes over the lifetime of the physical asset. The digital systems for digital twins should be able to handle these life cycles of digital twins. The sensor data from the products in operations can change the characteristics of the twins over its operating life. This is important for assets with long life, such as power plant equipment or an aircraft where the normal operating life is in tens of years. Even in a relatively short-lived product such as a smartphone, the battery life dwindles over 1–2 years.

The commonly used types of digital twins for a physical asset are as follows:

- As designed (engineering design of the asset)
- As manufactured (birth record of the asset)
- As installed (at the site where the asset is used, say in a factory or an aircraft, as delivered to the airline)
- As operated and maintained (changes in parts due to maintenance or product revisions)
- As retired (when decommissioned and could be used for secondary purposes)

Digital twins are helping in the digital transformation of manufacturing. The digital twin-based simulations of the *as-designed* twin can help to identify the right material and structure for the physical product. The overall goal is to account for variations in the supplier parts, as well as the throughput and quality considerations. Manufacturing processes are tweaked to reduce waste and product quality issues. The *as-manufactured* twin comes into play here. Supportability of the product is associated with the *as-operated* twin. It deals with the field operations of the asset. Product warranties and service contracts come into play here from the manufacturer's perspective. From the customer (owner or operator of the asset) perspective, the uptime, operating efficiency, and safety matter the most.

The digital twin system should be able to handle the digital twins over their life cycle, especially if it is a connected asset where the after-sales service and maintenance is provided by the manufacturer. Digital twins are often used by IoT systems to enhance the capabilities, such as predictive maintenance and asset optimization.

One area in industrial digital transformation that has seen a lot of development is predictive maintenance.

## Different types of maintenance

Maintenance is a set of actions taken to keep a machine working optimally. Broadly speaking, there are three categories for maintenance:

- Preventive maintenance
- Condition-based maintenance
- Predictive maintenance

Let's dive a bit deeper.

## Preventive maintenance

Historically, maintenance is driven by scheduled tasks that are based on a pre-determined time schedule. The actual status of the equipment is not important in such a maintenance plan.

The advantage of this approach is that it is simple to plan. However, the disadvantages of this approach are as follows:

- Sometimes, a maintenance event may happen too late (or too early).
- In some cases, maintenance occurring at a scheduled time may not be necessary.

Next is condition-based maintenance.

## Condition-based maintenance

This type of maintenance is based on the estimated conditions of the machine, typically monitored through inspection or sensors. For example, an oil quality sensor in a machine can provide real-time monitoring of oil degradation. Monitoring the oil condition using an oil quality sensor provides the ability to determine the optimal time to change the oil in the machine. Change the oil too early and the cost is significant; however, change it too late and the costs can be even greater! Sensors such as temperature, pressure, humidity, acoustic, magnetometer, and so on that are based on application requirements are used to bring real-time or batched information to condition monitoring logic implemented on a sensor node, edge, or the cloud. AI and machine learning algorithms can make this process adaptive. This logic raises an alert for maintenance and also triggers corrective action on the machine to prevent any damage.

## Predictive maintenance

In this case, maintenance actions are predicted in advance based on condition monitoring of the machine combined with a dynamic predictive model for failure analysis. A complete loop for predictive maintenance includes the data flow from the sensor node or edge compute solution, which could include raw sensor data or metadata that is transferred to the cloud, and dynamic predictive models that have access to large repositories of archived data and cloud compute platforms to execute predictive models. The biggest advantage of this approach is that maintenance is optimized for the life of the machine and production efficiency.

Next, we will learn about the digital thread and how it relates to the digital twin and the supply chain systems.

# The digital thread and the supply chain

An asset such as an aircraft depends on hundreds of parts suppliers. For instance, Boeing and Airbus rely on GE Aviation, Pratt and Whitney (Raytheon/United Technologies), and Rolls Royce for the engines, Honeywell for avionics, Panasonic for cabin systems, and Spirit Aerosystems for the fuselage. Hence, the digital thread is best suited to capture the digital representation of the entire value chain from product design and engineering to manufacturing, after-market, and product-in-use. It can connect the design collaborators, parts suppliers, and services partners with the manufacturer.

The digital thread aims to connect the whole supply chain of the asset, from manufacturing to operations of the asset in the premises of the customer or the operator. This is traditionally a siloed area where the flow of information is poor. The digital thread aims to capture the right information and make it available to the right place at the right time. When a problem arises for an asset, it could be due to the following:

- A design defect
- A manufacturing process defect
- A faulty part from the supplier in a specific batch during manufacturing
- Hard operating conditions in the field environment
- Excessive operations of the asset without proper maintenance
- Bad after-market part for maintenance and repair
- A skills gap in operations or repair

Complex assets can pose a variety of challenges, making it cost-prohibitive to keep it up and functioning properly. This cost of maintenance over a period of time can be a lot more than the cost of the asset. Digital thread systems can come to rescue here.

The Volvo Group, which manufactures over a quarter of a million trucks per year, utilized the concept of digital thread to transform its commitment to quality (Source: `https://www.ptc.com/en/case-studies/volvo-group-digital-thread`). Volvo deals with thousands of variations of engineering parts at its plant. For the 40 major checks that each truck goes through, over 200 variations are possible due to the complex supply chain involved. To deploy the digital thread, Volvo used a combination of AR, engine CAD, and **Product Life Cycle Management (PLM)** systems connected to manufacturing systems that digitally record the whole birth record for the asset – in this case, a truck. The digital twin is an integral part of the digital thread in a manufacturing scenario.

Volvo has also introduced the Remote Diagnostics system for trucks using the IoT platform. As a result, both the manufacturing side and the field operation side is digitized, leading to an end-to-end digital thread. When a truck encounters a problem in the field, the digital thread can help to pinpoint whether it is a result of any of the following:

- How it is being operated – for example, miles or load carried
- Environmental conditions of operations – for example, too hot or too cold weather or rough roads
- The batch it was manufactured in – that is, the plant location, supplier parts, and so on
- The environmental conditions in the plant, including the condition of the machinery in the plant
- The model of truck and design considerations

In this example, the digital twin can help with predictive maintenance on the field operations side, but diagnosing the issues that arise due to factors outside the product, such as the environmental conditions that the parts and manufacturing process are subjected to, requires the digital thread.

## Digital platforms

Digital transformation requires a delicate balance between digital technologies, business models, processes, customers, and various stakeholders. This ecosystem spans inside and outside the company. One way to bring this ecosystem together is through a digital platform. The software and cloud providers have created marketplaces around their offerings to bring the different stakeholders together. Some examples of these marketplaces, which are now seen well beyond the software industry, are as follows:

- **SalesForce AppExchange**: https://www.salesforce.com/solutions/appexchange/overview/
- **Oracle Cloud Marketplace**: https://cloudmarketplace.oracle.com/marketplace/
- **Amazon AWS Marketplace**: https://aws.amazon.com/marketplace
- **Microsoft Azure Marketplace**: https://azuremarketplace.microsoft.com/
- **PTC Marketplace**: https://www.ptc.com/en/marketplace
- **Honeywell Marketplace**: https://marketplace.honeywell.com/home

- **Intel Marketplace**: https://marketplace.intel.com/
- **Healthcare Marketplace Application – Healthcare.gov**: https://www.healthcare.gov/screener/

These marketplaces bring the domain-specific ecosystem together, around the main business of the main orchestrator. While the marketplace is often the external interface for the stakeholders to interact with these ecosystems, the management of the overall ecosystem can be quite complex. Digital platforms can help to harness the full potential of the transformation and the ecosystem.

On February 10, 2020, Rolls Royce announced its launch of Yocova, a data-led *digital platform* for the aviation industry. Singapore Airlines is one of the first major participants in Yocova. The term *digital platform* is over-used here; however, it demonstrates that the concepts of *marketplace* and *platform* have spread beyond the software companies to industrial giants. Yocova.com is meant to be a data exchange and collaboration platform for the aviation sector. This platform seeks to harness the power of the aviation ecosystem. It will provide an online space for the open and secure sharing of data and insights. It will allow stakeholders to collaborate and monetize data-driven assets and software applications. While Yocova is still in its infancy in 2020, it showcases that industrial giants such as Rolls Royce, which represents a sector of industry known for being conservative, is moving toward a digital platform to foster innovation via the ecosystem.

Apart from the Yocova initiative, Rolls Royce has launched other digital initiatives, such as **Motoren- und Turbinen-Union (MTU)** Go! (MTU is owned by Rolls Royce). While Rolls Royce is known for automobiles and aircraft engines, Boeing is one of the two largest aircraft manufacturers in the world. Boeing launched its AnalytX Platform in 2017. Boeing mentioned it had over 200 customers by October 2017 at the **Maintenance Repair and Overhaul (MRO)** Europe conference (https://boeing.mediaroom.com/2017-10-04-Boeing-Announces-Agreements-with-Seven-Customers-for-Analytics-Solutions).

Boeing's Analytx Platform is a good example of a digital platform. These platforms go beyond the capabilities of traditional IT systems and bring together the physical world, such as aircrafts being operated by the airlines, and the digital world – in this case, operated by the aircraft manufacturer Boeing. Analytx provides three broad sets of capabilities:

- **Digital Solutions**: Enhanced software capabilities for airline crew and fleet scheduling, flight planning and operations, maintenance planning, and inventory and logistics management.
- **Analytics Consulting Services**: New revenues via aviation subject matter experts who can help improve airlines' operational performance, efficiency, and economy.

- **Self-Service Analytics**: The ability to unlock the data behind the digital solutions for airlines to explore and discover new insights and opportunities, such as flight path optimization or fuel efficiency.

Boeing will be able to launch several other digital services in the future for the airlines and airports based on this foundational capability.

To harness the full power of digital technologies, digital platforms are required. These platforms may interface with the existing enterprise IT systems, such as **Enterprise Resource Planning (ERP)** including finance, supply chain, procurement, **Human Capital Management (HCM)**, **Customer Relationship Management (CRM)**, and other collaboration systems. Sometimes, the digital platforms may be built on top of the enterprise systems and extend the functionality to include capabilities such as IoT, AI with hardware acceleration, or **High-Performance Compute (HPC)** systems for engineering simulations. In addition, these systems can interface with capabilities such as AR/VR and blockchain.

Going back to the example of Volvo trucks, **Over the Air (OTA)** is another key capability to allow the software revisions and fixes to be pushed out to the trucks without the need to bring them to the repair shop. Volvo uses a digital platform to manage OTA and other similar requirements. Tesla cars are also equipped with OTA capabilities. Digital platforms augment the traditional enterprise IT platforms to embrace the digital technologies in the transformation journey. This *digital resource function* often falls in the CDO's responsibility area.

We have learned about the emerging technologies and how they are being used for industrial digital transformation in various sectors. While some of these technologies are already mainstream, such as cloud computing or 4G for communication, some are on the bleeding edge – for example, 5G. Digital technology is a shifting landscape, and a good understanding is required to evaluate its feasibility at any given point in time.

# Transformation case studies from consumer industries

Next, we will look at a few examples of digital transformation at work, in some consumer-centric industry sectors. We will see how these transformations are enabled by the emerging digital technologies from the prior section. Some of these transformations have been accelerated by the COVID-19 pandemic, at the time of writing this book.

## Peloton

Peloton has 2.6 million members worldwide at the time of writing. Their bikes represent a relatively recent digital transformation in the world of indoor cycling classes, which have moved them from the gym to the home. Peloton's Turkey Burn ride during the Thanksgiving holidays in the US draws well over 10,000 riders every year. It is a perfect example of the *servitization* of the exercise bike via digital technologies. The technology helps to recreate the high-end gym indoor cycling studio environment at home. The COVID-19 pandemic has pushed Peloton's digital transformation of this space even further. In April 2020, a single class drew a *live* audience of 23,000 people. Interestingly, this class was streamed from the instructor's home and not from one of Peloton's studios in New York or London.

Apart from the spin bike hardware innovations, Peloton uses the latest broadcasting technology in its built-in screens (see *Figure 3.6*). The connected sensors collect data to improve cycling for its bike users. The two sensors in the bike collect **revolutions per minute (RPM)** and resistance data when a user is cycling. The bikes have LED screens to display the sensor data and additional derived performance metrics, such as power, in real time. The riders can wear heart rate monitors as well if they want to do so. The Peloton bike tracks the progress over time for users. Using their own operating system in the console, the aggregated user data is sent to Peloton's cloud platform. Yony Feng, the CTO of Peloton, publicly shared in 2018 how their platform uses the public cloud to achieve its functionality (`https://aws.amazon.com/solutions/case-studies/Peloton/`):

Figure 3.6 – The Peloton digital experience [Source: `https://medium.com/@FelixCapital/peloton-the-netflix-of-fitness-joins-the-felix-family-4c26d789314b`]

Peloton is a good example of transforming the health and wellness industry by creating a unique combination of customer experience that members love and brag about through the leaderboard. Peloton launched Tread in 2018 to continue to innovate in this space. Being a home-based *group* experience, it was also perfectly positioned to capitalize on the *shelter in place* advisory during the COVID-19 crisis. This case study involves both the use of digital technology and business model change. By leveraging its data and applying AI to it, it can further build new digital revenue streams by partnering with its value stream. Some of the data and analytics-driven offerings in the future could include the following:

- Use riders historical streamed data to build a personalized recommendation engine for users that suggests rides and instructors based on user preferences, such as the day and time of the week.
- Use engagement and goals achievement information to evaluate the performance of their instructors.
- Peloton could partner with other wearable companies and leverage the user data to help promote the health and wellness of its members.
- Peloton could work with doctors and other healthcare providers to foster wellness for an entire family or employee groups.

Next, we will discuss rideshareing.

## Ridesharing

A rideshare service facilitates an arrangement in which a passenger travels in a private vehicle driven by its owner. This is typically arranged via a website or mobile app and there is a fee for the ride. The mobile app and the system behind it represent the technology enabler here, while the fact that the vehicle is not a commercial vehicle and the driver is not the professional taxi driver represents the business model change. The major companies in this category are Uber and Lyft from the USA, Didi from China, Grab from Singapore, and Ola from India. Together, these companies are responsible for the digital transformation of transportation in major parts of the world (https://ride.guru/content/newsroom/is-ola-taking-over-the-rideshare-industry).

The digital technology enablers of these rideshare services are as follows:

- Connected vehicle and driver, which is often via the consumer-grade smartphone running the rideshare app.
- Connected passengers via the smartphone app.
- Geo-location services to locate the proximity of the available vehicle and requesting rider.

- Maps with real-time traffic for optimal routing.
- Passenger and driver registration and profiles database with preferences.
- Pricing calculator and payment process, often cashless and cardless, via the in-app account.
- The ability of the vehicle to interact with local jurisdictions and rules, such as airport drop off or pickups.
- Push notifications and the enablement of communication between the passenger and driver with privacy in mind.
- In the near future, facilitating robo-taxis or autonomous driverless rides could be needed.

Let's consider the architecture of a generic rideshare platform (see: `https://static.thinkmobiles.com/uploads/2017/03/uber-app-backend.jpg`). The modular architecture enables capabilities to be added over time, such as electronic payments using third parties. The decoupling of technology tiers, such as the datastore, which is PostgreSQL, an open source database, can be easily swapped out with another database, whether open source or propriety. This makes it easier to maintain and enhance the digital platform over time. Uber had launched a self-driving truck business around 2016 but shut it down around 2018. In *Chapter 2, Transforming the Culture in an Organization*, we learned about the ability to experiment and pivot along the innovation journey. This is a good example of the fact that that every transformative initiative may not make business sense. However, Uber has successfully launched Uber Freights for logistics and Uber Eats for food delivery. Other similar business opportunities exist for such rideshare companies, such as providing transportation for school-age children and the elderly. Likewise, given that many retailers have curbside pickup, home delivery of goods ordered online could be done on-demand. Companies such as Amazon have experimented with Prime Now, with 1 to 2-hour delivery services in certain geographies.

# Nest

Nest thermostats are often seen as one of the pillars of the digital transformation of the home. Nest thermostats help to reduce the heating and cooling bills for residences. It does that by learning about the desired temperature and adjusting the temperature accordingly. Essentially, Nest reduces the waste of energy from residences by reducing the heating and cooling costs by 10 to 15%. It provides valuable information to the electricity value chain, such as utility companies, about the consumption pattern of energy. Finally, it has allowed Google, through its Nest acquisition for $3.4 billion in 2014, to become an important player in smart homes by extending its suite of intelligent products:

Figure 3.7 – A Nest thermostat (Source: http://www.flickr.com/photos/nest/6264860345/, License: CC BY-NC-ND)

The Nest thermostat shown in *Figure 3.7* uses machine learning to adapt to the acceptable temperature settings in the home. In addition, it uses motion sensors to figure out when there are residents in the home. The Nest family of products has grown into a suite of smart home products:

- Nest Guard
- Nest Detect (Guard and Detect work together to enable home security)
- Nest x Yale Lock (a key-free smart lock for the home)
- Nest Secure (home alarm system)
- Nest Connect (network range extender)
- Nest Protect (smoke and carbon monoxide alarm)
- Nest Hub Max (smart home display)

This suite of products again highlights how a digital platform can accelerate the offerings after starting with one product such as the Nest thermostat, in this case. Nest has an associated API ecosystem called Works with Nest (`Developers.Nest.com`). Nest creates a **Home Area Network** (**HAN**). It uses OpenWeave, which is an open source implementation of the Weave network application layer. OpenThread is an open source implementation of the Thread networking protocol by Google. OpenWeave can run on top of OpenThread. It uses Thread's reliable mesh networking and security. OpenWeave and OpenThread provide the IoT solution for the Nest family of products (see *Figure 3.8*). More information is available at `OpenWeave.io`:

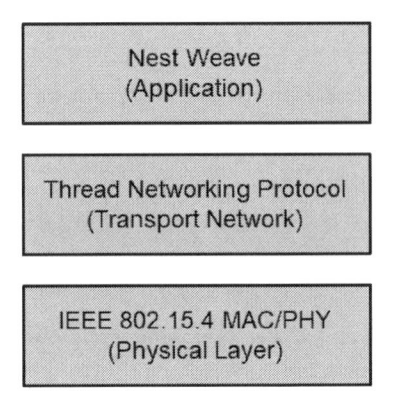

Figure 3.8 – Nest connectivity stack

The three case studies are examples of digital technology-led transformations in the **Business-to-Client** (**B2C**) sector. These examples are easy to understand from an end consumer perspective. From *Chapter 5, Transforming One Industry at a Time* onward, we will use these digital technologies for more complex industrial digital transformation case studies.

## Summary

In this chapter, we learned about the emerging digital technologies being used to enable industrial digital transformation. We learned that the key technologies for digital transformation include GNSS, IoT, cloud computing, AI, big data and analytics, blockchain, robotics, drones, 3D printing, AR and VR, RPA, and mobile technologies. We also learned more about these technologies and their applications through a series of case studies.

In the next chapter, we will learn about the current state of industrial companies and the challenges they often face. We will look at the business model and business process changes, as key enablers of the industrial digital transformation, alongside the cultural and technological changes.

# Questions

Here are some questions to test your understanding of the chapter:

1. Why are enabling technologies important to industrial digital transformation?
2. What are some of the key technologies that are enabling the current wave of digital transformations?
3. How would you identify new enabling technologies?
4. What is a digital twin and how are digital twins helpful in digital transformation?
5. What are some examples of the use of enabling technologies in the consumer sector?
6. How does the digital thread transform the supply chain and improve product quality?

# 4
# Business Drivers for Industrial Digital Transformation

In the previous chapter, we learned what kind of digital technologies are needed to help drive transformation and why they're needed, alongside the cultural and business-level changes required. We looked at several emerging technologies that are being used to solve problems that were previously harder to solve. We described some concepts, such as digital twins and digital threads, which have become more feasible due to the easy availability of emerging technologies and are often harmonized through digital platforms. Finally, we looked at some examples of these in use in business and consumer settings.

This chapter will go into the importance of the business process and business model changes to accelerate industrial digital transformation. We will see that often, business process optimization can drive productivity and cost savings, which allows the organization to experiment with business model innovations. In this chapter, we will learn about the following:

- Business process
- Business model
- The state of the industrial sector

- Major challenges in industrial companies
- Overcoming the challenges

# Business process

In this section, we will learn about the role of improving business processes or functional processes in the context of digital transformation. Improving the business process is often a formal management activity where functional experts lead the redesign to reduce friction and drive effectiveness or efficiency. This exercise often involves identifying the areas to improve and prioritizing the change based on the expected outcome in the form of productivity gains. These productivity gains are often internal to the company.

While undertaking business process improvements, a company may look at the following:

- **Inventory of current business processes**: Assess the state of the current business processes to stack-rank those that work well and those that are candidates for transformation.
- **Simplification of workflows**: Mature businesses may evolve into complex workflows and simplifying those may reduce costs.
- **Standardization**: Trying to reinvent the wheel can often create complexity and difficult-to-manage processes in different ways.
- **Improvement of customer experience**: Customers can be both external or internal stakeholders. Improved processes can often lead to better customer experience and profitability.
- **Risk reduction**: Process variability and sticking to industry best practices can reduce the risk to the business from both a product or service quality perspective, as well as a safety and compliance perspective.

Business process improvements may not directly add new revenues but provide a foundation toward overall organizational transformation.

The previously mentioned four-step approach to business process optimization can be applied to one problem area or business process at a time, to yield significant gains in productivity and cost reductions. You can find more details about this process at `https://www.bizjournals.com/boston/news/2018/04/01/5-ways-to-improve-your-business-processes.html`.

**General Electric (GE)** used a similar process to eliminate inefficiencies in procurements from suppliers who had multiple contracts with GE's different lines of business, as well as multiple contracts in different geographies. By consolidating this view of procurement from the suppliers across the entirety of GE, better processes and pricings were put in place.

## Transformation by business process improvement

Can the improvement of business processes be transformative for a company? Let's look at improving efficiency and overall effectiveness. Efficiency refers to doing things better and reducing waste. For example, submitting an expense report electronically is more efficient than mailing it by post, especially when a company has a distributed workforce. Even if employees send the expenses reports as email attachments and attach scanned copies of the receipts, it would be more efficient than via post mail. However, would this be an effective way of handling the expenses reports for a large company?

Even though the expense management reporting automation problem was technically solved a decade ago, 43% of companies still use manual processes (see `https://www.businesstravelnews.com/Payment-Expense/43-Percent-of-Companies-Rely-on-Manual-T-and-E-Systems`). Hence, we will use an easy-to-understand example here. An expense management system, whether homegrown or **Commercial Off-the-Shelf (COTS)**, can easily be used to do the following:

- Collect expenses and receipts.
- Apply some degree of expense policy validations (for example, a dinner expense over $100 needs additional explanation).
- Keep historical track of expense submissions and approvals.
- Allow the quick reporting of expense trends.
- Enhanced features such as corporate credit card integration and expense reimbursements to the employee's bank account.
- Fraud detection and prevention.

In the preceding example, we saw that to improve the business process in a company, we must look at both efficiency and effectiveness and often balance the two. It is often hard to drive both efficiency and effectiveness at the same time. In the prior example, efficiency can be quickly improved by moving from post mail to email for expense report submission. Employees can get used to that process quickly. On the other hand, launching a new expense reporting system may need time, training, and a cultural shift in the employees' mindset, especially if they perceive the discipline that the system requires as a tedious process. *Figure 4.1* shows the X axis as the strategic management dimension and the Y axis as the operational or tactical management dimension:

|  | Ineffective | Effective |
|---|---|---|
| **Efficient** | Business Becoming Obsolete | Thriving Business |
| **Inefficient** | Business Heading to Closing | Surviving Business |

Y axis: Operational/Tactical Management
X axis: Strategic Management

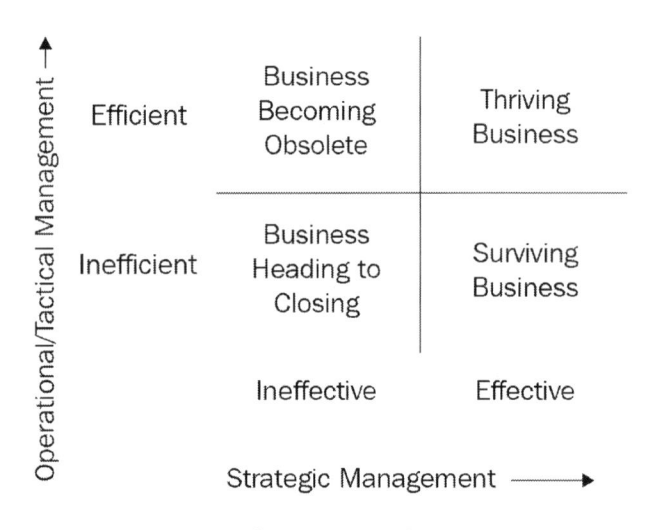

Figure 4.1 – Efficient versus effective business

The main takeaway from *Figure 4.1* is that pure efficiency only can lead a company toward obsolescence, as shown by the quadrant representing **Efficient**. A company can exist in survival mode if it is effective but not efficient. Hence, the fine balance to achieve both efficiency and effectiveness in business processes is the holy grail toward transformation. This is the approach that companies need to follow to tackle problems with business processes. It allows companies to achieve massive gains in their ability toward their desired outcomes on a more frequent and reliable basis. Companies can keep their focus on solving real customer problems and solving internal productivity problems.

Let's look at an example of a company called Custom Fleet. Custom Fleet provides vehicle fleet management and related services to enterprises. GE Capital divested from the Australia and New Zealand business of Custom Fleet in 2015 to Canada's Elemental Financial Corp. After this divestment, Custom Fleet had to quickly get off GE's systems. It moved to Oracle Cloud **Enterprise Resource Planning (ERP)** and **Enterprise Performance Management (EPM)**. Together, this drove business process efficiency at Custom Fleet. Heath Valkenburg, the deputy CFO of Custom Fleet, acknowledged how the integration of their financial processes with Oracle ERP and EPM allowed them an enhanced level of visibility into their fleet operations. The business users at Custom Fleet could look at the live data from hundreds of thousands of contracts, which led to more agile planning cycles. They were able to close their monthly books in half the time. Once they adopted Oracle **Human Capital Management (HCM)**, the productivity gain for their human resource team was in the range of 30–50%. This improved Custom Fleet's executive team's experience with the operations (source: `https://www.oracle.com/au/customers/custom-fleet-1-financials-cl.html`).

By improving its internal business processes, Custom Fleet was able to free up its resources and focus on innovative business offerings. For example, a Salesforce.com employee can *lease a vehicle as part of their salary package through Custom Fleet (Australia only)*. This is an example of a business model change on the part of Custom Fleet, to partner with large employers such as Salesforce.com, in this case, to grow its business of leasing cars.

Custom Fleet made other investments to improve its system processes by adopting **Application Programming Interface (API)** management for building a connected ecosystem. They adopted **Identity and Access Management (IAM)**. IAM allowed it to federate with its customers, thus providing secure and automated user access, functional privileges, and the provisioning of profiles and accounts. This improved IT-process capability allowed Custom Fleet to double the number of Fleet Office users within a very short period of time. We will learn more about business process changes in a later section of this chapter.

## Data-driven process improvement

Clive Humby, a British mathematician who was the brain behind Tesco Clubcard, a grocery supermarket loyalty program, coined the phrase *data is the new oil* in 2006. In the last one and a half decades, there have been many efforts to raise the hygiene and standards around the data quality and analytics derived from that data. The transformation process often requires business insights from traditional data and new types of data, such as unstructured data. In the car industry, insurance customers can now submit pictures of cars damaged in accidents to capture the environmental conditions and angle of impact of the involved cars.

Data poses an interesting paradox, as business users want more data but also quality, and the inability to draw insights from the sheer volume of data can be counterproductive. Streamlining business processes to collect and unlock insights from data, often via analytics, is key to business productivity. It requires training the data creators, such as insurance customers, car renters, and front office staff, to capture quality data at the point of operation. This can trigger the data pipelines to assimilate knowledge from the data, to provide business insights to the consumers of data. The data needs change with the maturity level of the business and requires you to think through the current, near-term, and longer-term data needs as the business marches along the transformation journey.

Let's apply this need for data and analytics to Custom Fleet. Historically, a fleet management company simply dealt with providing the right number of vehicles to the correct address of its corporate customers, on the agreed day and time. This simple car-matchmaking transforms into a more complex process when Custom Fleet is providing millions of vehicles, including commercial trucks and cars, to its multiple global corporate clients. In addition to capturing the vehicle fleet delivery information, Custom Fleet captures the information at the level of each ride, including vehicle utilization, driving habits, fuel utilization, and related attributes. Aaron Baxter, the CEO of Custom Fleet, said the following in 2017 (source: `https://www.theceomagazine.com/executive-interviews/automotive-aviation/aaron-baxter/`):

> *"We are trusted to provide data and insight to our customers that ensure their fleets are run efficiently, productively and safely. Unless you have the technology to deliver on that, you are going to be left behind."*

Such market dynamics drive companies such as Custom Fleet to transform their internal business processes from being just a vehicle-leasing company to a data- and analytics-driven company. As discussed in *Chapter 2, Transforming the Culture in an Organization*, these changes call for new digital talent, which would be data scientists, in the case of Custom Fleet. CEO Aaron Baxter further said the following:

> *"I never thought I would be hiring a bunch of data scientists. Historically, technology hasn't played a huge role in car leasing ... But there's a big global phenomenon going on in the industry today."*

These data scientists focus on the analysis of driver behavior, routing, driver safety, and fuel efficiency.

Custom Fleet invested $55 million into various kinds of innovation, including the new fleet-management system. How these investments enable business model changes for Custom Fleet will be covered in the following sections of this chapter. We will also look at Michelin in a similar context.

## Customer-driven process re-engineering

Enhancing the customer experience and meeting their unmet needs often requires an end-to-end mindset toward transformation. This entails a seamless process orientation across the organization silos. The traditional departmental silos in most large organizations make this a difficult task. Process improvements within silos often lead to incremental improvements only. We looked at the example of process change around the expense reports from postal mail to email. This is a big unmet need for frequent business travelers. In 2017, Revel Systems, airport retailer Pacific Gateway, and expense reporting software provider Expensify teamed up to launch an offering where airport travelers could drop off their receipts at airport kiosks and the expense report would be automatically filed by scanning those receipts and tying them to the traveler's corporate account. While this did not become mainstream, it did encourage large companies to transform the employee experience by adding tools such as a digital assistant on smartphones to allow the quick submission of expense reports from the field. Oracle has described the use of digital assistants/chatbots to quickly create expense reports here: `https://docs.oracle.com/en/cloud/paas/digital-assistant/use-chatbot/overview-digital-assistants-and-skills.html`.

*Figure 4.2* shows how a generic virtual or digital assistant can be used to develop a skill, such as one that can make expense report filing much easier. The figure shows that a variety of tools that enterprise users are already familiar with, such as Slack or Alexa, can be used to interact with the digital assistant, in this case. These digital assistant applications use the relevant skill to carry out the task with the backend systems in the enterprise, such as with the HR system or with the financial system – accounts payable and/or the expense reporting system:

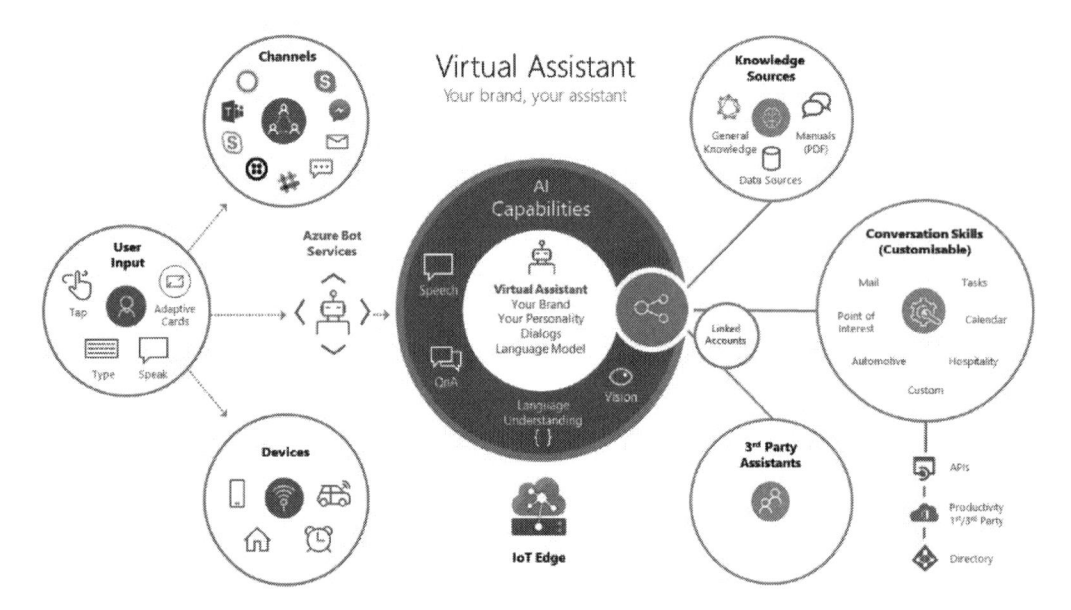

Figure 4.2 – Virtual assistant (Source: `https://stackoverflow.com/questions/57204473/remembering-context-and-user-engagement`, License: CC BY-SA)

The key takeaway from the example of the easy expense report filing process using a digital assistant is to build similar skills to automate other common business processes. Commonly used business processes that can be candidates to develop the relevant skills in digital assistants include the following:

- Manager requests and approvals
- Time-off and vacation inquiries
- Timesheets
- Employee onboarding
- Facility and equipment requests

- HR approvals
- Training
- IT and application access requests

Such a cross-departmental approach to looking at process management horizontally, across the silos with a focus on internal and external customers, can be truly transformative. Digital leadership, as discussed in *Chapter 2, Transforming the Culture in an Organization*, has to nurture a strategic sense to identify when incremental process improvement will suffice versus the need for more comprehensive and radical process reengineering. This quality is almost like the ability to *herd cats* to align the various corporate silos in favor of the customer experience and enhance the existing business processes and engineer new ones.

A good process frees up vital resources and people at the enterprises so that they can work on innovation and new offerings. Let's summarize this section as follows:

- Review the current business processes to identify the unmet needs and the functional gaps, to deploy existing or new IT/digital capability.
- Balance the effectiveness and efficiency, to undertake a business process transformation.
- When new IT/digital capabilities are introduced, look at where else it can make an impact – for example, the data scientist team can not only focus on operational data but also on enterprise data and behavioral data, to allow monetization models for data and analytics.

Can improved business processes become a source of new revenue? Can it help in reinventing the business model to build new digital revenue streams for product and services companies? This will be discussed under the business model changes.

# Business model

Can companies survive today by playing it safe? Disrupting yourself before the competition or the next start-up forces you to do that. Whitney Johnson, author of *Disrupt Yourself*, published by HBR Press, says the following:

> *"When you disrupt yourself, you are deciding to focus on who you can become, not on who you are."*

In the current competitive world, disruption is often the language of growth. Business leaders are looking for opportunities to create new value streams and transact in new markets. They resort to disruptive innovation as a means to accelerate that. For instance, Google monetizes their search engine based on what people are searching for. Using better algorithms to do that would be an example of incremental enhancements. However, with their Nest acquisition, Google has access to physical conditions in the residences of those using the connected thermostat or other devices from the Nest ecosystem. Having access to both the internet search information and home devices' information of consumers and being able to monetize that would be an example of disruptive innovation. Disruptive innovation can create a profound impact on the current market dynamics and similar ecosystems. Today, we see Google Nest and Amazon Echo competing to get a share of this segment of the consumers' homes.

Here are a few familiar examples of disruptive innovation:

- Movie rental businesses such as Blockbuster were disrupted when subscription by mail emerged. Netflix disrupted this market and then moved from physical media to the digital streaming of movies and shows.

- Amazon disrupted bookstores such as Borders and Barnes and Noble, using a similar order-by-mail system for books. Starting with books, Amazon later moved into e-commerce in a broader sense and later launched other digital services such as **Amazon Web Services (AWS)** for cloud computing.

- Companies such as Expedia disrupted travel agents for air travel, hotels, and other travel logistics. Airbnb has disrupted the traditional hotel business.

In all of these three examples, the incumbent was disrupted by non-traditional competitors. Industrial companies often had high barriers to entry because of heavy engineering, large plants, and related properties required, and the large economies of scale that they required to be profitable. The core industrial technologies do not change fast, and that often provided a security blanket to these companies. Consider steel manufacturing as an example, where it is difficult for a new entrant to gain market share quickly. However, the same sector has lately seen a *threat from the substitutes*. Another way to look at market substitutes is to consider them as disruptors. Rideshare companies are disrupting automakers and pose a threat to Tesla as well. Owning a Tesla implies owning an asset, whereas the success of rideshare industry leaders such as Uber and Lyft has been to stay asset-light. However, Tesla is eyeing the robo-taxi segment, as announced in early 2020.

The company intends to enable Tesla vehicles shipped after October 2016 to enable point-to-point autonomous driving with no humans taking over. This is possible as these models are equipped with necessary hardware, such as cameras and sensors, and would mainly need a software upgrade. This would allow the current owners of Tesla cars to offer peer-to-peer rides autonomously when they are not using their own car. This would mean a human driver is not needed to provide the ride. Tesla may roll out a smartphone app to facilitate peer-to-peer ridesharing. Tesla owners can schedule the time of day or week when they can offer their vehicle for this autonomous pool of rideshare vehicles and earn money from their idle car. This example shows that even a progressive company such as Tesla faces the threat of disruption from asset-light rideshare companies, but is flexible enough to tweak its own business model in *partnership* with its customers. Tesla owners could earn up to $10,000 per year, as per early estimates.

To continue the discussion of Custom Fleet and the automotive industry, let's look at the example of Michelin. Michelin makes tires, which is a tangible product that goes on the vehicles that Custom Fleet manages. Is it possible to *servitize* a tire? Michelin is one of the top three global manufacturers of tires. Tires, such as the 20.5R25 Michelin XTLA Radial Loader, are used in construction vehicles and earthmovers.

Michelin historically charges a price premium for its tires with the goal to create higher value for large vehicle fleet operators. In order to create value-added services for its customer base, Michelin looked at the **Tires-as-a-Service (TaaS)** model in 2016. For trucking fleet operators, fuel and tires are the two major elements of the operating costs, besides the human costs, which is in the range of $1.35 to $1.45 per mile in the US (see `https://www.imiproducts.com/blog/the-cost-of-trucking/`). The different cost elements may include the following:

- Maintenance and repair costs, in the range of $15,000/year
- The cost of tires, which is in the thousands per year, based on distance and weight carried
- Fuel cost, which is about 4x that of passenger vehicles
- The driver's salary, which is typically ¼ of the operating cost
- Insurance, tolls, and other hardware

Today **Michelin Fleet Solutions** (**MFS**) provides options such as **pay by the mile** for their tires instead of the upfront purchase of the tire. The use of sensors in the tires and vehicles can allow such automotive industry **Original Equipment Manufacturers** (**OEMs**) to charge based on consumption metrics such as mileage, actual wear and tear based on the load carried, or road conditions. Likewise, these companies can provide fuel and route advisories based on GPS technologies and the road or traffic conditions. This is a good example of a business model change to *servitize* the product – tires, in this case – to develop a new digital revenue stream. Fringe benefits to the fleet customer include reduction of the carbon footprint, in this case. Michelin participates in EPA's SmartWay program to help improve tires' design and benchmarks for fuel efficiency. See `https://www.epa.gov/smartway/learn-about-smartway` for details on the SmartWay initiative.

Michelin's CEO Florent Menegaux, speaking at UNESCO's NETEXPLO Innovation Forum 2020, compared digital transformation to surfing. Instead of fighting the wave, you want to ride it. In his viewpoint, for digital transformation to succeed, a radical human transformation is needed in parallel. The company's management plays a pivotal role in the alignment of the digital transformation to human transformation. In the TaaS example of Michelin, the reduction in carbon footprint shows a convergence of business outcomes and environmental outcomes, as a result of the transformation of the product – a truck tire, in this case. Michelin offers a similar service for race cars, where it adds four sensors per tire. These sensors collect real-time temperature and pressure information during a race. The receiver is powered by the cigarette lighter or USB port in the vehicle. The Track Connect App on smartphones provides relevant information and insights (see `https://www.michelinman.com/trackconnect.html`).

To embrace this convergence of people and technology, Michelin has a **Chief People Officer** (**CPO**), instead of a traditional **Chief Human Resource Officer** (**CHRO**). Its current CPO is PATS Jean Claude, who is based at Michelin's HQ in Paris. As seen in *Chapter 2, Transforming the Culture in an Organization*, the role of cultural transformation is as the precursor to business model transformation, and Michelin embodies that very well. It considers the company as not a rigid org-chart, but rather as a somewhat fluid and evolving model of relationships, like the neurons in the human brain. The strength of the company in its ability to change business processes and business models lies in the strength of the employees to create cross-disciplinary neural connections within the company.

To continue to transform Michelin, the company has set a goal to become a *connected mobility* company, from a pure tire manufacturing company. Today, Michelin manages over 1 million connected vehicles via its partnerships with NexTraq, Sascar, and Masternaut. By 2024, Michelin wants to have 160 million connected tires, mainly in the B2B space, such as track and earthmovers. Over time, the focus will shift toward B2C as well. Very often, tires are the only part of the vehicle that is constantly in contact with the group; they are key to sensing in a vehicle. The connected tires provide Michelin with data capital, which can help drive its ecosystem with partners. Michelin provides the TruckFLY mobile app (see `https://www.truckfly.com/en/`) to truck drivers, which helps them locate truck stops, gas stations, such as diesel stations, parking, real-time traffic updates of commercial vehicle interest, and the ability to be a part of the digital community of truck drivers (source: `https://www.michelin.com/en/news/today-a-leader-in-tires-tomorrow-a-leader-in-connected-mobility/`).

In the next section, we will look at how companies are reinventing themselves by shifts in their business models as part of their industrial digital transformation.

## Reinventing the business model

Companies such as Daimler are exploring and inventing new business models to prevent disruptions from rideshares and similar companies. Daimler is another company working toward digital transformation in the automotive industry. Overall, the automotive and trucking industry is changing fast. Daimler has come up with a car-sharing service called Car2Go. This is Daimler's entry toward providing a smarter transportation solution to cities. In addition, Ford's CEO has publicly shared that his vision for this 100-year-old automaker is to become a technology-led company.

In 2018, Ford announced that it would invest $11 billion into restructuring the company and laying the foundation of industrial digital transformation over the next decade, according to Bloomberg reports. This is Ford's way to strengthen its revenue via new products and services ahead of the expected vehicles sales slowdown by 2030 (see *Figure 4.3*):

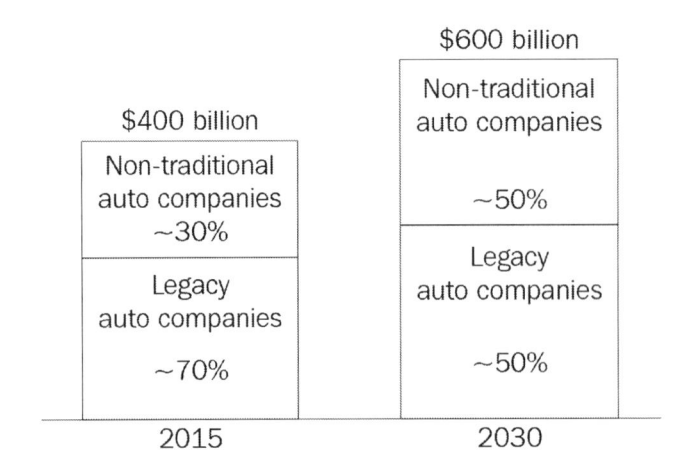

|  | 2015 | 2030 |
|---|---|---|
| Total | $400 billion | $600 billion |
| Non-traditional auto companies | ~30% | ~50% |
| Legacy auto companies | ~70% | ~50% |

Figure 4.3 – Revenue share and split for the auto industry

Such a strategic move by Ford, to align with the macro-economic trends in the industry, requires both a business model shift and technology-led products and services innovation. In the case of Ford, this would include initiatives similar to the Chariot shuttle-based ridesharing service in San Francisco, which it acquired in 2016, but ceased operations in 2019. Ford will also work toward **Electric Vehicles** (**EVs**) technology and its plans to launch with its **Autonomous Vehicles** (**AVs**). This would smoothen the transition to self-driving vehicles as those systems work better with EVs than the traditional internal combustion engines. Out of the total investment, $4 billion is earmarked for the self-driving auto business unit called Ford Autonomous Vehicles. **Advanced Driver-Assistance Systems** (**ADASes**) would be a step toward fully autonomous vehicles (Level 5). It will be useful now to review the different levels of AVs according to the **Society of Automotive Engineers** (**SAE**):

- **Level 0**: No automation. This describes our current everyday car.
- **Level 1**: Driver assistance. The vehicle can find the adaptive cruise control and lane keep assist to help overcome the driver's human driving fatigue.
- **Level 2**: Partial automation. The vehicle can handle two automated functions but needs a human driver in the car (Tesla Autopilot, as of early 2020).

- **Level 3**: Conditional automation. The vehicle can handle dynamic driving tasks but needs a human driver to intervene as needed (Tesla s/x/3 in limited scenarios, and the Audi R8, expected in 2020).

- **Level 4**: High automation. This vehicle can be driverless in most environmental conditions.

- **Level 5**: Full automation. This vehicle can operate entirely without a driver.

*Figure 4.4* shows the relationship between the different levels (Level 0 to Level 5) of AVs and the journey toward Level 5 of autonomous operations. This visual is important as it has profound implications on several of the examples that we have used in this book, such as the rideshare industry (for example, Uber), auto manufacturers such as Tesla, Ford, and Daimler, and OEMs, such as Michelin. Imagine Uber transforming into a robo-taxi company, where there are no human drivers for rideshare, or an Amazon Prime delivery truck stops by your house with no delivery driver in it. Or imagine a garbage collection service truck coming once or twice a week with fully automated services. This has profound implications on adjacent services, such as auto insurance, car rental services, gas stations, EV charging networks, and auto-repair services. Our example of Ford shows how the company is preparing for these changes within the next decade:

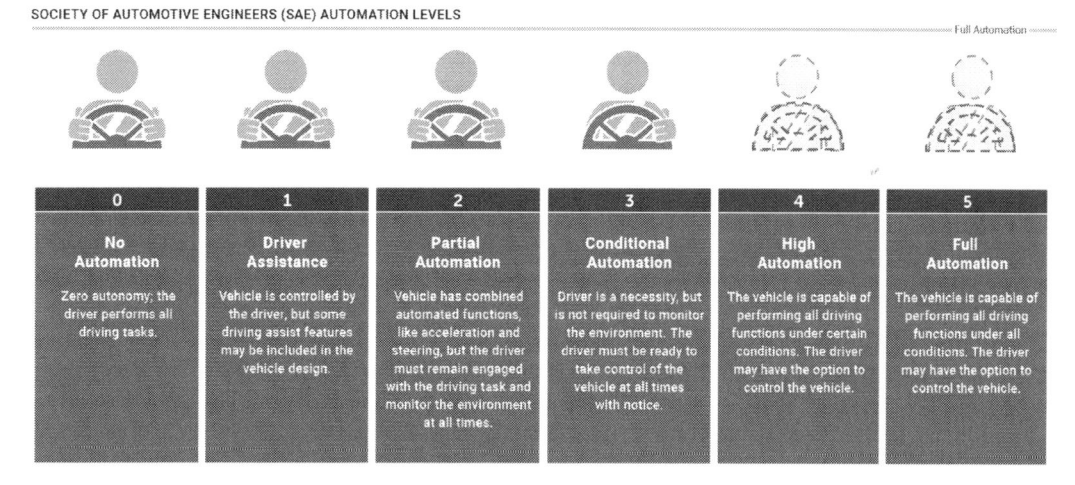

Figure 4.4 – The evolution of autonomous vehicles (Source: `https://scipol.duke.edu/track/s-1885-american-vision-safer-transportation-through-advancement-revolutionary-technologies-0`, License: CC BY-SA)

Ford has introduced the FordPass Connect app for car owners, which follows the same lines as TruckFly from Michelin. Smartphone apps such as FordPass provide roadside assistance to car drivers. FordPass Connect offers car owners capabilities including the following:

- **Check vehicle status**: Monitor fuel levels when away from the car or the next expected maintenance event.
- **Lock and unlock car**: Remotely lock and unlock your car – for example, if a car wash service arrives at your office garage, you can unlock it from your work meeting room.
- **Find your vehicle**: You've forgotten where you parked your car – sound familiar? Ford has an app for it!
- **Remote start**: The car can be scheduled to start at a certain time, which is good for preheating or cooling the car for comfort in extreme weather.

Further details can be found at `https://owner.ford.com/fordpass/fordpass-sync-connect.html`.

In summary, we can see that the automobile industry is treating Silicon Valley as the new Detroit in the US, and quickly transforming their business models and leveraging technology to stay relevant in the current age. It is very interesting to see how automakers are not only manufacturing the vehicle but also "manufacturing software applications," leveraging their ecosystems for consumption by their auto owners and riders.

## To cannibalize or not to cannibalize

Companies are often concerned that their new innovations may cannibalize their own cash-cow products and offerings. Let's take the example of the lighting industry. **Light-Emitting Diode (LED)** bulbs consume about 75% less energy and last 25 times longer than incandescent light bulbs – a good example of innovation from a technology and environmental perspective. However, GE, who practically invented the electric light bulb and sold it under GE Lighting, pretty much drove itself out of business after focusing on LED bulbs. Consumers do not have to replace their light bulbs as often and so do not buy as frequently. Philips Lighting also experienced similar consequences.

To prevent the type of disruption GE Lighting saw, it launched Current by GE in October 2015 as a line of business, which focused on a different business model. The goal was to develop recurring digital revenue streams from the LED light bulb and the ecosystem surrounding it. In this model, an LED light point transforms into an IoT node (see *Figure 4.5*). A light point does not usually have to worry about battery life on the IoT node. The IoT node has the ability to plug in different kinds of sensors. The applications built using this data are described in the following section. In a nutshell, the LED can be a basis for digital transformation for cities by virtue of sensing data from the IoT node. A software platform such as GE Predix and City IQ provides applications that in turn help to monetize the data, as well as improve law enforcement for the city:

Figure 4.5 – San Diego using GE's LED-based smart city solution [source: `https://readwrite.com/2017/03/11/san-diego-ge-io-cl4/`]

In 2017, the city of San Diego started working with Current by GE to transform the downtown area into a smart city. As shown in *Figure 4.5*, their vision was to convert the street lights into LED light points to conserve energy and provide IoT capabilities around the following:

- Smart parking and parking enforcement
- Traffic congestion management
- Law enforcement and resident safety
- Air quality, noise levels, and other specialized purposes

- Sensors using Bluetooth to count the volume of foot traffic by detecting pedestrians' smartphones
- Sound sensors for gunshot detection using ShotSpotter's technology (see `https://www.shotspotter.com/`)

The initial phase planned to install 3,200 *smartlight sensors*. The beneficiaries would include vehicle drivers, pedestrians, and cyclists, via the applications using the data and analytics enabled by this IoT solution. Over time, these insights can be monetized via further public-private partnerships. For instance, a rideshare company can correlate the pedestrian foot traffic with the proactive positioning of rideshare vehicles. Today, law enforcement can deploy officers based on patterns of congregations of people in the San Diego downtown area. This is a good example of the transformation of the business model of the light bulb to *servitize* it as an IoT node with the flexibility to add multiple sensors on it.

Over the years, we have seen business models change in different industry sectors. Here are a few examples:

- **HP printers**: Historically, printers such as the inkjet models were sold at a loss and the profit was generated by ink as a consumable over the lifetime of the device. To try to eliminate the use of aftermarket inkjet cartridges, HP cartridge protection was introduced, to help protect this revenue stream via the consumables.
- **Procter & Gamble's Gillette razors**: Razors often cost less than the cost of a few cartridges. This locks the users to the high-cost razor blades for the life of the razors.
- **Keurig coffee pods**: Another similar example, where the consumable is a coffee pod for the coffee machine. Keurig owned a patent on the K-cup coffee pods until 2012.

These are a few common B2C business models, to help generate recurring and high-margin revenue streams. These revenue streams are somewhat predictable as the sale of the main product is a leading indicator of the sale of the consumables based on the average usable life and general consumption models, such as a shave every day and a cup of coffee every morning. The key here is to maintain the customer relationship between the manufacturer and the customer after a single transaction representing the main product. Connected products and connected operations are the holy grail for closing the loop in many scenarios – see *Figure 4.6*. This sets the stage for the business model change:

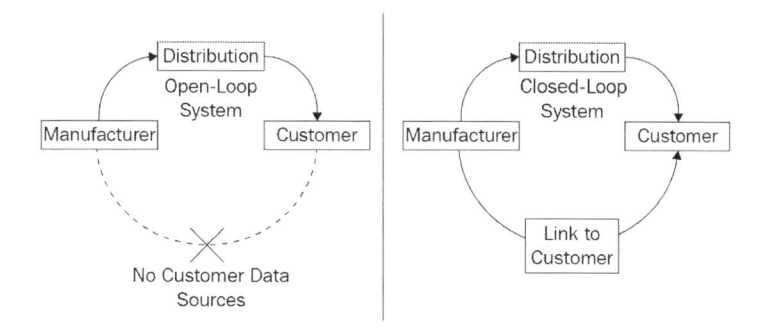

Figure 4.6 – The paradigm shift from open-loop to a closed-loop customer relationship

The preceding B2C examples have helped to tailor many B2B scenarios for recurring revenues. We are familiar with the service center selling auto manufacturers' genuine parts and maintenance services to car owners. All the previous scenarios mainly include selling a consumable that is a product to complement the main product. However, being able to sell recurring services and digital streams of revenues is often transformative in the B2B context. Let's look at a few examples where software offerings help to *servitize* the main product:

- **Apple iPhone**: Even though the iPhone is a stronger B2C use case, the App Store and iCloud are great examples of digital services generating recurring revenue streams, powered by software. As the economic cycles impact the sale of iPhone devices, the recurring revenues provide a steady stream of income for Apple, which is worth well over $1 trillion as of early 2020.

- **Square**: Square, which is a payment service provider, often provides the point-of-sale device for free or for less than $100, and charges about 3% of the transaction value as recurring service fees from the merchant (see *Figure 4.7*). This is mainly targeted toward the **Small and Medium-Sized (SMB)** segment. Overall, Square has transformed the electronics payment industry by democratizing the acceptance of various forms of payments for the SMB segment. Apart from the payment services, Square also offers financial and marketing services to its SMB customer base.

- **General Motors (GM) OnStar**: OnStar started as a roadside assistance service for owners of GM vehicles. Over the years, it has transformed into innovative offerings, including the delivery of Amazon packages to cars using the Amazon Key In-Car Delivery service. GM is working toward a new system called Global Connected Customer Experience, with integration with Google Voice Assistant.

- **CAT® Connect Solutions by Caterpillar**: Connected construction equipment provides value-added services for visibility, safety of operations, productivity at a job site, and equipment management for Caterpillar's customers. This is a B2B offering.

- **Kaeser Kompressoren**: Based in Corug, Germany, Kaeser offers Sigma Air Utility: Air as a Service. Industrial customers pay a fixed basic agreed price that provides a predetermined quantity of compressed air. If the customer needs larger quantities than usual, fixed consumption-based pricing applies to the additional quantities.

- **Johnson & Johnson**: Johnson & Johnson took over Verb Surgical at the end of 2019. Verb Surgical has a digital surgical platform with the goal of using a connected operating room and digital techniques to improve surgical outcomes. This allows revenue models such as charging the hospital or the surgeon for surgical equipment and digital procedures on a per-use basis.

The offering from Square is shown in *Figure 4.7*, with a smartphone app that has an attachment on it. It can be thought of as a Payment-as-a-Service business model:

Figure 4.7 – Square payment solution (Source: `http://gadgetynews.com/apple-selling-square-iphone-credit-card-swiper-turning-backs-on-nfc/`, License: CC BY-SA)

In *Figure 4.8*, we can see that this is an industry-wide trend to move to an as-a-Service model. An as-a-Service model is enabled by connected products, as well as, often, business model changes, where the goal is to wrap ongoing services around the product. iCloud allows Apple to wrap cloud storage services through the iPhone. The iCloud revenues, which is a form of Storage-as-a-Service, are estimated to be in the range of $5 billion/year. While this trend started in the software industry as the public cloud emerged, the servitization of physical products soon followed after. We looked at Air-as-a-Service and Tires-as-a-Service models in detail. This trend is likely to continue and demand business model changes for industrial companies to stay competitive and relevant:

| | Service Name |
|---|---|
| A | Air-as-a-Service (Kaeser Kompressoren) |
| B | Backend-as-a-Service (Mobile backend mBaaS) |
| C | Container-as-a-Service |
| D | Data-as-a-Service |
| E | Enterprise-as-a-Service |
| F | Function-as-a-Service / Furniture-as-a-Service |
| G | Games-as-a-Service |
| H | Hardware-as-a-Service |
| I | Infrastructure-as-a-Service |
| J | Juju-as-a-Service (Kubernetes service) |
| K | Kubernetes-as-a-Service (Rackspace) |
| L | Location-as-a-Service |
| M | Mobility-as-a-Service |
| N | Networking-as-a-Service |
| O | Operations-as-a-Service |
| P | Platform-as-a-Service |
| Q | Quality-as-a-Service |
| R | Recovery-as-a-Service |
| S | Software-as-a-Service |
| T | Tires-as-a-Service |
| U | Update-as-a-Service |
| V | Voice-as-a-Service |
| W | Workspace-as-a-service |
| X | Anything-as-a-Service (XaaS) |
| Y | Hybriss-as-a-Service (YaaS - SAP Hybris) |
| Z | Zenoss-as-a-Service |

Figure 4.8 – As-a-Service models in the industry

A few other examples include:

- **Global Technology Systems (GTSes)** – Battery-as-a-Service
- Kigali – Cooling-as-a-Service
- Citrix – Desktop-as-a-Service
- Combi Works – Factory-as-a-Service
- Geouniq – Geolocation-as-a-Service
- Philips, Current by GE and Tellco – Lighting-as-a-Service
- ProtoCAM – Manufacturing-as-a-Service
- Square – Payments-as-a-Service
- Uber/Lyft – Transportation-as-a-Service

We looked at several examples of how companies are reinventing their business models to transform themselves toward more continuous and predictable revenue streams with *servitization*. Next, we will look at the state of the industrial sector and its unique challenges.

# The state of the industrial sector

Compared to industries such as semiconductor manufacturing or automotive, the digital transformation of industrial processes is lagging in process industries (for example, oil, gas, and chemicals).

Process industry investment decision periods tend to be much longer as the potential risk associated with changing a production system in operation is always considered to be too high due to the interdependencies of processes. Changes can have an impact on a complex process system and lead, for example, to serious incidents, such as an explosion at an oil plant or chemical plant. In addition, no plant operator would want to alter a running system unless the anticipated benefits outweigh the risks substantially.

In January 2020, Honeywell CEO Darius Adamczyk discussed the software strategy of the company, which included the transformation to becoming a much more digitally modern company. This strategy consists of three components: data integrity, consistency, and, finally, common IT and platform architectures.

This move will allow Honeywell to make better choices and to use technology solutions such as AI and machine learning to further enhance internal capabilities. Another step in this process is the reduction of the fixed-cost footprint, which has started to vary significantly from fixed cost.

In recent years, Honeywell has given priority to digital transformation in the development process in an attempt to create a smart future and enable their customers on this path. The company plans to use **Industrial Internet of Things** (**IIoT**) technology to simplify e-commerce operations and facilitate the digital transformation of retail, distribution, logistics, supply chains, and storage sectors. In particular, Honeywell cited *smart supply chain solutions* such as connected logistics and intelligent warehousing as the key factors in the digital transformation of companies that are engaged in retail-related business.

Honeywell has indicated that it intends to carry out mergers and acquisitions in order to strengthen its cooperation with the integrators in the smart supply chain sector. The company also plans to intensify efforts in research and development to constantly improve the end-to-end solutions for the supply chain.

# Oil and gas industry

The petroleum and gas industry is known to employ state-of-the-art data, tools, and machinery. In terms of digital transformation and the use of real-time data and insights collected by connected technologies, the industry has, however, fallen behind. The *digital maturity* of the oil and gas business is at 4.68 out of 10, according to the MIT Sloan Management Review and Deloitte, which means that despite advanced technology in the industry, digital and connected technology is not adequately used. Digital transformation requires the integration of technology and its business practices at the core of the organization.

Data may be collected by oil and gas companies from a wide variety of sensors, such as sensors embedded in oil wells or machine-to-machine data. Digitally mature companies can gather important insights through the analysis of data acquired from multiple sources and gain a competitive edge. The average site has less than 10 GB of data associated with it, according to Ashok Belani, the technology chief at Schlumberger Ltd. Digital transformation is beginning to sweep over the oil and gas industry, with petroleum companies now realizing the impact and sustainability potentials, such as higher revenues, lower costs, improved security, and operations reliability.

## Chevron

Schlumberger, Chevron, and Microsoft announced a three-party collaboration to accelerate the development of innovative digital solutions and petrotechnology in September 2019.

Data emerges quickly as one of the most useful assets for every company, but it is often difficult to extract insights because the information is trapped in internal silo-like organization structures. Schlumberger, Chevron, and Microsoft will collaborate to develop digital applications that would enable Chevron to synthesize business insights from disparate data sources by processing, visualizing, and analyzing it. Once the value is proven for Chevron, it can be offered to their customers for new digital revenues. This solution is called a DELFI cognitive **Exploration and Production (E&P)** environment and uses Microsoft Azure.

In this case, the E&P domain knowledge comes from Chevron and Schlumberger, and Microsoft provides the cloud computing platform Azure and its other technical capabilities to speed up the solution development. The goal is to productize a cloud-based E&P solution for the oil and gas sector. Together, they want to ensure that the solution meets the **Open Subsurface Data Universe (OSDU)** data platform specifications for security and performance. Chevron technical experts will be able to enhance their abilities by building upon this open foundation.

The three phases of collaboration will consist of the following:

- Deploying the DELFI Petrotechnical Suite to create the development environment
- Development of cloud-based applications, using Microsoft Azure
- Development of the cognitive computing capabilities, which can be used by Chevron in its E&P value chain, in line with its business objectives

Let's take a look at the semiconductor industry now.

## Semiconductor industry

The semiconductor industry is characterized by short product life cycles with some incremental evolutional and product-to-product changes. We have seen new models of smartphones come out every 10–12 months. The semiconductor industry goes through technological changes at a fast pace. In this industry, innovation directly affects the product development process and hence, companies in this space are under constant pressure to move toward more agile supply chains. Hence, many decision-makers in the semiconductor industry follow the Agile methodology.

The semiconductor industry deals with a multitude of suppliers, ecosystem partners, and foundries as part of its supply chain systems. These entities produce and share a variety of information elements as part of the collaboration in the semiconductor ecosystem. This information interchanges and connections between the entities creates a multitude of challenges. This sets the stage for **Digital Supply Chain** (**DSC**) systems. DSC can add intelligence and efficiency to the process and drive new revenues and business value. The new methods for analytical and technological innovation can be used to improve DSC. The supply chain systems today consist of a sequence of stages through marketing, product development, production, and distribution before the product is eventually handed to the customer.

The DSC network will depend on several technology solutions for integrated planning and execution systems, smart procurement and warehousing, global logistic visibility, and advanced analytics. Through such transformation, digital manufacturing capabilities will allow the production of high-quality, complex semiconductor solutions in less time by overcoming the traditional handoffs and delays between different entities. Semiconductor companies will strive to reach the next level of operational transformation by leveraging data and analytics on the information generated across the channel relationships between the entities in the supply chain ecosystem.

In the next section, we will look at the current challenges that industrial companies face. Often, these challenges are a result of the legacy practices in place over several decades of existence.

# Major challenges in industrial companies

The process of digital transformation involves implementing new and emerging technologies in different aspects of a business. Any process that involves change is not easy. There are different challenges faced by industrial companies when going through the process of adopting digital transformation technologies. Some of the major challenges faced are described in the following sections.

## Lack of expertise

Digital transformation is not achieved just by choosing the best technical option. As discussed in *Chapter 2, Transforming the Culture in an Organization*, the right digital talent is critical to lead and execute a successful industrial digital transformation. Digital transformational change requires expertise in both technology and change management. Some organizations that seek transformations choose to bring in many outside consultants who generally tend to apply generic solutions as *best practices*. A company's internal staff will have intimate knowledge about what works and what doesn't in their daily operations. A combination of internal talent motivated toward digital transformation along with select, externally recruited talent would be more successful.

## Funding

Digital transformation requires a multi-year investment, and delivering on the promise of good ROI takes time. Generally, many business divisions would have to provide funding for the transformation projects for investments in technology, infrastructure, and services organization. All budget and infrastructure constraints should be carefully analyzed upfront in a cash-sensitive industry. Nevertheless, the creation of budgetary projections that are minimally different from real ones can be achieved by comprehensive preparation and a thorough understanding of emerging solutions and the organization's cultural climate.

## Legacy business model

Legacy business models are a challenge for industrial companies that have become very used to their own legacy systems and processes. Disruptions in well-established business models keep occurring with regular periodicity. Industrial companies often continue to operate in their comfort zone and are resistant to change. As a result, it is harder to change the age-old but proven business processes and reinvent the business model. To soften the impact of disruptive innovation, the use of digital technology can be first introduced to improve the internal business processes around the legacy system and showcase the business outcomes. As a next stage, the topic of new business model changes can be broached.

## Organizational structure

Significant structural and process changes are required in digital transformation. However, a powerful organizational culture exists in conventional manufacturing organizations and hence they may not be amenable to new workflows. Digital initiatives can face obstruction from several cultural factors of an organization, from long-term staff to risk-averse managers to corporate politics. An organization, through its digital processing initiative, can confront such challenges by drawing up a workforce transition plan. This program should include the digital transformation strategy and milestones, as well as scheduling messages to all stakeholders. It should also include identified gaps in skills.

Tight schedules and numerous resource constraints complicate manufacturing operations in industrial companies. Their management, therefore, does not accept any adverse effects on operations before they see any benefits from their digital transformation.

A constant reminder is needed to keep the mindset that workforce transition plans for digital transformations are a marathon and not a sprint. These plans should manage cultural change throughout the process.

## Lack of an overall digitization strategy

Industrial companies are under strong market pressure to provide their customers with products/solutions at a quick pace. Hence, these companies tend to concentrate more on tools and operational endpoints. They tend to ignore the value that their customers and their own companies can benefit from through process improvements. This trend may create additional challenges to digital transformation by abruptly shifting organizational structures and workflows without internal harmonization and operational readiness for them. It is important to first define what successful completion of digital transformation means when developing a strategy. A well-defined strategic plan calls for a vision of what the digitally transformed business will look like. It should also include corresponding methods used to monitor the accomplishment of milestones in the transformation journey. The digital vision of change should build on the foundation of the current core competencies and strengths of the business.

## Employee pushback

A false perception that digital transformation can endanger their jobs can cause employees of industrial companies to resist changes consciously or unconsciously. Employees might have another perception that the digital transformation might prove inefficient and then management will eventually give up efforts. Hence, leaders must acknowledge these concerns and stress that the digital transformation process will provide employees with the opportunity to upgrade their expertise to suit future markets.

## Outdated processes

Many industrial companies use traditional paper-based processes, which are manual and time-consuming. Industrial companies need modern and agile digital solutions to be efficient and they should offer employees a flexible approach to work seamlessly. Paper-based processes are the common sources of error and should be the first target for process improvement. A digital solution that has been well designed to be intuitive will improve productivity and commitment from employees and reduce training time. Smartphones and tablet-based solutions encourage employees to conduct business operations a lot more efficiently. This mobility allows the processing of transactions in real time and with better data accuracy.

## Lack of automation

Some industrial companies lack automation because of their legacy processes. The value of automation is that redundant and time-consuming tasks are eliminated. With the correct digital solution, these companies can automate and reject manual tasks so that product updates and response times can be sped up.

The following table summarizes the top challenges to industrial digital transformation by the size of the company:

| Top 5 Digital Transformation Challenges: Ordered by Company Size | |
|---|---|
| **Less than 1,000 Employees** | **100 – 1,000 Employees** |
| 1. Lack of Expertise to Lead Digitization Initiatives<br>2. Employee Pushback<br>3. No Overarching Strategy for Digitization<br>4. Business Partners Unable to Support<br>5. Limited Budget | 1. Employee Pushback<br>2. Organizational Structure Gets in the Way<br>3. No Overarching Strategy for Digitization<br>4. Limited Budget<br>5. Lack of Expertise to Lead Digitization Initiatives |
| **1,000 – 5,000 Employees** | **More than 5,000 Employees** |
| 1. No Overarching Strategy for Digitization<br>2. Lack of Expertise to Lead Digitization Initiatives<br>3. Limited access to required Technical Expertise<br>4. Employee Pushback<br>5. Limited Budget | 1. Lack of Expertise to Lead Digitization Initiatives<br>2. Organizational Structure Gets in the Way<br>3. No Overarching Strategy for Digitization<br>4. Limited access to required Technical Expertise<br>5. Employee Pushback |

Figure 4.9 – Results of a survey conducted by Jabil

Next, we will look at the changes needed to create an impact in industrial companies via the transformation.

# Overcoming the challenges

In *Chapter 3, Accelerating Digital Transformation with Emerging Technologies*, we discussed the rise of digital technologies and the digital platform. Along with the business model changes, we can lay the foundation for industrial digital transformation. Let's see how to overcome the challenges by putting together the digital technologies, cultural and organizational changes, business process changes, and business model transformations.

## Business model change by Tesla

Customers are more inclined to buy products and services that generate value for them. The automobile industry has worked on very similar principles for about a century now. They create a replacement market by offering a newer model with a few additional features, every few years, for their loyal customer base. As a result, the value of a used car drops drastically within the first 3 years. Industry estimates suggest 42% depreciation after 3 years for an average car in the US. Using Kelley Blue Book (see www.kbb.com) or similar sources, it is estimated that the residual value of these models of luxury cars after 3 years are as follows:

- Tesla Model 3 (-10.2%)
- Mercedes-Benz CLA (-47.7%)
- Audi A5 (-49.3%)
- Volvo S60 (-53.2%)
- BMW 3 Series (-53.4%)

Tesla clearly stands out in preserving value for the buyer. Tesla is able to preserve the value of its cars for the owners over its lifetime, by delivering new features **Over the Air** (**OTA**). Tesla does not fully rely on the hardware (mechanical parts of the car), but rather a combination of software and hardware, to deliver value, unlike traditional automakers. In the case of Tesla, the **Battery Electric Vehicle** (**BEV**) has very little maintenance needs apart from the tires and battery. Tesla is heavily investing in coming up with a million-mile battery using low-cobalt or cobalt-free battery chemical processes. In addition, Tesla purchased the company SolarCity in 2016 for $2.6 million to try to integrate energy generation, storage, and consumption for residential and commercial customers (see https://www.tesla.com/blog/tesla-and-solarcity-combine). This allows Tesla to bring BEV charging solutions to the homes of Tesla owners, as well as address power generation using renewable sources such as solar panels.

Tesla's example clearly shows that companies can leverage business model changes to drive industrial digital transformation and generate enormous value for themselves and their customers.

## Overcoming challenges using digital technology

During the COVID-19 crisis, many factory operations had to shut down for worker safety. This has accelerated a look at the proactive deployment of automation technologies in factory and supply chain operations, namely the following:

- Industrial robots and collaborative robotics or cobots.
- Autonomous materials movement using autonomous forklifts and cranes and high-payload drones.
- Sensing technology in protective gear for worker safety.
- Use of industrial IoT platforms for predictive maintenance and operations optimizations to reduce unplanned maintenance activities.
- Remote operations of physical systems are difficult. Most often, **Operation Technology (OT)** systems are not connected to IT systems and hence not accessible remotely.

However, attempts to make OT systems available for remote operations require higher levels of due diligence for cybersecurity, to preserve resiliency. Even progressive companies such as Tesla had to close their plants temporarily, similar to the other major automakers, during the COVID-19 crisis in early 2020.

In *Chapter 3, Accelerating Digital Transformation with Emerging Technologies*, we discussed various emerging digital technologies and the rise of digital platforms as key enablers of transformation, in combination with the business and cultural drivers. To reinforce that, a white paper by PTC mentioned that industrial digital transformation often fails when companies try to look for one silver bullet technology as the holy grail. Instead, industrial companies have to take a holistic approach to their digital transformation strategy and make multiple big and small bets.

Next, let's see how partnerships can help to overcome challenges.

## Overcoming challenges by partnership

Let's look at Baker Hughes, an oil and gas company that started in 1907 and has about 70,000 global employees as of early 2020. The oil and gas industry has gone through its own challenges due to falling oil prices, even before the COVID-19 crisis. Originally called Baker Hughes, in 2017, it became a part of GE Oil and Gas. The resulting company was called BHGE, or Baker Hughes, a GE Company. GE divested from BHGE in 2019, when it became Baker Hughes Company. Interestingly, in 2014, there were talks of its acquisition by Halliburton to form the largest oil and gas company. That move was blocked by the US Department of Justice by a civil antitrust lawsuit. One of the authors of this book (Nath) started his professional career in Halliburton in the 1990s.

Despite the changing landscape at the top of Baker Hughes and the sliding oil prices, it has continued its efforts to speed up the transformation of the oil and gas industry. With an approach to develop a broad portfolio of transformative technologies and solutions, it made several investments, ranging from AI, industrial IoT, sensors, and edge analytics to enterprise-scale AI. At the core of these investments is the goal to empower their customers to identify and extract the right data to improve operational productivity, efficiency, and safety in oilfield operations, such as a petro-chemical plant, shown in *Figure 4.10*. Such a plant has many complex systems and sub-systems, with thousands of sensors and measurable parameters.

In June 2019, Baker Hughes and C3.ai announced a **Joint Venture** (**JV**); see `https://bakerhughesc3.ai/` for more details. The following case study of Shell, to improve the reliability of petro-chemical plants, shows how a 100+ years old industrial company such as Baker Hughes is augmenting and accelerating the delivery of transformational outcomes via a joint venture. The group CIO of Shell, Jay Crotts, mentioned that Shell is a user of the C3.ai platform. Shell is embarking on its journey of industrial digital transformation with predictive maintenance as a step to improve its operations. C3.ai allows Shell to apply AI and machine learning, in this scenario.

Shell already had a strong partnership with Baker Hughes in oilfield services and related software services. Jay Crotts further stated that such initiatives bring the emerging digital technologies close to the mature oilfield technologies, to leverage the synergy between the two. This allows the convergence of Baker's oilfield domain expertise and C3.ai's competencies, to help drive innovative business outcomes, at a time when the crude oil prices are at historically low levels (source: `https://c3.ai/baker-hughes-and-c3-ai-announce-joint-venture-to-deliver-ai-solutions/`):

Figure 4.10 – Petro-chemical plant [source: https://www.pngfuel.com/free-png/ogate/download]

The JV between Baker Hughes and C3.ai brings BHC3 Suite capabilities to the oil and gas sector, such as the following:

- **Reliability**: Identify problems early and mitigate them.
- **Predictive Asset Maintenance**: The ability to prioritize maintenance tasks, balancing the risks and the budget.
- **Production Optimization**: Improve the productivity of oil wells and reservoirs.
- **Inventory Optimization**: Optimize operating costs, while minimizing stock-outs.
- **Sensor Health**: Ensure IoT systems/sensors are working properly.
- **Well Integrity and Health**: The ability to detect failures related to wells ahead of time or root cause analysis.
- **Yield Optimization**: Increase overall production from oil wells/reservoirs.
- **Energy Management**
- **Hydrocarbon Loss Analytics**

For further reading, you can visit `https://bakerhughesc3.ai/ai-software/`.

The industrial giants, such as Siemens, GE, and Honeywell, have chosen to mostly build their own capabilities, to drive the industrial digital transformation for their lines of businesses and their industrial customer base. As a result, we have seen these digital platforms and related ecosystem grow, mainly in the latter half of the last decade:

- GE's Predix Platform, including applications such as **Asset Performance Management** (**APM**) and the associated ecosystem.
- Siemens MindSphere facilitates digital applications for the fusion of the diverse sources of the oilfield operational sources to foster data-driven business decisions.
- Honeywell launched a digital platform with the goal of analyzing and optimizing oil and gas infrastructure by leveraging the collected operational data. This industrial IoT platform is named Honeywell Forge and was announced in 2019.

There are more such examples from the industrial giants. However, the key difference from the Baker Hughes story is that after separation from GE, it went for JV to accelerate a similar effort. Likewise, Rockwell Automation and PTC have partnered to launch combined solutions for industrial companies. Together, they offer FactoryTalk InnovationSuite. In the middle of 2018, Rockwell Automation decided to make a $1 billion equity investment in PTC. The series of examples here show that industrial companies have to continue to make a variety of big and bold bets to diversify their efforts toward digital transformation. No single silver bullet can ensure a successful transformation journey. This has been true for most B2C transformations as well. We have seen Google Nest take a series of steps and not just focus on the thermostat. Likewise, Netflix has moved from shipping DVDs to streaming movies to creating their own video content.

In *Chapter 7, Transformation Ecosystem*, we will discuss at length the impact of leveraging the partnerships and ecosystems to overcome various kinds of challenges in the industrial digital transformation journey.

# Summary

In this chapter, we learned about the need for improving the business process to drive productivity and cost-efficiency in industrial companies. New business models are often the basis of disruptive innovation, required to drive new revenues and stay ahead of the competition. Industrial companies, especially those who have been in business for a long time, face a multitude of challenges and are in the process of leveraging digital technologies and a cultural transformation to reinvent themselves. The process of reinvention can be a combination of organic initiatives or synergistic partnerships and acquisitions.

To summarize, we learned about the following:

- The need to continually tweak business processes in companies, while navigating the fine balance between the efficiency and effectiveness of the enhancements.
- The benefits of improved business processes in increasing both internal and external customer satisfaction.
- The need for business model improvements and reinventions to keep the disruptors away and add new digital revenue streams.
- The need for a variety of small and big bets on digital transformation initiatives, including strategic partnerships and JVs to orchestrate the ecosystem.
- Finally, we learned about the various ways to overcome challenges in the industrial digital transformation journey.

Part 1 of this book consists of the first four chapters, where we learned about *the what and the why* of industrial digital transformation. The next part of the book will focus on the *how* of the transformation and use detailed case studies from the commercial and public sectors. In *Chapter 5, Transforming One Industry at a Time*, we will showcase how to apply digital transformation to one industry at a time, using case studies from semiconductor manufacturing, construction, and related industries.

# Questions

Here are some questions to test your understanding of the chapter:

1. What are the main business drivers for industrial digital transformation?
2. What are the four steps to business process optimization?
3. What is the role of the new business model in driving transformation?
4. What are the common challenges in the semiconductor industry?
5. What is meant by an as-a-Service model?
6. What are some of the emerging digital platforms with applications in oil and gas and related industries?

# Section 2: The "How" of Digital Transformation

This part of the book provides case studies and a blueprint to develop an implementation plan for the transformation that can be used by mid-career professionals.

This part of the book comprises the following chapters:

- *Chapter 5, Transforming One Industry at a Time*
- *Chapter 6, Transforming the Public Sector*
- *Chapter 7, Transformation Ecosystem*
- *Chapter 8, Artificial Intelligence in Digital Transformation*
- *Chapter 9, Pitfalls to Avoid in The Digital Transformation Journey*
- *Chapter 10, Measuring the Value of Transformation*
- *Chapter 11, The Blueprint for Success*

# 5
# Transforming One Industry at a Time

In *Part 1* of this book, we covered some of the fundamental building blocks and emerging technologies as pertaining to industrial digital transformation. We looked at some of the reasons for developing a transformation strategy. There are several reasons for promoting the implementation of digital technology in industry. It is worthwhile looking at some examples across different industrial segments, to understand some of the motivation behind how we can identify opportunities for digital transformation. It is expected that, by the end of this chapter, you will be able to relate to some of the transformation examples presented, as well as be able to identify opportunities for transformation in your own respective industry. Specifically, we will look at a variety of instances where digital transformation has been applied, and, in each case, there are different considerations and methodologies that have proven themselves in practice.

In this chapter, we are going to explore the following topics:

- Transforming the chemical industry
- Transforming the semiconductor industry
- Disrupting industrial manufacturing
- Transforming buildings and complexes

- Transforming the manufacturing ecosystem
- Promoting industrial worker safety

# Transforming the chemical industry

The chemical industry is one of the largest groups of industries in the world, accounting for over $5.7 trillion of global **gross domestic product** (**GDP**) and over 120 million jobs (`https://cefic.org/media-corner/newsroom/chemical-industry-contributes-5-7-trillion-to-global-gdp-and-supports-120-million-jobs-new-report-shows/`), and touches almost every aspect of our lives. In this section, we will look at several instances where digital transformation has affected the industry over the years. We will first start with a historical example that shows digital technologies have been around for years, and will then move on to some of the newer use cases.

## Digitization of process control

Feedback control is widely used in the chemical industry for ensuring that the end product of the process is as desired. For example, in batch reactors, sensors monitor the evolution of the product and by-products, and reagents are adjusted in close to real time to ensure that the output of a batch meets the needed specifications. If these parameters are not controlled, the output could have different compound characteristics than expected and the entire batch would need to be discarded or reworked through additional processing and increasing material, labor, and tool costs. *Figure 5.1* explains the basic components of a feedback loop. In this simple example, a controller observes temperature deviation from a desired setpoint in a batch reactor and adjusts the coolant flow to keep the temperature as close to the setpoint as possible. This controller could be as simple as an on-off switch (bang-bang controller) where the valve is either completely open or closed, or it could be something more sophisticated to minimize tracking errors. Additional sensors, such as those monitoring pressure, could be utilized to measure the chamber pressure and avoid safety hazards. The concept is illustrated here:

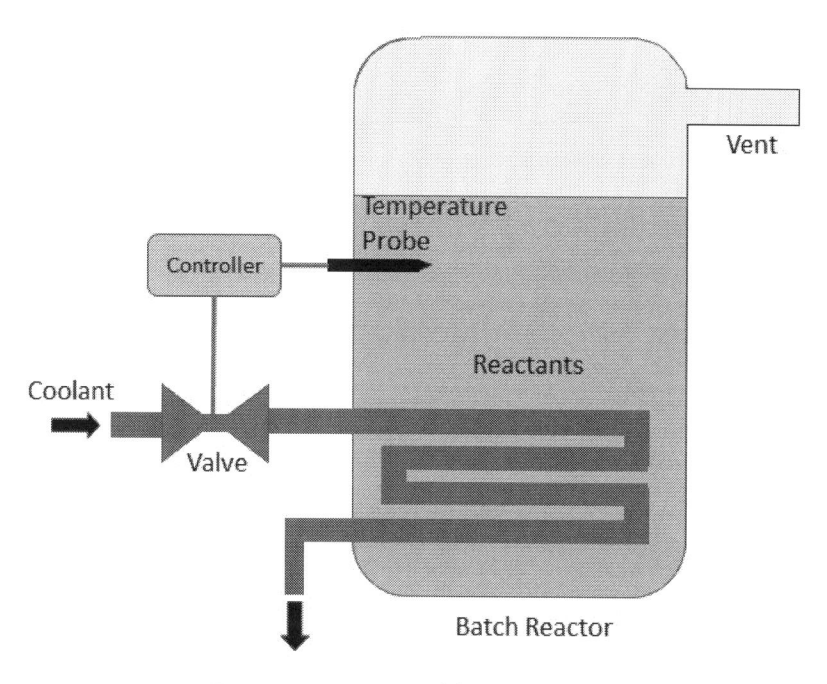

Figure 5.1 – Concept of feedback control

Initial application of feedback control was done via pneumatic systems and has evolved over time to enable the control of valves and actuators via electronic means. Electronics led to the advent of analog implementations of **Proportional, Integral, and Derivative (PID)** control wherein the regulation error is taken and is fed back as a sum of a scaled value (proportional), its integral, and derivative (see, for example, `https://www.csimn.com/CSI_pages/PIDforDummies.html`). By adjusting the scaling values assigned to each of these terms, different response profiles can be obtained, and these are usually tuned to provide rapid recovery from disturbances with a minimal overshoot and asymptotically zero regulation error. These loops tend to be univariate in the sense that they look at a single error measurement and control a single actuator. It is well known that this scheme results in inefficiencies since it treats each process stage by itself and does not consider cross-stage interactions. Given the time constraints involved, a process control solution that can simultaneously observe and control multiple process stages can, for example, preemptively compensate for incoming disturbances from an upstream operation.

This realization and the relatively (relative to computational time) slow dynamics involved led to the development of the field of **Model Predictive Control (MPC)** (see `https://www.mathworks.com/videos/series/understanding-model-predictive-control.html`), and even though the initial publications are over 30 years old, active research in this field continues to this day. *Figure 5.2* shows the basic concept behind how MPC works. Here, observations from multiple sensors are fed into a simulation model that forecasts the evolution of the system over a time horizon. The role of the optimization engine is to set the manipulated variable trajectories to minimize the cost (which typically reflects the regulation or setpoint tracking error, along with a term to smooth out the control action), as illustrated here:

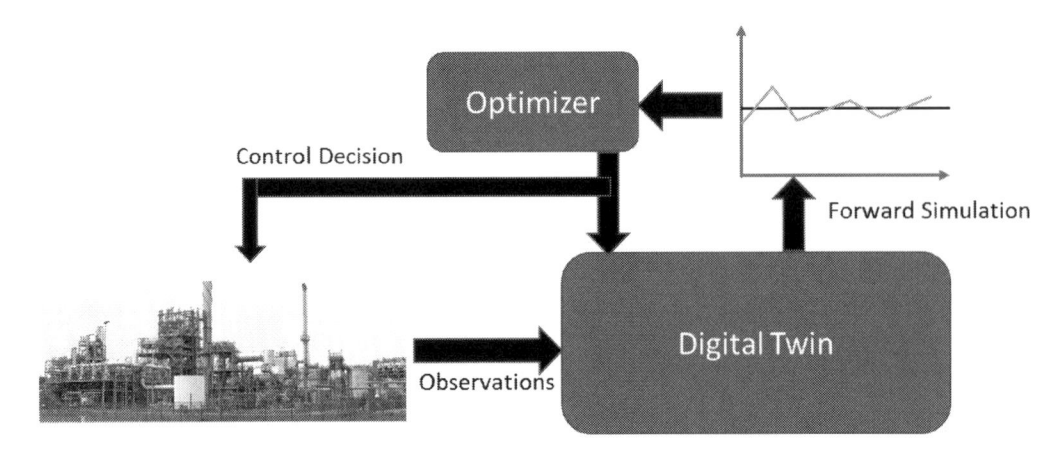

Figure 5.2 – Overview of the logic behind MPC

After this, the first recommended values of the manipulated variable are implemented, and the entire process repeats after shifting forward by one time step. Note that for most processes, PID controllers and hierarchical decision modules prove sufficient. However, in instances where there is high sensitivity to product quality and safety, or the need to tightly control by-products for environmental compliance, solutions based on MPC perform much better. Another advantage of MPC is that it automatically accounts for constraints on the actuators. (An integral controller, for example, can go into a state called wind-up, where the actuator has hit its limit but the error signal continues to add up due to integral action, which results in delayed recovery of the process. Various anti-windup schemes have been proposed in the literature, but MPC inherently does not suffer from this.) MPC has found wide use in complex chemical plants such as oil refineries and has truly shown the potential of computational power and industrial communication. Cloud connectivity of these controllers and the ability to have the complete process-floor topology will allow process engineers to view various stages of manufacturing remotely, and even across multiple plants.

It helps that there are several established vendors (such as Rockwell Automation, ABB, Honeywell, and AVEVA) who offer turnkey solutions, and the typical cost recovery period for these is less than a year. Additionally, the publication of several industrial challenge problems (for example, the Tennessee Eastman problem; see Downs, J. J. and Vogel, E. F., *A Plant-Wide Industrial Process Control Problem*, in *Computers & Chemical Engineering*, 17 (3): 245-255 (1993)) accelerated the development of complex control solutions that inherently depend on digitization, as it gave academic researchers practical test beds that exhibited complex interactions.

In addition to the true benefit of moving to a digital solution, the multivariate nature of MPC also inherently drives the development of robust communication technologies for field deployment. Oil refineries are sprawling complexes, and communication from various processing stages (for example, distillation columns, separators, evaporators) needs to go to a central location where the MPC algorithm executes. This has driven several industrial communication standards such as Fieldbus, Profibus, and the now-dominant Ethernet/IP (see www.odva.org). We will not delve into these here, but want to alert you to the fact that communication among various modules and standards to deploy this in an efficient and scalable fashion is key to enabling the implementation of digitization technologies in industry. Robust communication provided by these standards has led to the concept of a control room, wherein the entire operations of the plant can be effectively monitored from a single location. We will see this theme repeated as we look at other use cases later in the chapter.

# Digitization for inspection and maintenance

Given the sprawl of certain types of chemical plants—specifically, refineries and fertilizer operations and the web of piping carrying chemicals to and from them—it is a challenge to manually inspect and maintain the infrastructure.

In this scenario (as mentioned in *Chapter 3, Accelerating Digital Transformation with Emerging Technologies*), drones can prove invaluable in inspecting facilities. This area has been seeing an ever-increasing growth since 2017 as more and more companies embrace drones to address challenges related to inspecting hard-to-reach places such as flare stacks, overhead pipelines, and the inside of storage tanks where lingering toxicity may be of concern.

For example, Chevron typically inspected flare stacks at its Duri field via binoculars. This did not give a close-up view of the stacks, nor did it reveal any thermal patterns that could be of concern. In 2019, they contracted Terra Drone to inspect these stacks with high-resolution and thermal imaging cameras.

Other areas where drones stand out as viable instruments for inspection are in hazardous environments such as off-shore oil platforms, where they can efficiently perform inspection and imaging tasks on the underside of the platform.

In addition, drones can keep personnel out of confined spaces such as inside reactor vessels, where specialized training and additional personnel may need to be present outside the vessel (per safety regulations). Furthermore, drones can get inside pipes and ducts to inspect these from the inside—something that may be impossible for a person to do.

While drones can be very effective in inspection tasks, people are still needed to perform maintenance and repair activities. Given the size of the chemical plant, it is very inefficient to have personnel travel back and forth from a repair site to the control room, for example. Most communication to the control room (which typically is the place where the anomaly being inspected was detected) takes place via radio. However, this is where the power of video enabled through smart glasses has shown great success.

With **augmented reality** (**AR**) (see, for example, the following reference, which presents comprehensive use cases as far back as 2012: Nee, A. Y. C., Ong, S. K., Chryssolouris, G. and Mourtzis, D, *Augmented reality applications in design and manufacturing*, in *CIRP Annals – Manufacturing Technology*, 61: 657-679 (2012)), the person performing the work can not only talk but can also involve the engineer at the other end in the visual experience, while at the same time keeping their hands free to work on repairs. This allows for more effective troubleshooting as the expert is able to see exactly what is going on in the field. In addition, the maintenance worker is able to pull up repair manuals on the fly, as well as get pictorial information pushed to them to assist in faster repair turnaround without getting distracted from their work to look up information on a standalone device such as a laptop, phone, or tablet. In addition, smart glasses enable collaboration across geographies since they are not necessarily limited to the plant, and they can save on recovery times as the maintenance technician can connect directly with a field service engineer if needed without having to fly them to the site; of course, the IT department has to open up the appropriate firewall ports for such communication to be possible. Linde Gas has reported how smart glasses are helping to digitally transform workplace culture at the company by enabling instant access to expertise, especially for their plants located in remote locations.

# Monitoring for demand predictability and optimized delivery

Manufacturers typically want to outsource delivery management services to chemical suppliers so that they can focus on their core competency. For suppliers of commodity chemicals, remotely monitoring the status of tanks provides a win-win opportunity that makes this a benefit for both the customer and themselves. Firstly, this allows them to provide the customer with a real-time view of inventory status for their own internal production planning. Secondly, for the supplier, this provides a reliable data source to forecast demand and internally manage their own inventory and delivery schedules, to gain efficiencies in operation. In this situation, rather than waiting for the customer to contact them or periodically sending personnel out to report on remaining stock, real-time data allows suppliers to forecast customer consumption trends that can then be used to trigger planned replenishment as needed. Since these storage tanks are typically at locations where wired internet is not economical, they depend on sensors that transmit data via cellular connections to cloud servers. This allows data to be accessed by the customer through their own secure web portal, as well as data that can then be fed to the supplier's monitoring and forecasting algorithms. Access to this data enables the supplier to not only plan when to send tankers out to replenish tanks, but in case they have multiple customers in the service area, they can adjust the replenishment rates over time via optimization to ensure that the lowest number of tankers and trips are needed in a given time period, to service all customers. In fact, we can view this as a problem of minimizing the total load-weighted tanker mileage within a time horizon, and solve it to not only get the trip periodicity but also the optimized routing. *Figure 5.3* shows the entire data flow pipeline. In this instance, the supplier has limited replenishment to a weekly cadence, and the model has bucketed customers to match this up.

Suppliers have been adopting these methodologies over the past several years, and in many instances use this as a differentiating capability to win more customers. In the industrial chemicals space, PVS Minibulk (which is a division of Detroit, MI-based PVS Chemicals) has used monitoring systems provided by TankLink to efficiently plan and route deliveries, while at the same time they have avoided costly low-margin emergency deliveries.

The northeastern US accounts for a majority of residential heating oil consumption, and the last known data survey from the US Energy Information Administration (www.eia.gov) shows that in 2018, about 3 billion gallons of heating oil was sold to consumers. The demand pattern for heating oil is seasonal, since the primary use is for space heating, and demand is also dependent on the weather. Given the criticality of not running the tank dry, especially in the middle of winter, the consumer is motivated to partner with the supplier to enable remote monitoring. This motivates both suppliers and consumers to place sensors on tanks to enable remote monitoring. It also smoothens out any spurts in demand that may catch suppliers by surprise, along with providing the added assurance that heat will remain on in the house even if the customer decides to leave town. The data flow pipeline for remote monitoring can be seen in the following diagram:

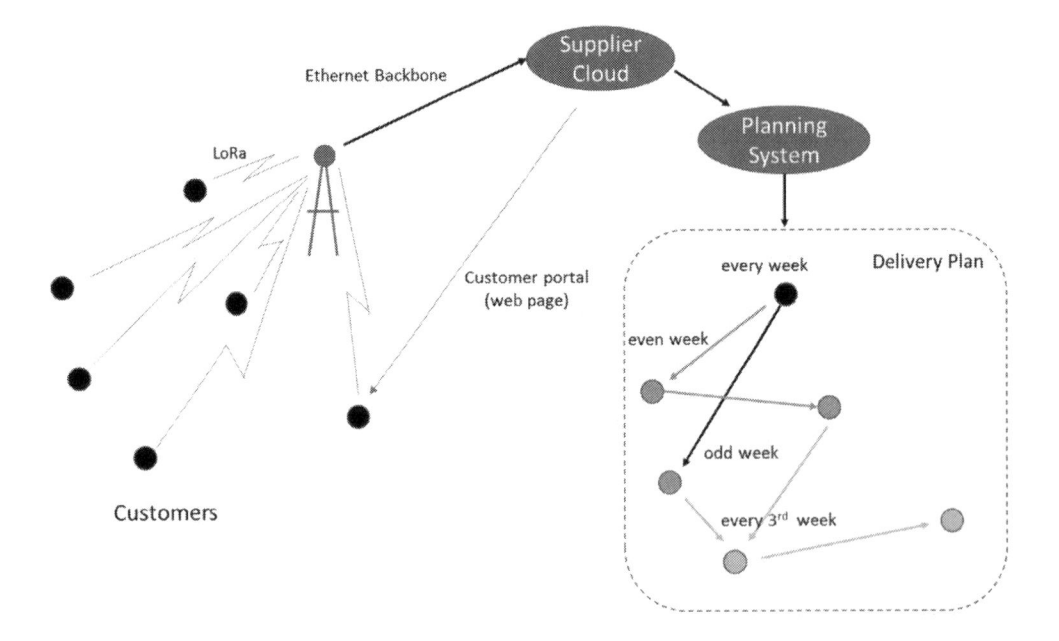

Figure 5.3 – Remote monitoring drives predictive replenishment of customer supplies

Remote monitoring is even transforming the beer distribution industry. BrewLogix has developed a keg base that will transmit the weight of the container to the supplier, along with a sensor that indicates the type of beer. This information is transmitted to the cloud via an internet gateway provided by Intel Corp. At a predetermined threshold, the supplier can trigger a delivery versus having the keg run dry, which is a risk with time-based rounds.

Lastly, large chemical companies also benefit from continuous monitoring of chemical usage and collection of data from their facilities. Air Liquide is a global company that delivers specialty chemicals—for example, to the semiconductor industry. They often run their own plants in locations close to major industrial clusters. Air Liquide has been developing remote monitoring technologies to detect potential issues early on in order to avoid supply disruptions to their customers, in addition to making decisions that help production efficiency in order to improve margins (Roy, A., Manoharan, J. and Zhang, G., *How Air Liquide Leverages on PI Technologies to Optimize its Operations — SIO. Optim program*, presented at *PI World*, San Francisco (2019)). This has also driven the development of **Remote Operation Control Centers** (**ROCCs**) at strategic locations across the globe, where Air Liquide engineers can monitor the performance of their operations.

In this section, we have seen how digital technologies can be leveraged for the purposes of improved operational excellence via a combination of digital twins and optimization techniques, and have in addition looked at use cases of AR and drones for the purposes of improving inspection and maintenance activities. The section lastly looked at how **Internet of Things** (**IoT**) sensors on the edge could be leveraged for monitoring inventory at customer sites to improve demand forecasting and to optimize replenishments, which results in better outcomes for both the supplier and the customer. In the next section, we will look at how digitization has been leveraged by the semiconductor industry.

# Transforming the semiconductor industry

In this section, we will focus primarily on the digital transformation of the semiconductor industry. The semiconductor industry permeates all aspects of society and accounted for over $400 billion in sales in 2019 (`https://www.statista.com/statistics/266973/global-semiconductor-sales-since-1988/`). The industry is responsible for driving remarkable miniaturization in electronic circuits, such that today's smartphones have more computational power than the original desktop computer and are about 100,000 times more powerful than the guidance computer that helped man land on the moon. In order to pursue this drive for integrating more and more functionality on a single piece of silicon, the industry must transform how it manufactures. Digitization has played a key role in this journey. In this section, we will be specifically looking at the following topics:

- Digitization and lights-out manufacturing
- Digitization for process monitoring and control
- Big data and digitization for yield management

Let's get started with it.

## Digitization and lights-out manufacturing

Lights-out manufacturing refers to a situation where the entire production line is fully automated and the only role of people in the factory is for maintenance or repair purposes. When looking at pictures of modern semiconductor fabs, they often show spotless aisles with overhead delivery vehicles and minimal people (see *Figure 5.4* for an example of this). In fact, a modern semiconductor factory with all the associated manufacturing complexity is a marvel of automation via digitization. However, this was not always the case. In this section, we will look at some of the key drivers and enablers that moved the industry toward lights-out automation. The following photograph shows a semiconductor fab:

Figure 5.4 – Picture of a wafer fab; overhead delivery vehicles can be seen moving along their tracks
(Courtesy of Intel Corp.)

Fundamental to understanding the reasons behind the move to this level of automation is the steady march of the industry to keep up with Moore's law. This was based on early extrapolations and predictions that the number of transistors in a device would roughly double every 2 years. Over the years, the industry has done whatever it takes to stay on this trajectory, and this was definitely the case in the mid-1990s when the move toward lights-out manufacturing was seeded.

The need to follow Moore's law and the associated increase in design complexity (related to the increasing number of smaller transistors per device) and cost led the industry to contemplate the transition from 200 mm silicon wafers to 300 mm ones. In a wafer fab, processing is done at the wafer level, whereby wafers are batched together into lots. The advantage of moving to a larger wafer size is the potential for the larger wafer area (300 mm has about two times the area of a 200 mm wafer), while most manufacturing costs are tied to the number of wafers moved. This would imply a 2X increase in the number of devices produced per wafer for a similar cost of moves. However, the net benefit is not 2X as there are other associated cost increases, such as chemical costs and equipment footprint increases. The reason 300 mm was chosen versus a larger wafer size was that, given the timeline, this was the maximum size the silicon wafer manufacturers could support due to the weight of the starting material to grow the crystal (reported to be between 300 kg and 450 kg). The projected weight of a single lot of 300 mm wafers was projected to exceed what could be ergonomically managed by a person. In addition, the success of ad hoc implementation of intra-bay delivery within 200 mm fabs at that time gave hope to the development of a standard framework for 100% of wafer deliveries in the factory.

## The importance of standards

In order to accomplish this transition, it was clear to the manufacturers that no one company could lead the transition given the costs and investments involved, along with learning from prior industry transitions from 100 mm to 150 mm, and then to 200 mm wafer sizes. This had to be an industry transition. Once this was realized, there was no need for anyone to push ahead, and all participants realized it was in their best interest to participate to the extent possible without giving away proprietary intellectual property. This led to the formation of a number of consortia to define the requirements, the key among them being I300I, which drove most of the existing standards through **Semiconductor Equipment and Materials International** (**SEMI**), which is the global standards organization for the industry (www.semi.org). Some of the standards the industry aligned to include the following:

- Standards around the wafer dimensions
- Standard lot size
- Design and dimensions for the lot carrier (often referred to as a **front opening unified pod** (**FOUP**)) and the associated load ports in the equipment. This is the standardized form factor for overhead delivery systems, as well as for stockers to store these carriers while they await processing.
- Enhancement to the communication standard for enhanced data collection

180   Transforming One Industry at a Time

- Standards for equipment performance monitoring, including defining equipment state models
- Standards for **computer-integrated manufacturing** (CIM)
- Process control systems standards

And the list goes on; refer to the SEMI website for a comprehensive list. The key takeaway is that the industry as a whole (the device manufacturers and the equipment suppliers) aligned itself to a set of standards that enabled rapid scale-up and deployment of 300 mm capabilities in the early 2000s. Several of the standards codified protocols for how equipment would interact with external factory systems, allowing enhanced data collection and control of the tools.

## Automated material handling systems and scheduling

The move to **Automated Material Handling Systems** (**AMHS**) and well-defined standards led to increased automation within the wafer fabs. AMHS is de facto needed to enable lights-out operations as it forms the backbone of material movement across the factory. *Figure 5.5* shows a manifestation of a simple layout where the following moves are allowed—intra bay: stocker-tool-stocker; inter bay: stocker-stocker. This was typical of initial implementations of automated material handling, and, as confidence in the methodology and system robustness has improved, alternate options such as direct tool-tool moves have also been implemented. However, for the purposes of this discussion, we will limit ourselves to the setup in the following diagram:

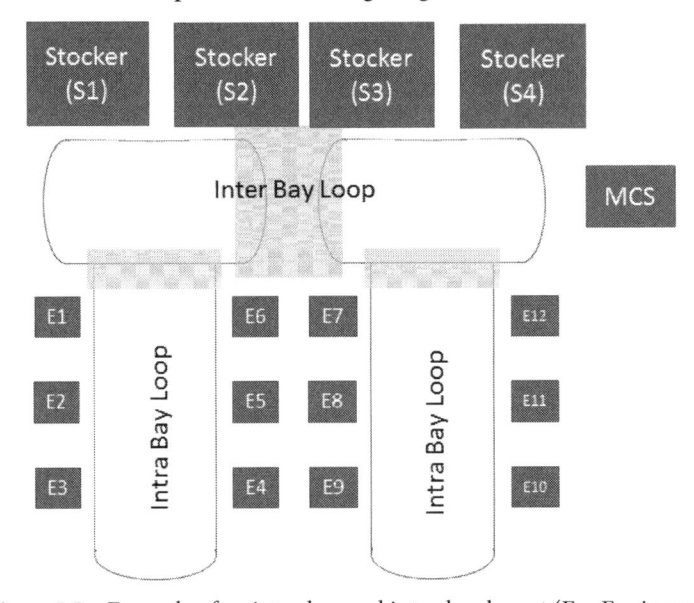

Figure 5.5 – Example of an inter-bay and intra-bay layout (E = Equipment)

The movement of overhead carriers is managed through a **Material Control System (MCS)**, which ensures that lots are transported from their source to their destination as quickly as possible without causing congestion or conflicts on the overhead rails.

The 300 mm equipment has a minimum of two load ports, which enables one of the load ports to always have a lot that is in process, while the FOUP at the other load port is replaced by the AMHS system. Initial deployments had simple algorithms to dispatch lots to tools based primarily on a pull (Kanban)-type solution that would move lots along as lots upstream depleted. *Figure 5.6* shows a flow sequence of this process, along with the key components. A simple *feed me* algorithm will trigger a lot pickup and replacement to the tool once the lot completes processing. One key interface component shown is the **Station Controller**—typically, there is one such edge device per process or metrology tool for local equipment control, data collection, and alarm monitoring. Physically, this can be positioned as a local computer sitting next to the equipment or it could be hosted in a data center, in which case a single server may control a whole bay of equipment simultaneously. This process is illustrated in the following diagram:

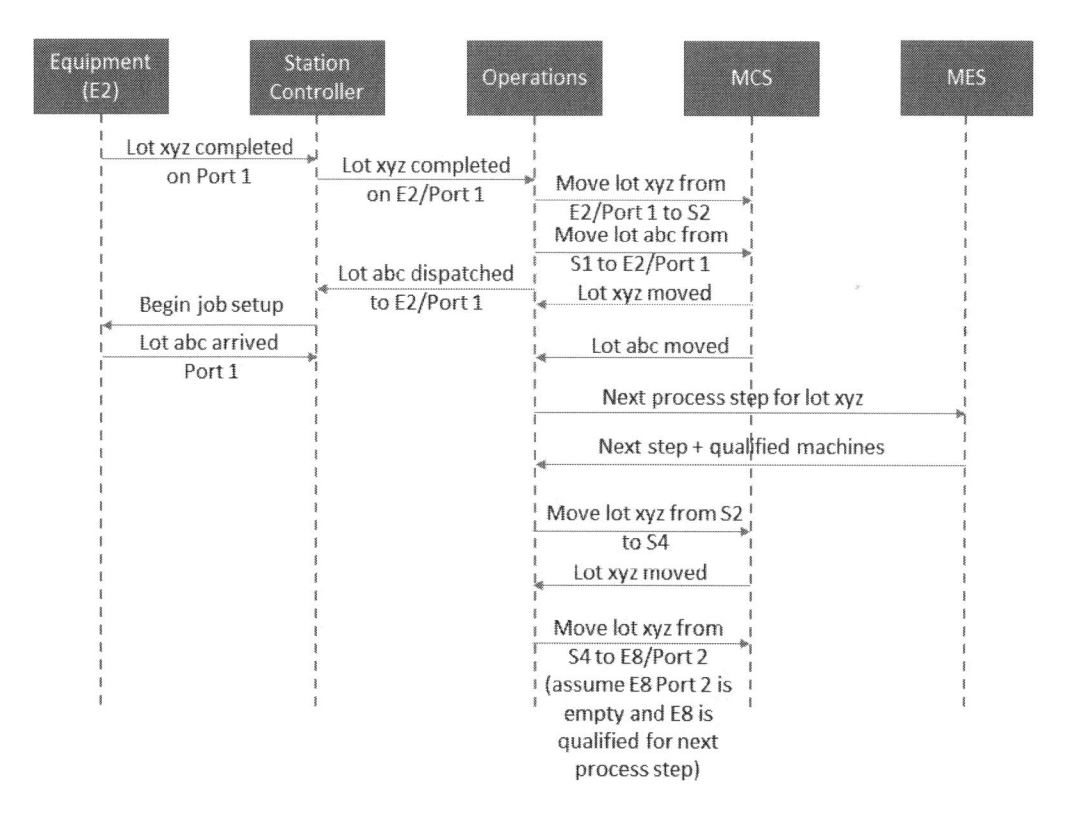

Figure 5.6 – Simplified material handling event sequence (equipment and stocker IDs are referred to in Figure 5.5)

As semiconductor processes have grown more complex, the **Operations** component shown in *Figure 5.6* has grown more sophisticated over time. Modern manufacturing processes have extensive time-window limits to manage yield (for example, to limit time between steps to avoid surface contamination). This has driven the need for more sophisticated decision systems tied around building a *digital twin* of the production line that can accurately predict how material will move downstream in the presence of probabilistic failure models, coupled with an optimization-based release policy that determines when lots can enter the critical time loops (Monch, L., Fowler, J. W. and Mason, S. J., *Production Planning and Control for Semiconductor Wafer Fabrication Facilities*, Springer, NY (2013)), such that they have a high probability of making it through the process steps in time.

The simulation-based approach is not amenable to immediate decision making and is typically executed on a periodic basis. The need for immediate decision making in the presence of any change in the factory situation has led researchers to investigate whether **deep reinforcement learning** (**DRL**) can be scaled up to this problem (see, for example, Waschneck, B., Reichstaller, A., Belzner, L., Altenmüller, T., Bauernhansl, T., Knapp, A. and Kyek, A., *Deep Reinforcement Learning for Semiconductor Production Scheduling*, in *Proceedings of the 29th SEMI Advanced Semiconductor Manufacturing Conference (ASMC)*, 301-306, NY (2018), which shows the results of applying this to a simplified scaled-down model of the manufacturing process). The following diagram shows a simplified view of how the scheduling problem can be modeled so as to make it amenable for **machine learning** (**ML**):

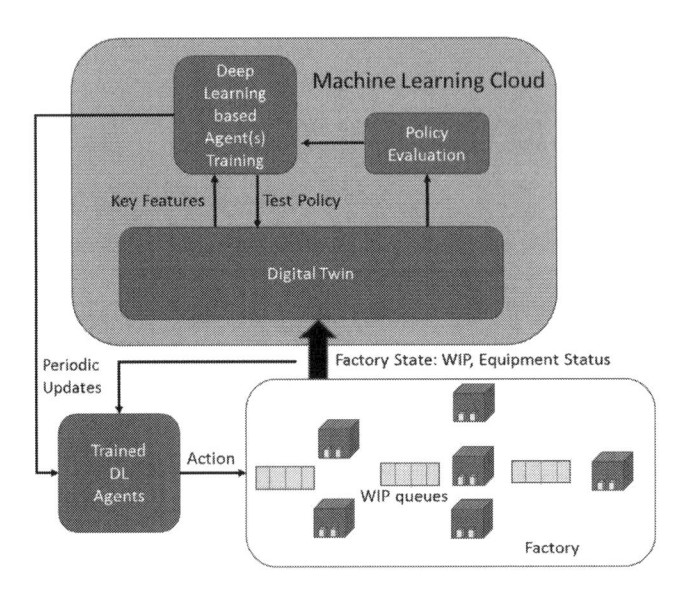

Figure 5.7 – DRL for factory scheduling

As shown in *Figure 5.7*, the **Agent(s)** observes the status of the **Work In Process (WIP)** across the line segment, as well as the status of the machines. In a brute-force method, this would form the agent's observation space. For any practical setting, the number of possible decision variables and observations would be overwhelming. This has led to active research in this area on how to either derive a limited set of features that aggregate the observation space to make it manageable or to partition the problem into many subproblems that can be trained independently. The key research open is to get solutions to these subproblems that can somehow coordinate among themselves to address the problem across the manufacturing line. This still remains an area of active research, and if a practical solution can be developed, it will go a long way toward the development of agile manufacturing control strategies.

As we note the power of digitization to achieve truly autonomous factories, we remind you that this would not have been possible without the strong industry-wide focus on standards. Without this level of standardization, it would have been impossible to achieve the economies of scale that have made this level of automation possible.

Next, we'll take a look at process monitoring and control.

## Digitization for process monitoring and control

In this section, we will look at applications of digital twins to enhance the performance of semiconductor processes, along with some potential applications of IoT devices. The process of manufacturing semiconductor devices requires extraordinary precision and repeatability. In addition, there is a constant challenge to keep defects (due to spurious particles) as low as possible. We will look at the potential for IoT to help with particulate control first, before focusing on the application of digital twins for improving the repeatability and performance of the manufacturing process.

## Applications of IoT and sensor data

We should note that, unlike chemical plants that we covered in the previous section, semiconductor fabs tend to be enclosed within a building and have a very high-speed wired Ethernet backbone. In addition, for the purposes of data collection for analysis, there is a need to attach context to the data—for example, the data needs to be tied to the specific wafer being processed, as well as the recipe in use during the data collection period. This makes the use of wireless IoT sensors particularly challenging. Given that there is a consistent effort to keep computer clocks synchronized across the network, the data can definitely be merged on a backend server. However, latency in taking action is unacceptable as decisions to abort the process or to prevent the process from starting need to be taken in a fraction of a second. So, the question arises: where can wireless IoT devices be applied, and what is their benefit? The key to identifying opportunities derived from the use of IoT devices is to focus on applications that are non-stationary (and hence cannot be tethered to mains power or be wired to Ethernet). We will look at one such example next. Other use cases involve monitoring the shock and g-force as material is moved either by overhead transport (as discussed in the preceding *Automated material handling systems and scheduling* section) or for monitoring and tracking inventory in warehouses.

## Case study of IoT sensors

If we look at the factory, there is one aspect of operations that is prone to drive particle generation as well as silicon defects, and this is the process of wafer handling. For example, during transport, even though the wafers are contained in a sealed FOUP, any excess vibration will cause them to rattle within their slots, and this in turn has the potential to generate particles. We would also like to monitor the transport cars as they move through the factory to detect wear and tear on the cars themselves, as well as to track alignment, to ensure that the wafers are subject to the least amount of shock. Additional handling within a process tool—for example, the robot arm that pulls out the wafer from the FOUP and then transfers it into the tool, as well as lift pins that are typically employed to lift up the wafer during processing—all contribute to potential wafer damage. CyberOptics (www.cyberoptics.com) and InnerSense (www.innersense-semi.com) have been manufacturing wafer shaped vibration sensors that communicate via Wi-Fi that can be periodically routed through the sequence of material handling steps to detect any excessive shock or vibration. This, however, needs to be done in place of production, and if the focus is on the automated material handling system, then this can be done via accelerometers attached to the FOUPs as well, for tracking its health without impacting production.

## Anomaly detection in time series

We now look at how ML can generalize detection of anomalies in sensor data—for example, detecting anomalies in the vibration data collected from the preceding example. Note that the examples given previously are but one type of sensor. Semiconductor equipment typically comes with sensors preinstalled to monitor critical process parameters (for example, temperatures; pressures; flow rates of key chemicals that are then communicated to the station controller via a standard communications interface (part of the suite of standards covered in the prior section). These perform as edge compute devices and can be augmented with appropriate accelerators such as graphic cards or **field-programmable gate arrays** (**FPGAs**). Traditional approaches to fault detection have been to have the engineer define limits of variation within a predefined window (*Figure 5.8*). This implies that the engineer has to have a prior knowledge about process performance, which is often not the case when a new process is being developed. In the following diagram, we can see that there are three windows defined that correspond to different steps in the recipe—in this case, they correspond to the period of time and to the sensor value of the oven:

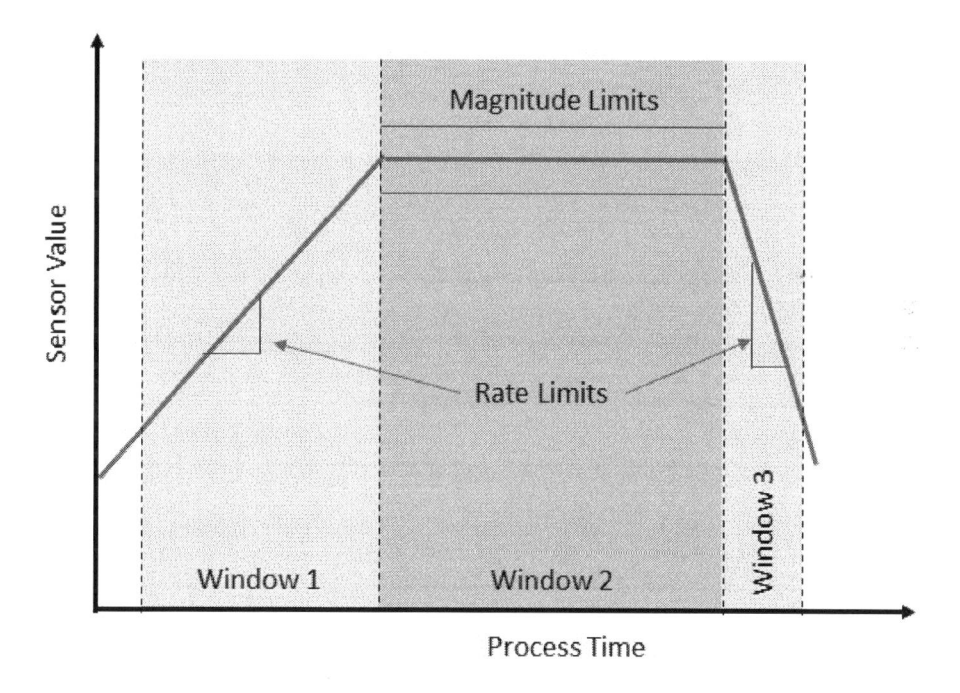

Figure 5.8 – Traditional methodology for defining limits to detect faults

The preceding diagram shows the oven going through a temperature ramp-up step, then spending time at a steady processing state, and then executing a ramp-down step. Here is an outline of the process:

- For the first window, the intent is to detect temperature measurements that deviate from the desired ramp rate.
- The second window detects deviation from the setpoint.
- The third window tracks the ramp-down rate.

For well-established processes, this methodology works well as there is sufficient prior knowledge to determine the features critical for process performance. We also note that the preceding methodology works well for what are called **point anomalies**—that is, they depend on a specific value of the signal being considerably different from others versus **shape anomalies**, which correspond to a period of the signal whose shape is different from that expected.

If the process is new, this often turns into a guessing game, and here is where the power of ML coupled with anomaly detection can be leveraged. In Wang, X., Lin, J., Patel, N. and Braun, M., *A Self-Learning and Online Algorithm for Time Series Anomaly Detection* in *Proceedings of the 25th ACM International Conference on Information and Knowledge Management (CIKM)*, 1823-1832, IL (2016), the authors present a highly scalable online self-learning algorithm that is not only able to detect point and shape anomalies but also identify the time window within which the anomaly occurs. The overall flow of the algorithm is shown in *Figure 5.9*. We note that the algorithm iteratively tries to find the optimal values of the tuple (**W,C,T**)—the cluster size (**C**) for computational efficiency; the best window size (**W**) to detect the anomaly; and the threshold (**T**) to call out an outlier, as illustrated here:

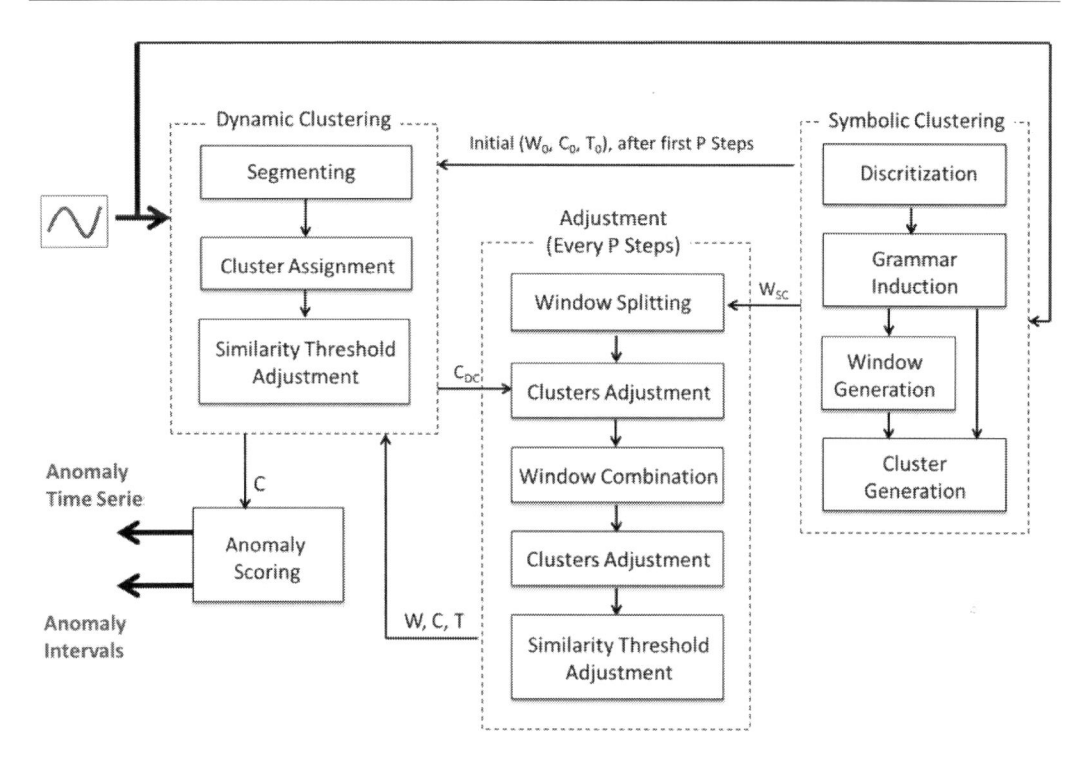

Figure 5.9 – Overview of the self-learning online algorithm for time series anomaly detection

The results of applying this algorithm to temperature data from an oven show some remarkable properties. The sample time traces and the detected anomalies are shown in the following figure, where the bold line indicates the specific time trace being detected as an anomaly:

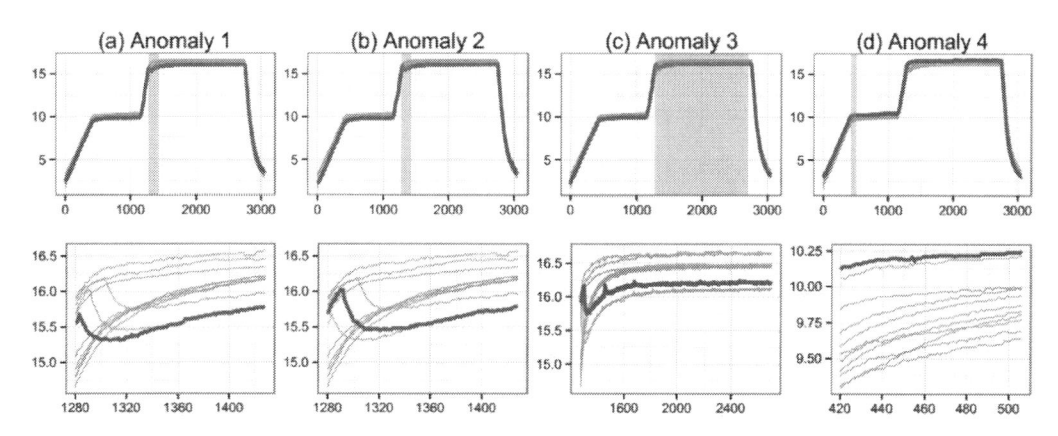

Figure 5.10 – Detection of point and shape anomalies in oven temperature data

Four anomalies are detected in the dataset, along with the windows corresponding to these anomalies, as shown on the top row of plots in the preceding screenshot. The bottom row shows the zoomed-in details of the anomalies picked up. The first three cases ((**a**)-(**c**)) show that shape anomalies are clearly detected by this method, whereas the final set of plots to the right ((**d**)) show that point anomalies are also detected. All these trace behaviors point to the need to retune the oven temperature controller. Detection of the shape anomalies would have been extremely difficult, if not impossible, if we were to have applied the traditional window-based methods.

### Sensor data for predictive maintenance

The final use case we will cover here is related to the use of sensor data to forecast maintenance. Typically, maintenance is either performed on a time or wafer count basis and is not really based on the consumption or wear of parts on the equipment. If parts are wearing down faster than expected, then the default action is to pull in the frequency of maintenance activities that incur additional non-productive time on the equipment. Some equipment is more amenable to monitoring for wear than others. For example, ion implanters have often been cited as examples where preventive maintenance can be implemented by monitoring the filament current. As the filament wears down, the filament resistance increases, and hence the current running through it decreases. This simple measurement can be used to forecast maintenance activity, which can then be slotted gracefully into the factory schedule. In addition, sensor data can be used for self-diagnostics on selected sub-systems or a full system. Note that we can also augment sensor data with machine alarm data or diagnostic logs to determine maintenance intervals.

### Digitization for process control

As we noted previously, the process of manufacturing semiconductor devices requires a high degree of precision down to the nanometer level. Furthermore, what exactly is happening on the wafer is typically impossible to observe in situ and is typically measured downstream once the wafer has completed processing and is moved over to a metrology tool. Some equipment supports inline metrology, where the wafer is measured as it immediately completes processing on the process tool itself, and investing in this capability is a trade-off with respect to the additional cost of metrology (the metrology module itself, but also the impact on process throughput if the module were to be in a non-processing state due to a fault) versus the tighter control that can be exerted on the process by eliminating delays in getting the measurements. In addition, inline metrology can often measure every wafer that is processed versus the standalone case, where typically only a few wafers are sampled.

## Virtual metrology

The lack of in situ metrology has driven considerable research into whether we can use the process sensor measurements to reliably infer what is going on at the wafer surface as it is processing. If this could be inferred reliably, then the processing conditions could be dynamically adjusted (for example, by using MPC, as covered in the *Transforming the chemical industry* section) to consistently achieve the desired outcome. While we have found several papers published annually on this topic, this has remained not too well adopted in the industry. There are several reasons for this, the primary one being that the model fidelity is not high enough to resolve processing error within allowable tolerances. **The National Institute of Standards and Technology** (**NIST**) has published a white paper that outlines some of these challenges (https://www.nist.gov/publications/virtual-metrology-white-paper-international-roadmap-devices-and-systemsirds). However, if we take a step back and demand less from these models, then there are options to implement a hybrid solution. For example, Patel, N., Miller, G. and Jenkins, S., *In situ estimation of blanket polish rates and wafer-to-wafer variation*, in *IEEE Transactions on Semiconductor Manufacturing*, 15 (4): 513-522 (2002), present how interferometry can be used to determine key process parameters needed for process control, as well as inferring the variability across a batch of wafers without needing excessive additional metrology. This methodology is robust, as has been proven via high-volume industrial data.

Given the current open issues in the wafer processing area, virtual metrology has found some success in the silicon packaging area, where the silicon is attached to an underlying substrate via solder reflow. *Figure 5.11* shows the results, wherein by collating the sensor measurements from the reflow oven, we can predict the temperature being experienced by the solder on the package via a digital twin model. This data is then used for anomaly detection to prevent misprocessing of the parts. The process is illustrated here:

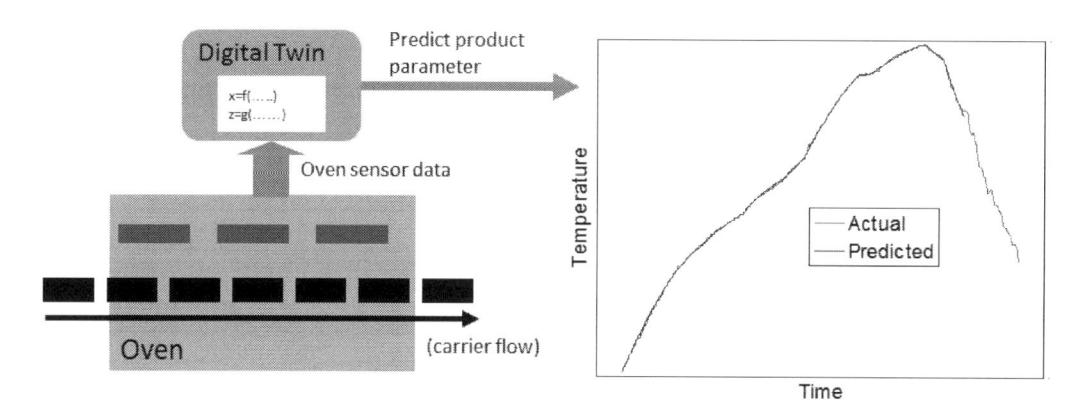

Figure 5.11 – Virtual metrology applied to predict solder temperature on a package in a reflow oven

Next, we will learn about digital twin and process control.

## Digital twin and process control

Given the preceding discussion, we now turn to the options available for keeping the manufacturing process on target in a repeatable fashion. Most control applications start with the development of a process model or a digital twin that can explain the impact of the process inputs to the outputs. One of the key enablers of process control applications was the same standards effort we covered earlier as part of the 300 mm transition.

In the past, process recipes used to be stored in a binary format, and considerable reverse engineering was involved in determining what bytes of the file needed to be changed to adjust the processing parameters. With the 300 mm SEMI standards, the concept of variable recipe parameters was introduced, and these could be adjusted prior to the start of processing via well-defined commands from the station controller. Texas Instruments has published a number of use cases related to process control, and we will look at a specific one related to control of a batch thermal process. The following figure presents how such a scheme would work for a vertical furnace used to deposit silicon nitride (note that all equipment communication is routed through station controllers, which are not shown for clarity):

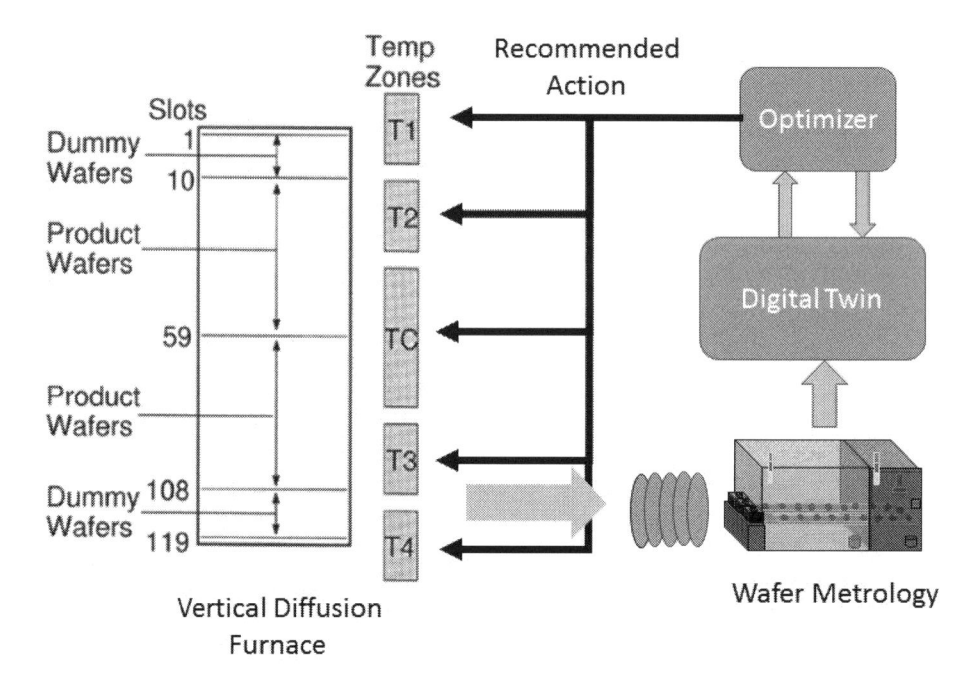

Figure 5.12 – Scheme for controlling a vertical diffusion furnace from downstream metrology data

The furnace can support two different processing steps (based on recipe), and the thickness and uniformity of the deposited film is controlled by manipulating the processing time as well as the zone temperature profiles during processing. At the end of the process, each lot has a wafer in its FOUP measured at the metrology tool. Note that if the furnace is not fully loaded, no additional dummy wafers are placed, and hence the dynamics of the process also depends on the number of full lots being loaded into the furnace. A digital twin of the furnace models the furnace behavior. In addition, the digital twin is also updated by measuring the deviation of the actual versus predicted performance of the furnace. The following figure shows that optimizing the recipe via the digital twin yields much tighter control of the deposited film thickness:

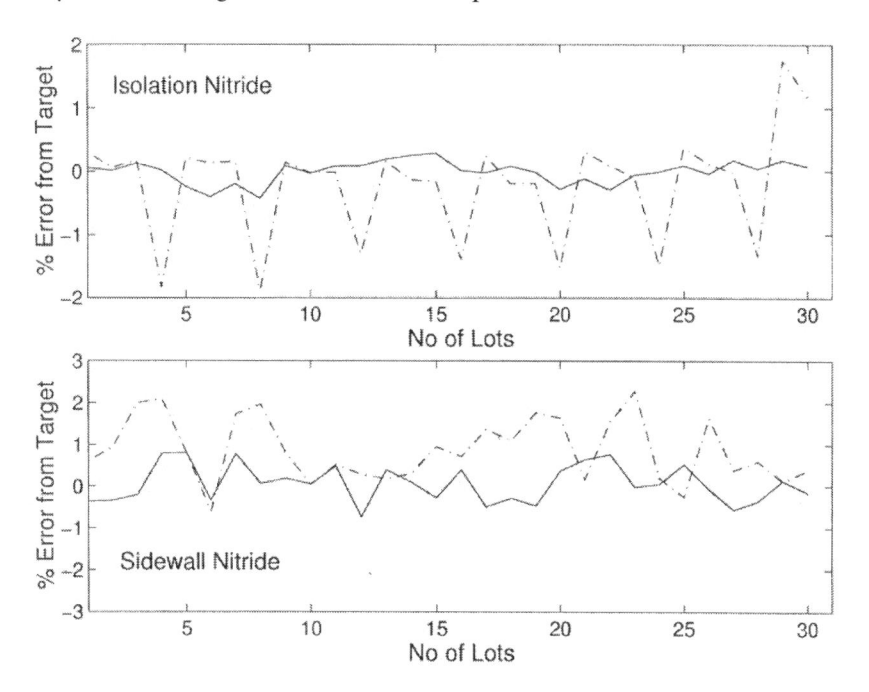

Figure 5.13 – Impact of optimized recipes on process performance

The data is collected for 30 lots prior to the control solution implementation and for 30 lots after. Over a 2X reduction in error range is achieved, resulting in improved process yield.

# Big data and digitization for yield management

In this section, we will look at three specific use cases of how digitization can be applied to the problem of yield management. We will look into the application of upstream data to forecast downstream product yield; in the case of a yield excursion, a big data technique that can quickly help troubleshoot root cause—that is, what are the root causes leading to the excursion (for example, raw materials, or process parameters); and lastly, the application of machine vision and edge computing for visual inspection. Yield refers to the total sellable units versus the total number of units per wafer.

## ML for yield prediction

Process and test data is continuously collected as the product moves across the manufacturing line. Examples were provided previously on monitoring the processing conditions in equipment, as well as the application of a digital twin to drive process repeatability. For semiconductor device manufacturing, however, there are additional electrical tests that happen during the course of processing that can be used to predict the final behavior of the part. The following figure shows the overall process flow inclusive of wafer fabrication, die singulation, packaging, and final test:

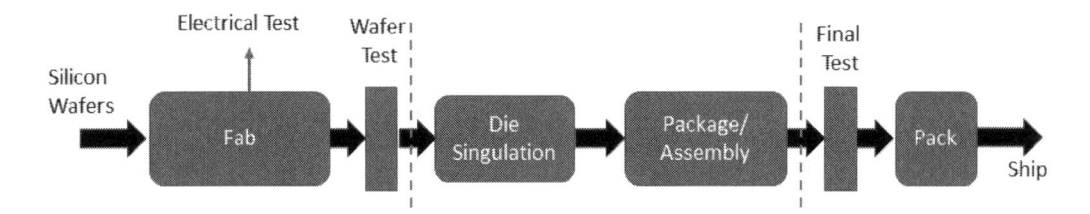

Figure 5.14 – Overall semiconductor product manufacturing flow (vertical lines indicate material may be cross-shipped to different manufacturers if the company is fabless)

The intent of yield prediction is to prevent die that have a high likelihood of failure from being picked after die singulation and being sent on for packaging and testing. This yields considerable savings in manufacturing costs as less scrap is built. Even a few-percent reduction in scrap can provide significant return, since packaging and testing can add up to 50% to the cost of the final product. Note that the data collection and model development poses special challenges if different steps of the process are performed across different companies. In this situation, the (potentially) fabless semiconductor company needs to aggregate data from multiple wafer and final test companies and have interfaces to push the decision back to the die singulation or packaging/assembly house.

In 2007, Intel proposed a ML methodology to predict wafer level final test yields for its chipset products based on Gradient Boosted Trees (Yip, W. K., Law, K. G. and Lee, W. J., *Forecasting Final/Class Yield Based on Fabrication Process E-Test and Sort Data*, in *Proceedings of the 3rd Annual IEEE Conference on Automation Science and Engineering*, 478-483, AZ (2007)). This utilizes upstream data from electrical and wafer test to predict the final functional test outcome. Researchers from **Massachusetts Institute of Technology** (MIT) working with SanDisk Semiconductor recently published the results of using RUSBoost models (where **RUS** stands for **Random Under Sampling**) to forecast die yield for memory stacks (Chen, H. and Boning, D., *Online and Incremental Machine Learning Approaches for IC Yield Improvement*, in *Proceedings of the 2017 IEEE/ACM International Conference on Computer-Aided Design (ICCAD)*, 786-793, CA (2017)). In their approach, the forecasted good die would be routed through a high-end packaging and test process, as the end product using these was expected to have a higher overall performance. In contrast, die tagged as likely to fail would be stacked into low-end parts via a low-end cheaper process as, post testing, these would have a higher likelihood of failure. Based on the stack height, they predicted up to a 20% gain in final product yield. In both of the preceding examples, the need to deal with an unbalanced dataset and concept drift is highlighted.

The following figure shows one manifestation of how this could be implemented as a central enterprise capability. It assumes the case of a fabless manufacturer, whereby packaging and test strategy decisions are transferred to outsourced manufacturers as decisions (hiding the data and model details). If there is sufficient trust, we would ideally want to push the data and the models so that the decisions would be based on the latest learnings:

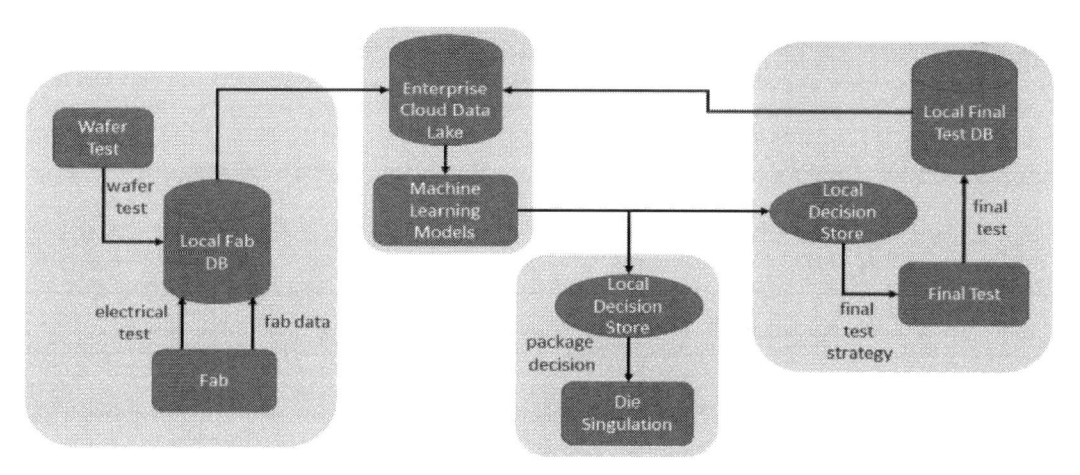

Figure 5.15 – Distributed architecture for yield prediction; the figure shows fab, singulation, and final test potentially occurring at different physical locations, and using different suppliers

We note that the use of different assembly options by the MIT researchers is an excellent way to fully leverage the ML model. Given that no model can give a 100% accurate prediction, allowing for such options enables us to optimize the decision threshold to maximize expected returns. Furthermore, this also allows us to continue to observe the outcome of all our decisions so as to continuously train the model in the face of concept drift.

## Big data for yield troubleshooting

In manufacturing, we often face the situation of sporadic yield excursions or a burst in customer returns. In both these cases, it becomes important to quickly identify potential root causes so that engineering teams can start further troubleshooting and implementation of corrective actions. This problem can be viewed as a generalization of anomaly detection, wherein we are trying to isolate anomalous measurements and product routing through the manufacturing line. Note that the fact the product shipped indicates that there were no alarms or excursions reported as it was being processed. Hence, the excursion is most likely due to subtle shifts in process performance or a combination of factors. However, we can take advantage of the identified sample to specifically look for anomalies. One of the first steps we can take is to generate time sequence plots, where the $x$ axis is the date time stamp and the $y$ axis is the sequence of processing operations. If all the units clump up together then it points to a potential operation to go investigate further, as it indicates the first degree of commonality. However, this does not account for any fluctuation in process performance, nor the fact that given these were detected as a yield excursion in a short time span, most of these units probably ran through the line at about the same time.

Given the volumes of data generated, it is important that the algorithms developed be as scalable as possible. In the case study presented next, researchers from George Mason University in association with Intel Corporation developed a highly scalable association rule-mining solution that can be leveraged for this purpose (Khade, R., Lin, J. and Patel, N., *Finding Meaningful Contrast Patterns for Quantitative Data*, in *Proceedings of the International Conference on Extending Database Technology (EDBT)*, 444-455, Lisbon, Portugal (2019)). One requirement for association rule mining is to discretize the continuous variables—determining the correct bin boundaries is important, and in this case study, this has been addressed. We note that this is an infrequent computation step and does not have a significant impact on the overall algorithm scalability. The overall architecture to enable this is shown in *Figure 5.16*. The idea behind this approach is quite straightforward. The system on a daily cadence continues to build up its concept of normal baseline performance of the manufacturing line (population characteristics). This concept consists of learning the probabilities of values of categorical and continuous attributes, along with their combinations (that is, paired attributes). When a dataset is submitted to the system for analysis, it is able to quickly identify (in seconds) contrast patterns between this sample and its concept of the population, as illustrated here:

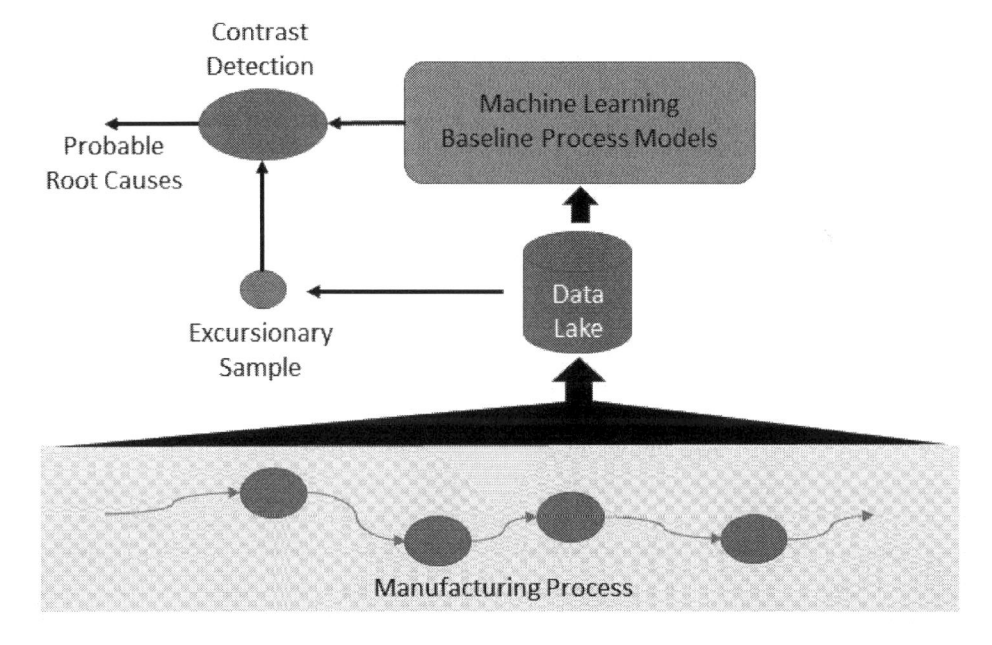

Figure 5.16 – Architecture for rapid contrast mining of excursionary samples

The example presented in Khade, R., Lin, J. and Patel, N., *Finding Meaningful Contrast Patterns for Quantitative Data*, in *Proceedings of the International Conference on Extending Database Technology (EDBT)*, 444-455, Lisbon, Portugal (2019) shows that for the sample of units that failed at final test, the system was able to identify that the root cause could be attributed to a specific placement head on the chip attach module that handles all units going through the back lane of the reflow oven. Furthermore, it also identified that there were abnormalities in the temperature experienced by these parts that pointed to the need to retune the oven temperature controllers. The effects were subtle enough that they did not trigger any inline monitors to alarm.

## Digitization of inline inspection

Over the past few years, there has been a tremendous interest in computer vision techniques for the purpose of object recognition in images. Anywhere we look, there are examples of successful outcomes when using these to identify objects in pictures. Compared to manual inspection, where there is considerable operator fatigue resulting in a large variation in the detected and classified defects, any computational solution will provide consistent results.

From an inline inspection perspective, there are two aspects we need to address. First is the ability to accurately detect defects, and second is the need to classify these for the purposes of process improvement activities. In addition, there is also a need to execute this inspection with high throughput. While we can get high-fidelity images from standalone inspection tools, we cannot expect any solution that drives pervasive inspection on processing tools to achieve this level of image fidelity. We should look at the fab and packaging/test separately, the reason being that for the former, there are dedicated inspection tools at multiple points in the manufacturing flow, and these take high-fidelity images of the wafer. Intel has reported great success in applying ML to classifying defects on wafers (`https://www.intel.com/content/www/us/en/it-management/intel-it-best-practices/faster-more-accurate-defect-classification-using-machine-vision-paper.html`).

Furthermore, the need to detect very fine defects and the variety of packages running through the manufacturing line makes any solution based purely on **deep learning** (**DL**) infeasible as the amount of data required for training would be formidable. In the past, traditional image processing techniques were leveraged for defect detection and classification—for example, Said, A. and Patel, N., *Die Level Defect Detection in Semiconductor Units*, in *Proceedings of the IEEE Advanced Semiconductor Manufacturing Conference (ASMC)*, 130-133, NY (2013) present how, using a line scan camera imaging tray of parts moving on a conveyor, we can develop very accurate defect detection and classification algorithms for the die area.

With current advances in DL, we can couple the algorithms from the preceding reference that segment the image into regions and send these regions to a deep **convolutional neural network** (**CNN**) to classify the defects. Since the image is pre-segmented, the images presented to the network are consistent over time, which helps in scaling up the solution. In this sense, traditional image processing takes care of the part-to-part variability, while DL is able to improve classification accuracy. Note that we will still have a highly unbalanced dataset, as in any stable process the number of defective units will be very small. The following figure shows a potential architecture where edge clients capture and process the image; the images are then saved off into a database, and the training engine accesses these images to execute periodic training runs:

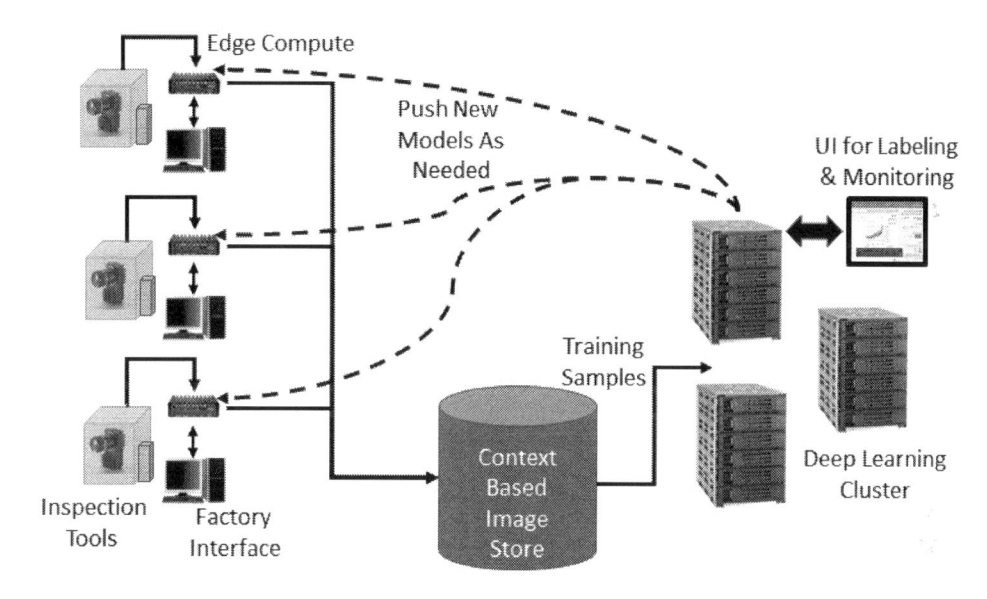

Figure 5.17 – A general architecture for implementing DL-based inspection solutions

If the models improve by a sufficient amount, they are then pushed to the edge clients, and the training cycle repeats at a periodic interval. This is an active development area in the industry, and unfortunately not a lot has been published in the open literature.

We would like to point out that explainability is a key difference between DL models and traditional image analysis algorithms. This has to do with the black-box nature of the DL models. If there is any change in the process (for example, raw materials) that impacts the background or contrast seen in the picture, a DL model may need to be retrained—an expensive process—versus adapting to this via a quick threshold adjustment in traditional image analysis. This is less likely to happen on wafer inspections but is highly likely when inspecting units during assembly.

In the previous section, we looked at several examples of how digitization is being leveraged by the semiconductor industry in its drive toward autonomous manufacturing, dealing with tighter tolerance requirements in the process, managing process yield, and driving more flexible inspection. In the next section, we will look at several other examples of how digitization is disrupting manufacturing, including driving greater flexibility and faster design cycles, and—more importantly—by keeping the supplier engaged with the customer after the sale, for mutual benefit to both parties.

# Disrupting industrial manufacturing

Having focused on semiconductor manufacturing, we will now look into areas and case studies in industrial manufacturing. Here, disruptions refer to innovations and new paradigms being introduced to manufacturing. In the context of this book, this will refer to any manufacturing activity that deals with machining, or assembly of products.

## Flexible manufacturing

Manufacturing plants can be characterized into broad categories, based on the volume they can produce and the variety of parts they manufacture. These can be categorized into the following:

- **Low mix/high volume**: In this case, the plant is turning out a few part varieties at high volume. This would, for example, be the case for dedicated assembly lines.
- **High mix/low volume**: In this case, the plant has relatively small production capacity but can manufacture a large variety of parts. Manufacturers that make custom parts in low volume are an example of this.
- **Low mix/low volume**: This is the simplest case of all—the plant has limited production capacity and is dedicated to making a limited variety of parts.
- **High mix/high volume**: This is the most complex manufacturing scenario as a variety of parts are being run through a plant that has large production capacity. This is the specific case we will examine further in this section.

In high mix/high volume manufacturing, we not only have to deal with the volumes, but also with frequent changeovers that occur as equipment needs to be reconfigured to run different types of parts. In order to support the need for switching between products, it is imperative that the machine should allow itself to be reconfigured via a process recipe that depends on the requirements of the product. Furthermore, efficient introduction of new products and removal of obsolete products requires close integration between the **Manufacturing Execution System** (**MES**) and **Product Lifecycle Management** (**PLM**) system. The following figure presents a high-level block diagram that shows the integration across multiple modules in the factory via an information bus:

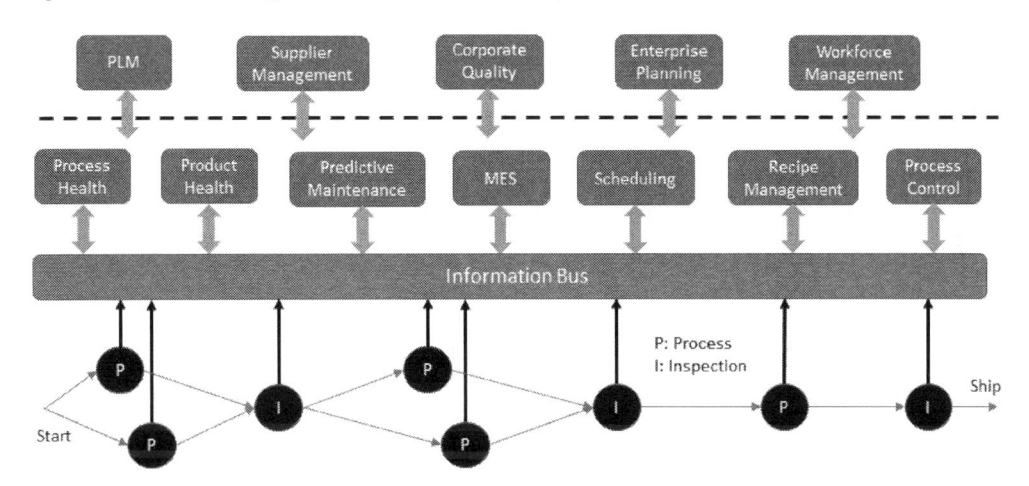

Figure 5.18 – Systems for the smart factory

Siemens AG has made their plant in Amberg, Germany a showcase of these technologies. The Amberg plant makes **Programmable Logic Controllers** (**PLCs**), and after an employee places an initial bare circuit board on a smart workpiece carrier, which is identified via **radio-frequency identification** (**RFID**), the rest of the process is completely automated. Data on the workpiece configures the equipment to meet its needs. As components are placed on the board, data feeds to the inventory management system ensure there is always a supply in stock. Inline inspection and testing automatically upload their data. Workers at the plant focus on improving the system by looking for opportunities to improve the processes or detect patterns in data that will enable them to further reduce defectivity levels. With its level of digitization, the plant is able to produce 1 million products per month with a 24-hour lead time and with a 10-defects-per-million outgoing defectivity level. Siemens reports a ninefold increase in overall plant efficiency, as reported in Deren, G., *Empowering the Digital Transformation via Digitalization within the Integrated Lifecycle*, presented at the *Model Based Enterprise Summit*, NIST, MD (2018).

PCBWay (www.pcbway.com) is a **printed circuit board** (**PCB**) manufacturer based in China, with their factory located in Shenzhen. They make custom prototype PCBs for customers and promise a week turnaround on most orders (and up to 24 hours for expedited orders), and a minimum quantity of five boards. All interactions with the company happen online—the customer uploads their design in a predefined format on PCBWay's website, then there is a design check done by PCBWay, after which the customer is sent a notification of any changes and a request to pay. After payment, the PCB moves into production and is shipped to the customer on completion. The system automatically generates test programs to ensure that the final PCB passes all electrical checks before shipment, and the customer is shown the status of their order as it makes it through the manufacturing process via PCBWay's website.

Tesla's Fremont production line can dynamically adapt processing to produce either a sedan or a **sport utility vehicle** (**SUV**), while at the same time incorporating preordered customizations to that specific chassis.

## Design prototyping of mechanical parts

Gone are the days when we would, for example, design a part, send it to a local manufacturing shop to build the first article, and wait for weeks to receive it back for further iterations on the design. Now, in a matter of a day, we can 3D print most small parts for an initial fit check, and only when the part design is finalized does it get sent out for manufacturing. This had added tremendously to the efficiency of getting new designs completed. For example, 3D printing has been extensively utilized by Nike as part of its *Express Lane* initiative to speed products to market. They have reported a four times reduction in **time to market** (**TTM**) leveraging this technology. In fact, 3D printing also allows for quickly developing and implementing custom jigs and fixtures on the factory floor.

In addition to 3D printing, we can also leverage the digital twin models of our product to visualize and evaluate other aspects of the design. For example, in the case of an electronics module, we can envision the heat generation and transmission within the casing and identify any potential cooling issues. We can also look at the thermo-mechanical stresses induced on various components to ensure that they will not impact product reliability. The same can extend to other mechanical designs. For example, Pyga Industries (www.pygaindustries.com), a bicycle maker based in South Africa, used Siemens' Solid Edge simulation software to ensure that the bicycle's suspension could withstand the stresses placed on it as the user navigated the toughest terrain.

By tying into preexisting parts of our existing PLM systems, digitization of the design process can also help quickly source parts for the prototype from existing qualified suppliers. Furthermore, such a system would keep supplier explosion to a minimum, allowing us to continue to leverage volume pricing from a few sources. Several design software companies provide modules for this integration. For example, Dassault Systèmes' SOLIDWORKS computer-aided design software (www.solidworks.com) offers a `PARTsolutions` plugin that will interface into your existing PLM system to ensure that designers can search the existing parts database and avoid duplicates. It also offers an approval process to add new parts into the database, to prevent an uncontrolled growth in supplier diversity.

## Techniques for preventing downtime

In this subsection, we will look at techniques for preventing disruptions in industrial manufacturing. This can be viewed as an extension of the preventive maintenance topic covered under the previous section, as the basic principles remain the same. There are other disruptions related to the supply chain and facilities that will be covered in the subsequent sections. The key enabler for predicting disruptions is to have the necessary sensors for data collection embedded on the processing tools. We can also look at options to add on wireless sensors if the equipment did not support integrated sensors for the parameter of interest. Here, we will look at several sensors that can help predict disruption so that timely maintenance can be performed before there is damage to the workpiece or an unscheduled equipment downtime that is disruptive to the overall flow of material in the factory.

In most machining operations, the obvious parameter to measure is the vibration signature. This can be done via a two- or three-axis accelerometer, depending on the degrees of freedom available on the part being monitored. For example, a lathe spindle can be monitored by a two-degrees-of-freedom accelerometer, whereas a cutting tool may need three degrees to capture all the forces being exerted on it. Applications of vibration monitoring include monitoring the sharpness of cutting tools. As the edge wears down, the vibration signature changes. In addition, vibration sensors can also detect out-of-round situations on spindles.

Acoustic sensors measure the sound generated by the machining process. Subtle changes in the sound signature can point to changes in the process behavior—for example, a workpiece rattling during processing due to wear in the clamps over time.

In addition, we can measure other parameters such as the power consumed by various motors on the machine, as well as flow rates and temperatures of coolant fluids, and infrared measurements of the temperature around the cutting tool and work piece.

All this data can be combined to develop a fingerprint of the process, and this can be used to match machine tools or to also detect deviations that can possibly lead to work piece damage or unscheduled downtime.

Ford Motor Company has been using Marposs's (www.marposs.com) Artis monitoring technology for monitoring the equipment used for cutting transmission gears. They named Artis as one of the top four finalists in their *2019 Global Manufacturing Technical Excellence Awards*. Compared to the traditional piece-count tool replacement practices, the new monitoring system has helped achieve a 30%-to-80% improvement in tool life, as well as helping reduce overall manufacturing costs due to less unscheduled downtime, less time spent dispositioning non-standard material, and scrap avoidance.

## Value beyond the product

So far, we have focused our case studies around what happens within the manufacturing plant. However, there are other use cases of digitization that go above and beyond the factory. One such application of digitization is to gather (potentially in real time) information about the product after it has been sold to a customer. This allows collection of data that can be used to do the following:

- Alert the manufacturer about impeding problems and returns so that they can work with the customer ahead of time to schedule maintenance or repairs.

- Understand how customers are using the product, which can be fed back for future product design revisions.

- Provide a service to the customer to more efficiently manage the use of the product and to differentiate the offering.

This capability is becoming more and more prevalent as manufacturers work with customers to ensure that they have minimal unscheduled downtime and can get need-based maintenance scheduled ahead of time, resulting in a better customer experience.

GE Aviation provides a service to its airline customers where GE collects data from jet engines on airplanes operated by the airlines via GE's Predix platform. Given the large quantity of data collected, this is typically downloaded via a wireless interface once the plane is on the ground. The data collected can be used to compare engine performance to other engines in the customer's fleet. By analyzing the data, GE engineers can predict the need for maintenance and avoid unscheduled downtime and schedule disruptions for the airline's customers. They can also identify opportunities for fuel savings via optimizing when the engine compressor needs to be washed, using their *Water Wash Optimizer* application. The washing of the engine at the right time can increase the **Time on Wing (ToW)** of the jet engine. In other words, washing the engine with water and the right mix of chemicals, at the right time, can improve the time between maintenance of the engine that requires downtime and large expense. This is done in a way that has no adverse impact on the reliability of the engine operations. It often also helps to improve the fuel efficiency of the engine. In the end, by monitoring the use of their product by their customer, they are able to provide customers better operating efficiency, along with more time in the air for their assets.

In the area of heavy machinery, John Deere offers a service that monitors their equipment in the field. Monitoring equipment allows them to detect anomalies before they result in a breakdown. By comparing data across the fleet, they can develop more efficient maintenance and repair protocols. Technician visits can be scheduled ahead of time in coordination with the customer to address potential issues or to provide maintenance services as needed. The following diagram shows the architecture, highlighting the importance of feeding the alerts to the local dealership, who can then coordinate next steps directly with the customer:

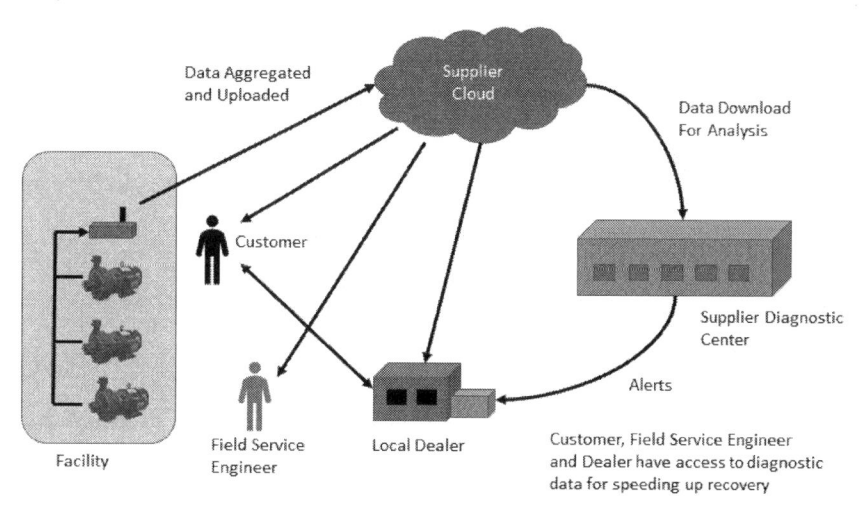

Figure 5.19 – Connected equipment architecture with local dealership support

Caterpillar goes further than just providing equipment monitoring alone. They also offer sensors in the cabin to monitor the operator for fatigue and distractions. This enables greater job site safety as customers can arrange shifts to minimize fatigue.

Even customers of stationary equipment can benefit from monitoring. For example, Cummins, which manufactures generators, provides continuous monitoring of customer assets through their PowerCommand Cloud solution. In the residential space, Enphase Energy, which supplies microinverters for the solar power industry, has been providing monitoring of their customers' solar system performance through their Enlighten offering. In the case of issues with power production, their system sends alerts to residential customers, with details of the problem. The customer can access their data through Enphase's web portal and track their system performance down to each solar panel.

Oftentimes, we also come across cases where the customer may not be willing to share information with the manufacturer. In such cases, it is still helpful to provide tools to the customer to enhance their asset management and to ensure they get the most out of their purchase. This is less beneficial to the supplier as they miss out on actual use data for driving future improvements, but there are still benefits if the customer is able to utilize the tools in terms of goodwill, making them less likely to switch to competitors, especially if they need to redo the training and processes associated with the monitoring tools. For example, Intel Corporation provides Intel Data Center Manager as a licensed utility that customers can use to track power and thermal performance of their servers. This allows customers to optimize data center cooling, optimize power consumption, detect potential hardware issues, and identify zombie servers (that is, servers that are serving no useful purpose).

In the previous section, we looked at examples where companies have leveraged digitization to drive greater manufacturing flexibility, speeding up the design process, improving end product quality by monitoring the machining process, and—lastly—providing not just a product to the customer, but also additional services that provide mutual benefit to both the supplier and the customer. So far, we have focused on the manufacturing process and data flows from equipment and products. We will next look at how digitization can be leveraged by use cases tied to buildings and complexes.

# Transforming buildings and complexes

In previous section, we looked at various use cases tied to factory and physical assets. We will now look at buildings and facilities. In this section, we will focus on the following two aspects:

- Monitoring of facilities via digitization
- Smart buildings

So, let's get started.

## Facility monitoring

The primary objective in the digitization of a facility monitoring function is to ensure that the facilities operate most efficiently in generating industrial output and minimize the costs associated with unexpected downtime. This objective must be achieved without compromising on safety of personnel and by maintaining compliance with industry-specific regulations.

Most common monitoring of industrial facilities looks at temperature. Digitally connected temperature sensors can provide information on various working spaces and industrial zones in buildings. Similarly, digitally connected pressure and humidity sensors can generate the needed information about the human comfort index for the respective locations. **Volatile Organic Compound** (**VOC**) sensors are used to detect presence of dangerous VOC gases such as benzene, formaldehyde, toluene, methylene chloride, and ethylene. It is important to constantly track levels of such compounds because they are harmful to human health.

Another aspect of facilities monitoring that can be enabled by digital transformation is the ability to track objects or people inside a facility. There are a variety of solutions available for indoor asset tracking. Some solutions use reader-based technology, which scans passive tags (such as RFID) attached to objects and tracks the asset. Another available option is a beaconing solution, where an active **Bluetooth Low Energy** (**BLE**) tag is attached to an asset and its position is tracked based on its distance from nearby beacons in the facility. There are a variety of other technologies that use similar signals such as Wi-Fi, **ultra-wideband** (**UWB**), and ultrasonic.

Another aspect is to monitor ancillary systems to ensure that they are operating at peak efficiency. One example of such a system is to monitor the remaining operating life of air filters in **heating, ventilation, and air-conditioning** (**HVAC**) systems in a facility. Usually, filters in HVAC systems are changed periodically at a fixed interval of time. This approach does not consider the current condition of filter. If the filter gets clogged sooner than the set date for replacement, then the HVAC system will operate with a lower efficiency until the filter is changed. Air quality will be poor and operating costs will be higher during this time. A digitally connected differential pressure sensor-based air filter quality indicator can be used to monitor the status of all filters in a facility. This will allow the facilities operator to schedule filter replacement tasks.

## Smart buildings

In an industrial setting, smart buildings provide better control of operations and help conserve resources such as water and energy. Smart buildings' implementations vary across industries and use IoT technologies enabled by a decade of development in connectivity solutions and cloud analytics. Digital transformation is being applied to building automation systems that manage HVAC systems, fire detection suppression systems, flood control, lighting, physical access controls, and security systems.

Digitization of indoor maps for industrial buildings can be used in transformation efforts to enable a multitude of applications, including workspace management, maintenance planning, emergency planning, security, and location-based alerts. Blueprints of building maps or AutoCAD drawings can be digitized for integration with automation **application programming interfaces** (**APIs**), where floorplans and the position or state of industrial equipment/assets can be updated in real time.

Human presence detection sensors, ambient light sensors, and indoor air-quality sensors integrated in a digitally connected building management system can be used to adjust HVAC systems and lighting with zone-based control in order to deliver a more comfortable working environment and reduce operational costs. Desk and other building sensors are being added for COVID-19-related contact tracing. They also allow utilization of working space to be tracked, especially as working from home is becoming more prevalent. Enlighted, a Siemens company, has done some pioneering work with such sensors (`https://www.enlightedinc.com/press-releases/enlighted-launches-game-changing-building-iot-sensor-for-corporate-real-estate/`).

Manufacturing and facilities are typically part of a larger supply chain. We will now look at how the supply chain can benefit from digital transformation.

# Transforming the manufacturing ecosystem

A factory or production facility is just one piece within an enterprise. In the preceding sections, we looked at various use cases of how digitization can help prevent unforeseen disruptions and help with agility. In this section, we look at how digital transformation can help with managing variability and disruptions into systems that feed production and take the product and deliver it to customers—that is, the supply chain.

## Concerns in supply chain management

We first start with a look at the supply chain. This is shown in the following diagram. As we see here, there is one pathway wherein material is flowing into the enterprise:

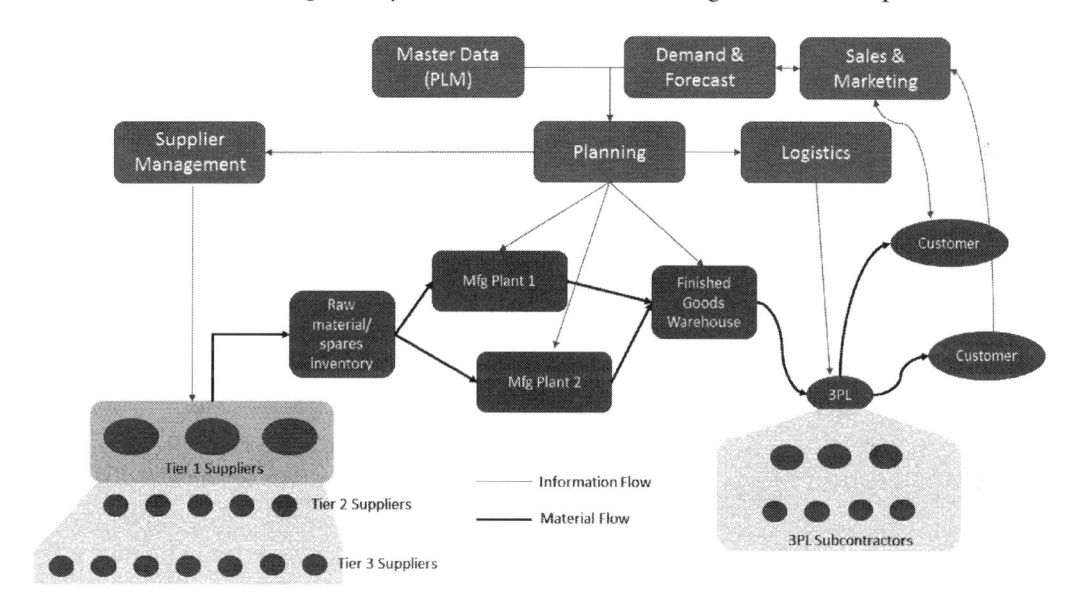

Figure 5.20 – Overview of the supply chain

The plant transforms it to a saleable product, and there is another path where this product is delivered to customers. Encompassing the entire process is the demand signal that drives all the planning activities within the enterprise. Planning can be broadly broken up into short-term, mid-range and long-term plans, described as follows:

- **Long-range plan**: This is a plan based on forecasted demand over a multi-year horizon. This plan defines if new facilities need to be started up, if there is going to be anticipated product mix changes that may require retooling of existing facilities, if additional suppliers need to be qualified to meet expected purchase orders, or if new distribution centers need to be opened up as the product market expands.

- **Mid-range plan**: This plan is based on a forecast over the next 6 to 18 months and is used to make decisions related to workforce size/training, outsourcing decisions, and to potentially look at revisions of existing products to boost sales.
- **Short-term plan**: This typically has a less than 3-month horizon and is primarily planning for execution. The intent is to ensure there is sufficient inventory of raw materials and production capacity to meet the immediate demand.

It is clear that planning activity is centered on anticipated demand, and forecasting this as accurately as possible is critical in order to avoid costly decisions, especially with regard to the mid-range and long-range plans. Incorrect forecasts can leave the company with idle new facilities, an excess or unqualified headcount, and commitments to suppliers to purchase unneeded raw material. In fact, inventory stocking policies set stock levels in direct proportion to the variability in demand, and hence this increases the cost of material on hand, either in terms of raw material or finished product.

On the delivery side, the transport of goods to the customers is often outsourced to **third-party logistic providers** (**3PLs**). They, in turn, could further outsource their business to subcontractors. Very soon, it will become difficult to know who has physical possession of the product containers. For example, Hanjin Shipping used to be one of the top 10 container carriers in terms of capacity. When it declared bankruptcy in 2016, it severely impacted small customers who unknowingly had their goods on one of their ships. The ships could not unload as there was no one to pay the dock fees, causing severe disruption in the supply chain.

Lastly, on the supply side, we need to monitor not just our tier-1 suppliers but also potentially their suppliers (tier-2) who may impact them. This impact is not just in terms of sourcing disruptions, but may also impact the company's reputation. Even if the tier-1 supplier is not involved in ethical violations (for example, child labor or sourcing conflict minerals) but the tier-2 supplier is involved in these activities, the media will usually point the spotlight on the tier-1 supplier as it has a more prominent name. For example, a tier-2 supplier for several clothing brands was caught using child labor. However, the media focus was primarily on the clothing brands, who had to vigorously defend themselves.

# Role of digitization

We will now look at examples of how digitization helps with several of the concerns listed previously. We first look at a general data lake architecture with the appropriate data sources and consumption avenues in *Figure 5.21*. Most of this information is available through supplier-provided APIs and is first formatted into structures appropriate for storage in the data lake. Consumers of this information are DL-based sentiment analysis tools, supply chain risk monitoring solutions, demand forecasting, sales and marketing, and supplier management modules. The architecture is as follows:

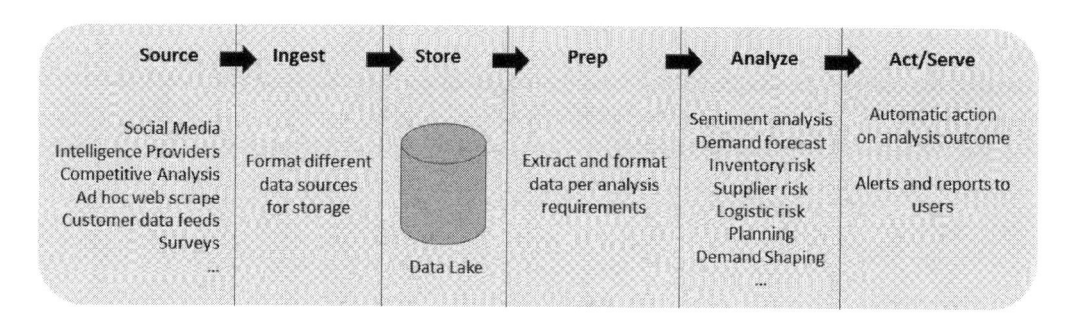

Figure 5.21 – Data lake concept for data aggregation for supply chain analytics digital transformation of demand forecasting

Gone are the days when we used time series for demand forecasting. Time series were good—at best—for short-term trends as they are based on historical data, and, as conditions outside the enterprise change, this historical data may no longer be relevant. We can augment historical patterns with additional real-time data that comes from digitization of the supply chain (often termed demand sensing) to not only improve our short-term forecasts but to also use this information to shape the demand so that we can better utilize our assets.

For low-volume specialty products, we can look at the utilization of assets at the consumer's site (for example, through data feeds tied to remote diagnostics) to determine when a direct consumer will be placing orders for new equipment, for example, or to forecast repair parts that need to be produced. On the high-volume consumer side, looking at market intelligence and sentiment analysis we can better predict how specific products are being perceived in the market and sales, and marketing can target where they want to direct energy to shape demand, either by advertising, social media engagements, new product introductions, or via pricing adjustments. Proctor & Gamble, for example, collects data from point-of-sale terminals, combining this with data across retailers, warehouses, and in the channel to determine demand for its consumer products as well as to set safety stock levels. They have reported over a 50% reduction in short-term forecast errors. PepsiCo has been using social media data to track changing consumer behavior, and this is fed into new product development. Note that even with demand sensing the focus is on the short- or, at best, medium-term forecasts. However, even in the short term the impact is substantial, especially if they are tied to an automated operational planning process that can react with agility as the forecast updates.

## Digitization for risk management

It is often the case that social media announces events before official news channels can cover them. For example, in 2015 when there was a chemical plant explosion in Zhangzhou, China, the news first broke on social media. This gave alert companies time to evacuate their employees ahead of the general rush for transportation as more companies started their own evacuations. In this situation, hours matter, and those who had information on tap were able to act on it faster. Nowadays, it is common to find news on social media first, even from journalists or world leaders, ahead of it making it into the official news channels. Although this does offer a more immediate avenue to access information, we need to be careful to put appropriate checks and balances in to avoid malicious messages and bots disrupting our supply chain operations. Social media platforms are continuously developing mitigation strategies against such messages, and this still remains an active area of research (Kudugunta, S. and Ferrara, W., *Deep neural networks for bot detection*, in *Information Sciences*, 467 (October): 312-322 (2018)).

In addition to the preceding information, we can use market intelligence feeds to keep track of supplier (and their suppliers') health. These systems can constantly be looking at incoming information to search out sentiments, keywords, or phrases that may be indicative of potential risk to the supplier, such as strikes, government actions, lawsuits, and so on. DHL has developed its Resilience360 supply chain risk management platform (https://www.resilience360.dhl.com/) that provides this capability among many others for overall supply chain risk management.

Lastly, the preceding concepts can be adapted to managing in-house corporate risk. By moving data onto a cloud-based platform, there is improved transparency and access to information versus having to dig it out of someone's computer. In addition, outlier detection algorithms can be implemented on this data trove to look for abnormal activities such as unusual expenses or abnormal patterns of system access, and these in turn could serve as alerts to the **chief financial officer** (**CFO**).

# Promoting industrial worker safety

As the industries march on their digital transformation journey, worker safety cannot be overlooked. In this section, we will look at how digital technologies can be leveraged to improve the culture of safety and at how, in some cases, safe operations can be a competitive advantage. There have been US government *Fair Pay and Safe Workplaces* guidelines that required companies to focus on worker safety, especially in large construction sites (https://www.federalregister.gov/documents/2014/08/05/2014-18561/fair-pay-and-safe-workplaces).

Some of these laws and executive orders change over time, but the importance of industrial worker safety is paramount. No transformation can be successful if it risks life and property. As a result, a few areas have emerged for the use of digital technologies to promote industrial worker safety. Some of the hazards at workplaces are listed as follows:

- Factory operations where workers have risk of exposure to toxic gases, high temperatures, and so on
- Construction sites where large equipment is used near humans
- Oil rigs and platforms where natural hazards are common
- Mining operations
- Humans working with industrial robots (cobots)

While the deployment of a technology solution in many of these scenarios might seem like an overhead cost, we will look at scenarios where these solutions can be the foundation of a productivity boost as well, leading to real industrial digital transformation. In the construction industry, the projects are often required to do the following:

- Have safety reporting procedures, such as any unsafe actions at a job site and any near misses—The overall goal is to track, detect, and be proactive about the prevention of potentially unsafe actions.
- Improve regulatory compliance—There are many national and local regulations to improve the productivity of any degree of automation for incident logging and processing. Likewise, automation for policy enforcement—such as worker without a valid license cannot operate a crane—can improve regulatory compliance.
- Analytics and diagnostics—Insights around safety policies and diagnostic information in the case of safety mishaps can be very useful and reduce manual enforcement and related tasks.

Next, let's look at digital solutions in this area.

## Designing a worker safety solution

Such capabilities are found in digital applications that are broadly called Industrial Worker Safety or Connected Industrial Worker solutions. Some of the features of such a solution include the following:

- Real-time worker location—This includes a) Identify worker position by project and site location and b) Overlay worker and equipment position on job site map.

- Monitor workplace to prevent accidents—The goals include detecting proximity of worker to hazards and preventing accidents, as well as monitoring environment for high temperature and gases.

- Safety policy enforcement and incident analytics—This would include investigating the root cause of safety incidents and near misses, correlation analysis, and rule-based actions on real-time sensor data analysis.

For commercially available solutions see `https://www.oracle.com/internet-of-things/iot-connected-worker-cloud.html`.

*Figure 5.22* shows a typical construction site with heavy equipment in the top center, a hazard such as a pit at the bottom, and a construction worker next to it. A trainee worker is on the left and the supervisor is on the bottom right. A Connected Industrial Worker solution enhances the safety of operations on a job site. It can also transform the construction business by improving worker productivity and by providing context-sensitive information about the project, on a timely basis. The information collected from such a solution can be used to do the following:

- Track time and attendance automatically at job site.

- Ensure that crew assigned for specific job site stay together and close to their assigned foreman or supervisor for feedback and guidance.

- Analyze actual time spent on tasks and patterns of the movement of crew members to come up with more efficient procedures.

- Better scheduling and resource allocations for future tasks and projects.

- Better supporting data for billing and demonstrating the milestones in the construction project.

Let us look at the construction site here:

Figure 5.22 – Construction job site

Let's look at how some of these technologies and solutions apply to a construction site. There are connected wearable gears such as a hard hat or jacket, or a wearable badge with sensors that can record environmental temperature, gas levels, or even detect a fall by sudden change in altitude. Likewise, a connected watch or other wearable device can be used to detect body temperature, heat rate, or related vital signs. The key point is that such wearable items are connected through an IoT application, to provide actionable insights.

Connected wearable technologies are common in life outside of a work environment. Today, our watches tell us much more than the time of day—with a quick peek, we can check our heart rate or the temperature outside, as well as our next appointment.

214 Transforming One Industry at a Time

The job site shown in *Figure 5.22* may be shown in the Connected Industrial Worker application, as shown in *Figure 5.23*. The concentric circles denote different types of people. The equipment and hazards can be represented by different icons, and ovals denote the zones around it for safety purposes. An onsite supervisor, or even a remote control center, can monitor the job site through such an application. They can set up rules and different types of reports and views to monitor the safety of operations as well as productivity, as illustrated here:

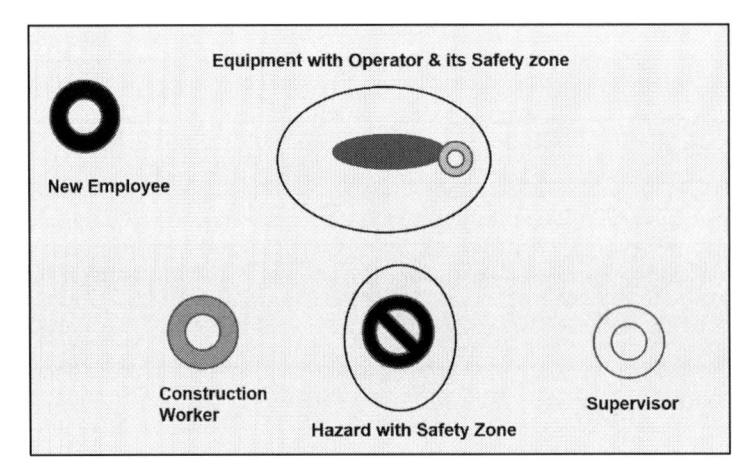

Figure 5.23 – Connected Industrial Worker application dashboard view

The system would need 3D rendering capabilities to show the actual location of workers, as well as sensors with the ability to detect a worker who fell by means of detecting a rapid change in altitude versus gradually climbing up or down. An illustration of 3D rendering can be seen in the following figure:

Figure 5.24 – Need for 3D rendering and fall detection capabilities (Source: http://civilengineerthoughts003.blogspot.com/2015/09/general-safety-in-construction-site.html, License: CC BY-NC-ND)

The application should generally provide smartphone capabilities as well, so workers and supervisors can use these while at the field location. The smartphone application may also show the schedule for the day or allow requests to change shifts and schedules.

Why do we believe such a Connected Industrial Worker application is an enabler of industrial digital transformation? This solution can easily scale for all the job sites of a large or global construction company. The actual wireless connectivity and the network backbone may vary according to the local availability of the connectivity options. However, the application framework can run on a digital platform and connect to other parts of enterprise applications such as project planning, project financials, and **Human Capital Management (HCM)**. The safety capabilities can provide a construction company a competitive advantage over its industry peers, and, often, government or large commercial construction projects require such features. The boost in productivity is due to connected features that help to monitor actual progress as well as provide context-specific instructions to workers. Some routine activities such as time cards can be automated when a worker signs off from the smartphone app or can be enabled with a single click.

In this section, we have looked at ways to transform the workplace, while making industrial workers safer and more productive.

# Summary

In this chapter, we covered use cases of how industrial digital transformation has been applied to the chemical, semiconductor, and manufacturing industries, along with its application to buildings, facilities, and the supply chain. We remind you that even though we tied these use cases to specific industries, they can be adapted in general to any industrial enterprise. We hope that these use cases, along with the associated links and references, will enable you to map digital transformation into your organization's own specific industries and situations.

In *Chapter 6, Transforming the Public Sector*, we will learn about the transformation process in the public sector. We will cover transformation initiatives at different levels of the public sector—namely, federal, state, and local—with regard to defense as well as education in the US and globally. We will learn the challenges that arise when we try to scale public sector transformation across the country and around the world, and even in space!

## Questions

Here are some questions to test your understanding of the chapter:

1. Why are the main outcomes from industrial digital transformation in the chemical industry?
2. How is industrial digital transformation driving lights-out manufacturing?
3. What is the role of digital transformation in supply chain management?
4. How can we make buildings and facilities smarter?
5. How can industrial digital transformation make workers safer and more productive?

# 6
# Transforming the Public Sector

In *Chapter 5, Transforming One Industry at a Time*, we learned about the outcomes of industrial digital transformation in the chemical and semiconductor manufacturing sector. We saw how the supply chain is being transformed and how buildings and facilities are becoming smarter. Finally, we saw how industrial worker safety and productivity are being transformed. In this chapter, we will build on the introduction to public sector digital transformation in earlier chapters. We will learn how the public sector differs from the private sector and how those differences present additional challenges to digital transformation efforts. We will also review examples of digital transformation across the public sector, at the state, local, and federal level, as well as in education in the US and globally. Finally, we will learn about the challenges of scaling government transformation across organizations and around the globe. In a nutshell, we will learn about the following:

- The unique challenges in the public sector for industrial digital transformation
- The enhancement of the citizen experience through digital transformation
- Digital transformation at a national and global scale

# Unique challenges of industrial digital transformation in the public sector

Digital transformation is not easy. There are many challenges faced by organizations that initiate a digital transformation effort. In *Chapter 4*, *Industrial Digital Transformation*, we discussed these challenges in some detail. While the public sector faces all the same digital transformation challenges as the private sector, the public sector faces an additional group of challenges. The laws and rules that govern the way that the government buys products and services, hires staff, and manages projects, along with the cultures that have evolved in the public sector, can slow or stop digital transformation efforts. In this section, we will discuss some of those challenges and how we can mitigate them to ensure the success of public sector digital transformation efforts. These challenges include the following:

- Access to new technology
- Government culture
- Hiring challenges – processes and pay and skill gaps
- Budgets and technical debt

We will discuss each challenge and how the government is responding to these challenges.

## Access to new technology

Traditional government procurement processes have substantially hampered the ability of government agencies to access new technologies in a timely manner. Typically, public sector organizations acquire new technologies through competitive procurement processes. The purpose of the government's competitive procurement process is to ensure that the government receives the best value for taxpayers' money. In addition, the procurement rules are designed to ensure that the process is fair to all vendors who wish to sell to the government and to avoid corruption. Unfortunately, sometimes the rules that are designed to ensure the efficiency and effectiveness of the government have the opposite effect.

In the vast majority of organizations, these processes usually take at least 6 months and, in more challenging situations, can take several years. On average, public sector procurements comparable to those that can be executed in days or weeks in the private sector take several months to a year. An example of the complexity of the government contracting process can be seen on the USA.gov site: `https://www.usa.gov/become-government-contractor`.

Traditional competitive procurement processes involve fully documenting the requirements for a solution, whether that is strictly a hardware purchase, a **Commercial Off-the-Shelf (COTS)** or **Software-as-a-Service (SaaS)** purchase, or custom development. Those requirements are then used to create a **Request for Proposals (RFP)** (see `https://www.usaopps.com/government-bids.htm` to see a collection of government RFPs). Responses to the RFP are evaluated by a committee that selects a vendor, usually based on the lowest cost, technically acceptable bid. This does not always result in the best solution being purchased or a successful implementation. Because the procurement process takes a long time, long-term contracts are generally awarded to vendors. While, at least in theory, these contracts are performance-based, there tend to be few incentives for those incumbents to perform well, as the cost of change is very high and the incumbent vendor knows there is a low risk of being replaced before the end of the contract term.

Government leaders have been trying to speed up this process for years, as it inhibits not only technology projects but also a wide variety of government activities. There are a number of approaches that have been developed over the past few years that have been helpful in speeding up the procurement of technology. Agencies can establish pools of vendors that are pre-qualified to sell a particular product at an agreed price. This is accomplished by competitively bidding long-term contracts that allow the agency to spend up to a maximum amount over a contract term but that do not guarantee business to any individual vendor. With these contracts in place, staff can then order the products, such as servers and laptops, that are on the price list at a pre-negotiated price. These contracts can be created by the federal government, states, and local governments, as well as non-profit organizations whose mission is to support the government.

Unfortunately, these contracts are generally limited to a handful of vendors per technology and generally don't provide access to the latest technologies. There are frequently limits in how many or which agencies can access the contracts, either in the terms of the contracts or due to restrictions placed on agency staff by their procurement organization. Specifically, some procurement organizations choose not to use outside contracts. The contracts also have ceilings, which limit the total spend on the contract, terminating the contract when that ceiling is exceeded. Similar contracts can be used to purchase services, although restrictions on *like for like* – which require the same services to be provided over the same period of time – and other restrictive contract terms can limit the usefulness of such vehicles when acquiring services. Consequently, most organizations can only use their own multi-award contacts to acquire services.

Over the last several years, government technology and procurement teams have begun to find creative ways to both follow procurement law and gain access to new technology. These solutions have included the following:

- Technology innovation labs
- Challenge-based procurement
- Multi-award vehicles
- Contests and hackathons

Let's look at all of these in detail.

## Technology innovation labs

One approach that public sector teams have been using to gain access to new technologies is innovation labs. Apolitical, a non-profit organization dedicated to helping modernize government, lists dozens of government innovation labs around the world at the national, state, county, and city level. These labs are dedicated to evaluating new technologies, such as IoT devices and machine learning, that can provide public benefit and are rapidly deploying those technologies into local communities. These labs generally have special procurement authority to accept free services and to run low-cost pilots without following the government entity's standard procurement processes.

One such example of an innovation lab is SMC Labs in San Mateo County, in the Bay Area, California (see `https://smclabs.io`). One of the outcomes of this lab is the air quality sensing project (see `https://openmap.clarity.io/?viewport=37.477778,%20-122.220819,10.6`). Another example, from Canada, is Ontario Digital. It is driving multiple digital government and related initiatives for its citizens.

In addition to technology innovation labs, progressive agencies are setting up procurement innovation labs. For example, the US **Department of Homeland Security (DHS)** created a procurement innovation lab to help speed up the adoption of new technologies. DHS employees can work with consultants in the lab to evaluate and refine their innovative procurement approaches to make sure that the approaches are both legal and successful.

## Challenge-based procurements

Rather than traditional RFPs that define a specific solution to a problem and request bids that respond to that specific solution, challenge-based procurements present a problem statement and ask the vendor community to respond to that problem by proposing solutions. Challenge-based procurements often require vendors to deliver a proof of concept as part of their proposal, with most or all of the evaluation criteria based on whether the proof of concept meets the agency's needs. This approach not only reduces the up-front time that would usually be spent defining detailed requirements but also allows vendors to propose innovations that apply new technology and other new ideas without requiring the government agency to be familiar with that technology or idea in advance of the procurement.

The city of Toronto, Canada, has put its own unique spin on challenge-based procurements by creating partnerships with firms that are selected through the challenge-based procurement process. They allowed start-ups that had good ideas but lacked implementation resources to participate in the program. The start-ups were able to grow their capabilities throughout the prototype phase to the point where they were ready to deliver when it was time for the implementation phase. If the start-up was unable to scale, the city could choose a different implementation partner, assuring them that the idea could still move forward.

## Multi-award vehicles

A multi-award vehicle or pre-qualified pool establishes a pool of suppliers that have demonstrated that they have the ability to deliver a broad set of products or services defined in a request for proposals. For example, a pre-qualified pool composed of vendors who provide a wide range of software and hardware development services could be created. These vendors are fully vetted, and an agreement is put in place defining the terms and conditions of any engagements, and setting rates and prices, or, in some cases, maximum rates and prices that may be further negotiated for specific projects. The goal of a multi-award vehicle is to have as many vendors as possible as part of the pre-qualified pool. Then, when a product or service is needed, an expedited secondary competition is completed among the vendors in the pool.

The speed of the secondary competition, a matter of days or weeks rather than months or years, to set up the initial vehicle can significantly reduce time to deployment for new solutions. Greg Godbout, the US Environmental Protection Agency CTO during the Obama administration, called this process *buying at the speed of need*, meaning that these vehicles allow federal agencies to purchase products and services when the need is identified, not months or years later. While multi-award vehicles are generally used to access technical staff, they are also used to access hardware, services, and other new technologies.

## Contests and hackathons

Many public sector agencies use hackathons and other types of contests to engage developers and inventors who would not ordinarily bid on government contracts to design, develop, and deliver new technology for the government. Hackathons and other contests are generally of short duration and relatively low cost, with prizes of a few hundred or thousand dollars. While these competitions don't generate completed and ready-to-deploy products and services, they do generate ideas and deliver technologies that the government would likely not see for several years using traditional procurement approaches. Technology and solutions delivered through hackathons and other contests can be further developed and refined by government staff, or another procurement method can be used to retain the project's creator. One such example is the US **Government Services Administration (GSA)** hackathon 2019 (see `https://www.challenge.gov/challenge/gsa-hackathon-2019`).

## Government culture

We often say that the government is comprised of a lot of really good people who want to do great work but are constrained by a system that is optimized to ensure that no one breaks the law, rather than to ensure that work gets done. That is no more evident than in government culture, which places so many constraints on staff that it seems at times to be expressly designed to foster mediocrity. There are several characteristics of the historic government culture that must be changed to foster digital transformation in government, including a culture of risk aversion and compliance, gaps in skills and pay, and inappropriate decision-makers. Specific cultural issues and mitigations that will be discussed in this section include the following:

- Risk aversion
- Compliance culture and misaligned incentives
- Inappropriate decisions and decision-makers
- Organizational fatigue

Let's look at these issues in the following sections.

## Risk aversion

In the US, the government workforce has more legal protections than any other group of workers in the country. On top of that, most government employees in the US are unionized. Those government employees who are not unionized have equivalent protections and rights to unionized employees. Therefore, it is ironic that civil servants are also among the most risk-averse knowledge workers in the country. The government's long and bureaucratic processes that tend to result in long lead times and large contract awards create high stakes that make risk-taking feel particularly dangerous. There are certainly parts of the digital transformation process, such as the procurement process, where individual risk-taking should be avoided. Risky activities that go badly during a procurement process could result in a procurement process being restarted from the beginning or, in the worst case, civil or criminal liabilities. However, the risk aversion generated by the real risk associated with activities such as government procurements seems to extend to all areas of the digital transformation process.

In addition to the risks perceived by employees, most government leaders do not convey support for risk-taking. This aversion to risk inhibits the government's ability to deploy new technology, which is inherently risky. It is important for government leaders who wish to foster innovation to reduce risk by breaking down projects into small and lower-cost activities focused on proving the value of that new technology first – that is, creating proofs of concept and minimum viable products. In addition, government leaders must demonstrate their support for employees who take reasonable risks to deliver value. This requires an open dialogue expressing support for risk-taking and setting up guardrails so that employees understand what is permissible and what is forbidden.

## Compliance culture and misaligned incentives

Government entities often value compliance with rules and processes over achieving results. This is the result of the fact that *what gets measured gets managed*. What is measured in government is frequently whether a project has a plan, rather than whether working products are delivered, and whether a project is on budget, rather than whether the budget is being wisely spent.

The Federal IT Acquisition Reform Act scores federal CIOs on their assessment of projects. If a federal CIO rates many of their projects as failing, they receive an *A* on that metric because they are perceived to be honestly assessing risk. If they resolve the underlying problems and start reporting their projects as on track, they will receive a lower grade. The CIO is rewarded for identifying the problem, but they are penalized if they resolve the problem. To accelerate the delivery of new technologies, agencies need to begin measuring what new technology they deliver and how rapidly and successfully it is delivered to the public. To accelerate digital transformation, agencies need to move toward measuring performance, rather than compliance.

## Inappropriate decisions and decision-makers

All organizations, public and private, suffer from the problem of decisions being made by individuals who do not understand the problem or solution or who have objectives that are in conflict with the needs of the public or others in the agency due to their specific metrics and incentives. However, this problem is more pronounced in the public sector.

Historically technology management has been decentralized within public sector organizations, resulting in small groups of technologists scattered throughout agencies, often managed by mid-level managers or executives who do not understand the technology or the value of modernization, centralization, or data sharing. Without the pressure to make a profit, the potential for the wrong individual to make a decision is magnified. Politically motivated decisions, whether by the small *p* of organizational politics or the large *P* of electoral politics, are much more likely. These decision-makers frequently don't understand the value that digital transformation will bring, believe that technology investments are too costly, or they simply prefer the status quo.

To combat the problem of inappropriate decision-making, CIOs must put structured decision processes in place that drive organizations to make fact-based decisions about project selection, budgeting, and planning and that consider the risk and returns from each investment under consideration. CIOs must ensure that customers and others that are impacted by technology decisions are involved in the decision-making process and understand the cost and benefit of each solution so that educated project selection decisions can be made.

## Organizational fatigue

As you may have gathered from reading this section up to this point, getting things done in government is extremely difficult. Hiring people, buying technology and services, and managing people are far more complex and time-consuming activities than in the private sector. Many people believe that civil servants are lazy or stupid. That is not the case. Rather, most are extremely dedicated and mission-driven. However, the sheer effort required to make things happen quickly in government is exhausting and eventually results in career civil servants giving up their efforts to effect change. Over time, most government employees simply give up trying to change the system and wait for work to be handed off to them when the previous person in the value chain has completed their work, rather than attempting to simplify processes to deliver faster results.

If we doubt the artificial obstacles inhibiting the success of government staff, we need only to look at the speed at which the government was able to act at the beginning of the COVID-19 pandemic, or, for that matter, during any declared emergency. When a state of emergency is declared, two critical things happen. The first is that procurement rules are suspended, and the government is able to buy supplies and services the same way as the private sector to speed up their ability to meet critical needs. The second is that, like any group in a crisis, the vast majority of employees stop worrying about politics, organizational boundaries, and conflicts between management and bargaining units and focus exclusively on delivering essential services to the public. Both the system and the people rise to the occasion.

While transformation leaders can't permanently waive procurement rules, they must find ways to reset their culture and instill a sense of urgency among their teams, even when not in a crisis, so that government projects can be delivered faster and at a lower cost, while meeting customer needs more effectively.

# Hiring challenges – process and pay and skill gaps

Most government employees are paid substantially less than their counterparts performing similar jobs in the private sector. This pay rate is not indicative of the value of the work being performed, as many government employees perform roles that are of incalculable value to society or of the skill of individual employees, as most are as highly skilled as their private sector counterparts. It is simply a decision that has been made to pay government employees less than their value on the open market. Whether this decision is fair or rational or whether pensions, job security, working conditions, and the opportunity to be of service are sufficient to offset this lower pay is a subject for a different book. But the fact that this exists is an issue that impacts government transformation.

Government pay is generally not merit-based but rather is based on time in the position. Increases occur annually as defined by a pay structure, regardless of performance, and bonuses are rare in public service. This structure incentivizes employees to stay in their positions to achieve annual pay increases and to look for more highly graded positions to advance their pay once they have exhausted all the steps on their current pay structure, regardless of whether they are enjoying their current position or the new position is of interest to them. While it may not seem entirely rational to seek a promotion even when an employee is enjoying their work, most employees are at least somewhat motivated by the extrinsic reward of pay increases. In addition, many government employees work in areas where the cost of living is very high and choose to seek promotions to improve their quality of life or simply make ends meet.

In addition to lower pay, government employees do not receive the perks that their private sector colleagues, especially their colleagues in the technology sector, enjoy. Governments are generally barred from providing any gifts to their employees, including the free coffee and holiday parties, that most individuals working in the private sector take for granted. While laws vary between jurisdictions, in most cases, it is illegal for government employees to accept anything of value from vendors, in most cases not even a catered lunch at a briefing center. Public sector employees are also subject to rigorous financial disclosures and restrictions on their ability to invest in private sector companies.

This pay disparity means that government service generally attracts two types of people: those who are intrinsically motivated to serve and are willing to accept the pay gap to do so and those who accept the pay gap to achieve the better work-life balance and job security that is generally afforded by government jobs.

Once someone decides that they want to work for the government, they must go through a lengthy interview process and possibly obtain security clearance. Government interview processes are very structured and take much longer than private sector hiring processes. This results in a much longer time from when someone applies for a position to when they receive a response and complete the hiring process than in most private sector organizations. In addition, the way that the government evaluates candidates is different than in the private sector, resulting in many highly qualified candidates who don't understand public sector hiring being screened out early in the process. Finally, security clearances for certain jobs may result in long delays between an offer and a start date. The result of all of these process hurdles is that many individuals who are interested in government jobs accept positions in the private sector before the government agency can make an offer or sometimes even schedule an interview.

## Responding to hiring challenges

Given all these challenges, it is not surprising that there tend to be substantial gaps in the skill of government employees who are expected to design, implement, and manage solutions based on new technologies. While these challenges are large, there are solutions that organizations are using to close the skills gap.

## Training

Many agencies are investing in training programs to bring their employees up to date on new technologies such as IoT, machine learning, analytics, and **Robotic Process Automation (RPA)**. They are investing in certifications such as **Information Technology Infrastructure Library (ITIL)** and **Project Management Professional (PMP)** and development methodologies such as **Scrum** and **Kanban** (see https://www.digite.com/kanban/what-is-kanban/). Agencies are using in-house training courses, online training, conferences and courses, and university degree programs to deliver customized training to each employee. As many private sector companies have reduced their training and development budgets, this allows public sector agencies to differentiate themselves from the nearby companies that they are competing with for talent.

Most public sector organizations recognize that bringing in a mix of individuals, including new college graduates, staff from other public agencies, and individuals from the private sector, helps them achieve the mix of skills that they need to be successful.

## Streamlined hiring for high-demand positions

Many public sector agencies, especially the federal government, have created special, streamlined hiring processes to allow positions that are in high demand to be filled more rapidly. For example, in federal government, a department or agency may request direct-hire authority, allowing the agency to bypass much of the hiring process for critical jobs where there is a shortage of candidates. In these cases, the agency is able to hire in a manner similar to the way that the private sector hires.

## Hiring preferences

Most public sector entities have some preferences for underrepresented minority groups, veterans, and individuals with disabilities. Those preferences frequently allow managers to hire any candidate that meets the position requirements and is a member of a class receiving preference. In recognition of their service to their country, the federal government gives a significant preference to veterans. This preference can be used by federal hiring managers to quickly hire qualifying veterans.

## Special hiring authorities

Finally, many organizations have special authorities that allow managers to hire limited-term employees using streamlined processes. These are government employees, not contractors. However, their appointment to government service is term-limited and the individuals in these positions don't have any underlying status with the government agency. Since they lack status as a permanent employee, if they want to move to another job in the agency, they must apply in the same manner as someone who is not employed by the agency. These term-limited positions can range from a few months to a few years. In some organizations, these are formal fellowship programs such as the Presidential Innovation Fellowship or the Presidential Management Fellowship. In other cases, an organization may be able to fill any position with a limited-term employee. These positions are especially helpful to organizations that want to bring specific new expertise into their organization as they can hire individuals with that expertise who can train their existing staff, while also learning about how the government operates from the rest of the team. Successful limited-term employment programs grow both expertise within the government and understanding of the government within the private sector.

Public sector organizations that are successfully transforming are using some or all of the preceding approaches to training and hiring to increase their likelihood of success in adding new staff with new skills to their teams.

# Budgets and technical debt

Limited government budgets can interfere with the ability of public sector agencies to implement their digital transformations. In most places, including the civilian agencies of the federal government and most state and local agencies, government budgets have been declining for decades, while the need for services has increased. Even the best funded government agencies have more demands on their budget than they have funding. Agencies must deliver basic services, run the agency's internal processes, and meet the political objectives of their elected officials and the community. Agency IT organizations must balance delivering transformative products and services with maintaining and updating existing technologies.

Unlike the many digitally native start-ups, most government agencies have been around for a long time. In most cases, agencies existed before the computer age started, and, while not generally early adopters, agencies have historically followed the private sector in the implementation of new technologies, resulting in an enterprise architecture that is a collection of older technologies, from mainframes to microfilm, along with modern and cutting-edge technologies. Unfortunately, while agencies are slow to adopt new technology, they are even slower to upgrade and retire old technologies.

As a result of budget constraints and the sheer amount of technology in place, many public sector agencies are carrying a great deal of technical debt. While the idea of technical debt was once only applied to taking shortcuts in software development, it is now broadly understood to include not only poorly designed code but also obsolete software and hardware.

In a conversation in April 2020, one public sector CIO noted that they were still trying to eliminate the technical debt from the great recession that started in 2008 when the COVID-19-induced recession hit them with new technology needs and another budget cut. Recessions bring an increased need for government services at the same time that funds become more scarce. CIOs must identify digital transformation solutions that allow their agency to retire technical debt. Using Agile methodologies to deliver that transformation allows CIOs to incur costs in small chunks and receive working products at every step of the process. The result of the Agile approach will be solutions that cost less and are delivered faster than using traditional methodologies.

# The digital divide

The digital divide describes a situation where a portion of the population does not have access to computing technology and/or broadband internet. While this does not exclusively impact access to public sector services, private sector organizations are not obligated to ensure that every member of the public is able to use their product. On the other hand, the public sector has a unique mandate to serve everyone. This means that even if the government can provide a service electronically, if some of the public can't access that service electronically, the government needs to provide that solution in another way that is accessible to every member of the public. This means government agencies must maintain two versions of many processes for the foreseeable future.

While the digital divide is described as one thing, there are really two digital divides. One digital divide is rural. Bringing broadband to rural areas has been cost-prohibitive, as there have not been enough residents in certain areas to allow telecom providers to recoup the costs of delivering service to those areas. This is not a new problem in the US where the deployment of new technologies is concerned. This was an issue for the distribution of electricity in the first half of the 20th century, and telephone service in the second half of the 20th century. This problem has been solved in the past by the federal government designating services as essential and providing subsidies to expand the services to underserved rural areas. A similar federally driven solution will likely be necessary to deliver broadband to underserved rural communities. This aspect of the digital divide may not impact local governments in areas that are exclusively urban and suburban.

The second digital divide is an economic divide. In many areas – urban, suburban, and rural – there is plenty of access to broadband but many residents either can't afford broadband access or don't have an internet-capable device, or both. In fact, while the percentage varies, every municipality has residents who can't afford broadband internet access. Local and state governments can help solve this problem through public broadband initiatives and community partnerships to get low-cost or free broadband service and internet-capable devices to members of the public who can't currently afford the service, and the equipment required to access the internet.

The digital divide became even more apparent during the COVID-19 pandemic when government offices around the world suddenly closed. Some services, such as obtaining a new driver's license, simply were not available, while others, such as obtaining a building permit, were only available to those who had broadband internet access. The result was not only redoubled efforts by municipalities to transform and digitize government services but also a spotlight on the digital divide. Many municipalities rolled out short-term solutions, such as extending Wi-Fi from public buildings into parking lots, locating school buses with wireless access points in underserved communities, and deploying millions of computers to students throughout the K-12 system. The pandemic also launched calls from leadership in municipalities such as LA County and the city of Oakland to identify ways to deliver internet access to everyone in their communities.

While all these complexities add additional challenges for the public sector, agencies are able to utilize the strategies described in this section to mitigate those challenges and deliver innovative solutions, albeit more slowly than in the private sector.

Now that we have discussed the challenges that are specific to digital transformation in the government, we will learn about how the public's expectations of government are changing and how government organizations are finding ways to overcome challenges and deliver better services to the public.

# Transforming the citizen experience

Now that we have discussed the challenges specific to government digital transformation, we will cover what the delivery of government services looks like and how government digital services are transforming that experience through a group of case studies. These case studies will describe government digital transformation across a wide range of domains and technologies. The responsibilities of governments are extremely broad and even though we will discuss a significant number of technologies in this section, we will not be able to exhaustively cover the uses of technology in the delivery of government services.

## The role of government services

The government performs a tremendous number of services for the public. The federal government does everything from providing a standing army to protect the country from those who would wish us harm, to ensuring food safety to making sure the banking system works. While state and local governments don't have to worry about raising an army, they also have a broad mandate, ensuring public safety, providing infrastructure, delivering the services that enable the social safety net, and providing services that make the day-to-day lives of residents more enjoyable, such as parks and much more. Finally, public schools, both K-12 and higher education, ensure that students receive an education that prepares them to be productive citizens.

## What citizens expect from the government today

We all live in a digital world today. We expect to be able to get nearly anything that we want or need on the internet. Our expectations, or at least our desires, don't change when we interact with the government. We expect that we should be able to access virtually any government service online and that the experience should be easy, fast, and intuitive. That is, we expect that the government should work like the private sector. While the government has not met that mark entirely, it is undergoing its own transformation to utilize digital technologies, and the rate of that transformation is accelerating.

## Transformation across the government

While the government performs a vast array of activities, for the purpose of this section, we will break those services down into several verticals or types of services provided by the government to collect revenue, protect the public, and enhance the quality of life. Within each vertical, we will look at examples of how the government is transforming the way that it serves the public. The specific verticals that we will cover are as follows:

- Government operations
- Military
- Public safety
- Healthcare
- Social services
- Transportation
- Resident services
- Education

- Environmental protection
- Utilities

We will close this section with a discussion of smart cities. The discussion of smart cities is a glimpse into our future when cities will use information and communications technologies to enhance the livability and sustainability of cities by collecting data through IoT devices, communicating that data over a network, and analyzing the data to understand conditions and respond to problems and opportunities.

## Government operations

In the short term, government budgets are fairly inflexible. Revenues tend not to deviate a great deal over the short term, except in the case of sudden changes, such as natural disasters. In addition, when fees are collected for government services, those fees rarely fully recover the costs of services. For example, in most jurisdictions the cost of issuing a new driver's license does not recover even the incremental cost of issuing a single driver's license, much less the full cost of operating the Department of Motor Vehicles. Therefore, the government cannot improve "margins" by completing a higher volume of transactions. In addition, unlike the private sector, where savings generated by efficiencies are often recouped as corporate profits or employee bonuses, government cost savings can be reinvested back into government programs.

Therefore, it becomes obvious that the more efficiently governments operate their services, both internally and public-facing, the more services they are able to deliver to residents. At the same time, we have learned that there are many bureaucratic challenges to success in government that make program delivery difficult, time-consuming, and expensive. For this reason, any digital transformation that delivers efficiency is extremely important to the effectiveness of the government.

### The state of Nebraska

Ed Toner, CIO of the state of Nebraska, has made effectiveness a cornerstone of his digital transformation. In a recent blog post, Ed noted the following:

> *"At the State of Nebraska we focus on introducing efficiencies, consistency and reliability in everything we do."*

The state's digital transformation has included a great deal of basic blocking and tackling to prepare for the future. They consolidated IT teams across the state into one state-level IT agency and consolidated infrastructure operations into two state data centers. Servers were virtualized and data archived, reducing operating costs further. The actions reduced cost and complexity, opening the door to better data access and improved processes.

Unifying the technology organization and systems, as well as removing the technical barriers within the data center, allowed the state to integrate data across many state agencies, including Health and Human Services, the Department of Revenue, the Department of Motor Vehicles, 911, and the State Patrol. Removing silos allowed agencies to use data analytics to gather insights across what previously were insurmountable data barriers. Better data analytics allows the state to draw inferences across datasets and better serve the residents of Nebraska.

To improve both internal and public-facing processes, the state selected OnBase as the platform to automate their previously paper-based workflows and dedicated an entire team to automating workflows. Most importantly, before any processes were automated, the IT department's lean six sigma team worked with the process owners to streamline the business process. Only then did the OnBase team begin the process of automating workflows. Improved workflows resulted in cost savings to the state and a better user experience for the end users, whether employees or the public.

As a result of this extensive preparation, the state of Nebraska was able to rapidly modernize internal processes, as well as a number of customer-facing processes. A few examples of customer-facing services that have benefited from the state's increased IT effectiveness include the following:

- *Electronic filing of air quality reports*: The Environmental Quality Agency decreased the wait time for approvals dramatically – from several weeks to several days – and reduced the administrative burden on the public by allowing applicants to file electronically instead of on paper.

- *Online access to the* **Women, Infants, and Children (WIC)** *program*: The state brought client access to the WIC assistance program online, reducing 23 paper forms and allowing staff to better serve clients by providing a single comprehensive view of client data across all parts of the program.

- *Paperless cattle inspections*: A paper-based process that could require weeks to identify cattle has been replaced with an electronic process. Nebraska brand inspectors carry iPads to photograph, register, and collect payments for 6.6 million head of cattle each year.

In 2020, the state began applying robotic process automation to back-office processes to continue their digital transformation journey.

## Military

The US **Department of Defense (DoD)** is the largest employer in the country. In total, there are nearly 2.9 million uniformed and civilian employees in the defense department, which includes the major branches of the military, as well as the National Security Agency and a number of other functions.

### Air Force software factories

While much of the digital transformation work of the military is classified and, therefore, unavailable to the authors, there is one very successful program that we will discuss. Within the air force, the Chief Software Officer, Nicholas Chaillan, is dedicated to creating a digital air force. One of the programs that Chaillan and his team have created is the Software Factory program. The air force has created eight software factories, each dedicated to a different aspect of the air force mission. These factories deliver cutting-edge capabilities to support the success of airmen on base and in the field. The eight factories span the breadth of the air force mission.

The software factories are augmented by three additional capabilities:

- **PlatformOne**, a centralized team providing DevSecOps-managed services to teams throughout the air force.
- **CloudOne**, a centralized team providing cloud infrastructure at a variety of classification levels and with **Authority to Operate (ATO)** DoD programs.
- **DSOP**, the DoD enterprise DevSecOps initiative that provides guidance and support to programs across the DoD.

The implementation of software factories has resulted in a more nimble and cost-effective air force.

## Public safety

Public safety encompasses a variety of public services, including police and fire services, courts, jails, and prisons, as well as ambulance and emergency dispatch services. This vertical also includes technologies deployed in government facilities and public spaces to ensure the safety of government employees and the public.

## Temperature and crowd detection

As the world reopened after the unprecedented shelter-in-place orders associated with the COVID-19 pandemic, public health officials around the world recommended checking the temperatures of individuals entering public spaces to reduce the risk of infected individuals coming into close proximity with others and spreading the virus. While most organizations started with manual temperature sensing, it quickly became clear that manual temperature checks would be impractical. Not only would an individual need to be present at every entry to check temperatures, but those individuals would become bottlenecks at peak traffic times. In addition, conflicts soon developed with people refusing to have their temperatures checked.

In addition to checking temperatures, officials responsible for public buildings and spaces needed ways to monitor that spaces were not overcrowded and that individuals were complying with requirements to wear masks.

While the need for temperature monitoring in public spaces was new to much of the world, it was not new to governments in Asia that had used remote temperature monitoring technology during the SARS, H5N1, and MERS outbreaks. To meet the need to track temperatures, ensure that spaces were not overcrowded, and monitor mask compliance, vendors deployed new and updated versions of thermal imaging solutions used during earlier health emergencies. Since many airports in Asia had deployed these solutions in the past, it is not surprising that during the COVID-19 pandemic, solutions were first deployed in China and other parts of Asia, followed by airports around the world, including airports in the US. As of the time of writing, hundreds of jurisdictions in the US are evaluating thermal monitoring solutions as part of their plans to reopen government offices and restore services. *Figure 6.1* illustrates the components and operation of a thermographic imaging solution:

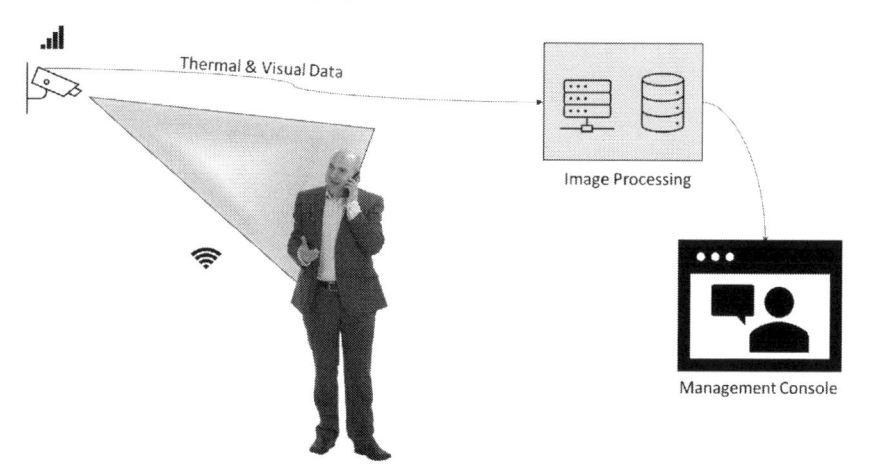

Figure 6.1 – Remote temperature monitoring

When a thermal monitoring solution is installed in a location, individuals who pass by within range of the camera have their temperature checked unobtrusively by the camera. Individuals can pass by the camera at normal speed and in groups. There is no need to stop or to pass by the cameras one by one. Any individual who has an unusually high temperature is flagged. An image of that individual is provided to a human operator to take action appropriate for the location and policies in place.

Temperature sensing is accomplished with thermographic cameras that focus on specific points on the human face. Specific locations on the face are selected to increase accuracy and reduce false positives or negatives. Cameras recalibrate automatically every few minutes to account for the ambient temperature outdoors and reduce false positives for people entering the building from outside. Cameras deliver temperature data and images over cellular or Wi-Fi to a server that uses AI to process the temperature data. Where solutions are local and attended, such as monitored building entrances, the operator is notified on-screen when an individual appears to have a higher-than-normal temperature. For centralized solutions that monitor many cameras, an operator can be notified by SMS, which can include the image of the individual.

AI-enabled facial recognition can be applied to identify whether all individuals in a space are wearing masks. If individuals are not adhering to requirements for mask use, the system can alert an operator, who will then follow their organization's processes to resolve the situation. One or more cameras can be used to provide full coverage of large spaces, such as meeting rooms and transit platforms. When crowds form that do not allow appropriate distance between individuals, the system will notify an operator to take action to reduce the density of people in the space.

## Healthcare

While a great deal of healthcare is delivered by the private sector, a significant portion of the population is served by public hospitals run by states, counties, and the federal government. In addition, the public sector is responsible for delivering public health services, also known as population health services, a mandate that has been pulled into the public limelight by the COVID-19 crisis.

Healthcare delivery and support services, especially in hospitals, are increasingly performed with the assistance of digital technologies. Complex surgeries are now assisted by robotics, while patients are monitored by a wide array of internet-connected devices, including everything from EKGs to thermometers. Within hospitals, robots are used to free up pharmacists and reduce errors by dispensing medications from hospital stock automatically when a physician enters a request in a patient's electronic medical record. Modern medical care has been transformed by the **Internet of Things (IoT)** delivering a myriad of data to medical providers as part of electronic medical records that can then be shared with providers around the world to ensure continuity of care. Based on the size of the global healthcare industry, there is a lot of room for digital transformation in this sector.

## Telemedicine

While IoT provides powerful capabilities to medical providers in doctors' offices, hospitals, and extended care facilities, the true power of IoT becomes apparent in telehealth applications. The most basic application of telehealth is to provide virtual doctor visits, including specialist consultations. *Figure 6.2* provides a conceptual diagram of telehealth in use. While telehealth visits were first used to treat rural areas without sufficient primary care doctors or to provide access to specialists unavailable in the local area, the use of telehealth spiked during the COVID-19 pandemic, when it was used to reduce the risk to both healthy patients and those with underlying medical conditions by limiting their visits to providers. Telemedicine was also used to treat COVID-19 patients with mild symptoms, as shown in this video from the Israeli health service: `https://www.youtube.com/watch?v=MkpO5CIk6i8`:

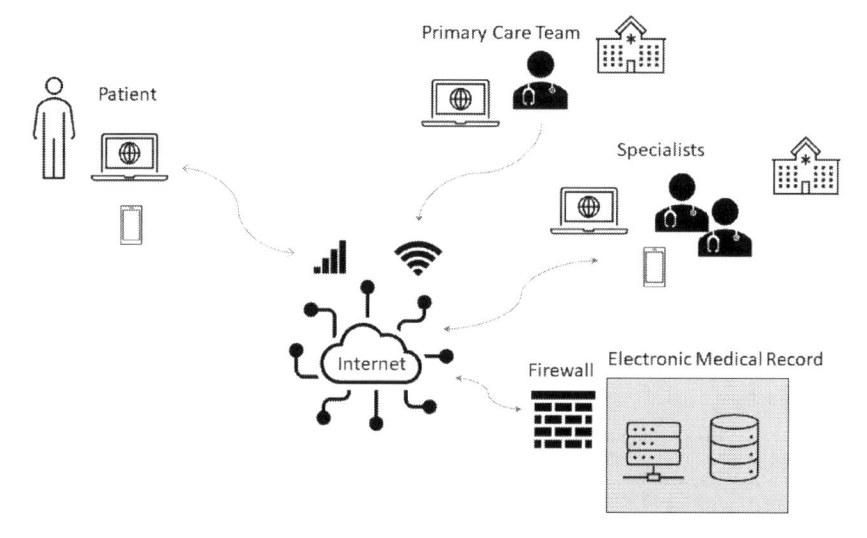

Figure 6.2 – The ecosystem of a telemedicine visit

A remote patient visit requires only that the patient has access to a telephone or computer with a camera and to broadband internet. Patients engage in video visits with their primary care team, including physicians, nurses, nurse practitioners, and physician assistants, and with specialists as needed. The care team can write prescriptions, order tests, and update the patient's medical record all remotely. The care team is also able to view test results and engage in follow-up activities, all without the patient entering their office.

Virtual care team visits are augmented by the explosion of IoT devices that can be used to monitor patient health and compliance without the patient returning to a doctor's office or hospital:

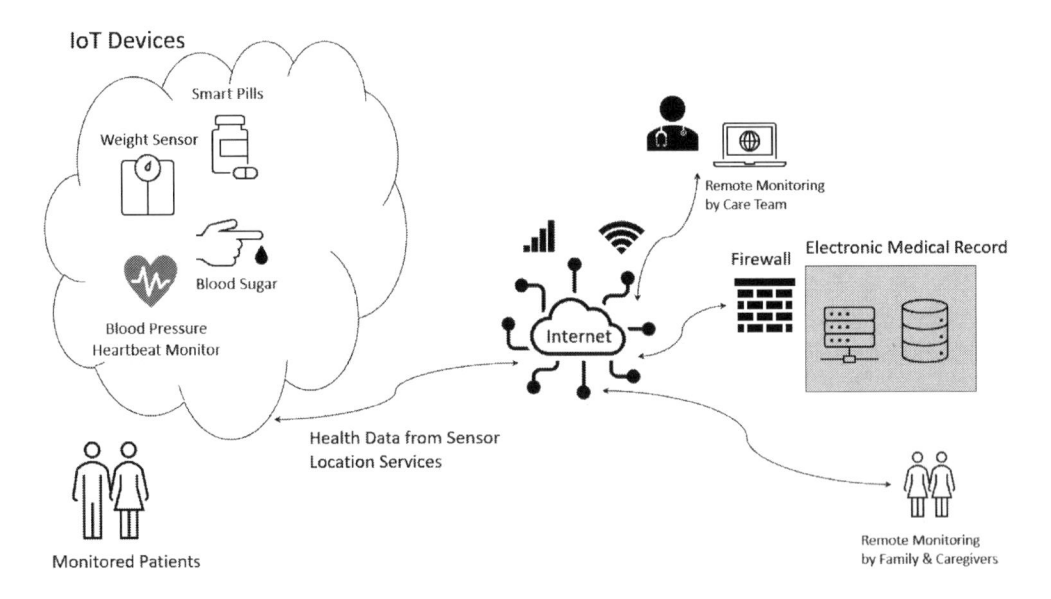

Figure 6.3 – IoT enables healthcare

IoT has endless applications for home healthcare and monitoring. The health of patients being treated for cancer is monitored at home by Bluetooth-enabled scales and blood pressure cuffs. Smart insulin pens track the time and dosage of insulin delivered to a patient, along with their blood sugar, and recommend the time and amount of their next dose. Emerging medical technologies include ingestible sensors that are included in pills to track medication compliance and contact lenses that measure blood glucose levels. *Figure 6.3* shows how IoT devices enable remote medical care by enabling both the healthcare team and family members to track the health of patients with chronic conditions. These capabilities both improve outcomes and reduce the cost of chronic care by ensuring that emerging issues are identified earlier, allowing intervention before issues become serious.

## Social services

Governments provide a social safety net through a variety of public services that include unemployment assistance, food assistance, protection for children and elders, and assistance to help move people from homelessness into permanent housing. The modernization of social services has been as simple as replacing paper coupons with debit cards to deliver food assistance and as complex as aggregating data across medical fields, social services, and law enforcement to find individuals at risk of slipping through the social safety net.

## homelessness

According to the US Department of Housing and Urban Development, after declining from 2007 to 2016, the number of homeless individuals started rising in 2017. As of early 2020, over 600,000 people are homeless in the US. The situation is especially acute in expensive coastal cities. Digital tools are crucial in the fight against homelessness.

California's approaches range from requiring developers to provide below-market-rate housing to directing funding toward building new homes specifically to house the homeless. In order to enable those policy initiatives, California needs data. Local communities provide an array of services to the homeless and track each member of the homeless population in their community to ensure that those individuals receive the right services. Services are provided by an array of community organizations organized into a **Continuum of Care** (**CoC**) for each county.

Each CoC collects a great deal of information about the individuals they serve. Historically, that data has remained at the local level within each county. This becomes a problem when individuals move between counties, impacting their continuity of services as well as the census of homeless individuals in the state. The state is currently developing a solution that will aggregate data across the state and then use master data management to deduplicate the data and ensure that each individual has a full case history available in any county where they need services. This solution utilizes a wide array of transformative digital technologies beyond simply big data, including data visualizations to drive insights and **Geographic Information System** (**GIS**) analytics to locate homeless populations.

Analytics tools allow local agencies to understand more about both individuals and the homeless community as a whole. Access to good data allows caseworkers to make data-driven decisions to help those they support. In San Francisco, case workers are able to access homelessness data via a mobile app and then perform assessments and connect the homeless with resources on the spot.

Other innovative projects underway include a joint project between UCLA and Los Angeles to use predictive analytics to identify individuals who are at risk of falling into homelessness in the near term. Once identified, local service agencies could provide cash assistance and wrap-around services to help individuals and families stay in their homes. A similar project is underway in New York as a collaboration between NYU's Center for Urban Science and Progress and the Women in Need foundation.

## Transportation

Governments have a broad transportation mandate, from ensuring the safety of air, train, and road travel to providing roads and managing traffic flow to reduce congestion. The government provides the critical infrastructure that allows people to move freely, safely, and efficiently.

Technology has been used on our roadways for many years. The most common use of technology has been radar, to identify the speed of individual cars and ticket those individuals who exceed the speed limit. More recently, red-light cameras have been added to the traffic enforcement arsenal. Red-light cameras automatically take a picture of the license plate and the driver of vehicles that pass through red lights and automatically send a ticket if the image of the driver matches the registered owner of the vehicle. These technologies probably do more to frustrate drivers than to improve their experience, regardless of their impact on road safety. There are, however, uses of technology in transportation that improve our experience on the roads, even though we are likely unaware that the technologies exist.

### Traffic management

As our roads become more crowded, the imperative to move people more efficiently has come to the forefront. While trip reduction, carpooling, and public transit help reduce congestion on our roads, technology is also a critical component to keeping us moving. Technology is used throughout our road network to manage congestion, ensure that lights are optimally timed, and predict traffic jams.

Santa Clara County, located in the heart of Silicon Valley, has a population of nearly 2 million residents and swells daily with commuters from out of the county and travelers from out of the area, resulting in substantial traffic congestion. Thankfully, the county of Santa Clara combats this congestion with one of the most sophisticated traffic management systems in the country.

While the county government is only responsible for managing traffic on roads in unincorporated areas and seven expressways that cross the county, the expressways are critical to the smooth operation of roads across the county. High levels of congestion on the expressways would ripple across the county, eventually resulting in gridlock. To combat this ever-looming crisis, the county of Santa Clara has deployed hundreds of cameras and sensors on expressways across the county. The data provided by these IoT devices is routed to the county's traffic management center and then to a cloud-hosted data analytics solution, where it is analyzed. The resulting information is used to adjust the timing of 130 traffic signals across the county.

Traditionally, traffic signals have been preprogrammed with a handful of time-of-day and day-of-week programs. While the program at 9 AM on Monday morning was different than the program at 4 PM on Saturday afternoon, it was the same every Monday morning and every Saturday afternoon. It did not account for daily events, such as traffic accidents, heavy rain, or even slow-moving pedestrians. Smart road networks have changed that paradigm.

Using the information provided by the cameras and sensors, signal coordination plans are automatically adjusted to optimize traffic flows based on current conditions. Signal coordination plans are adjusted in real time as needed, up to every cycle of a light. In addition, special sensors are embedded in roadways that can identify when bicycles are at an intersection. When the sensors recognize a bicycle, signal timing is adjusted to ensure the bicyclist has adequate time to cross the intersection. Similarly, rather than placing a set timer on crosswalks, microwave sensors track pedestrians in the crosswalk, and, using edge computing to reduce lag time, can extend the time before a traffic light changes, to ensure that the pedestrian safely reaches the other side of the road.

The Santa Clara traffic management system also employs edge computing to predict traffic 15 minutes into the future. The predictive data is published to the county's website, allowing residents to check traffic and adjust their departure time earlier or later to avoid heavy traffic.

## Resident services

The vast majority of the residents of any state, county, or city have very limited interactions with their government and are generally unaware of when they are using government services. They pay taxes, drive on roads, visit parks, and apply for permits. While they appreciate that the police or fire department exists, they may go years without interacting with them. As we discussed earlier in this chapter, these residents want their experiences with the government to be just as simple and technology-enabled as their experiences working with private sector companies. State and local governments are meeting these requests with services designed to make government transactions easier and internet-enabled.

## Non-emergency reporting (311) applications

In many municipalities, 311 is the number that members of the public can call to report non-emergency issues, such as potholes, street-light outages, illegal dumping of waste material, and graffiti. These were designed to be one-stop solutions. Unfortunately, this is often a frustrating experience, as individuals are frequently told they have called the wrong jurisdiction and are offered little or no help finding the right one. Many jurisdictions are replacing or augmenting call centers with mobile applications designed to streamline the experience of interacting with the local municipality. Many reporting applications are built on *open 311* or commercial platforms that have open APIs and can integrate and exchange data with nearby municipalities:

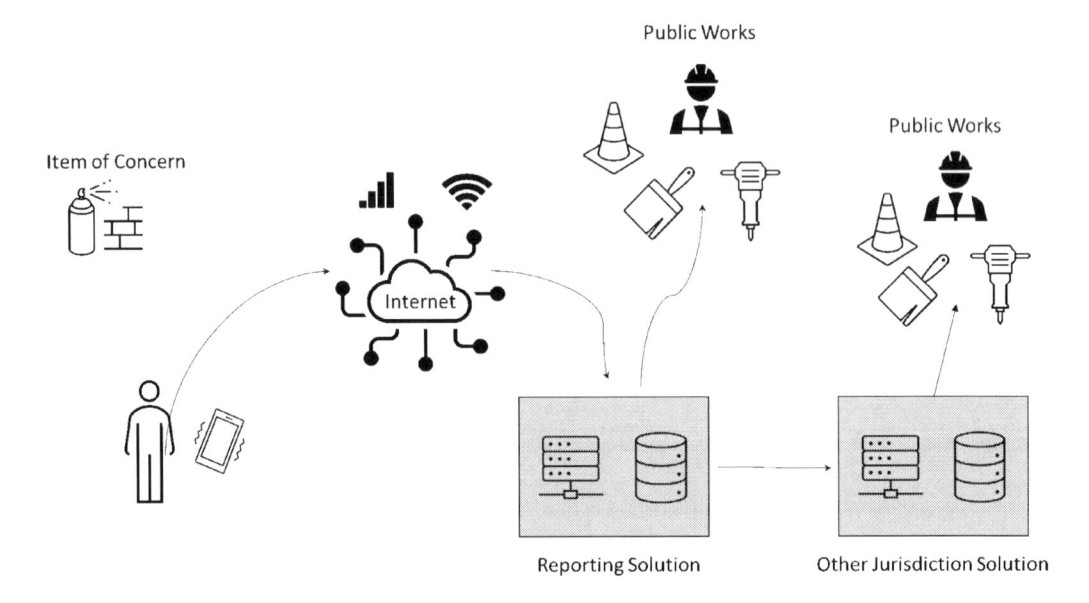

Figure 6.4 – 311 applications

In *Figure 6.4*, we see a municipal reporting application in action. A resident of the community finds evidence of graffiti and uses the reporting application installed on their phone to contact their city or county and report the graffiti. If the graffiti is within the jurisdiction that received the request, it is automatically routed to the public works department for cleanup. If the address is in a different jurisdiction, the request is routed to that jurisdiction. If the two jurisdictions have compatible solutions, the message is sent directly to their solution. If not, most reporting solutions will automatically generate an email with the request to be sent to an appropriate contact in the jurisdiction where the problem lies. Most jurisdictions will also update the requester on the status of their request in the app.

## Online permitting and remote inspections

Historically, the process of obtaining a building permit has required that the person requesting the permit appear in person at a city, county, or sometimes state office to file paperwork and pay fees. They must then return later with their plan documents for those plans to be inspected. Frequently, an appointment is required, which may not be available for several days or weeks. Once the plans have been reviewed, changes are usually requested. After the changes have been made, yet another trip to the permitting office will be required for review and, hopefully, final approval. For complex projects, the visit to the permit office may be repeated several times before the permit is issued.

Online permitting completely revamps the permit process by eliminating all trips to the permitting office. When a member of the public wants to apply for a permit, they fill out the permit application and pay the fees online. When the plans are ready, they are submitted to the permitting agency electronically. Once the plans have been received at the permitting office, they are routed internally. Unlike paper plans, multiple individuals can review the plans at the same time. Feedback can be sent to the requester incrementally as individual specialists complete their permit reviews. Updates are returned electronically, and the permit can be issued electronically with a paper copy mailed to the requester if it is required.

As a result of this completely online process, many hours of time and a great deal of expense are saved by requesters. In addition, permitting agencies do not have to maintain paper files of building plans or digitize plans as they are submitted, saving time, money, and space and reducing the instances of lost or misplaced plans to zero.

Municipalities are also transforming their inspection processes. To reduce the risk of inspectors being injured, a few agencies have implemented drone inspection of roofs and other features located high up on buildings. *Figure 6.5* demonstrates a drone inspection:

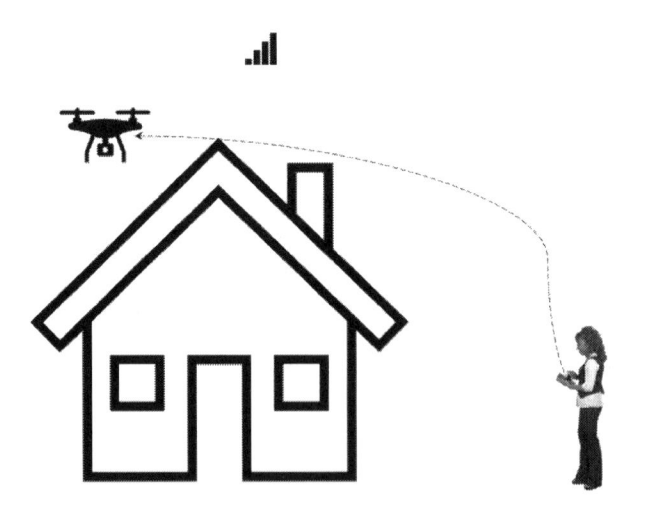

Figure 6.5 – Drone inspection

The drones can be manually flown by the inspector or follow a pre-determined route programmed based on the building plans. Drones transmit live images of the roof or other features to the inspector's computer or tablet over the cellular network. The inspector can review the footage live and save the footage for later review.

During the COVID-19 outbreak, building inspectors began conducting completely remote inspections. Using a video chat or teleconferencing application, inspectors direct contractors, or homeowners to the location that requires inspection. The contractor or homeowner shows the location to the inspector and takes pictures as requested by the building inspector. Once the inspection has been completed, the inspector reports their findings and requests changes or signs off on a successful inspection. After any corrections have been made, the reinspection is completed the same way and the certificate of occupancy is issued.

## Education

Since the advent of the internet, digital technologies have been disrupting the educational experience. Much like the implementation of technology throughout business and government, educational technology has transformed education in phases of increasing value and disruption. The term for this spectrum of change in education is the **SAMR** model, with the initials representing **Substitution, Augmentation, Modification, and Redefinition**. *Figure 6.6* describes each of the stages of the SAMR model:

| Stage | Description | Examples |
| --- | --- | --- |
| Substitution | Replaces activities performed by hand with activities performed using a device. The method of teaching is not functionally changed. | Using word processors to type assignments or writing on an overhead projector slide instead of a blackboard. |
| Augmentation | The addition of technology enhances the learning experience. | Using advanced features of a word processor, such as cut and paste, spell check, or graphics, or enhancing presentations with graphics and other advanced features. |
| Modification | Teaching tasks are partially or entirely redesigned. | Flipped classrooms where students watch recorded lectures at home and work on assignments in the classroom |
| Redefinition | Technology creates brand new methods of instruction that were not possible without technology. | Classrooms connected via video conference to other classrooms around the world to complete lessons that require engagement or collaboration between classrooms. |

Figure 6.6 – The SAMR model

The goal of digital transformation in education is to bring as much value as possible, which means traveling up the value chain from substitution all the way to redefinition. During the rest of this section on education, we will use examples to discuss the disruption created by online learning and how online learning can exist at each level of the transformation value chain.

## Online learning

Distance learning has been a popular concept in education for decades, if not centuries. The earliest form of distance learning was the correspondence course, where, as the name suggests, students corresponded with their teachers via postal mail, and the only technology involved may have been the mail delivery method, or more recently, a word processor. Later, courses were sent to students via videocassette or broadcast over closed-circuit television. It has only been in the last several years that online education as we know it today, with students and teachers sharing a virtual classroom, has come into existence.

While the last several years have seen a significant expansion of online learning, the COVID-19 pandemic resulted in the closure of campuses around the world, both in K-12 and higher education, forcing virtually all education online overnight. The most basic form of online learning, the *substitution* of a virtual experience, makes heavy use of transformative technologies, including virtual meeting spaces and online learning management systems where students collect assignments and turn in work. In many schools, however, online learning provides features that *augment* the classroom experience, adding social media-like features, such as virtual office hours, threaded discussions, and group chats, as well as online tests and quizzes and automated plagiarism-checking and assignment-scoring.

When teachers go beyond augmentation to *modification*, they apply the online tools to fundamentally change the way they teach. Teachers may flip their classrooms, preparing lectures for students to review in advance of class and using class time to work through problems, as well as breaking students into small groups in online breakout rooms so that they can collaborate.

Finally, reaching the level of *redefinition*, online learning is used to implement personalized learning. Guided by a machine learning algorithm with support from the classroom teacher, each student is provided customized educational experiences based on their subject matter mastery, learning styles, and interests. While teachers monitor progress, meet with students, and modify assignments to ensure that the learning experience is appropriate, the incorporation of machine learning allows far more customization than an individual teacher could provide for a classroom full of students.

The recent shift of nearly every classroom in the world online will profoundly impact teaching and learning over the next decade, even after students return to the physical classroom, as many teachers will continue to use the technologies they have embraced during the pandemic. Unfortunately, the shift to online learning has highlighted the *digital divide* between those who have access to broadband internet and those who do not have access to broadband internet. To ensure that the online education experience is shared equally by all students, school districts, cities, counties, and states are working to provide internet access to all students, regardless of income or location.

Typical solutions implemented to increase access include providing internet access in public buildings, such as schools, libraries, and community centers. As discussed earlier in this chapter, during the pandemic, this delivery method was challenged. Districts and municipalities began pushing their wireless signals into parking lots and parks, and parking Wi-Fi-equipped buses in low-income or low-access neighborhoods. None of these public Wi-Fi solutions are adequate to create an equitable experience for all students. One of the continued challenges that we face is extending broadband internet access to rural areas and delivering access to low-income families. The US government has solved similar problems by recognizing them as essential and subsidizing the expansion and delivery of the service. However, as of the time of writing, the problem remains unresolved.

## Environmental protection

The government is charged with the stewardship of the environment, including the development and enforcement of regulations and cleanup of the environment when it is damaged to ensure that we are all able to enjoy clean air, land, and water. In the US, protection of the environment is shared by the states, local government, tribes, and the federal government in a structure referred to as **cooperative federalism**. As with the other verticals we have discussed, the field of environmental protection is broad and the examples that we explore will only cover a fraction of the possible applications of technology to improve our natural environment and health.

### Story maps

Environmental data is fundamentally place-based. Environmental impacts happen in specific locations over a long or short period of time. Understanding the impact of specific events at specific locations is crucial to our ability to respond to disasters, keep the public safe, and remediate contamination. Story maps are a powerful tool for understanding and communicating environmental impacts and coordinating action.

Story maps rely on GIS data combined with existing maps and charts, data analytics, narrative text, images, and multimedia content to convey information about the status of a location in an easily understandable way. While we are discussing story maps in the context of environmental protection, GIS data can be leveraged to share powerful information about any dataset that is place-based.

Some examples of the use of story maps to communication environmental status include the following:

- Lead in drinking water is a well-known and serious problem in the US. The US **Environmental Protection Agency (EPA)** created an interactive story map to allow individuals to learn about projects to educate the public, reduce risks, and eliminate lead service lines across the country: `https://epa.maps.arcgis.com/apps/Cascade/index.html?appid=989f006a15f14256ad8bdfd837016453`.
- The US EPA has published a national map of **Per- and Polyfluoroalkyl Substances (PFAS)** contamination. PFAS is a chemical used in Teflon and other products. It doesn't break down naturally and is known to accumulate in the human body and result in adverse outcomes. Consequently, the EPA has been tracking contaminated sites and has shared a map here: `https://www.ewg.org/interactive-maps/pfas_contamination/map/`.
- Camp Minden is a site in northwest Louisiana that was used for explosives recycling. After an explosion, the owners of the site filed for bankruptcy and abandoned the site. The Louisiana national guard took ownership of the site and collaborated with the US EPA to track air quality around the site to ensure public safety. They also took on the disposal of the waste. The EPA regional office created a story map to communicate the status of the cleanup and the environmental impacts on the community: `https://www.epa.gov/la/camp-minden-explo-story-map`.

The EPA uses other tools to communicate the state of the environment to the public, including the highly visible Village Green project.

### The Village Green project and beyond

In 2013, the US EPA kicked off a project to create a public demonstration of the ability of air quality sensors to monitor common pollutants in real time and inform the community through live updates on the web and through a mobile app. As you can see from *Figure 6.7*, the Village Green was intentionally a large structure. Sensors were mounted in a weather-tight locked box behind the park bench and the entire solution was powered by solar panels mounted on top. While the solution was too large and expensive for broad deployment, it provided a proof of concept and, through its visibility, a source of discussion and education for the community. A total of 10 Village Green installations were placed in cities across the US and at the US embassy in Beijing, China:

Figure 6.7 – Village Green in Durham, NC. Photo by the author

The Village Green contained sensors that measured PM2.5., which is particulate matter with a diameter of less than 2.5 micrometers, ozone, black carbon, nitrogen dioxide, volatile organic compounds, wind speed, temperature, and humidity. The sensors took measurements every minute. The data was analyzed by a computer located on the bench and transmitted over the cellular network to EPA servers, analyzed for anomalies, and then made available on the EPA or local partners' websites and mobile apps. The EPA open sourced the Village Green design so that members of the public can build their own Village Green.

> **Important note**
> If you would like to build your own Village Green air quality monitoring station, the EPA has provided full instructions to design, operate, and maintain your station at `https://cfpub.epa.gov/si/si_public_record_report.cfm?Lab=NRMRL&dirEntryId=340116`, along with an hour-long training video at `https://www.youtube.com/watch?v=iF7Cr33S0zM&feature=youtu.be`.

This proof of concept has evolved into environmental monitoring via low-cost sensors that can be attached to a cell phone or deployed into the environment on the ground or in a body of water. Government entities around the world use low-cost air and water quality sensors, often in locations that would be difficult to reach to perform manual monitoring, to track environmental conditions. Sensor data is processed, and members of the public are automatically advised of hazardous conditions.

## Utilities

Utility companies are adopting new tools and solutions of digital transformation and progressing toward a data-driven future. The use of transformational technology in utilities can be seen in the generation, transmission, and distribution of energy. In addition, the electric meters that are on consumers' premises are also becoming more intelligent.

## Smart metering

Smart meters and communication networks that enable two-way communication between a utility company and the consumer are an important part of this transformation. The best-understood business driver for smart metering is accurate billing and saving labor costs of performing physical meter readings. Smart meters can give customers much better visibility into their use of electricity, resulting in lower usage.

The electric utility market is changing, with a large increase in consumers buying electric vehicles and networked smart appliances. These customers want the ability to connect their electric vehicles to the grid, and remotely control their smart appliances. With a greater number of such devices and the progressive maturing of these technologies, the shapes of both the demand and load curves for utility companies are going to change dramatically. Adding to the mix **Variable Renewable Energy** (**VRE**) sources (rooftop solar system) and utility business model changes will accelerate a need for more detailed real-time measurement electricity usage. These requirements have driven the development of smart meters and **Advanced Metering Infrastructure** (**AMI**).

## Italy – Enel Distribuzione

Two decades ago, during the process of the liberalization of the energy market, Italy's largest utility company Enel decided to make fundamental changes in their business, which resulted in transformation of electricity market in Europe. Enel took these market dynamic changes as an opportunity to make fundamental changes to their energy distribution system, business processes, and customer relationship management. One of the fundamental changes that Enel made was the introduction of smart metering, called a *telegestore* system. The major components of the *telegestore* system are a smart meter, a gateway with a modem and concentrator installed in every secondary substation, and a central system that gathers and manages data and communication with gateways.

Between 2001 and 2006, Enel installed 33 million smart meters for 100% of its customers in Italy. In 2004, nearly 8 million smart meters were installed. Enel completed the *telegestore* project at a cost of $2.6 billion in 2006 with the installation of 33 million smart meters for Italian households and businesses. Nearly two decades later, with 33 million of these smart meters in operation, the *telegestore* system is still the largest smart meter installation in Europe. The project's success has triggered the movement toward the development of smart meters, and this system serves as a valuable prototype for other utilities that are trying to develop and deploy smart metering solutions. This system is approaching its end of life, since the engineering components in this system are now almost 20 years old.

Since 2017, Enel has been transitioning to the second generation of smart meter called Open Meter. *Figure 6.8* shows an architecture diagram for Open Meter, which provides additional new features, such as smart home energy management and dynamic tariff optimization:

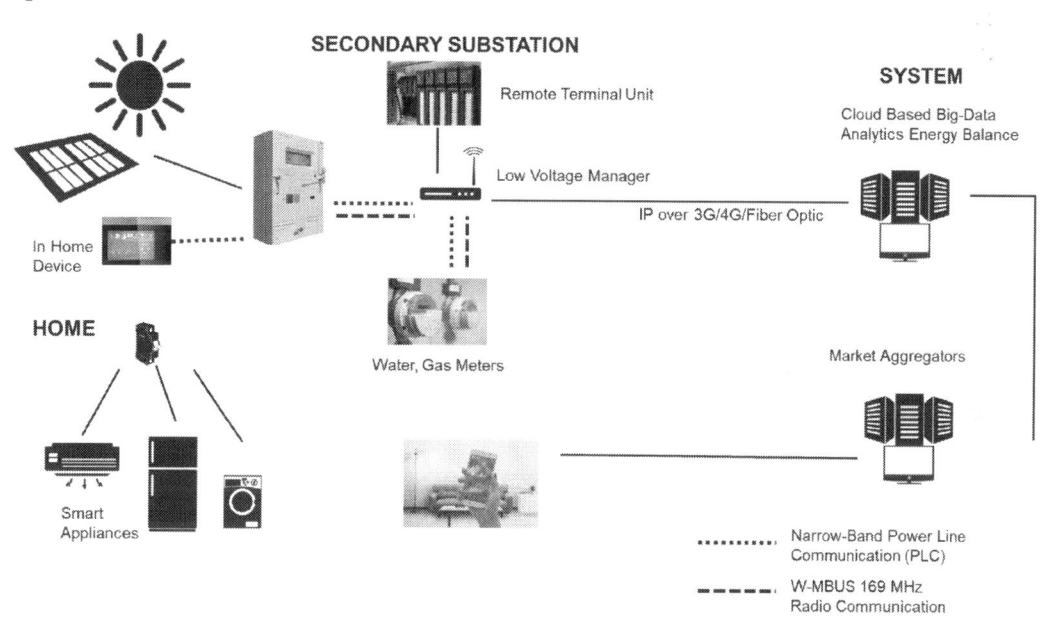

Figure 6.8 – Open Meter architecture

The new smart meter also has the functionality to continuously monitor grid **Quality of Service** (**QoS**) and detect network faults in real time. These meters have two communication paths, including power line communication and **Radio Frequency** (**RF**) in order to meet regulatory network security requirements. As per IoT Analytics, 141 million smart meters were shipped worldwide in 2019. The **Compound Annual Growth Rate** (**CAGR**) for this market is 7%.

The Enel case study of smart meters shows the scale that is required for industrial digital transformation when we talk about the whole country. In the next section, we will look at some national and global-scale digital transformation scenarios.

## Smart cities – Lake Nona, Florida

Successful smart city development depends on multiple factors, such as capital investment, technology expertise to deploy solutions that match different requirements, and municipal involvement with the community to achieve the goal of providing smart services and generating return on investment. The Lake Nona community, located 10 miles from Orlando International Airport in Florida, is a 17 square mile smart city development enabled through public-private partnerships. This development has a 650-acre health and life sciences business park, a sports training and performance district, smart homes, and smart office buildings that have high-speed ubiquitous connectivity. This community also has business incubators and accelerator programs.

The medical city constituents of this community include the following:

- The **University of Central Florida** (**UCF**) health sciences campus
- The University of Central Florida College of Medicine
- Nemours Children's Hospital
- The University of Florida Research and Academic Center
- Orlando VA Hospital and SimLEARN Center
- The Sanford Burnham Medical Discovery Institute

It also has the following sports training facilities:

- US Tennis Association National Campus (which is the largest tennis campus in the world)
- Johnson & Johnson's Human Performance Institute
- Orlando City Lions major league soccer training facilities

Private-public partnerships were developed between the University of Central Florida, the city of Orlando, developer Tavistock Group, and several technology companies mentioned in the next section. Let's now look at how digital technology is involved here.

## Digital connectivity

A key aspect of infrastructure design for this smart city development includes wireless and fiber optics networks that enable 1 Gbps digital connectivity to communicate across the entire population of the community, including the medical city, retail enterprises, and residents. Partnership with technology companies that have communication networks as their core business was a major reason for a successful deployment of network connectivity, including wireless and fiber optics networks to medical facilities, homes, offices, and schools. The connectivity technology partners include Cisco, all major cellphone carriers, GE, Corning, and Summit Broadband.

This infrastructure allows a wide array of network-connected sensors that enable smart services, such as the following:

- An app that alerts users about available parking spaces near retail establishments in the community
- Control of streetlights based on the presence of pedestrians in the area
- Health and wellness apps driven by sensors in smart homes

The networking infrastructure consists of the fiber optic infrastructure, cell towers, a **Distributed Antenna System** (**DAS**), a communications head end for four major carriers, and the cable video services transmission center. Cellular connection points are distributed in various buildings across the community for high QoS for cellular and Wi-Fi solutions. All major carriers use common connectivity infrastructure.

In Lake Nona, Verizon is testing solutions enabled by 5G wireless technology for a variety of applications, such as healthcare, public safety, and connected responsive retail experiences.

## Smart homes

Smart homes in this community have 1-gigabit connectivity to enable a wellness platform. This platform and associated apps allow the management of a variety of functions, including home security and the monitoring of health-related parameters, such as sleep, nutrition, and senior care. The starting point for this wellness platform is data generated by a connected sensor and IoT technology solutions in the home.

Most of the residents of the community are participating in a long-term initiative being conducted by Johnson & Johnson and Nemours to study comprehensive health habits and wellness issues. IoT solutions in these smart homes help to study a wide range of health-related parameters, such as physical activity and the variations in weight and blood pressure.

These smart homes are designed using the **Wellness Home Built-On Innovation and Technology** (**WHIT**) initiative. A high-level view of such a home is shown in *Figure 6.9*. More details are available at www.MeetWHIT.com:

Figure 6.9 – Connected Smart Home

Using IoT solutions enabled by distributed sensors, these homes are designed to serve as living spaces that also become tools for health monitoring and improvement.

Different aspects of health that can be monitored by WHIT include the following:

- Human activity and performance
- Sleep quality and quantity
- Chronic conditions
- Nutrition
- Relaxation

This smart home allows the possibility of securely sharing individual health parameters, which are tracked by various IoT solutions, directly with physicians. The availability of real-time data and feedback from physicians can enable actionable information for residents. Data available from the wellness platform can drive a health dashboard at home and the respective apps on the user's mobile devices. Actionable information and recommendations on physical activity, sleep quality and quality management, stress management, and nutrition can contribute to the improvement of health.

One important aspect of the WHIT wellness platform is that it allows testing new technologies and solutions and evaluating their health outcomes in an established community. Such capabilities in the wellness platform can help in creating new innovations to support aging in place.

### Smart buildings

Commercial buildings in the Lake Nona community are served by a fiber optic ring network. Capacity management for cellular connectivity, wireless coverage, and cable service is an important feature of reliable QoS for diverse applications in the medical city, sports training district, and retail establishments. All buildings are equipped with network-connected sensors to monitor energy usage, lighting conditions, air quality, and human presence. Building automation systems and HVAC systems in these buildings optimize energy consumption while maintaining the human comfort index in the indoor environment.

### Autonomous shuttle

The Lake Nona community is deploying an autonomous shuttle service with a fleet of 10 passenger capacity electric vehicles from Navya to provide first/last mile of transportation. These electric shuttles are equipped with a LiDAR sensor, cameras, a GNSS system, and vehicle odometry sensors for maintaining the precise positioning of the vehicles and constant awareness of their environment. A digital road network map of the community is used by vehicle positioning and route planning software for location awareness on the route in order to navigate effectively through different conditions.

In this section, we looked at a variety of ways that digital transformation is improving the everyday experience of residents of communities across the US. In the next section, we will discuss transformation efforts on a national and global scale.

# Transformation on a national and global scale

Often, organizations start a pilot to test out a transformative idea. One such pilot was done in Barcelona, Spain, where environmental sensors recorded the noise and the pollution levels in residents' homes. The data was encrypted and shared anonymously with the communities in Barcelona. This data helped influence city-level decisions. As part of this pilot, the technical issues related to gathering, storing, and controlling the stream of sensor information were resolved. This was under the **Decentralized Citizen-Owned Data Ecosystems (DECODE)** initiative (see `https://decodeproject.eu/pilots`). Do all grassroots-level transformative projects and pilots succeed and scale? In this section, we will learn how digital transformation initiatives can be scaled to national and global levels.

# Airports as the first line of health defense

Air travel is a global industry with revenues exceeding $2.7 trillion. Will airports and aircraft become the first line of health screening? Global and domestic air travel can speed up the spread of a pandemic, as seen in the case of COVID-19 in early 2020. Cruises and other forms of travel, such as driving across a border, can also contribute to this rapid spread. Let's focus on air travel here. For a long time, in international airports, customs and immigration authorities have put systems in place to assist the national authorities. These systems help in verifying the nationality and visa credibly of flyers with the use of a passport, in combination with biometrics such as fingerprints and access to any past terrorism or suspected terrorism and money laundering or smuggling type of activities. This problem has been solved to a reasonable degree on a global scale via the cooperation of countries and their customs and border protection agencies.

In the last two decades, globalization and travel have accelerated the spread of epidemics such as SARS (2003), bird flu (2005), swine flu (2009), and the Zika virus (2016). This calls for airports and airlines to become the first line of healthcare defense. Given the proven framework for the verification of nationality and immigration status that exists today, the same can be extended to incorporate the verification for *eligibility to travel* based on health criteria. Apart from immigration-based screening, there is already good infrastructure to check for objectionable goods – for example, the US does not allow raw plants and animal products to prevent the spread of diseases to both humans and plants. In a nutshell, by reusing and extending the existing global infrastructure, we can easily scale the transformation. Many airports already use biometrics data, so those stations can be extended to record accurate temperatures of humans or do other tests that can be done non-invasively. Again, this first line of defense can be used to separate people into *green* and *red* health channels analogous to customs channels that travelers are already familiar with (see *Figure 6.10*). The concept of a health or immunity passport is in the very early stages of discussion by the **World Health Organization** (**WHO**) (see `https://www.who.int/news-room/commentaries/detail/immunity-passports-in-the-context-of-covid-19`). Such an immunity passport will rely on individuals who test for the presence of the antibodies for SARS-CoV-2 to freely travel or return to their workplace. Again, if such an immunity passport goes into effect, it would heavily rely on the processes at airports to check and enforce it. For instance, just like a TSA pre-check in the US, a person with *immunity* could bypass the health screening at an airport:

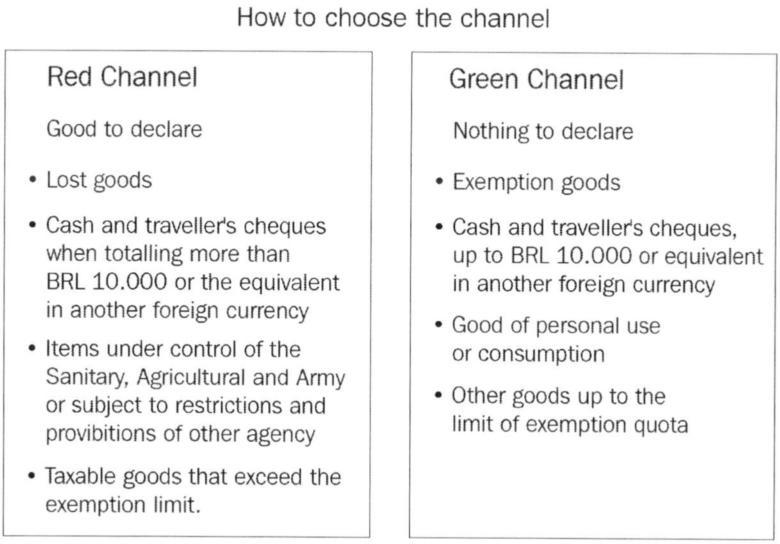

How to choose the channel

| Red Channel | Green Channel |
|---|---|
| Good to declare | Nothing to declare |
| • Lost goods | • Exemption goods |
| • Cash and traveller's cheques when totalling more than BRL 10.000 or the equivalent in another foreign currency | • Cash and traveller's cheques, up to BRL 10.000 or equivalent in another foreign currency |
| • Items under control of the Sanitary, Agricultural and Army or subject to restrictions and provibitions of other agency | • Good of personal use or consumption |
| • Taxable goods that exceed the exemption limit. | • Other goods up to the limit of exemption quota |

Figure 6.10 – Red and green channels

Airports have previously already been screening people at the port of entry whenever there was a threat of the spread of epidemics or infectious diseases. However, often, these are manual efforts that cannot easily scale to large numbers. This is one area of opportunity for technology providers to innovate.

The screening of airline baggage for explosives and other dangerous goods has led to improved technologies that have been deployed on a global scale in the last decade. We need to maximize the reuse and extension of this airport infrastructure to add screenings with the goal of healthcare in mind. While since 2010 the US immigration process does not require screening for **Human Immunodeficiency Virus (HIV)** infection, it was required prior to that (see `https://www.uscis.gov/archive/archive-news/human-immunodeficiency-virus-hiv-infection-removed-cdc-list-communicable-diseases-public-health-significance`). Likewise, when medically required, countries and international ports of entry are likely to be regulated by laws with public health in mind. These laws may change over time, one way or the other, with the advice of epidemiologists and other medical experts.

According to an article by Boston Consulting Group, in 2018, national-level digital transformation initiatives succeeded only when the government took an Agile approach, with the governance of the initiatives that go along with the vision set from the top. At the same time, governmental initiatives need to make sure there is enough engagement on the ground for the transformation to succeed. In other words, too much centralization of power may not help a digital transformation succeed.

## Digital India

To drive digital transformations successfully, government leaders have to provide top-down leadership and inspiration. They need to provide governance models for the success of the transformation initiatives to ensure engagement down to the lowest levels. US president Gerald Ford (1974–77) believed that *the real purpose of government is to enhance the lives of people*. The Digital India plan by the Indian government is one transformation initiative with a vision from the top. Its vision is to empower the transformation of India into a knowledge economy and a digitally empowered society (see *Figure 6.11*). With India having a population of 1.35 billion in 2020, Digital India is a really large-scale digital transformation initiative:

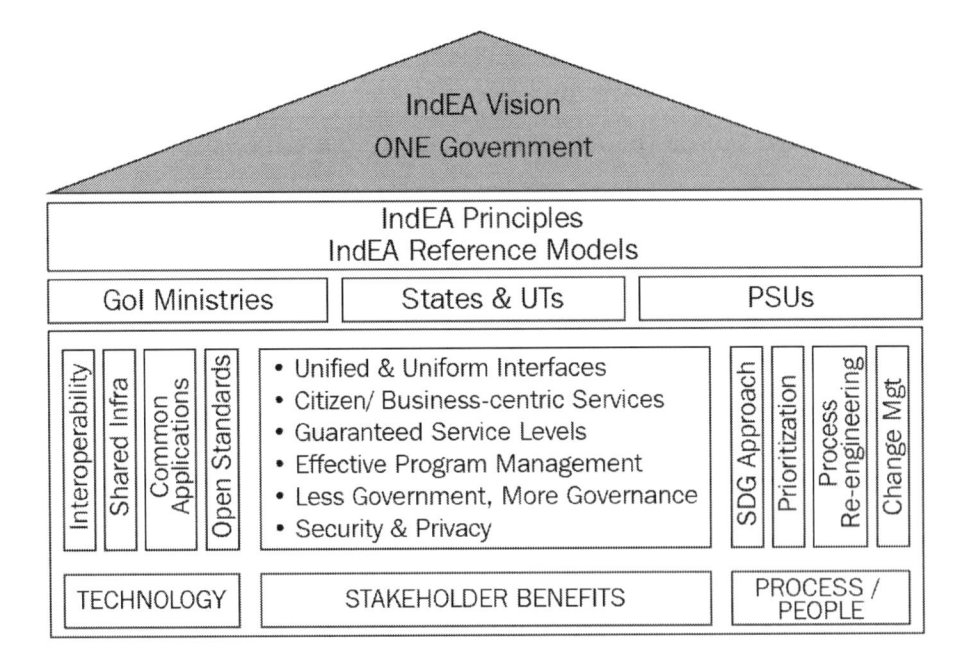

Figure 6.11 – The India Enterprise Architecture vision

The Indian government has also provided a suitable governance mechanism via the four categories of performance measurement:

- **Vision**: Goals, service portfolio and delivery, and resources
- **Citizen**: Benefits, service levels, quality, and accessibility
- **Process**: Individual and organization efficiency, cost effectiveness, management, and innovation
- **Technology**: Information and data, reliability, availability, security, and privacy

The preceding performance reference model provides a balanced governance framework and measures to track the goal of the Digital India transformation initiative. This is the basis of the **Business Reference Model (BRM)** shown in *Figure 6.12*:

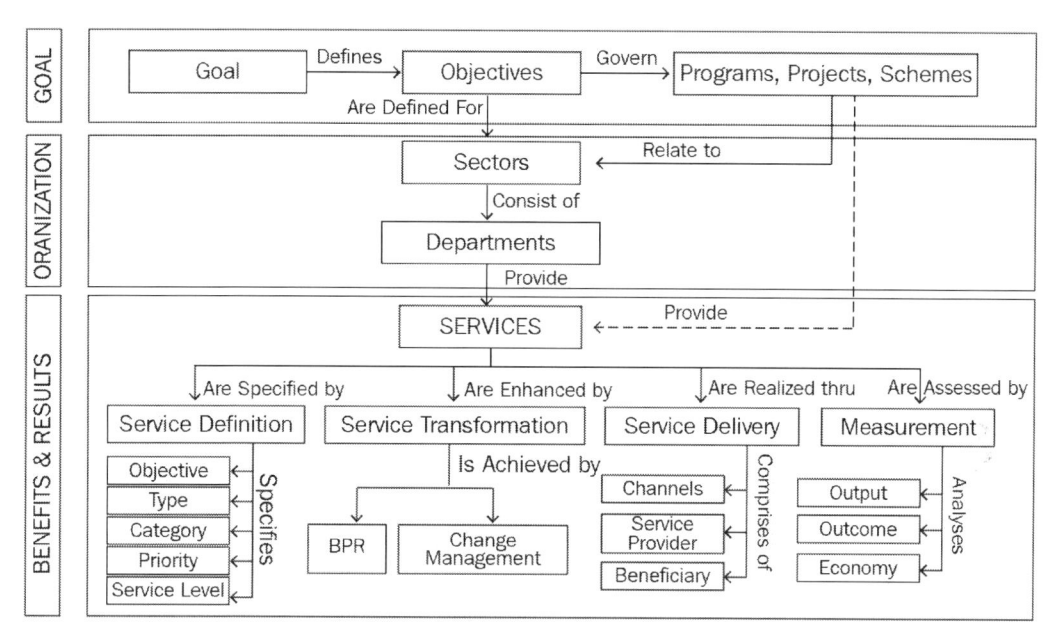

Figure 6.12 – The BRM for Digital India

The BRM defines the business vision required to fulfill the purpose behind the Digital India transformation initiative. It carries the vision down to the objectives as it relates to the sectors and the departments of the government in India. It defines the functions and services for citizens and internal stakeholders. The BRM helps to identify the list of services that apply across the government groups of departments. It then helps to abstract these services to a collection of uniform processes and government workflows. Overall, we can see that the vision from the top with the right set of governing enterprise architecture and business framework can set the right stage to foster engagement from the individual departments. At the same time, it can help to scale the transformation across such a vast country. As of 2019, one of the initial success stories of the Digital India initiative is digital identity (Aadhaar) for over 1.38 billion Indian citizens. Over 200 million new bank accounts were opened to allow the digital transfer of funds (Jan Dhan). There are over 1.2 billion mobile phones in India (Mobile). This initiative is called the **Janadhan-Aadhaar-Mobile (JAM)** initiative and is a big digital transformation as the country aims toward reaching a $5 trillion economy from its current levels of about $3 trillion (see https://www.pmindia.gov.in/en/government_tr_rec/leveraging-the-power-of-jam-jan-dhan-aadhar-and-mobile/).

## Smart cities mission in India

The smart cities mission is another such initiative from the Indian government that started in June 2015 (see `http://smartcities.gov.in/content/`). 100 cities were identified for the initial phase of this smart cities transformation initiative. The main objective is to build a core infrastructure that provides smart solutions to improve the quality of life for its citizens, including a clean and sustainable environment. This top-down program targets a sustainable and replicable smart cities model for the rest of the country. The initial list of 100 cities for this transformative initiative can be found at `http://smartcities.gov.in/content/spvdatanew.php`. An example of a smart solution is e-mobility in Bhopal, India. Under this program, electric vehicles will be introduced for mass transit, in a city with a population of about 1.8 million.

To compare the scale of government initiatives across countries such as India, China, and the US, let's look at these numbers. As of early May 2020, about 110 million Americans received a stimulus check under the $2 trillion **Coronavirus Aid, Relief, and Economic Security (CARES)** Act (see `https://home.treasury.gov/policy-issues/cares`). Likewise, only about the top 10 cities in the US have a population of over 1 million, compared to about 50 such cities in India and 160 cities in China. We can see that the scale can vary vastly by population and the amount of money involved, from initiative to initiative, but is very large compared to most private sector initiatives.

## Smart cities in China

China established its smart cities digital transformation journey when it included it in its 12th 5-year plan, as early as 2011. Subsequently, Chinese cities such as Beijing, Shanghai, Guangzhou, Hangzhou, and a few others have started to transform themselves. The following table goes into the details of how digital technologies play a role in smart city transformation in China. The table maps each major digital technology with its role and major use cases:

|  | Definition | Role | Use Case |
|---|---|---|---|
| IoT | Communication network between devices | Collecting data | monitoring (surveillance) and control |
| Cloud Computing | Expandable/shrinkable "lake" to provide unified computing resources | Processing data, providing application services | Data centers, software and information service platforms |
| Mobile Internet | Wireless communication network | Transporting data, providing mobile application services | Mobile applications (mobile office work, mobile law enforcement) |
| Big Data | Ultra-large amounts of data with different structures, able to be used to illuminate data with valuable information | Data mining, data visualization | Industry and government intelligentization |

Figure 6.13 – The role of digital technologies in smart cities in China (source: `https://www.uscc.gov/sites/default/files/2020-04/China_Smart_Cities_Development.pdf`)

The smart city development explanatory model (*Figure 6.14*) summarizes the approach of the Chinese government, which provides the vision and the necessary governance and support from the top. At the same time, the leadership provided by a strong city mayor is extremely important for *engagement on the ground*. According to Statistica, the number of smart homes in China is expected to grow from 14.2 million in 2017 to about 116 million by 2024:

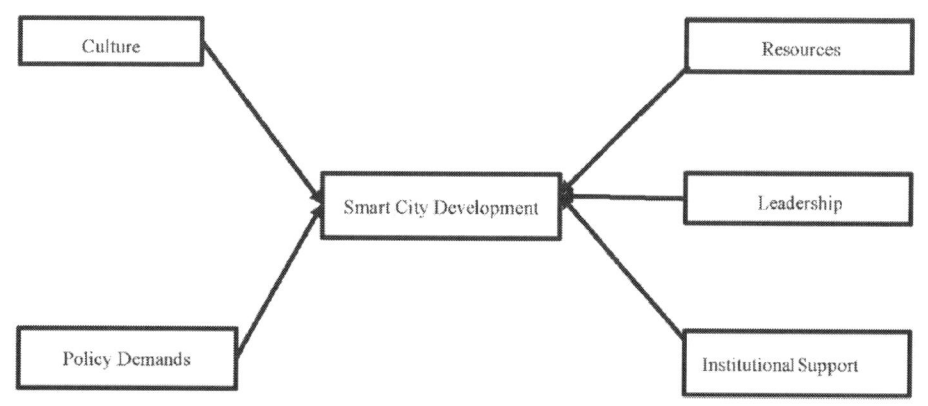

Figure 6.14 – Smart cities explanatory model of performance in China

These explanatory models help to track and evaluate the progress and success of digital transformation initiatives on a national scale. In the case of China's smart cities transformation, they are being used to understand the variances in implementation and achievements of the outcomes in different cities.

## Coronavirus control in New Zealand

New Zealand has a population approaching 5 million. In early June 2020, their prime minister Jacinda Ardern announced that New Zealand had no active cases of coronavirus. As a result, they were able to open schools, public gatherings, and domestic travel back to normal levels. They had over 1,500 people infected, resulting in about 22 deaths, as of June 2020. After discovering the first case on February 28, New Zealand introduced one of the toughest border restrictions in the world, by March 14, which required anyone who entered the country to self-isolate for 14 days. At that time, they had only 6 cases. The country implemented a testing strategy that had very high coverage compared to the US and European countries (see `https://www.health.govt.nz/our-work/diseases-and-conditions/covid-19-novel-coronavirus/covid-19-current-situation/covid-19-current-cases#lab`). Prime minister Ardern said the following:

> *"Decisive action, going hard and going early, helped to stamp out the worst of the virus."*

According to data from `www.ourworldindata.org`, as of June 12, 2020, New Zealand has almost 64 tests per 1,000 of the population compared to the other extremes, such as Brazil, who has 2.3 tests per 1,000 and India, who has 4 tests per 1,000. To summarize, the example of how New Zealand handled the coronavirus outbreak is a good example of a nation delivering rapid and transformative outcomes to its citizens following some of the principles we have discussed in part 1 of this book:

- **Process changes**: Strict enforcement of isolation, the closing of borders early on, and regulations to control the effectiveness of testing kits.

- **Technology**: Testing for coronavirus is a new medical *technology*. Instead of relying only on propriety testing kits that were in short supply, New Zealand's Ministry of Health and local universities looked at ways to source reagents and testing hardware from Asia so that the generic supplies could be used with these machines. The Ministry of Health also released the NZ COVID Tracer app in May 2020 (see `https://www.health.govt.nz/news-media/media-releases/nz-covid-tracer-app-released-support-contact-tracing`).

- **Culture**: According to a poll, 88% of New Zealanders trust that their government would make the right decisions about controlling the coronavirus at a national scale. Hence, these cultural factors that are unique to New Zealand resulted in a very high level of public cooperation to help control the spread of the disease. Instead of using strong laws to control the spread of the virus, the New Zealand prime minister Jacinda Ardern said "Be strong and be kind." People gave priority to the children of front-line workers to go to daycare and schools.

- **Business model**: While New Zealand heavily depends on tourism, with it bringing an estimated revenue of $112 million per day, they decided to put that on hold to invest in the welfare of its citizens and focus on strong recovery to protect the tourism industry in the longer term. Airbnb reported a massive increase in domestic travel booking starting in late May 2020 (see `https://www.newshub.co.nz/home/travel/2020/05/airbnb-data-reveals-massive-increase-in-new-zealand-domestic-travel-bookings.html`).

In the preceding sections, we learned how digital transformations operate at a national and global scale. We saw how the national governments can set the vision, provide the resources and the governance for the transformation initiatives, and empower the agencies and the private sector at the suitable levels.

# Summary

In this chapter, we learned how digital transformation initiatives apply to the public sector globally. These initiatives primarily target the welfare of citizens and similar stakeholders, who could be temporary residents and tourists, in some cases. Unlike the commercial sector, these transformations are not primarily driven by profit motives but provide the opportunity for the private sector to provide transformative solutions and economically benefit from that. In the next chapter, we will learn more about public-private partnerships, in the context of the ecosystems for industrial digital transformation. We will also learn about the consortiums and the partner and channel ecosystems created to accelerate industrial digital transformation.

# Questions

Here are some questions to test your understanding of the chapter:

1. What are some of the challenges that public sector organizations face when executing digital transformations and how are they different from the challenges faced by the private sector?
2. What is technical debt?
3. How is digital transformation changing the citizen experience?
4. What are some examples of how the government has used digital technologies to improve the citizen experience?
5. What are the building blocks for smart city transformations?
6. How can a local digital transformation initiative be scaled to a national level?

# 7
# The Transformation Ecosystem

In the previous chapter, we learned about how digital transformation is changing the public sector. We discussed the specific challenges of digital transformation in the public sector and how agencies are overcoming those challenges. We also reviewed case studies of the use of new technologies in the public sector. Finally, we explored transformation at a national and global scale, examining transformations that had a broad reach across a nation or around the world.

In this chapter, we will learn about the need for an ecosystem-centric approach for an effective industrial digital transformation project. We will learn that even large, global companies may not have all the skills and resources for transformation and have to often rely on partners and ecosystems to accelerate their transformation journey. We will learn how to identify who the right partners are to provide complimentary skills and capabilities in order to accelerate the pace of transformation. We will look at the following:

- How to move the needle in industrial digital transformation projects
- What is the role of proper partnerships and alliances in digital transformation?
- What is the role of ecosystems and consortiums in industrial digital transformation?

# Moving the needle in industrial digital transformation projects

In this section, we will look at how industrial digital transformation is often seen as a *team sport*. The necessity for teamwork runs not only across the lines of business inside the company, but very often across companies, including partners, customers, and other stakeholders in similar industrial sectors including start-ups. Some have compared industrial digital transformation to nothing short of the historical European Renaissance. After all, the first Industrial Revolution started within two centuries of the Renaissance. We will look at several examples of these types of teamwork. Often, such strong collaborations can effectively *move the needle* for digital transformation. An enterprise, on its own, can try to transform itself and then make an impact on its customer base, but often, to make an impact in the whole industry sector, it *takes a village* (for more information on this idea, see `https://www.channelpartnersonline.com/blog/it-takes-a-village-to-achieve-digital-transformation/`). The following diagram reflects the role of ecosystems in industrial digital transformation:

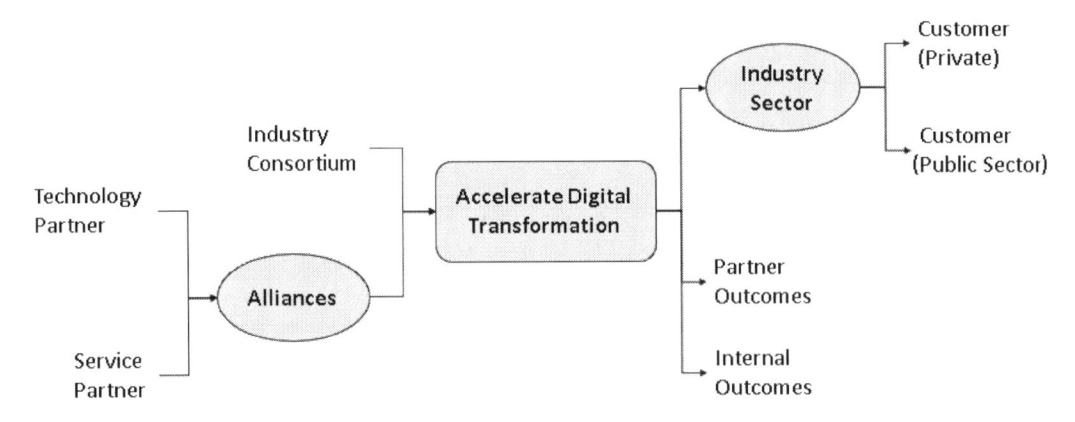

Figure 7.1 – Role of ecosystems in industrial digital transformation

*Figure 7.1* shows that by leveraging the ecosystem, such as industry consortiums and alliances, the whole industry segment can be transformed. When individual companies work on their transformation, they typically improve internal outcomes and influence some of their customers. Often, research institutions such as the **National Institute of Standards and Technology** (**NIST**), universities, and countries are actively involved in such consortiums and alliances. However, in this chapter, we will look at the acceleration of outcomes for segments of industry, so let's dive in and look at examples of transformation from different industries.

## Shipping industry

A network of like-minded and synergistic organizations can accelerate transformative initiatives by providing complementary skills and create a strategic roadmap for the given industrial sector. Along with CargoSmart, Oracle is driving the acceleration of the industrial digital transformation of the shipping industry, via the creation of the **Global Shipping Business Network (GSBN)** (for more information, see `https://www.maritime-executive.com/article/nine-companies-sign-up-for-global-shipping-business-network`). GSBN is exploring how a blockchain-based platform can add efficiency to the exchange of logistics and cargo data across the whole supply chain. Nine different ocean cargo carriers and terminal operators are getting actively involved in this initiative. The ultimate goal is to drive the industrial digital transformation across the whole network of logistics stakeholders by reducing friction, thereby improving efficiency in the system. Stakeholders may include the shipper, multi-model carriers, port operators, customs agencies, and freight-forwarding service providers. The following are some of the examples of the forms that need to be filled in the shipping industry:

- The **bill of lading** documents a carrier's acknowledgment of the cargo for shipping purposes.
- A **commercial invoice** is used in international trade and is issued by the seller or exporter to the buyer or importer and serves as a contract and proof of sale.
- The **certificate of origin** provides the attestation that the listed product meets the criteria that it originates in a particular country.
- The **inspection certificate** is often completed by a government agency or its delegate to confirm that that the goods were inspected.
- The **Destination Control Statement** is usually mandated by the **Export Administration Regulations (EAR)** and the **International Traffic in Arms Regulations (ITAR)** and states that the exported products are destined for the country indicated in the other shipping documents.
- The **Shipper's Export Declaration (SED)** serves two purposes: firstly, as a record of U.S. exports, used for government statistics and reporting, and secondly, as a regulatory document for cargo of a value exceeding a certain threshold.
- The export packing list is the list of product and packaging details for each shipment.

The use of blockchain-based solutions adds efficiency and trust in the shipping logistics industry, which is full of paperwork. See *Figure 7.2*. IBM and Maersk have jointly developed a platform called TradeLens, which leverages blockchain as well (for more information on this, see `https://www.tradelens.com/platform`). However, one of the challenges posed by the proliferation of blockchain technologies and such consortiums is that soon, there will be multiple competing platforms, which could create islands of information. Examples of such multiple blockchain technologies are Hyperledger and Ethereum, both of which are popular, but there is not much interoperability between them at the moment:

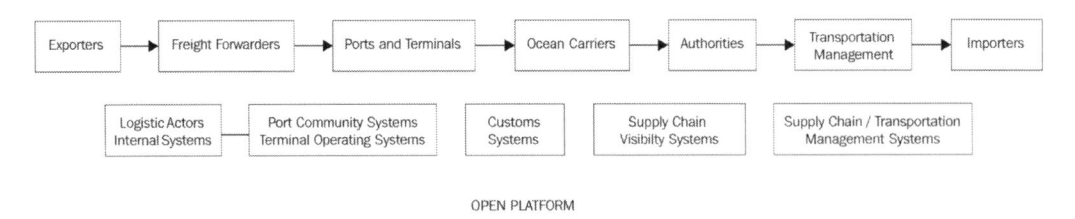

Figure 7.2 – How blockchain adds efficiency to the shipping industry

*Figure 7.2* shows how open platforms can be used by different stakeholders across the logistics industry to exchange information. The use of blockchain adds a layer of trust in the platform. Blockchain has been used for scenarios including tracking and tracing in multiple industrial sectors. Now, let's look at the application of blockchain in helping with the traceability of food, and more specifically, in the recall of contaminated food.

# Farm to folk

Digital technology can be used to track where the food ingredients originate from, and how they are packaged, stored, and shipped all the way from the farm where they are grown until they arrive on the plate of the consumer. The ability to trace contaminated food all the way back to its origin is critical for managing recalls and preventing the spread of food poisoning:

Figure 7.3 – Food poisoning

In September 2018, Walmart and Sam's Club mandated their fresh and leafy vegetable suppliers to provide tracing of their produce back to the farm using the blockchain technology by September 2019. This action was prompted by the related outbreaks in the industry; see *Figure 7.3* for more information. According to Walmart, when tracing contaminated food products, blockchain reduces the week-long effort to 2.2 seconds (see `https://corporate.walmart.com/media-library/document/leafy-greens-on-blockchain-press-release/_proxyDocument?id=00000166-0c4c-d96e-a3ff-8f7c09b50001`).

IBM is working with Walmart on this blockchain initiative. In addition, IBM and Walmart are working with Merck and KPMG, in a US **Food and Drug Administration** (**FDA**) program, for the identification and tracing of prescription drugs. Oracle is working with Certified Origins Italia to ensure olive oil is tracked from the bottling facility to the port of arrival in the US via a blockchain-based solution. This is the *meeting of the two chains*; that is, the supply chain and the blockchain, with the goal of keeping food safe.

Next, let's look at the transformation that the automobile industry is going through, with the emergence of partnerships around autonomous vehicles.

## Autonomous vehicles

In 2016, BMW Group, Intel, and Mobileye partnered up to accelerate the development of autonomous cars (for more information, please see `https://newsroom.intel.com/news-releases/intel-bmw-group-mobileye-autonomous-driving/#gs.900gj8`). BMW Vision iNEXT targets 2021 for the production of autonomous vehicles. In March 2017, Intel acquired Mobileye for $15.3 billion, one of the largest acquisitions of an Israeli company. In May 2020, Intel acquired Moovit for $900 million. Moovit provides **Mobility-as-a-Service** (**MaaS**) solutions for urban transit. Intel is also working with IEEE on a formal model for safety considerations in automated vehicle decision making (*IEEE 2846*; see `https://sagroups.ieee.org/2846/`). Bosch is also a stakeholder in the development of autonomous cars (see `https://www.bosch.com/stories/autonomous-driving-interview-with-michael-fausten/`).

The preceding examples show how multiple organizations can come together to accelerate transformative outcomes. Let's next look at how Mercedes and NVIDIA are working together to develop the software architecture for autonomous cars. Such software-defined vehicle architecture will use the NVIDIA DRIVE platform underneath the hood. Mercedes plans to roll out a fleet of vehicles with upgradable automated driving features by 2024. These vehicles will have many software-defined vehicle features, such as the following:

- Driver-assist and safety features
- Automated driving between regular routes for known address pairs
- The purchase by subscription of other driving features using **over-the-air** (**OTA**) updates

In 2017, PACCAR, a large truck manufacturer, and NVIDIA announced a collaboration. PACCAR's CEO, Ron Armstrong, mentioned that their company was exploring driver-assisted and automated driving systems with NVIDIA. Given that there are 300 million trucks globally, this can have a big impact on the distribution industry.

A related concept in the trucking industry is called **driver-assistive truck platooning** (**DATP**). Platooning allows the coupling of two or more trucks traveling together using connective technologies. This increases fuel efficiency and safety, and helps to reduce the carbon footprint (see `https://www.acea.be/uploads/publications/Platooning_roadmap.pdf`). Companies including Volvo, Daimler, Scania AB, Continental Automotive, Peloton Technology, and NVIDIA are also working closely to accelerate platooning in the trucking industry, and Europe is leading in that regard over other parts of the world. MAN Truck Germany is also working on the platooning of trucks (see `https://www.truck.man.eu/de/en/Automation.html`).

## Partnerships for transformation

Partnerships are critical to transformation both in the public and private sectors. In the public sector, organizations often have to forge public-private partnerships to accelerate transformation. This section will go into the details of these partnerships.

## What are public-private partnerships?

A public-private partnership is a cooperative arrangement between at least one private sector organization and at least one government agency. In recent years, these relationships have transformed to include non-profit organizations such as healthcare providers and educational institutions, **community-based organizations** (**CBOs**), and business improvement districts. Public-private partnerships are usually, but not always, long-term arrangements. The purpose of these partnerships is to complete large and complex projects or deliver services to the public. True partnerships, where public and private interests are balanced, can transform potentially confrontational relationships into collaborations that are focused on achieving shared goals. One example is the City of Sacramento, California, entering into a public-private partnership with Verizon in 2017 to build next-generation 5G infrastructure. This effort has included deploying Wi-Fi to the city's 27 parks by the end of 2020, a resource that has been extremely valuable during the COVID-19 pandemic.

Public-private partnerships are different from supplier relationships not just because they tend to be long term, as noted in the preceding paragraph, but also because they are not transactional. The word *partnership* is critical in the description of the relationship, as it describes a mutual commitment to collaboratively solve problems and the mutual assumption of risks and rewards.

Public-private partnerships are most commonly used to finance, develop, and run projects such as roads and public transit systems, parks, convention centers, and sports facilities. These partnerships can accelerate project completion as well as attract major businesses to a city or state. Public-private partnerships usually involve the private company providing the initial funding for the development of a public infrastructure project and usually managing its implementation in exchange for a revenue stream over a period of time. Private-sector companies can bring innovative technology to projects, resulting in agencies implementing technologies sooner than otherwise would have been possible, resulting in improved public services at a reduced cost.

In recent years, public-private partnerships have begun to evolve in different ways, most notably to implement technology projects such as smart cities. Public-private partnerships for technology implementation can be short- or long-term and may be formal or informal.

## Preparing for and structuring a public-private partnership

The development of a public-private partnership that supports public-sector digital transformation must begin by crafting a clear understanding of the community's strengths and challenges. This assessment will provide the context to identify new capabilities that will be developed, along with identifying partnership opportunities and potential partners. Each opportunity (for example, smart parking structures or smart gas meters) must be scoped out to understand the cost and benefit, as well as the technical capabilities that will be delivered and the skills required to implement the project. Benefits should be defined in clear terms and should include the metrics that will be used to measure the project's success.

Once a set of projects has been identified, the municipality must assess its readiness to implement those projects. The municipality must ensure that the services and capabilities required to support the new smart services, such as sufficient connectivity and storage capacity, are in place. Finally, after a municipality has defined its projects and ascertained its readiness, it can move on to defining and creating partnerships.

Once a municipality has identified and vetted a project that is appropriate for a public-private partnership, it must then identify potential partners. Next, it will define the concession or revenue-sharing arrangement and legal framework and select a partner.

What we just described has been the traditional way that public-private partnerships have been structured. This structure was necessary for legacy partnerships that involved large construction projects. This model still works for projects that are initiated and led by municipalities and most public-private partnerships evolve in this general manner. However, as we will see in the next section, technology projects lend themselves to a wide range of project structures and are initiated by a range of stakeholders.

## Examples of public-private technology partnerships

Jonathan Law, a partner at McKinsey and Company, said "*Once you've seen one public-private partnership, you've seen one public-private partnership,*" meaning that the variety of opportunities for the private and public sectors, as well as non-profits and universities, to work together for mutual benefit is endless. In this section, we'll attempt to convey the breadth of possible partnerships and partners and then discuss a couple of examples in a bit more detail.

The following list includes a number of examples of public-private partnerships centered around smart cities, the most common technology-related public-private partnership. The partnerships listed highlight the variety of partners that can be involved as well as the ways that partnerships can be formed:

- A new city, Belmont, is emerging outside Phoenix, Arizona. Backed by Bill Gates and other investors, the entire city will be wired with a high-speed network and have ubiquitous sensors to support smart city technologies including autonomous vehicles.

- A partnership of the New York City Department of Information Technology and CityBridge, a consortium that includes Qualcomm, CIVIQ Smartscapes, and Intersection, are implementing a project called Link NYC that is installing free public Wi-Fi kiosks in former telephone booths throughout New York City.

- The City of Amsterdam's smart city initiative was started by a non-profit that has become progressively more enmeshed with the government, with the founder now serving as the CTO of the city. The initiative began at a time when the city was not interested in smart city projects. A set of entrepreneurs prepared a number of pilots and demos that captured the imagination of members of the public. Once the public was engaged, the government got engaged as well.

- In Kentucky, the Robert Wood Johnson Foundation, Propeller Health, and the University of Louisville's Institute for Healthy Air, Water, and Soil have created a project that funds smart asthma inhalers that capture the location where they are used. The data will be used to create a database that identifies high-risk locations throughout the city of Louisville.

- Columbia University is wiring parts of Harlem to provide internet access. Widely available connectivity is needed for that part of New York City to compete economically and support its residents.

- The city of Copenhagen and Hitachi are exploring how to monetize datasets that can be used to create applications that will serve residents.

- The city of Charlotte, NC, has partnered with Duke Energy, Cisco Systems, and Charlotte Center City, a non-profit organization dedicated to the development of Charlotte's urban center to improve sustainability across the spectrum of energy, air, water, and waste. This network is continually expanding and now encompasses a range of partners including Itron, CH2M Hill, Verizon, Enevo, and the University of North Carolina – Charlotte.

- For its smart nation initiative, Singapore is incubating solutions within the government with the intention of spinning them out of the government with sustainable revenue streams.

- Mexico City is working with a non-profit organization to implement earthquake detection solutions.

- Abu Dhabi has partnered with a Swiss company to determine how to deliver equitable telemedicine in a financially sustainable way.

Now that we have surveyed the landscape, let's look at three public-private partnerships, ranging from simple to complex in more detail.

### Billboards save lives

Every year Florida residents and visitors must cope with a range of natural disasters including hurricanes, floods, and tornadoes. Florida is particularly vulnerable to hurricanes and natural disasters due to the state's 1,200 miles of coastline and areas with limited road access. The state's emergency management department recognized that fast and easy public communication is a key component of emergency response. The state must be able to warn residents and visitors of emergency conditions, including road closures and evacuation routes.

In 2008 following a series of severe hurricanes, the leaders of the **Florida Outdoor Advertising Association (FOAA)** recognized that advances in digital technology that enabled quick changes of computerized billboards could also enable Florida's law enforcement and emergency services agencies to use billboards to improve public safety. FOAA approached the State with an offer to make billboards available and by the end of the year, billboards were being used to display AMBER alerts, posting fugitive wanted signs, and delivering information about flash flood notices and warnings during severe weather.

Industry members and the state jointly created policies for posting alerts. In addition, FOAA joined the State Emergency Response Team to ensure uniform and fair usage of billboards. In an emergency, the **Florida Department of Emergency Management (FDEM)** contacts FOAA to request digital billboard positions, specifying the geographic area and time frame for the alert. FOAA uses a pre-approved template to create the alert. FOAA members then post the alerts to specified billboards and tracks the display times and locations to support program metrics.

The first major activation of the partnership was for tropical storm Fay in August 2008 in response to widespread flooding. In that case, 37 different messages were displayed across 11 counties over the course of 10 days on over 75 billboards. The system has been activated numerous times since then and has surely saved countless lives.

## Partnership for Next-Generation Vehicles (PNGV)

PNGV was formed in 1993 as a cooperative R&D program between the US government and USCAR, which included Chrysler Corporation, the Ford Motor Company, and General Motors Corporation. The government's efforts were led by the Department of Commerce and included the Departments of Energy, Transportation, Defense, and the Interior, along with the **Environmental Protection Agency (EPA)**, the **National Aeronautics and Space Administration (NASA)**, and the **National Science Foundation (NSF)**. PNGV was formed at a time when there was great concern over the loss of global market share by the big three US automakers, resulting in a renewed focus on manufacturing competitiveness.

While a case study of a project begun in 1993 may seem dated, we include the PNGV case study because it reinforces the idea that some technological innovation takes a long time. The government tends to be exceedingly patient, but the private sector is not. Therefore, examples of cases where industry members made a long-term commitment to technology investments are important and enlightening.

The goals of PNGV were to do the following:

- Improve the competitiveness of the US in vehicle manufacturing through the adoption of new technology, including agile and flexible manufacturing.

- Convert research into commercially viable innovations for conventional vehicles. Research areas included fuel efficiency and emission reduction.

- Develop a vehicle that was three times more efficient than a comparable 1994 model sedan, which would be a fuel efficiency of approximately 80 miles per gallon.

While all three goals were considered to be important, the primary focus was to deliver a more fuel-efficient vehicle with the plan to select a technological approach by 1997, reveal concept vehicles in 2000, and deliver prototypes in 2004. A diesel-hybrid approach was selected and concepts were delivered on schedule in 2000. However, it was determined that the approach was not viable, as the vehicle could not meet increasing emissions standards, the market was moving toward sport utility vehicles and away from sedans, and the vehicle equipped with the diesel-hybrid technology could not be manufactured at a competitive price. The final challenge for the program was the introduction of gasoline-hybrid vehicles to the US market at the same time by Toyota. Gasoline-hybrid became the de facto standard for high fuel efficiency and emission reductions until the plug-in electric vehicle was introduced.

After the program ended without meeting its primary goal, a **National Academy of Sciences** (**NAS**) panel evaluated the program and concluded that the program had been successful. NAS concluded that substantial proprietary R&D activity had been generated. In addition, work from the PNGV program, in cooperation with the US Advanced Battery Consortium, resulted in commercial applications, including the nickel-metal hydride battery that powered the gasoline-hybrid vehicles that ultimately spelled the demise of the diesel-hybrid development program. The program also spurred technology investments by manufacturers who were not involved in the partnership. Takeshi Uchiyamada, who led the development of the first-generation Prius, has publicly stated that Toyota's investment in gasoline-hybrid vehicles was spurred by the PNGV program.

While not fully successful, this public-private partnership resulted in substantial investment and innovation by both the program partners and competitors who perceived a threat to their market share as a result of the program. In addition, rather than ending the program, the participants retooled their partnership as a new entity, the FreedomCAR consortium.

## Columbus smart city project

In 2016 Columbus, Ohio, was the sole winner of the **Department of Transportation** (**DOT**) *Smart City Challenge*, receiving a $50-million-dollar grant as a result. The Columbus proposal, which bested 77 other applicants, envisioned improving access to jobs through improved mobility and reliable transportation, better neighborhood safety, and more environmentally sustainable development methods throughout the city.

The Columbus Partnership, a non-profit organization comprised of 75 CEOs in the Columbus area, was an initial backer of the grant proposal, pledging both financial support and visibility to demonstrate to the DOT that there was community support for the initiative. The City of Columbus then matched the grant through their Smart Columbus Acceleration Fund, with over $600 million in private investment and public investment to date and a goal of $1 billion in commitments by the end of 2020. Partners contributing to the fund have included AEP, AT&T, Cardinal Health, Drive Capital, Honda, the State of Ohio, the City of Columbus, and the **Central Ohio Transit Authority** (**COTA**).

Smart Columbus investments so far have included the following:

- Enabling all COTA buses with Wi-Fi and mobile payment technology
- Modernizing the city's vehicle fleet with highly efficient electric vehicles
- Deploying smart street lights throughout Columbus

- Building an autonomous vehicle testing center at the Ohio State University
- Nearly $200 million made in grid modernization investments in preparation for electric vehicle adoption

These efforts are clearly only the beginning of the City of Columbus' smart city initiative. The funding model employed in this program is worth noting. The initial private support led to a public grant, which spurred additional private sector investment. This positive reinforcement loop follows the same pattern we saw in the previous case study about the PNGV partnership. Successful, and sometimes even unsuccessful, public-private partnerships deliver results to both the public and private sectors and accelerate progress in both.

In the next section, let's look at the commercial partnerships.

# Partner programs

Partner programs enhance the ecosystem around a company's products and service offerings. With the proper partnership in place, the time and cost to develop and market solutions can be drastically reduced. For example, a company with new offerings of digital services can partner with a **System Integrator** (**SI**) in a win-win partnership instead of building a whole new professional services' arm. GE Digital developed an extensive Ecosystems and Channels Program, involving partners of multiple types for industrial digital transformation. The major categories were as follows:

- Technology partners
- **Independent Software Vendor** (**ISV**) partners
- SI partners
- Telecommunication partners
- Resellers

Let's now look in detail at each type of partnership.

## Technology partners

The technology partners included companies that provide digital technologies, such as the following:

- Intel, HPE, and Dell, for the edge or gateway devices for IoT.
- SAP and Oracle for enterprise software and the IT-OT integration (where **OT** stands for **operations technology**).

- Microsoft, since Azure was used as one of the public cloud platforms for GE's Predix platform for IoT.
- Others in this category included Cisco, STMicroelectronics, NVIDIA, and Apple for hardware and related categories.

Next, let's discuss ISV partners.

## ISV partners

This category included companies who were to build the market-ready solutions on GE's Predix platform. NEC was one such company that used AI and machine vision to build a solution for recognizing non-serialized parts in manufacturing. For partnership announcements, see https://www.nec.com/en/global/insights/article/2020022525/index.html.

Other smaller companies were also part of the ISV program, and offered their solutions via GE's marketplace.

## SI partners

The SI partners included Accenture Digital, Deloitte Digital, Tata Consultancy Services, Infosys, Wipro, Ernst & Young, and similar companies. Such companies provide advisory and implementation services to their industrial customers. Such SI partners helped in GE's internal transformation as well as in the industrial sector for the joint customers, who had relations hips with both GE and the SI partner.

## Telecommunication partners

Telecommunication companies are a key part of Industrial Internet of Things (IIoT), providing the connectivity for the system to work. AT&T and SoftBank were part of this category. AT&T was the key partner for the San Diego smart city initiative. Other emerging areas for partnerships included private **Long-Term Evolution** (**LTE**) coverage such as in the Port of Los Angeles.

## Resellers

Resellers often have trusted relations hips with the enterprises for their hardware, software, and professional services needs. They help to facilitate the commercial agreements between multiple parties and may provide other value-added functions, such as managed services. Softtek and GrayMatter were part of this category.

The preceding example showed how GE Digital built its partner ecosystem around its digital platform. In the next section, we will learn more about the role of consortiums to drive industrial digital transformation.

# Ecosystems and consortiums

Let's look into the role of ecosystems and consortiums in industrial digital transformation. Often the consortiums can be non-profit bodies but are often actively championed by large for-profit companies aiming to unify the different stakeholders around a common goal. Let's look into this area in more depth.

## Consortiums

A consortium is an association of multiple companies including large enterprises, non-profit companies, start-ups, governmental agencies, and individuals, with a specific purpose. The purpose of a consortium may be to evangelize a specific topic, for advocacy, or to create standards and operating processes for the benefit of its members and stakeholders. Sometimes the enterprises and for-profit member companies of the consortium may compete with each other as they may be doing business in similar industrial domains. As a result, we often see co-opetition, which is cooperation + competition. Many consortiums have emerged, mainly in the last decade, that support the vision of industrial digital transformation in some form or the other. We will list a few technology consortiums here and then deep dive into a few that are relevant to digital transformation:

- The **American Institute of Aeronautics and Astronautics (AIAA)**: Focuses on shaping the future of aerospace (see http://aiaa.org).

- The **Autonomous Vehicle Computing Consortium**: See https://www.avcconsortium.org/members and https://www.businesswire.com/news/home/20191008005138/en/New-Consortium-Develop-Common-Computing-Platform-Autonomous.

- The **Car Connectivity Consortium** (CCC): The CCC involves many car companies as well as Apple, all of whom are working on initiatives such as digital keys (see https://carconnectivity.org/).

- The **Cloud Foundry Foundation**: Launched in 2011, it counts EMC, VMware, and GE among its prominent members.

- The **COVID-19 HPC Consortium**: IBM, Dell, Intel are working with government and research institutes for the high-performance computing resources around the pandemic projects (see https://covid19-hpc-consortium.org/).

- **Data Processing and Analysis Consortium**: About 400 European scientists and software engineers created this to support the activities of the European Space Agency.

- The **Digital Twin Consortium (DTC)** started in 2020 and is driven by companies including Microsoft, ANSYS, Lendlease, and Dell.

- The **Enterprise Ethereum Alliance**: Created in 2017, when a total of 30 Fortune-500 companies, start-ups, and research groups around blockchain got together.

- **Global System for Mobile Communications Association (GSMA)**: GSMA started in 2007 and will be a big influencer for 5G-related technologies. It has about 1,200 members.

- The **Government Technology and Services (GTS)** coalition: The GTS is a non-profit body (see https://www.gtscoalition.com/about-us/government-technology-services-consortium/).

- The **Industrial Internet Consortium (IIC)**: The IIC started in 2014, when industrial and technology companies including GE, Intel, IBM, Cisco, and AT&T got together to evangelize IIot. The IIC currently has around 200 members.

- **International Air Transport Association (IATA)**: IATA started in 1945 and involves the major airlines of the world. It sets the technical standards for airlines.

- **International Electronics Manufacturing Initiative (iNEMI)**: iNEMI is a consortium of leading electronics manufacturers, and research institutes such as universities and government agencies, with a focus on board-level electronics.

- **Joint Center for Energy Storage Research (JCESR)** started in 2012, under the auspices of the US **Department of Energy's (DOE's)** Energy Innovation Hubs (see https://www.jcesr.org/).

- The **Linux Foundation**: It started in 2000, when Open Source Development Labs and the Free Standards Group merged together with the goal of standardizing the Linux operating system.

- **Manufacturing USA**: This comprises 14 public-private organizations and is sponsored by NIST (see https://www.manufacturingusa.com/).

- **Open Data Center Alliance**: Intel helped to start this association in 2010, with the goal of developing open standards for cloud computing. It grew to over 100 members and was later closed down.

- **Open Fog Consortium**: It started in 2015 with companies including ARM, Cisco, Dell, Intel, Microsoft, and Princeton University. It grew to over 50 members, then became part of IIC in 2018.

- The **Open Platform Communications Foundation**: Well known for the OPC **Unified Architecture** (**UA**), released in 2008, which is a platform-independent service-oriented architecture for machine-to-machine communication (see `https://opcfoundation.org/`).

- The **OpenPOWER Foundation**: It was created in 2013 around IBM's hardware systems, and later in 2019, it became part of the Linux Foundation.

- **SEMI** (formerly **Semiconductor Equipment and Materials International**): A semiconductor-related group with about 2,000 members (see `https://www.semi.org/en/about/organization`).

- **US Advanced Battery Consortium** (**USABC**) was started in 1992 (see `http://www.uscar.org/guest/teams/12/U-S-Advanced-Battery-Consortium-LLC`).

- The **World Wide Web Consortium** (**W3C**): This started in 1994, and has over 400 members working toward the development of standards and guidelines for the World Wide Web.

The preceding list is meant to be a representative list of consortiums and similar organizations, where multiple public and private companies come together, to accelerate transformation in their given industrial sectors. Let's look at the role of the IIC in detail.

## Industrial Internet Consortium

The IIC was formed in 2014, to bring together companies of different sizes from across the globe, along with large and small technology innovators, government bodies, and academic institutions, with the goal of accelerating the development of best practices, testbeds, adoption, and widespread use of industrial internet technologies. Bill Ruh, who was then VP of GE Global Software, explained that the IIC was created to help develop a common terminology and reference architecture for industrial internet technologies. In addition, the IIC encouraged the collection and documentation of common use cases in industrial domains. These lead to development of testbeds in sectors including aviation, transportation, healthcare, and energy with the goal of rapid adoption of **IIoT** by business users. The aspiration was to make IIoT solutions as easy to use as the commercial plug-and-play software that is common in the enterprise IT world. The members of the IIC organized themselves into working groups and task groups, which worked on areas such as digital twins and digital transformation. The authors of this book have actively participated in the IIC's Testbeds programs and working and task groups.

One of the areas where the IIC created a quick impact was its aforementioned Testbeds program (for more information, see `https://www.iiconsortium.org/testbeds.htm`). One of the authors of this book (Nath) has worked extensively on some of these testbeds; namely, the following:

- Asset Efficiency Testbed
- Industrial Digital Thread Testbed
- Smart Airline Baggage Management Testbed

More details about these testbeds are included in the book *Architecting the Industrial Internet*, by *Shyam Nath*, *Robert Stackowiak*, and *Carla Romano*, published by *Packt* in 2017. We will look at the Smart Airline Baggage Management Testbed here, which involved the following organizations:

- IATA, the consortium of airlines we briefly mentioned earlier
- GE – Digital & Aviation
- M2MI Corporation
- Oracle
- SigFox
- STMicroelectronics

This combination of differently sized companies worked toward a solution for the IATA industry regulation that went into effect in 2018. This regulation is called *IATA Res 753* and is related to efficiency in airline baggage management. The airlines and airports were the main stakeholders (see `https://www.iata.org/en/programs/ops-infra/baggage/baggage-tracking`). The IIC testbed is a good example of how multiple parties came together to prototype a solution applicable to the airline industry. This prototype was demonstrated to several airlines.

Next, we will look at examples of partnerships and alliances in industry.

# Partnerships and alliances in digital transformation

Solutions needed for industrial digital transformation require contributions in several distinct areas of expertise. These include the following:

- Semiconductor companies
- Software solutions providers
- Hardware/software development-tool companies
- SIs
- **Original Equipment Manufacturers (OEMs)/Original Design Manufacturers (ODMs)**
- Service providers
- Distributors

An ecosystem or a partnership program brings many of these contributors together to collaboratively develop and deploy solutions in response to varying requirements for diverse industrial applications.

There are different industrial organizations that play another important role in developing standards. Let's now look at a selection of these.

## International Electrotechnical Commission

The **International Electrotechnical Commission (IEC)** is a global standards organization that focuses on electric and electronic products, systems, and services. The IEC played a key role in the development of standards for units of measurement, such as gauss for magnetic field strength and hertz for frequency. It was also the first to propose the system of standards that later came to be known as the SI System, *Système International d'unités* (which literally translates to *International System of Units* in English).

The IEC uses a consensus-based standards development and conformity assessment systems approach. These International Standards publications from the IEC are utilized for the development of national standards. They are also used as references in preparing international tenders and contracts (see `https://www.iec.ch/standardsdev/publications/is.htm`).

The IEC and **International Standards Organization (ISO)** have formed a **Joint Technical Committee (ISO/IEC JTC 1)** to focus on standards for information and communication technologies. These standards are directed toward digital transformation efforts that will utilize technologies such as AI, IoT, cloud computing, cybersecurity, biometrics, and multimedia information, among others.

The IEC is headquartered in Geneva, Switzerland, and has regional offices around the world.

## Jedec

Jedec is a microelectronic industry alliance with over 300 member companies and a focus on developing standards. The technology focus areas for Jedec are as follows:

- Main memory
- Flash memory
- Mobile memory
- Lead-free manufacturing
- **Electrostatic Discharge (ESD)**

Embedded-memory devices play a very important role in digital transformation. Jedec is collaborating with MIPI Alliance for the development of a power-efficient data transport mechanism for its interconnect layer offering compliance with the Universal Flash Storage standard.

Jedec is headquartered in Arlington, Virginia.

## SEMI

SEMI is an industry association of over 2,000 companies involved in the design, manufacturing, and supply-chain management of semiconductors. SEMI develops a wide variety of standards for automated semiconductor fabs. Semiconductor companies have been developing digital twins (as described in *Chapter 3, Accelerating Digital Transformation with Emerging Technologies*) that provide high-fidelity representations of fab operations including frontend, assembly, and backend testing. Such initiatives for smart manufacturing are ROI-driven. As an industrial association, SEMI has brought together a smart manufacturing technology community that facilitates information sharing and collaborative problem-solving for the smart manufacturing domain. This community has a Smart Manufacturing Advisory Council made up of a group of industry leaders.

Let's continue to look at the alliances from the technology sector.

## Edge AI and Vision Alliance

The Edge AI and Vision Alliance is an industry partnership made up of more than 100 member companies that focus on the adoption of edge AI and embedded computer vision in diverse end products based on these technologies. Embedded computer vision is being adopted in different digital transformation efforts for diverse applications including facial recognition for biometrics, industrial robots, and vehicle component manufacturing. The Edge AI and Vision Alliance organizes conferences and events to provide practical insights and technical information that product developers can use to build products with embedded vision functionalities. The Alliance brings together the embedded vision technology and edge AI suppliers with new customers and partners.

## National Electrical Manufacturers Association

The **National Electrical Manufacturers Association (NEMA)** is a trade association of 350 electrical equipment manufacturer companies in the US that focus on seven industrial segments, listed as follows:

- Industrial products and systems
- Transportation systems
- Building systems
- Building infrastructure
- Utility products and systems
- Lighting systems

NEMA publishes Standards and Technical papers focused on these areas. In the next section, we will explore the ecosystems of a selection of semi-conductor companies.

# Semiconductor company ecosystems

Using the example of STMicroelectronics, we will deep dive into the specifics of semiconductor manufacturer ecosystems and how they generate value for stakeholders.

## STMicroelectronics ecosystem

STMicroelectronics and its ecosystem partners provide complete hardware and software development environments, reference design boards, tools, and software libraries to support rapid prototyping of semiconductor solutions resulting in complete systems as products. Semiconductor components from STMicroelectronics used for building consumer, automotive, and industrial solutions include the STM32 microcontroller/microprocessor, sensors, actuators, connectivity, security, GNSS for location, power management, motor control, and standard I/O peripherals. *Figure 7.4* pictorially shows the parts of this ecosystem, which includes stackable hardware development boards, software solutions for vertical applications, development tools, cloud service solutions, partner programs, and a community for developers:

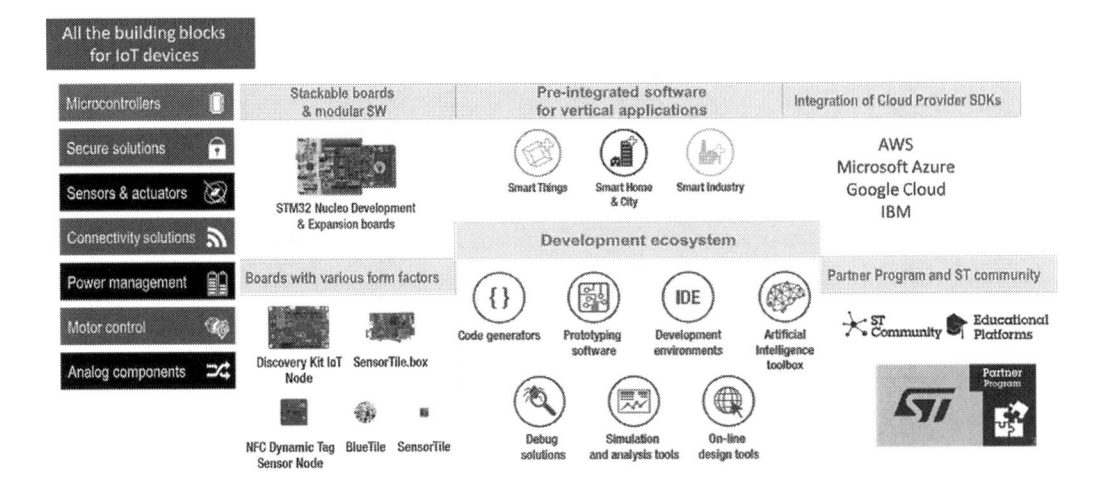

Figure 7.4 – STMicroelectronics ecosystem – components for complete solutions

This ecosystem allows the integration of cloud services with the edge components and devices, in collaboration with various partners.

**STM32 Open Development Environment** (**STM32 ODE**) is provided to develop applications based on microcontrollers/microprocessors and ST semiconductor solutions, allowing developers to verify their design assumptions and move quickly from ideas to a proof of concept. This development environment contains interoperable hardware and software components that cover the main domains such as sensing, connectivity, power management, motor control, and audio. The software suite includes drivers, middleware software libraries, and complete application software to create a design with ST products.

# Nucleo ecosystem

The Nucleo ecosystem is built with STM32 Nucleo boards that can be conveniently expanded with a wide range of application-related hardware add-ons (including the Arduino Uno Rev3 and ST Morpho connectors; Nucleo-32 includes Arduino Nano connectors) in order to quickly test a solution with STM32 Nucleo creation boards. These expansion boards provide functionality for the following:

- Sensing: MEMS motion, environmental sensors, and imaging
- Audio: MEMS microphones
- Connectivity: BLE, Sub GHz, Wi-Fi, and NFC
- Location: GNSS
- Move or actuate: Motor control
- Power management: USB Type-C power delivery, LED drivers, and power switches

The Nucleo platform benefits from the STM32 **Hardware Abstraction Layer (HAL)** software library and complete software examples for their respective development boards that work with most commonly used IDEs such as IAR EWARM, ARM Mbed, GCC/LLVM, and Keil MDK-ARM:

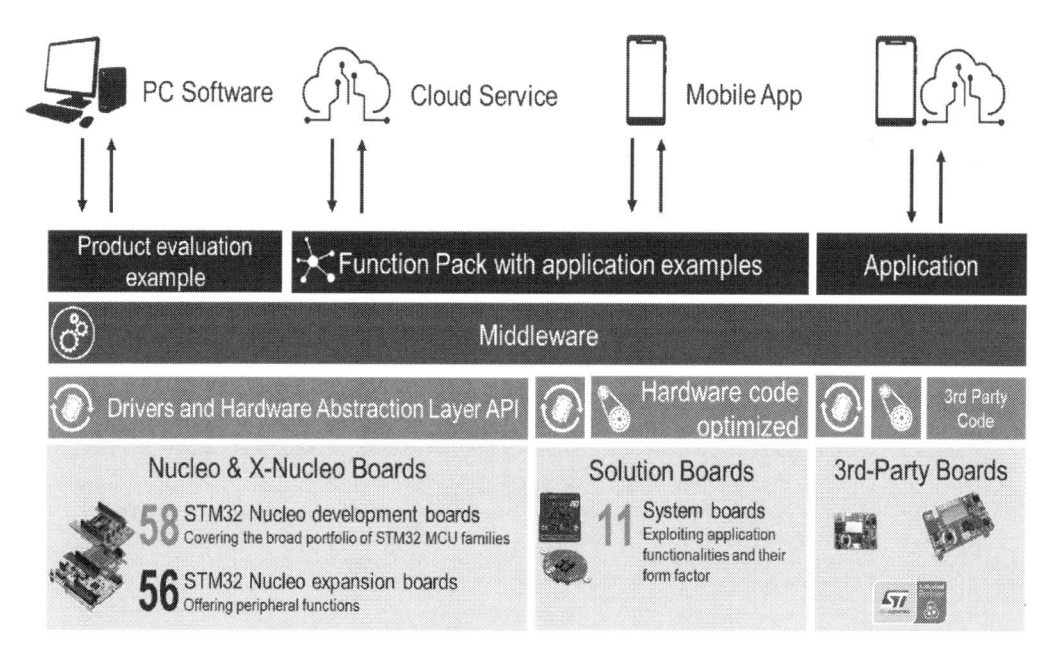

Figure 7.5 – STM32 ecosystem overview

Let's look at the STM32Cube ecosystem in the next section.

## STM32Cube ecosystem

The STM32Cube ecosystem provides a software framework for STM32 microcontroller and microprocessor devices. It is designed both for users seeking a full STM32 development environment, and for those who prefer to use IDEs, such as Keil or iAR; different components of the STM32Cube (such as STM32CubeMX, STM32CubeProgrammer, and STM32CubeMonitor) can be easily incorporated into these supported IDEs. *Figure 7.5* shows the hardware platforms and software stack that allow developers to build a complete application. It includes a complete collection of PC tools that are needed for the entire development process.

STM32CubeMX is a GUI-driven tool that allows the configuration of STM32 microcontrollers and processors, including setting up peripherals, configuring GPIOs, setting up the clock tree, and DDR configuration.

STM32CubeProgrammer is a software tool supported on commonly used OSes, such as Windows, Linux, and macOS, used to programming the STM32 products.

STM32CubeMonitor is a software tool used to monitor and visualize program variables at runtime in order to fine-tune or debug STM32 applications.

The MCU Package within STM32Cube contains embedded software that drives the peripheral of the selected microcontroller or microprocessor. Each package provides standard drivers.

The STM32CubeExpansion package contains embedded software components and libraries for functionalities such as sensing, audio, motor control, power management, and connectivity that are built with appropriate microcontrollers/microprocessors. These packages are provided by STMicroelectronics as well as selected partners.

Now let's look at the partner programs that are widely utilized by semiconductor companies.

# Partner programs

The ecosystem of hardware and software solutions for semiconductor company product portfolios is enhanced by a partner program that helps customers in their development of prototypes and complete products. New business models and revenue streams may be defined through a collaboration between a semiconductor company and its partners. Partner programs offer enhanced technical coverage for small- and medium-sized companies, therefore generating more business by connecting various stakeholders from several areas of expertise and different geographic locations. Closer collaboration between the technical teams of a company with the partners' teams increases compatibility and added value to the respective product offering.

## STMicroelectronics Partners Program

The **STMicroelectronics (ST) Partner Program** has more than 280 companies participating in it. ST certifies and promotes collaboration between ST and its partners on joint marketing activities, advanced technical solutions, and high-value business projects.

Products and services available in the ST Partner Program include the following:

- Hardware and software development tools
- Embedded software
- Cloud solutions
- Modules and components
- Engineering services
- Training

Through this program, partners gain early access to product roadmaps and prototypes that allow a quick start in the technical development of products and services. The ST Partner Program also enhances collaboration between partners to help them propose combined offers to end customers.

## ARM Partner programs

ARM develops architectures for computer processors and licenses them to other companies that develop their own products, such as **System on Chip** (**SoC**) circuits. Such SoCs are used in a wide variety of devices such as mobile phones, tablets, sensor nodes, connectivity chips, and many others.

## ARM AI Partner program

There is a lot of development activity in the area of on-chip implementation of AI and machine learning. ARM has developed an extensive AI ecosystem available through this partner program that offers various tools, algorithms, and applications. Companies including Xilinx, NVIDIA, and AMD are also contributing to the hardware acceleration of AI.

## Mobile technologies

ARM architecture-based processors are extensively used in mobile phones. This partner program counts 1,000 companies as members with a very diverse business focus spanning hardware and software development tools. Partners work with ARM on content creation projects and building new experiences such as AR/VR.

## Security

ARM has partnered with companies that are leaders in security building-block products and services. Through this partnership program, companies can work together to build a solution that encompasses a secure combination of hardware and software.

## Automotive

In this partnership program, ARM partner companies collaborate on computational requirements for automobiles. Partners can collaborate to create hardware and software solutions for complex automotive applications including **Advanced Driver Assistance Systems** (**ADAS**) and autonomous systems.

## Infrastructure

In this partnership program, ARM ecosystem partners collaborate on building IoT devices and infrastructure building-block products and services. Those partner companies with hardware and software expertise work together to help create innovative ARM-based solutions.

We looked at several partner programs in the previous section. Let's also look at the potential downsides of the ecosystems and partner programs we've seen.

## Caution

There are overheads in managing and coordinating with multiple parties, as such relationships often require collaborative working agreements. The participants have to balance the protection of intellectual property that may be generated in such activities with the speed of execution. When a joint solution is offered to the end customers, the purchasing, implementation, and support processes could be complex in such scenarios. The cybersecurity risks of such transformative solutions have to be kept in mind as well.

## Summary

In this chapter, we learned about the critical role that ecosystems and partnerships have in creating a transformative impact within a given industrial sector. We've seen how multiple companies and government agencies can work together with academia to accelerate industrial digital transformation.

In *Chapter 8, Artificial Intelligence in Digital Transformation*, we will look at the role of AI and machine learning in digital transformation. We will look at how data and analytics in combination with AI can help to deliver new kinds of transformative applications.

## Questions

Here are a few questions to check your understanding of this chapter:

1. Why are partnerships needed for digital transformation?
2. What is a consortium?
3. Are partnerships and ecosystems only relevant for private companies?
4. What are some examples of partnerships in the autonomous vehicle industry?
5. Name a few partnerships in the semiconductor industry.

# 8
# Artificial Intelligence in Digital Transformation

In the last chapter, we learned about the ecosystem approach to industrial digital transformation. We saw that ecosystems of partners and other stakeholders is key to moving the needle for transformative initiatives. As a result, a number of large companies often drive these initiatives across groups of large and small companies, consortiums, government agencies, and academia, with the goal of accelerating the transformation across industry segments.

In this chapter, we will learn how **Artificial Intelligence (AI)** is the key to industrial digital transformation initiatives. We will investigate different aspects of AI and how it drives business outcomes when applied to relevant data. We will cover the following topics in this chapter:

- The difference between AI, machine learning, and deep learning
- Applications of AI in industry
- Organization change influenced by AI

# The difference between AI, machine learning, and deep learning

Let's start with definitions of AI, **Machine Learning** (**ML**), and deep learning in order to get a better understanding of each of these technologies. *Figure 1.4* in *Chapter 1, Introducing Digital Transformation*, shows different fields of research that fall under AI and the approximate timeframe when they gained popularity.

## Artificial intelligence

AI is the field of study and its applications that utilize computers to perform tasks that are generally accomplished with the help of human intelligence. These tasks can include perception using visual, audio, and tactile/haptic inputs, pattern recognition in motion/environmental sensor data, and decision-making.

## Machine learning

ML is a subset of AI as a field of study. Algorithms used in ML are trained using large amounts of data tagged with associated and relevant real-world information. ML algorithms are being used in a variety of applications, such as automatic defect classification and predictive maintenance of equipment deployed in complex processes of the semiconductor industry. These algorithms can keep improving with newer data.

## Deep learning

Deep learning is a subset of ML. Algorithms used in deep learning are inspired by the function of the brain, and are called **Artificial Neural Networks** (**ANNs**), which process input data through multiple layers to extract progressively higher-level features. Deep learning algorithms using computer vision technology are being used in robotics applications to sense their surrounding environment in order to safely work with humans.

*Figure 1.4* in *Chapter 1, Introducing Digital Transformation*, pictorially shows the relationship between these three different fields of study. Now, let's explore different types of ML algorithms.

# Choices in ML algorithms

ML algorithms have been developed over the past 6 decades. The initial development of these algorithms was constrained by the available computational power and memory in the early part of this development process. However, the pace of development has picked up since the late 1990s. Hence, there are a variety of algorithms that are available and can serve the requirements of diverse applications in industrial digital transformation. *Figure 8.1* shows a high-level comparison of ML algorithms:

## Types of Machine Learning Algorithms

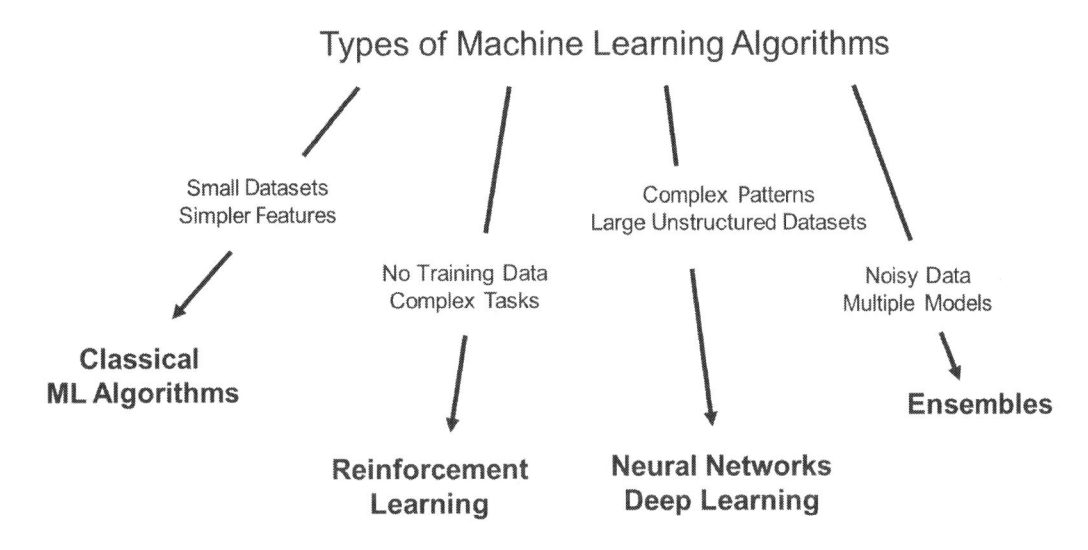

- **Classical ML Algorithms** — Small Datasets, Simpler Features
- **Reinforcement Learning** — No Training Data, Complex Tasks
- **Neural Networks Deep Learning** — Complex Patterns, Large Unstructured Datasets
- **Ensembles** — Noisy Data, Multiple Models

Figure 8.1 – Comparison of ML algorithms

As stated earlier, ML algorithms are developed using large amounts of data. Classical ML algorithms can be used for industrial applications when the features used for ML tasks, such as pattern recognition, are not complex. If the industrial process or system is very complex for mathematical modeling, then **Reinforcement Learning** (**RL**) algorithms can be used when there is a possibility of using a trial-and-error-based approach to learn using the system. In applications where the quality of data available for training the algorithms is not good and the features are complex, then ensemble methods of ML algorithms can be used. Image and audio recognition problems require large amounts of data for training and use complex features, and hence neural networks or deep learning algorithms are generally used for such applications.

An exhaustive list of ML algorithms and their descriptions is available on Wikipedia at `https://en.wikipedia.org/wiki/Outline_of_machine_learning#Machine_learning_algorithms`.

Classical ML, RL, and ensemble algorithms are described in the next section.

## Classical ML algorithm categories

ML algorithms can be utilized to complete tasks such as detection, classification, predictions, or making decisions. There are two broad categories of ML algorithms: supervised learning and unsupervised learning. *Figure 8.2* shows a pictorial view of the classical ML algorithms:

### Classical Machine Learning Algorithms

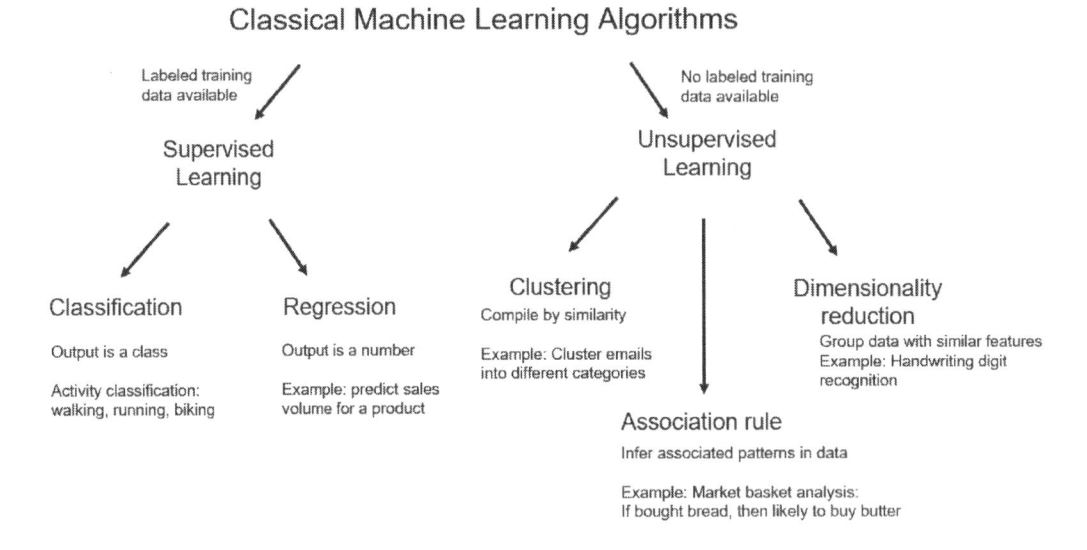

Labeled training data available → **Supervised Learning**
- **Classification** — Output is a class. Activity classification: walking, running, biking
- **Regression** — Output is a number. Example: predict sales volume for a product

No labeled training data available → **Unsupervised Learning**
- **Clustering** — Compile by similarity. Example: Cluster emails into different categories
- **Association rule** — Infer associated patterns in data. Example: Market basket analysis: If bought bread, then likely to buy butter
- **Dimensionality reduction** — Group data with similar features. Example: Handwriting digit recognition

Figure 8.2 – Classical ML algorithms

Supervised learning algorithms require labeled input data for the ML algorithm training process. Labeling indicates that training data is tagged with the best-known information about the state of the system at the time of data collection. Some examples of supervised ML algorithms are linear regression, logistic regression, K-NN, decision trees, random forest, and naïve Bayes. Supervised and semi-supervised algorithms are being applied for applications such as predictive maintenance and quality inspection in industrial environments. Unsupervised learning algorithms can develop patterns without any labeling or tagging information in training data. Some examples of unsupervised learning algorithms are clustering and dimension reduction algorithms. K-means clustering can be applied to assist in solving crimes and will be discussed in this chapter.

## RL algorithms

RL algorithms refer to a class of sequential decision-making algorithms where learning occurs through interaction with the environment in order to maximize a numerical reward signal. These algorithms are different from supervised learning algorithms. In the case of supervised learning, the process of learning occurs using a training set of labeled data that has been compiled using an expert mechanism that applies labels based on real-world observations. RL algorithms are different from unsupervised learning algorithms, which usually find hidden patterns in collections of unlabeled data. RL algorithms can be applied to a system with a dynamic environment where an agent (or agents) interact with the environment. The main components of an RL algorithm are a policy, a reward signal, and a value function. In some instances, a model of the environment may also be used when available. Based on the current state of the environment, the agent takes an action, guided by a policy and expected reward. The value function defines the aggregate reward an agent can expect in the future, based on the current state of the system.

There are a variety of RL algorithms consisting of combinations of the use of a model, value functions, and policy basis; for example, evolutionary RL algorithms do not utilize value functions. In the case of **Inverse Reinforcement Learning (IRL)** algorithms, there is no reward function. IRL algorithms learn the reward function, and these types of algorithms find applications for problems, such as decision-making in autonomous driving where IRL learns the reward function from human driving behavior. RL algorithms find their application in diverse industrial processes, such as controllers in petroleum refineries and chemical processes.

Manufacturing processes in various industries, such as the semiconductor industry, are becoming more complex. Consider a few unique challenges in the semiconductor industry, as follows:

- Product diversity and different production processes associated with them.
- Frontend processing can have thousands of individual processes that can last for weeks.
- Stringent quality requirements for processes with nodes in single-digit nanometers.

Production planning and the coordination of different processes need decision support systems. RL algorithms driven by policy, a reward signal, and a value function can be applied for these decision support systems. In the case of semiconductor industry frontend/backend operations, the model of the environment can also be available since this is a heavily researched area. Here, production engineers have to constantly make operational decisions in an ever-increasingly complex environment due to smaller lot sizes and product diversity in order to optimize the production process. This is an area where RL algorithms can help with order-dispatching system decisions. The objective of such a system is to achieve customer **On-Time Delivery** (**OTD**) while reaching the throughput and cycle time objectives for sustained profitability of operations.

## Ensembles

Ensemble learning algorithms use a combination of different models in order to improve ML performance. They can also be considered as meta-algorithms.

A combination of base ML algorithms in an ensemble algorithm can be achieved in multiple ways. One of the commonly used ensemble algorithms is a collection of a random forest of decision trees (a classical ML algorithm). Some of the ensemble methods commonly used are discussed in the following sections.

### Voting

The final output of the ensemble model is derived from outputs or predictions from each algorithm. Different voting schemes can be applied to each of the constituent algorithm outputs. In the case of majority voting, the prediction with more than 50% of votes is selected for final output. In the case of weighted voting, the votes for different models are weighted differently.

### Averaging

Here, the outputs from base-level algorithms in the ensemble are averaged to produce the final output. Weighted averaging techniques can also be applied based on the performance of base-level algorithms.

### Bootstrap aggregating (Bagging)

This method uses a bootstrap sampling technique to compile the training data subsets that are used in training constituent base algorithms, such as decision trees. The final output is produced by using a voting method for classification purposes and an averaging method for regression.

## Boosting

In this case, the constituent base algorithms are connected and trained sequentially to improve the overall accuracy of the ensemble.

## Stacking

Stacking uses another ML algorithm, such as a meta-classifier, to combine the output of each of the constituent algorithms in the ensemble to produce a final output.

Additional details about ensemble learning algorithms are available at `https://en.wikipedia.org/wiki/Ensemble_learning`.

## Deep learning

Deep learning algorithms are based on the structure of ANNs. With advances in computational frameworks and the widespread availability of devices such as GPUs that enable implementation of ANNs, deep learning algorithms are increasingly being used for applications in image processing and audio processing. Deep learning algorithms achieve higher accuracies in applications such as image classification as compared to classical ML algorithms. The performance of deep learning algorithms keeps improving as greater amounts of training data become available. The most popular deep learning algorithms are the following:

- **Deep Neural Network (DNN)**
- **Convolution Neural Network (CNN)**
- **Long Short-Term Memory Network (LSTM)**
- **Recurrent Neural Network (RNN)**
- **Deep Belief Network (DBN)**
- **Deep Boltzmann Machine (DBM)**

For reference, see `https://towardsdatascience.com/defining-data-science-machine-learning-and-artificial-intelligence-95f42a60b57c` and `https://www.albeado.com/products-and-technology.html`.

In the next section, we will look at the applications of AI in various industry sectors, including in the public sector.

# Applications of AI in industry

Let's explore how AI is being applied in areas such as manufacturing facilities, quality control and inspection, and predictive maintenance.

## AI in factories

AI can enable the digital transformation of manufacturing and factories in many ways. Applications of AI increase productivity in the manufacturing process, improve the quality of products, optimize the use of warehouses, and allow predictive maintenance for many functions in the factory. A sensor is the first key enabling component for AI implementation in a factory. Data can also be available from **Programmable Logic Controllers** (**PLCs**), SCADA systems that monitor and control processes/equipment, quality monitoring systems, alarm systems, and even **Enterprise Resource Planning** (**ERP**) systems. There is a wide array of sensors available to collect data at every stage of production in the factory. These sensors can measure many important parameters, such as temperature, vibration, acoustic emission, pressure, humidity, acceleration, velocity, displacement, force, torque, magnetic field strength, proximity, and others. Sensor data is processed on the edge or gateway, in the cloud, or in a distributed fashion in a combination as per the architectural needs.

## AI for predictive maintenance

Industrial operations customarily use schedule-driven maintenance as a method to ensure that equipment or systems are operating at their peak efficiency. Corrective maintenance is done if there is an unscheduled failure of a part or equipment. Consider the example of an automotive factory. The **Automated Imaging Association** (**AIA**) states in a Vision Online article that the cost of 1 minute of downtime is $20,000 in an automotive factory manufacturing high-profit automobiles (https://www.visiononline.org/vision-resources-details.cfm/vision-resources/Remote-Vision-System-Monitoring-Unleashes-Predictive-Maintenance-Capabilities/content_id/6181). AI-based predictive maintenance solutions can prevent such unplanned downtime in the factory.

Industrial operations stakeholders are motivated to minimize the business risk of unexpected system failure and unplanned downtime. They would like to obtain better visibility into their systems through the following:

- Obtaining an estimate of the **Remaining Useful Life (RUL)** of various critical and non-critical equipment down to the serviceable component level.
- The ability to detect anomalies in the system and predict the failure of equipment in the near future.
- Receive recommendations on maintenance actions to sustain the achievable peak efficiency of equipment.

Predictive maintenance solutions provide a balanced approach to maintenance resulting in cost savings through improved utilization of equipment operating at peak efficiency for the maximum utilization of the component lifetime.

It is important to note that in order to benefit from the advantages of AI-driven predictive maintenance, the business use case needs to be predictive in nature and relevant operational data with sufficient quality should be available for this system. For example, a predictive maintenance algorithm for an engine would require time-series sensor data (with accurate timestamps) from all of the sensors monitoring the performance of the engine, along with operational settings and wear states of different engines that are used for the collection of this data. The underlying assumption is that the performance of all machines degrades over time.

Rotating machinery, such as electric motors, generators, pumps, and turbines, are part of critical equipment in an industrial operation. Predicting parameters such as **Mean Time to Failure (MTTF)** for this equipment can enable operations managers to ensure that there is no unplanned failure of equipment. Failure probabilities on machines that are close to failure can allow plant operators to monitor these machines closely and plan the shortest downtime of the plant for maintenance or the replacement of equipment. There are many high-impact applications of these predictive maintenance methods in the utility industry.

As described previously, the success of AI algorithms depends heavily on the availability of the sufficient quality of relevant data for the system. This data should include normal operation data patterns, degraded operation data, and failure data patterns. Relevant high-level information about machines, such as maintenance and failure history, operating conditions, and ideal operating characteristics, is also needed to prepare the predictive maintenance AI models. Considering the example of rotating machinery, sensor data can be collected from speed detectors, temperature sensors installed at various locations, such as bearings, accelerometers to detect vibrations, electrical parameters (such as voltage, current, and phase), and oil pressure as per the configuration of the machine. This data can be transferred through a wired or wireless connection to the edge, gateway, or cloud depending on the selected configuration. Domain experts can identify the relevant data, including the required sensor data at the required frequency, and ensure that the required data with sufficient quality is available. Data scientists and domain experts can collaborate to prepare the predictive models.

Predictive models can be developed for the following functions:

- To estimate the probability of equipment failure within a specified time
- To estimate the range of time of failure along with the most likely root cause
- To estimate the RUL of the system

There are multiple options for the choice of algorithm to be used, from classical ML algorithms to deep learning algorithms. An LSTM network is one such example of a deep learning algorithm.

The performance of a selected algorithm can be evaluated using a combination of metrics, such as the following:

- **Precision**: This is the ratio of true positive identification to all relevant instances of failure. Hence, the higher the precision of the prediction model, the lower the false positive rate will be.
- **Recall**: This is the true positive rate, which corresponds to true positives that are correctly identified by the model. Higher values of recall will indicate that the prediction model is accurate in identifying true failure.
- **Receiver Operating Characteristics (ROC) curve**: This is a plot of true positive rate (recall) versus the false positive rate of the model for the selected operating conditions.

Next, let's look into the use of AI in quality assurance.

# AI in quality assurance and inspection

Quality assurance is an important part of the industrial process. Manufacturing processes vary significantly depending on the industry and application. However, all manufacturing processes that utilize equipment will have common **Key Performance Indicators** (**KPIs**) to achieve a reduction in six big losses, as follows:

- Equipment failure
- Planned stops for setup/adjustments
- Idle time
- Reduced speed
- Process defects
- Reduced yield

There are two parameters that are also commonly used by industrial processes that include manufacturing: **Overall Equipment Effectiveness** (**OEE**) and **Overall Line Efficiency** (**OLE**). OEE is an indicator that is used to monitor the productivity of equipment, and is also utilized to drive process improvements. OLE is computed through the aggregation of OEE for various equipment in the production line. OEE is based on three factors: **availability**, **performance**, and **quality**. OEE is computed as *OEE = Availability X Performance X Quality*, where *Availability* is the ratio of operation time to planned production time, *Performance* is the ratio of (ideal cycle time X total count) to the operation time of equipment, and *Quality* is the ratio of good part count to total part count in production.

Cycle time is the time required to produce one part. Planned production time is the total time equipment will be producing parts as per the plan. In discrete manufacturing operations (such as automobiles, smartphones, and airplanes), an OEE score of 85% is considered world-class, and many companies use this score as a suitable long-term goal. A score of 60% is typical for discrete manufacturers, and a score of 40% is typical for companies that have just begun tracking and improving the performance of their manufacturing processes.

More details about OEE can be found at www.OEE.com.

The OLE of manufacturing processes that utilize multiple equipments is dependent on factors such as the cycle time of each equipment, and hence the calculation of OLE is more complex. A simple estimate of OLE can be computed using the weighted average of OEEs of different equipment in the production line.

Several quality management methods have been developed over the years and have been successfully utilized in diverse manufacturing operations, from semiconductor companies to automotive manufacturing, to improve OEE. **Failure Mode and Effect Analysis (FMEA)**, **Total Productive Maintenance (TPM)**, and Lean manufacturing are some examples of such methods. The well-known **Toyota Production System (TPS)** has been used as a model by countless other industries that have benefitted from enhanced product quality and improved manufacturing processes.

Digital transformation is enabling a transformation of these quality management methods as well. Real-time computation of availability (for OEE) is possible for a production line instrumented with distributed sensors described in the previous section. This sensor data (which may include image, audio, and other application-specific parameters) would allow real-time estimation of quality through the use of ML and AI algorithms. These algorithms would also be able to generate predictive warnings if the quality of production drops below target levels. Examples of image processing for monitoring quality are described in the next section.

# AI in image recognition for quality of inspection

Machine vision can be used both for quality inspection during manufacturing processes in the factory as well as for inspection of physical assets in the field. Let's look at a few different examples:

- **Borescopes in jet engine maintenance**: **General Electric (GE)** Aviation, uses a borescope for inspecting the aircraft jet engines at the airports without taking the engines off the wing. The borescope uses optical systems using a flexible tube that can be inserted inside the engine to record the internal surface conditions. These images are taken by illuminating the surface to take high-precision images. These images could be a video or may use other forms of imaging not visible to the human eye. These algorithms are based on DNNs. These are applied to these recorded images to look for surface damages or micro-fractures that could be a result of the multiple flight cycles that the engine has undergone since the last maintenance in the shop. The borescope inspection is a non-destructive testing process that can provide a good leading indicator of when the engine would require maintenance and at the same time assure the safety of the next flight. The ability to do the borescope inspection of the jet engine, without taking it off the aircraft wing, helps to increase the **Time on Wing (ToW)** of the engines and overall reduces the downtime for the airline due to maintenance events. See `https://www.geaviation.com/commercial/truechoice-commercial-services/on-wing-support` for more details.

- **Aircraft inspection by drones**: In 2019, Austrian Airlines used autonomous drones for the inspection of the fleet of aircraft, using the technology developed by a French company called Donecle (see https://www.donecle.com/solution/#inspect). The drone can inspect a narrow-body aircraft, which is often used for domestic flights, in an hour. It collects very high-resolution images of the entire external aircraft body and applies AI to it to detect any anomalies. This process can detect any impact of lightning strikes on the aircraft or any regulatory gaps, or pinpoint the areas that may need further human inspection. This can automate the service ticket for the aircraft engineers and technicians according to the observed issues.

Next, let's look at the use of AI in healthcare, logistics, and other domains in the subsequent sections.

## AI in medical domain image recognition

Healthcare and medical imaging pose a few interesting opportunities for the application of AI:

- **AI in healthcare**: Deep learning techniques such as CNN are being used to assist physicians in skin cancer diagnosis. In a 2017 article in Nature (see https://www.nature.com/articles/nature21056), scientists demonstrated the classification of skin lesions using a single CNN, by using about 129.5 thousand clinical images. This dataset had images representing about 2,000 different diseases. A CNN was used for binary classification of the two scenarios – first, common skin cancer detection between keratinocyte carcinomas versus benign seborrheic keratoses, then second, identification of the deadliest skin cancer between malignant melanomas versus benign nevi. This is an interesting scenario since one of three melanomas arise from the benign, melanocytic nevi. Yet, the vast majority of melanocytic nevi will never end up in melanoma.

    The CNN results were compared against 21 board-certified dermatologists. The CNN's performance was comparable to the human experts for both of the preceding classification scenarios of skin cancer. This is a good testimonial of how AI and machine vision can be transformative in cancer detection and treatment.

- **Deep learning in radiology**: Medical imaging such as X-rays often involves the exposure of humans to radiation. As a result, it is important to reduce multiple incidences of imaging. Often, the only way of communicating between the physician and the imaging technician is through prescriptions or the doctor's orders. A sample diagnostic imaging order form can be found at `https://www.legacyhealth.org/-/media/Files/PDF/Health-Professionals/Referral-forms/Imaging-Order-Form-7-2014.pdf`.

    This form indicates that **Computed Tomography (CT)** – head CT – is needed; it does not provide details of the brain screen protocols. As a result, the imaging technician would use their best judgement to complete the procedure. Then, the ordering physician looks at the imaging reports a few days later and determines that additional CT views are needed. This further exposes the patient to radiation and also delays the treatment. To prevent this conundrum, AI is being applied to medical imaging, at the time of taking the images, to help decide, based on the outcome of the first image, which additional slices may be needed. While this is in the early stages of use in the medical industry, this is yet another transformative use of AI and machine vision for medicine. This can cut short the multiple iterations of medical imaging and reduce multiple exposures to nuclear radiation (see `https://www.gehealthcare.com/long-article/how-ai-and-deep-learning-are-revolutionizing-medical-imaging`).

- **IBM Watson Expert**: Humana has used IBM's AI-based service, now called Humana's Voice Agent, since 2019 to handle provider calls. Humana is one of the largest US medical insurance companies; they receive over 1 million calls annually from their providers. With the help of the AI-based Voice Agent, they were able to streamline these calls and improve provider experience. In this solution, AI is used to interpret the real intent of a provider's telephone call. The system verifies the provider's access level for any privileged information and then decides how to best deliver the requested information (see `https://www.ibm.com/watson/stories/humana/`).

Next, let's look at the use of AI in warehouses and distribution centers.

# AI for the dynamic optimization of warehouse operations

Modern warehouses are a critical component of the economy today. CNBC reports that the US may need an additional billion square feet of warehouse space to accommodate booming e-commerce demands (https://www.cnbc.com/2020/07/09/us-may-need-another-1-billion-square-feet-of-warehouse-space-by-2025.html).

Modern warehouses are managed using sophisticated management systems. Some of the common functions in a warehouse are as follows:

- Receiving goods
- Inspection and acceptance of goods
- Barcode scanning for individual **Stock Keeping Units** (**SKUs**)
- Picking
- Put-away
- Order assembly
- Packing goods
- Slotting
- Cycle counting
- Shipping goods

A warehouse management system directs and validates each step in the movement of goods in the warehouse and capturing and recording all inventory movement. Warehouse management systems can be a standalone system, part of supply chain execution modules, or part of ERP systems. There are options for cloud-based warehouse management systems available as well.

Warehouses are increasingly installing many sensors for different operations. Forklift detection sensors can monitor the movement of forklifts when they move in and out of a trailer. Dock monitor sensors can provide information on when trucks arrive and leave the warehouse. Automated material handling systems such as instrumented conveyor and sortation systems have been in use in warehouses for a long time. Metadata from these systems is now available in warehouse execution systems. **Autonomous Mobile Robots** (**AMRs**), described in *Chapter 3, Accelerating Digital Transformation with Emerging Technologies*, are being adopted in modern warehouses. These robots are in constant wireless communication with robotic control systems. There is also increased use of computer vision using cameras installed in selected locations in warehouses to enable the tracking of movement of goods. AI applications are making warehouses more dynamic and responsive.

AI methods are used to process the data gathered from these varied sensors from multiple systems and unstructured data from ERP systems to detect patterns and make specific recommendations on the following:

- The rate of replenishment of different inventory items
- Inventory movement and management to fine-tune logistics and material handling
- Pick-and-pack processes for improved productivity
- Shorter walking routes for personnel
- Optimized path planning for AMRs in the warehouse

Companies such as Honeywell offer systems for these modern warehouses. Honeywell Intelligrated is an example of one such system that includes automated material handling and robotics systems.

The large amounts of data generated by AI systems are turning into assets for businesses. Next, let's look into a couple of examples of how these data assets are being monetized.

# Monetization of data assets for high-value business scenarios

AI solutions are dependent on large amounts of data. Digital transformation and the application of AI are generating large amounts of data, which are regarded as important assets by businesses.

With the rapid proliferation of IoT devices and mobile devices with sensors, these devices are generating data at a rapidly increasing pace. In many instances, this data is labeled with contextual information. Data from traditional transactional systems, such as SABRE for airline systems, continues to generate valuable data assets. Google, Amazon, Facebook, and Apple have all created platforms that generate massive amounts of data for these companies through the use of platforms such as Google's search engine, Facebook's social media platform, Amazon's online retail site, and Apple's mobile and computing devices.

## Data assets

Data assets continue to be generated through a wide variety of data, which includes contextual and user profile information. Ridesharing companies use AI-based algorithms in their platforms to match drivers with riders, optimizing the routes, and dynamically pricing the ride. At the same time, these ridesharing companies continue to get pick-up and drop-off location information of riders that utilize their platform and services. Food and grocery delivery platforms, such as DoorDash, Uber Eats, GrubHub, and others collect additional contextualized data with user profile information.

Semiconductor companies that are adopting digital transformation are continuing to generate a myriad of data from manufacturing, supply chain management, and customer engagements.

## Data monetization

There are two avenues for monetization of data assets for business: internal and external.

Businesses use data internally to improve the manufacturing processes, quality management, products and services, and customer satisfaction. Mobile phone companies use the data they collect to develop new products and services for their subscribers and improve their operations. Mobile phone companies also generate revenue by offering this anonymized and aggregated data to a wide variety of customers, such as digital ad agencies, retailers, public transportation agencies, government agencies, and healthcare organizations. This is an example of the external monetization of data assets.

## Business case study

John Deere, the world's largest farm equipment manufacturer, and Cornell University created a partnership on Ag-Analytics (`https://news.cornell.edu/stories/2017/09/cornell-digital-ag-program-integrates-john-deere-operations-center`).

The farm equipment sold by John Deere has a large number of sensors installed. Through these sensors, a large amount of location-tagged data is generated by farmers when they use their equipment to till fields, plant seeds, and harvest crops. This data is transferred through John Deere's data operations center securely into the Ag-Analytics platform.

This platform offers free tools to farmers, which provides them with valuable information for their farms on the following:

- Crop insurance calculators
- Forecasting tools
- Real-time yield forecasting
- Risk-management tools
- Data on soil and weather
- Satellite vegetation data

The key takeaway regarding monetization via AI is that the companies should leverage AI as a means or as a digital tool and not as the end goal when making it part of industrial digital transformation. In other words, adding the capability to apply AI is not enough unless it makes an improvement in the business outcomes and is quantifiable for top-line or bottom-line revenues.

Next, let's look at the use of ML at the edge.

## ML at the edge

ML can be done in the core or cloud system or at the edge. In this context, edge refers to the machine or the sensor inside or mounted on or near the device. ML is applied at the edge, rather than waiting for the data to be transported to the cloud or the core backend server. While applying the model or inferencing in the edge is often used, an emerging area is doing the model building or learning at the edge for certain limited cases. See *Figure 8.3*.

Let's see how ML at the edge works.

## Micro-electromechanical system sensors framework

These days, there are numerous examples of IoT devices that are being used in a wide variety of applications. These devices in smart homes manage security, energy consumption, and appliances. Factories are optimizing operations and costs through predictive maintenance, as described earlier in this chapter. Smart cities are deploying different types of IoT devices, such as smart parking sensors to pollution monitors installed on streetlights. ML- and AI-based solutions that are built with **Micro-Electromechanical System (MEMS)** sensors, connectivity, and **Microcontrollers (MCU)** are proliferating.

A lot of current deployments of IoT devices use an architecture where the raw sensor data is sent to a cloud solution with large processing and archiving capabilities. This approach requires significant data bandwidth and computational capabilities. This architecture results in higher latencies to IoT devices because raw data containing audio, video, or image files from millions of IoT devices is sent to the cloud for processing.

In applications that require very low latencies for good user experience, the cloud-based architecture might have some limitations where responsiveness is important. In such applications, on-edge computational solutions are needed to minimize transport delays and to deliver a better user experience. The on-edge architecture utilizes MCUs for computations. MCUs are tiny, low-cost computational devices often found as a core computational unit in the latest generation of IoT devices. MCUs contain one or more processor cores, memory, and programmable input/output peripherals. More than 30 billion MCUs were shipped in 2019 globally. MCUs are used in embedded systems in all kinds of applications in automobiles, mobile phones, medical devices, home appliances, and IoT devices. These MCUs deliver high computational performance at extremely low power consumption and can run on tiny batteries for months.

Over the past few decades, the computation power of MCUs has increased significantly, while the power consumption has been reduced. MCUs with an ARM Cortex M4 core can execute AI algorithms such as DNN in real time to process an audio signal. In the cloud-computing architecture, MCUs are primarily responsible for sensor data acquisition, batching, labeling, and sending this data to the cloud infrastructure. This is not an ideal utilization of compute resources for MCUs that are typically clocked at hundreds of MHz.

A distributed computing approach significantly reduces the bandwidth requirement for transferring sensor data when the edge computing capabilities in MCUs or sensors are utilized. This approach also provides an added advantage where the user data, as personal source data, is locally processed and only metadata is sent to the cloud. This approach is particularly beneficial for applications involving medical devices or fitness devices:

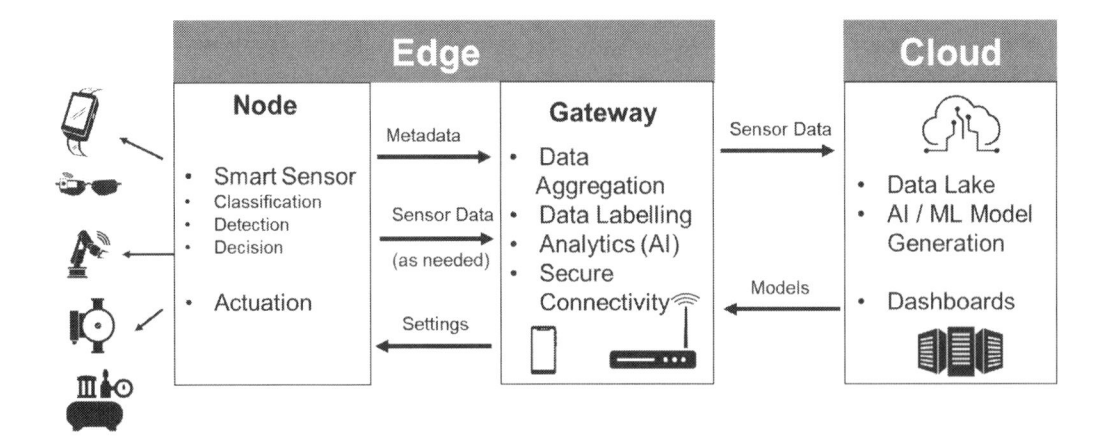

Figure 8.3 – Cloud and edge computation

*Figure 8.3* shows an architecture that depicts the interactions with the physical world with sensing and actuation through nodes on the edge, and data archiving occurs in the connected cloud.

STMicroelectronics offers MCU solutions from a wide portfolio of STM32 MCUs and sensors, such as LSM6DSOX, which has a built-in ML core and finite state machine and a Cube.AI toolkit, which allows AI solutions such as DNN to be prepared for implementation on the MCU.

STMicroelectronics offers advanced inertial sensors that have the capability to execute decision trees in the built-in ML core of the sensor. This capability allows the user to develop a variety of applications for consumer devices such as smartwatches or industrial devices such as wireless sensor nodes where power consumption for applications needs to be minimized. These advanced sensors, such as the LSM6DSOX and ISM330DHCX, are increasingly being used to build solutions with an *always-on* user experience with extremely low current consumption, in order of single-digit micro-amps for sensor applications, such as activity tracking, gesture recognition, and vibration monitoring. These sensors also have internal memory and a high-speed I3C serial interface. Storing sensor data on the sensor and transferring it in batches over a high communication rate I3C bus will reduce the wake-up period of the interfacing MCU, thereby saving energy. A decision tree or a finite state machine can be downloaded into the sensor to build functionality such as human activity tracking, gesture recognition, or vibration monitoring in an industrial application.

Middleware for this sensor allows easy integration with popular mobile platforms, such as Android, which are commonly used to build smart devices for consumer, industrial, and automotive applications.

Next, let's look into Field Programmable Gate Arrays (**FPGAs**), which are also used in edge solutions.

## FPGAs in edge analytics

Companies such as Intel and Xilinx manufacture FPGAs, which are semiconductor devices that have **Configurable Logic Blocks** (**CLBs**). These can be easily connected via programmable interconnects. FPGAs can be used for the hardware acceleration of CNN deep learning applications. However, FPGAs also consume 3 to 4 times less power than **GPUs**. That makes FPGAs a good candidate for use in AI on the edge (see https://www.usenix.org/system/files/conference/hotedge18/hotedge18-papers-biookaghazadeh.pdf).

One use case of FPGAs for inferencing in machine vision is on factory floors. Often, it is not practical to send a large number of images to the cloud-based system in near real time for analysis for production quality. In such cases, FPGA-based edge-computing systems provide a feasible option for local inferencing. In addition, FPGA-based smart cameras are being used for video surveillance applications.

Let's look at some public sector examples of AI.

# AI in the public sector

In this section, we will look at the use of AI and ML in the public sector. Let's begin with the topic of law enforcement and crime.

## Detecting gunshots

According to the CDC, there were about 40,000 firearm-related deaths in the US in 2017 (see https://www.cdc.gov/nchs/fastats/injury.htm). Apparently, 80% of gunshot incidents go unreported. A company called ShotSpotter (see http://www.shotspotter.com/technology/) had developed a technology that can be used by law enforcement. Gun violence has serious consequences on society and the national economy. According to a 2019 study by the US Joint Economic Committee, the economic impact of gun violence is about $229 billion yearly. This kind of technology relies on multiple sensors for acoustic detection and then calculating the precise location of the gunshot. A few other companies in this space are Databuoy, AmberBox, ZeroEyes, and Shooter Detection Systems.

ShotSpotter uses a combination of the acoustic sensors that are on buildings or light posts and algorithms to detect a gunshot and notify the law enforcement department responsible for that area. This automates the process and gives a more precise location of the gunshot. The system triangulates the sound of the gunshot and uses the timestamp of the gunshot for the distance traveled by the sound to locate the origin. Advanced techniques using AI can help to identify multiple shooters in an area or a series of shootings by the same person. This company provides a mobile app called Respond to law enforcement personnel so that they can get the relevant information when on the move. Due to the use of ShotSpotter, the time to respond to gunfire incidents has reduced tremendously, and law enforcement teams can be sent to the right place. Many gunshots would otherwise go unreported, and ShotSpotter helps to bridge that gap as well. The city of San Diego started using ShotSpotter in 2016. They experienced a reduction in gunfire incidents in 2019 compared to 2018. Some of the sensors used in this process are mounted on the LED light posts in San Diego downtown that act as LED nodes.

ShotSpotter is a good case study of digital transformation, in the public sector, with the goal to make the citizens safer. The company ShotSpotter uses cloud technology to run its solution and has an annual subscription revenue model. It charges mainly by the per-square mile of the deployment of the ShotSpotter solution in the city or the campus. This is a great example of AI-driven digital revenues powering business model transformation. ShotSpotter was recognized by the US Department of Homeland Security for its offering.

Let's look at another scenario for use of ML for detecting crime sprees.

## Detecting crime sprees

According to a paper published in 2013, about 1% of the population in Sweden was responsible for 63% of violent crimes (see https://www.ncbi.nlm.nih.gov/pmc/articles/PMC3969807/). This is true for the US as well. A very recent scenario in California involved Joseph James DeAngelo Jr., who is known as the Golden State Killer. He was caught in April 2018 and was responsible for three crime sprees leading to a total of 13 murders, 50 rapes, and over 100 burglaries. These crimes were committed between 1974 and 1986. The three different crimes sprees were named the following:

- The East Area Rapist in the Sacramento, California area
- The Night Stalker in Southern California
- The original Night Stalker

Since often a series of crimes will be committed by a small number of culprits, the identification of crime sprees is useful in solving a number of crimes together. One of the authors of this book (Nath) applied ML to crime sprees while working with a law enforcement agency in Louisiana. The details of the work can be seen in the paper here: http://cs.brown.edu/courses/csci2950-t/crime.pdf.

Detectives and the police department often have a huge backlog of unsolved cases. According to FBI data, less than 20% of property crimes (those involving burglary and theft) get solved. The use of AI and ML, including a geo-spatial plot of the crimes and using the K-means algorithm for clustering, can provide much-needed assistance to law enforcement officers in solving crime faster. In this case, the clusters of crimes were plotted with color-coding. This allows the detective to see which set of crimes have similar characteristics according to the clustering algorithm. For example, a series of break-ins in gas stations over a few days, within 20 miles of each other, could be an example of a crime spree. The detectives can start to focus on these clusters first and use their experience to look for more information to confirm whether it looks like an act carried out by the same set of criminals. This determination now helps to build the evidence from each of the crime incident reports, to develop a richer set of evidence against the same criminal group.

Next, let's look at more recent trends in the use of AI and computer vision to help law enforcement.

## Computer vision and law enforcement

Let's look at SenseTime, a company that was created in Hong Kong in 2014. Today, it is one of the highest-worth AR companies in the world, valued at over $7.5 billion. SenseTime is working on facial recognition technology. It is reported to own a massive computing network consisting of 54 million GPU cores spread over 12 GPU clusters.

The Beijing Daxing International Airport in China became operational in 2019 and was developed at a cost of $179 billion. It will use SenseTime's AI-based **Intelligent Passenger Security System (IPSS)** system for passenger management at the airport. IPSS uses face recognition to allow passengers to self-verify that they have the required valid identification and airline ticket. It will also tag airline baggage to prevent any lost bags.

Another company, SITA, has developed a similar solution called SITA SmartPath for use at the airport (see `https://www.sita.aero/solutions-and-services/solutions/sita-smart-path`). This solution also uses facial recognition technology, as seen in the following figure:

SELF-SERVICE CHECK-IN → SELF-SERVICE BAG DROP → SECURITY SCREENING → BORDER CONTROL → SELF-SERVICE BOARDING → ASSISTED BOARDING

Figure 8.4 – The SITA Smart Path solution for airport automation

We would like to caution against recent issues due to bias in AI and the use of such technology in controversial issues. SenseTime was blacklisted by the US government in 2019 as it was believed to be involved in human rights violations against a Muslim minority group in China. In June 2020, IBM announced it would stop research and development of facial recognition technology. In the same month, **Amazon Web Services (AWS)** also put a 1-year moratorium on the use of its technology called Rekognition by police agencies (see `https://blog.aboutamazon.com/policy/we-are-implementing-a-one-year-moratorium-on-police-use-of-rekognition`). In recent times, this technology has been scrutinized for racial bias and privacy. An MIT study looked at the commercially available system with the capability of recognizing the gender of a person. The study found that the error rates for recognizing dark-skinned women were 49 times higher than that for white men. Likewise, the US Department of Commerce found that the error rates for African men and women compared to Eastern Europeans were higher by two orders of magnitude.

## AI in aviation

For predictive maintenance of aircraft jet engines, AI has been used in various ways. We looked at the use of computer vision via the borescope. Next, let's look at the use of AI via the digital twin of the jet engine. One of the authors of this book (Nath) has described this in a blog post here: https://blogs.oracle.com/datascience/applying-industrial-data-science%3a-a-use-case.

In *Figure 8.5*, the *Y* axis is the **Exhaust Gas Temperature** (**EGT**) and the *X* axis is time. The EGT plot is a good indicator of how long the parts inside the engine are exposed to high temperatures. The sensors inside the jet engine record this. As the aircraft takes off from the runway, its engines are subjected to excessive amounts of stress as it climbs, until it reaches cruising altitude. The laws of physics and material science tell us that when matter is subjected to very high temperatures for an extended period of time, it becomes prone to failure. With each takeoff, the interior of the engine goes through similar high-temperature exposure:

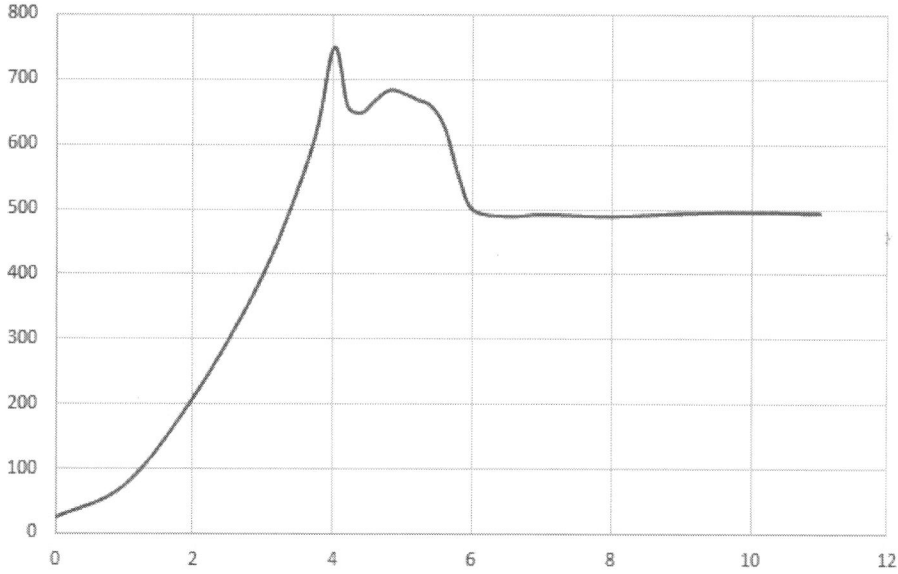

Figure 8.5 – An aircraft jet engine's EGT plot

The domain knowledge of how the jet engine is designed gives us the physics-based analytics model. The observed sensor readings give us the statistical model. The two together, along with the knowledge of the jet engine and its sub-components, give us a unique digital twin of a specific engine. With this AI-based digital twin, we can make intelligent decisions about when to service the engine or how to optimize the fuel efficiency of the engine.

Since the digital twin of the jet engine helps to provide an indication ahead of time of the maintenance activities of the aircraft and its engine, it can be used for intelligently scheduling the aircraft or the engine for **maintenance**, **repair**, and **overhauls**, often referred to as **MRO** activities. Based on insights from the digital twin and the borescope inspection, the repair shop may already be prepared with the spare parts that may be needed and know what kind of maintenance activities are needed. In theory, this is similar to a surgeon knowing ahead of the surgery what to expect while performing the procedure on the patient in the operating room, due to diagnostics tests and imaging done ahead of time.

Next, let's look at the impacts of AI on an organization's structure and culture.

## Organizational change influenced by AI

For the success of the AI-driven transformation, the change management of the organization and the AI initiative has to be coordinated. For the success of AI, the benefits should be clear to the different stakeholders in the organization. One way is to involve the employees in the early pilots using AI. For instance, an AI-powered digital assistant could be rolled out for health and wellness to the employees. This would allow them to experience it first hand. For knowledge workers, they can be encouraged to improve their AI knowledge at their own pace. Many free resources are available due to the rise of **Massive Open Online Courses** (**MOOCs**), as well from companies, such as the following:

- Dell – Education Services (see `https://education.dellemc.com/content/emc/en-us/home.html`)

- Intel – AI courses under the AI Developer Program (see `https://software.intel.com/content/www/us/en/develop/topics/ai/training/courses.html`)

- Oracle – AI/ML for Developers (see `https://developer.oracle.com/ai-ml/`)

- STMicroelectronics – educational materials and embedded ML (see `https://www.st.com/content/st_com/en/campaigns/educationalplatforms/iot-edu.html` and `https://www.st.com/content/st_com/en/support/learning/stm32-education/stm32-moocs.html`)

These examples showcase the democratization of education and allow employees at all levels to learn about AI and feel a part of the company's AI-led transformation. In a recent Deloitte study titled *Thriving in the era of pervasive AI*, three groups of AI adopters were defined after interviewing over 2,700 IT and line-of-business executives globally:

- **Starters**: This group consists of about 27% of those surveyed and includes those who are just experimenting with AI adoption.
- **Skilled**: This group consists of 47% of those surveyed and have seen a moderate level of success due to AI adoption.
- **Seasoned**: This group consists of about 26% of those surveyed and are the leaders in terms of AI adoption with a larger number of AI deployments and a mature pool of digital talent to support those deployments.

These AI adopters are in various stages of incorporating ML, deep learning, machine vision, **Natural Language Processing** (**NLP**), and **Robotic Process Automation** (**RPA**) for the following reasons:

- To gain a competitive advantage
- To enable new business models
- To optimize and enhance business processes
- To automate or make employees more productive

In order to gain a competitive advantage, companies have to think of creative ways to put AI-led initiatives to work. Airbnb uses AI in many creative ways. In its case, the competition is from traditional hotels, but it tries to improve the overall guest and host experience. Here are a few ways that Airbnb is using AI:

- **To evaluate whether a guest can be trusted**: Hosts offer their primary or secondary homes to *unknown* guests. The home may be their highest-value possession, so it is important to ensure that their property is safe. AI algorithms applied to the guest act as Airbnb's own form of a background check, based on the information available, with the goal of keeping the hosts safe.

- **Message sentient**: Guests often send time-sensitive questions to the host, as they may be traveling. AI is used to understand the intent of the messages via the Airbnb app and often automated responses are generated.
- **Ranking of experiences**: Due to the COVID-19 pandemic in early 2020, Airbnb suffered a big setback as the travel industry crumbled. However, Airbnb quickly started a new offer called Experiences, which do not require travel (see `https://www.airbnb.com/s/experiences/online`). To make the Experiences feature relevant to the guest, Airbnb has deployed search ranking based on ML to display the *most relevant* experiences to their guests.

This is a good example of how AI-led transformations are encouraging creative ways of thinking in the modern industry landscape. This, in turn, drives companies to make the right kind of changes internally, to take advantage of the AI-led opportunities. However, a company such as Airbnb is digital-native and agile. We saw that the company is quick to try out new business models, such as Experiences, as well as is savvy in the adoption of AI. This can be a challenge for large and traditional companies.

When GE Aviation started working with data scientists with aircraft engine data, the black-box approach of using ML to find anomalies was a big challenge for aviation engineers. Aviation engineers are used to explaining the behavior of the jet engine based on the laws of the physics and material sciences. When a root cause analysis is done for parts failure, the explanations should be in line with the physical properties of materials. When data scientists looked at ML models created from sensor data and pointed out the anomalies or actions for predictive maintenance, the black-box models were not human-explainable. To provide an example of a human-understandable model, let's go back to the example of EGT, used earlier in this chapter.

When certain GE engines required more frequent servicing than normally expected, data scientists were able to correlate those engines to aircraft flying over certain destinations. However, that was not sufficient to explain why engines running on certain routes should have more issues than on other routes of similar duration. This is one example where aviation engineers were hesitant to act on data that is not easily explainable by the known properties of the engine or its components. To overcome such situations, GE Aviation collocated some engineers with the data scientists from GE Digital at San Ramon, California. This way, the aviation engineers and data scientists could work together and bring the two perspectives together to solve problems faster. When the two groups worked together under one roof, they were quickly able to come to the physics-based explanation of the real problem. The engines that were often flying on routes to places with hot deserts in the summer, such as Saudi Arabia or Phoenix in the US, were those that required servicing more often. This was the result of the fine sand particles entering the jet engine and adversely impacting the fan blades and other internal structures, especially when there was a sandstorm when the engine was running or during the takeoff. The following two references further explain the adverse impact of dust on the engines:

- https://www.wired.com/2015/06/ge-uses-sand-around-world-test-jet-engines/
- https://blog.geaviation.com/product/sand-and-sky-how-engineers-are-improving-the-way-airliners-engines-cope-with-the-most-extreme-natural-conditions/

This section provided good examples of how enterprises need to be flexible to bring different groups of people at the same level as they adopt AI. In GE's case, moving some of the aviation engineers to collocate with data scientists was a good example of the positive organizational impact of AI as the company went ahead with its industrial digital transformation journey. These measures later helped GE Aviation create an aviation digital unit and launch new AI-powered digital services for airlines.

## Security considerations for industrial digital transformation

The application of AI and ML is heavily dependent on relevant data. In the scenarios of applying AI to enterprise systems, the data often originates in databases that are fairly secure. Often, this enterprise data is moved to data warehouses and datamarts for **Business Intelligence** (**BI**), analytics, and AI/ML. This process is well understood and can be secured by following the IT best practices. However, as we embark upon the industrial digital transformation journey, additional security concerns arise, namely the following:

- For effective use of AI/ML, we often need connectivity to physical devices to gather data, such as from Programmable Logic Controllers (**PLCs**) on the factory floor or to other industrial controls systems and operations that create vulnerability.

- This data, once gathered, or the data at rest, is vulnerable to exposing the nature of the operations of the company and their competitive advantages.

- Digital twins also can be hacked to gain insights into the trade secrets and operating procedures that create competitive differentiation from other companies.

The digital transformation journey calls for increased awareness of security considerations. According to the June 2020 survey titled *Digital Transformation & Cyber Risk: What You Need to Know to Stay Safe* by the Ponemon Institute, 82% of the 883 respondents, consisting of IT security and C-suite executives, agreed that digital transformation has caused a minimum of one data breach. Some of the causes of such breaches are increased speed of change, moving to the cloud, increased use of IoT, decentralization of IT, and outsourcing to third parties. The Ponemon report states that "*A successful digital transformation process requires IT security to balance securing digital assets without stifling innovation.*" Hence, it is important to budget for proper cyber security initiatives as part of the transformation.

To minimize the risk during the transformation journey, we recommend reading from a few resources, such as the following:

- **Industrial Internet Consortium** (**IIC**): Industrial internet security framework for IoT – see `https://www.iiconsortium.org/IISF.htm`.

- **National Institute of Standards and Technology** (**NIST**): A cybersecurity framework – see `https://www.nist.gov/cyberframework`.

- **Cloud Security Alliance** (**CSA**): **Cloud Controls Matrix** (**CCM**) – see `https://cloudsecurityalliance.org/research/cloud-controls-matrix/`.

- **European Union Agency for Cybersecurity (ENISA)**: Threat landscape for 5G networks – see `https://www.enisa.europa.eu/publications/enisa-threat-landscape-for-5g-networks`.

Leveraging a cybersecurity framework will avoid reinventing the wheel, the quest to improve the security posture during the transformation journey. In the next section, let's look at the ways of securing the software development process, as often, new software applications are developed in an agile fashion for the transformation process.

## The rise of DevSecOps

**DevSecOps** stands for **development, security, and operations**. DevOps brought the developers and system administrators closer. DevSecOps embeds security at each and every stage of the development and deployment life cycle. *Figure 8.6* shows the difference between the DevOps and DevSecOps:

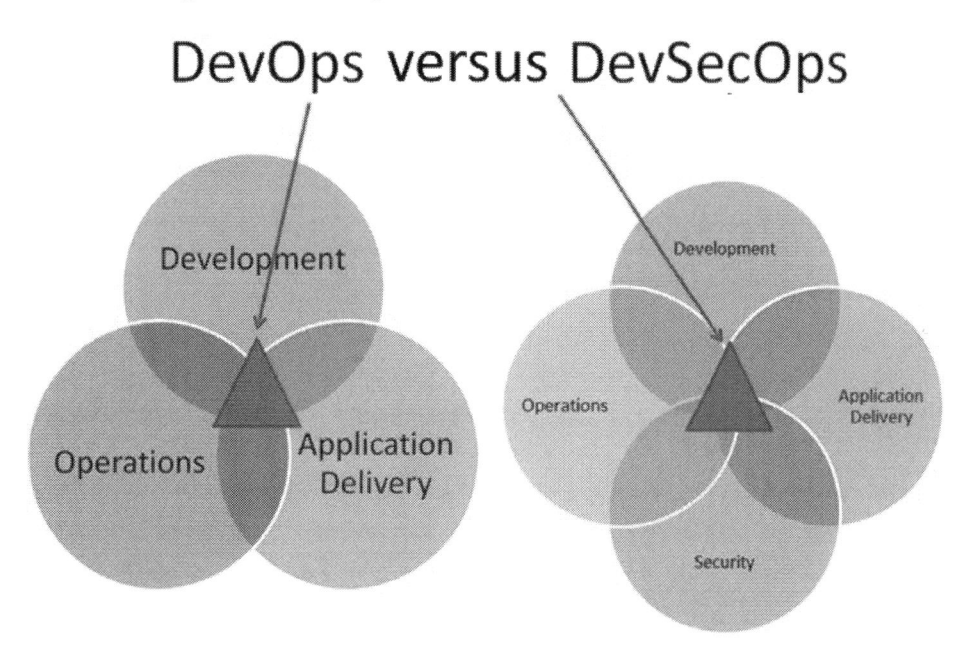

Figure 8.6 – DevOps versus DevSecOps (Source: `https://commons.wikimedia.org/wiki/File:DevOps_vs_DevSecOps_Mginise.jpg`, License: CC BY-SA)

The digital transformation journey may include new software development at a fast pace. As a result, it is critical to embed secure practices in the core of the agile development cycles. Let's look at the application security testing tools. The commonly used terminology for testing include the following:

- **Static Application Security Testing** (**SAST**) analyses the static code to identify vulnerabilities.

- **Interactive Application Security Testing** (**IAST**) analyses the code and its behavior when running, either by humans, instrumentation, or automation.

- **Dynamic Application Security Testing** (**DAST**) helps to detect the vulnerabilities in web applications while they are running in simulation or production.

- **Runtime Application Self-Protection** (**RASP**) helps to detect attacks on an application in real time and protect it from malicious input or actions. Over time, RASP can be used to continuously monitor its behavior, leading to the identification of attacks and mitigation without the need for human intervention.

In the following table, let's compare these different software application testing tools (source: *Synopsis Guide to Application Security Testing Tools*):

|  | SAST | IAST | DAST | RASP |
| --- | --- | --- | --- | --- |
| Phase | Development | Quality Assurance (QA) Testing | Testing, production | Production |
| Speed | Instant to hours | Instant at the runtime | Hours to days | Instant at the runtime |
| Continuous Security Testing | Yes | Yes | No | Yes |
| CI/CD Integration | Yes | Yes | No | No |
| Integration | IDEs, build tools, and issue trackers | Build tools, test automation, issue trackers, and APIs | None | Language runtime, application server |
| Accuracy | Medium | High | Medium | High |
| Actionability | High | High | Low | High |

The use of AI and ML for application testing is still evolving. A review of the potential of AI and ML in test automation was published in October 2019. See `https://link.springer.com/article/10.1007/s11219-019-09472-3`.

In the next section, we will look at the evolution of AI to safeguard industrial systems.

# AI for cybersecurity

As more and more systems are digitalized and connected to the internet during industrial digital transformation initiatives, cybersecurity is becoming a very important consideration in overall solution deployment planning and strategy. Installation of sensing, actuating, and computing solutions that are connected to the internet for applications in smart buildings, smart homes, and smart industry implies that there is a potential for cybercriminals to gain access to these systems and cause cyber mayhem with physical world implications.

Cyberattacks on smart buildings mostly target their building automation systems. Computers systems in smart buildings control and manage **Heating, Ventilation, and Air Conditioning** (**HVAC**) systems, elevators, lighting, alarms, security systems, and water supplies. Malicious cyberattacks, such as spyware, worms, and ransomware, have been used to target smart buildings.

Industrial processes and systems in most smart industry applications utilize **Supervisory Control and Data Acquisition** (**SCADA**) systems, PLCs and IoT nodes, gateways, and edge compute devices. These systems are generally connected to production control system networks and are generally physically separated from the corporate or business network. However, this physical separation is not possible when smart industry applications require the enabling of deeper visibility into data acquisition systems and control systems for diverse applications for predictive maintenance to a smart supply chain. Hence, **Industrial Control Systems** (**ICSes**) are now susceptible to cyberattacks. Cyberattacks using malicious worms, such as Stuxnet, Duqu 2.0, and others, have been used to cause damage to computer systems used in different industries.

AI algorithms are being deployed to prevent cyberattacks and improve cybersecurity for many different applications. Network intrusion detection and prevention is one of the critical applications to secure internet traffic from malicious traffic entering the corporate or industrial/production control systems. AI algorithms such as DNNs are utilized to defend a network from cyberattacks by dynamically updating algorithms that detect malicious internet traffic and prevent it from affecting the network.

Botnets are used to launch denial-of-service attacks on networks. A cluster of internet-connected devices running one or more bots can also be used to steal data and conduct industrial espionage. ML algorithms such as Bayesian classifiers and **Support Vector Machines** (**SVMs**), deep learning techniques, and ANNs are used in botnet detection.

ML algorithms such as random forest and SVMs are used in forecasting hacking incidents and cybersecurity incidents. Supervised ML algorithms, such as decision trees, logistic regression, and random forest, and deep learning algorithms such as DNNs are used in fraud detection. Google uses neural networks and logistic regression tools for email classification for spam filtering in Gmail.

## Summary

In this chapter, we learned about the different paradigms of AI. We looked at the various industry use cases of AI, from factories to public safety. Finally, we looked at what kind of changes AI is driving in organizations as they are adopting it for digital transformation. Some of these changes create a need for increased awareness of cybersecurity. However, the use of AI to improve the security posture is an emerging area, and in the near future, we will be able to leverage it to a greater extent.

In *Chapter 9*, *Pitfalls to Avoid in The Digital Transformation Journey*, we will look at some of the early indicators of failure in industrial digital transformation initiatives. We will look at some examples of such failures and try to categorize the main reasons for those failures. Overall, that should help plan transformative initiatives with early interventions and reduced risk of failures.

## Questions

Here are some questions to check your understanding of this chapter:

1. What is the difference between AI, ML, and deep learning?
2. What is ShotSpotter technology used for?
3. What are the possible downsides of using AI-based facial recognition technology?
4. How is AI used in factories?
5. What is the role of the MOOCs in evangelizing AI?

# 9
# Pitfalls to Avoid in the Digital Transformation Journey

In *Chapter 8*, *Artificial Intelligence in Digital Transformation*, we learned about AI, machine learning, and deep learning. We looked at various applications of AI across the public and the private sector. We looked at AI at the edge for specific use cases. Finally, we looked at the organizational changes that often occur as a result of the adoption of AI.

In this chapter, we will learn how to identify when digital transformations are failing and the possible reasons for their failure. We will look at specific examples from the last few decades and evaluate the failure and success of those transformations. Understanding the causes of previous failures will help us to identify situations that could result in project failure in the future, and correct the project's course to improve the chances of success.

In this chapter, we will cover the following main topics:

- Indicators of failure
- Failed transformations

# Indicators of failure

Failed transformations can take many forms. They can include individual projects that do not achieve the expected business value or those that never reach completion and must be restarted. Failed transformations can have more dire results, causing a company to lose its competitive advantage with an entire product line, or even an entire company to file for bankruptcy. Failed transformation efforts, and the collapse of whole companies due to these failures, can provide us with valuable lessons. Let's look at the leading indicators of **Industrial Digital Transformation** (IDT) failures in the following sections.

## Lack of an industrial digital transformation strategy

Did the organization develop a strategy for transformation, or it is still a collection of proof of concepts? Let's list some of the reasons that a conversation about IDT might begin in a company:

- To check the box in an annual report or a PR event that the company had an active digital transformation initiative.
- Someone from the C-suite visited a trade show, came back, and pitched the idea of transforming the company simply because others are trying to do the same.
- A group of executives were lured into a Silicon Valley trip to meet the start-ups, unicorns, and innovation centers of large companies who claim to have started their own IDT journey.
- A management consulting company made an unsolicited pitch to help transform the enterprise.
- Some employees who won the innovation or software hackathon are very passionate about it.

While the aforementioned reasons can support a digital transformation journey in an enterprise, these are not sufficient reasons for a company to kickstart its IDT.

The lack of an evolving IDT strategy in an enterprise is often a recipe for disaster. According to a Celonis 2019 survey of 450 executives, 45% of the C-suite did not know how to initiate their digital transformation strategy (see `https://story.celonis.com/square-one-research/` for more information).

While it may be hard to pin-point the end state of the transformation, the strategy needs to provide a framework that can evolve with time. Volkswagen's experience is an example of a top-down digital transformation strategy. The company will invest $4 billion by 2025 and is in process of building its digital platform. It is also targeting $1.1 billion in new digital revenues by 2025. This digital platform will allow the company to produce digital devices on wheels and make car owners part of this new digital ecosystem. This platform allows Volkswagen to deliver new experiences to the customer via WePark, a parking app with billing; WeDeliver, an app for courier companies to deliver packages to the trunk of the car in the absence of the owner; WeExperience, to recommend fun activities in the area around the parked car; and eventually WeShare, a car sharing app (see `https://www.volkswagenag.com/en/news/stories/2018/08/volkswagen-develops-the-largest-digital-ecosystem-in-the-automot.html` for more information).

Honeywell is another good example of IDT. Currently, its software revenues exceed $4 billion, out of which $1.5 billion is **Industrial Internet of Things (IIoT)**-related applications. Its strategy consists of the following:

- A digital platform called Honeywell Forge, announced in 2019
- A strong focus on the cybersecurity of **Operations Technology (OT)** systems (see `https://www.sitsi.com/honeywell-its-digital-journey-transforming-industrial-software-centric-company-my-key-takeaways` for more information)

Let's look at other critical indicators of the health of transformations.

## Other indicators

Let's look at a few other indicators of failure in digital transformation initiatives:

- The board does not pay attention to, and provide oversight for, the digital transformation and leaves the effort in the hands of management. This prevents top-down support.
- An inward focus versus industry sector trends: For example, Blockbuster looked at stopping late fees as a $200 million loss in revenue, rather than seeing it from the customer's perspective.

- A mismatch of planning versus doing: Improper use of **Minimum Viable Products** (**MVPs**) and lessons learned from *fail-fast*.
- Too much emphasis on technology and not enough emphasis on cultural shifts: A 2018 report by Jabil found that 74% of the respondents think cultural challenges are bigger than technology challenges for transformation.

**General Electric (GE)**, Ford, and **Procter and Gamble (P&G)** undertook major IDT initiatives in the mid-2010s. In all the three cases the CEOs, who were instrumental in the transformation strategies of their companies, abruptly resigned or retired in the middle of the journey:

- Jeff Immelt, CEO of GE, stepped down on August 1, 2017, and then resigned as chairman of the board on October 2 of the same year.
- Mark Fields, CEO of Ford, stepped down in August 2017.
- A.G. Lafley, CEO of P&G, stepped down in October 2015.

Given that most transformation initiatives succeed only when they have top-down support, an abrupt change at the CEO level is a major leading indicator of the failure of an IDT. Often, these changes are also associated with rapid fluctuations and falls in share prices for public companies. Sometimes, companies come out with a restatement of earnings in the middle of the transformation, which can be another red flag. In April 2018, GE restated its 2016 earnings, reducing them by $220 million and its 2017 earnings by $2.2 billion. While it can be argued that stock prices and restatements of earnings are not directly related to the success or failure of transformation initiatives, the combination of these adverse factors requires further scrutiny of the transformation strategy.
A restatement of accounting statements is very likely to open a can of worms with investor groups and stakeholders (see `https://www.cnbc.com/2018/04/13/general-electric-earnings-restatement-.html`).

Another leading indicator of trouble is when the average employee of the company undergoing transformation is not able to clearly explain the *why* of the transformation. The employees are often asked to change how and what they do, and it's hard when they do not understand the reasons behind it.

GE had aspired to transform into a *digital industrial* company, the first of its kind, around 2012. This led to the creation of GE Digital, with its California headquarters in San Ramon, out of what started as a software **Center of Excellence** (**CoE**) in September 2015. Several billion dollars of investment went into this IDT. We will look in more detail at GE in the subsequent section of this chapter.

Finally, a transformation that is focused on digital technology only, and does not clearly quantify the **Return on Investment** (**ROI**) for stakeholders, is also on the path to failure. We can learn valuable lessons not only from the companies that did not succeed in their initial transformation journeys, but also from the companies that missed the opportunity to transform. In the next section, we look at some of these examples.

## Digital transformation failures

Revisiting some of the *failures* from the last two to three decades will help us understand some of the pitfalls for large-scale transformation or the lack of it. We will group these failures in companies into their related industry segments. When we think of the telecommunication sector, we often think of companies such as Motorola, Nokia, BlackBerry, AT&T, MCI/WorldCom, and so on. In this section, we will discuss the failure of three mobile phone companies, where each of them achieved market dominance and then failed due to a combination of reasons.

Let's start with Motorola first.

## Motorola

Established in 1928 as the Galvin Manufacturing Company, with products such as battery eliminators, the Motorola brand was born in 1930 when the company started to sell car radios. Motorola has numerous accomplishments to its name. In 1940, Motorola created the first walkie-talkie. Motorola created its first pager in 1956. Motorola's radio pagers, based on the concept of the walkie-talkie, were used by hospitals in New York City where doctors could receive radio pages within a range of 25 miles. In 1969, Neil Armstrong spoke the first famous words from the moon, *"one small step for man, one giant leap for mankind,"* over Motorola's radio technology. In 1973, Motorola developed the first cellular mobile phone and received FCC certification for the first commercial cellular phone, known as the DynaTAC 8000X, in 1983. Motorola also developed cellular phone infrastructure, including **Base Transceiver Stations** (**BTSes**) and equipment that is installed in towers. With this first-mover advantage, Motorola sold the largest number of mobile phones every year globally until 1998. Launched in 2004, the Motorola RAZR was the best-selling mobile phone in the US market, with more 130 million phones sold over a period of 4 years. However, Motorola was not able to see and adapt to transformational trends at the time. Motorola's market share in mobile phones dropped from 21% in 2006 to 6% in 2009. After the success of the Motorola RAZR, which was a well-designed mobile phone, there was a need for a transition to devices that would also offer data-driven services to meet the changing expectations of consumers. During this period, RIM BlackBerry had started to offer mobile phone solutions with push-email solutions. Email service was beginning to become popular with businesses and individuals. RIM BlackBerry offered secure server-based solutions that allowed secure emails and instant messaging solutions for employees of corporations. These features allowed BlackBerry devices to be positioned as business tools and the company quickly gained market share.

Motorola was focused on mobile phone hardware. It was very successful with analog technology and later with digital technology (such as the Motorola RAZR). However, Motorola was not focused on a transition to building devices where software solutions would be critical to the successful adoption of the overall mobile solution from the customer's perspective. Motorola designers wavered on selecting an operating system for their mobile phone offerings. Until 2003, Motorola phones used a proprietary OS. Starting in 2004, Motorola A-series phones were based on the Linux OS. Starting in 2005, Motorola Q was offered with the Windows Mobile OS. The user experience of these devices was poor. This is ironic considering that Motorola was one of the first companies to adopt the techniques and tools for process improvement and controlling the quality of output, known as Six Sigma. Motorola made a switch to the Android operating system and launched the Motorola Droid phone in November 2009. This phone was offered with a touchscreen and a slide-out keyboard. By this time, Apple had already launched its game-changing mobile phone, the iPhone, in 2007, which transformed this industry. Motorola had incurred losses to the tune of $4.3 billion during the period from 2007 to 2009. With the launch of the Motorola Droid phone in 2009, and the follow-up devices, the Droid 2 and Droid X phones, Motorola started to gain market share again. However, in 2011, the company was split into Motorola Mobility and Motorola Solutions. The success of the Droid phones that were based on the Android platform was appealing to Google. In May 2012, Google acquired the consumer-device-focused Motorola Mobility portion of the company for $12.5 billion. Some of the mobile phones, such as the Moto G, launched by Motorola Mobility while operating as an independent company under the ownership of Google, were successful. However, Motorola Mobility continued losing market share, and was later sold to Lenovo in 2014 for $2.91 billion.

Next, let's look at BlackBerry.

### Research-In-Motion BlackBerry

**Research-In-Motion** (**RIM**) is the company credited with developing the first mobile phone with secure email. RIM started with a two-way interactive pager in 1996. In 1999, RIM launched an email pager called the BlackBerry 850. BlackBerry steadily gained market share based on the strength of their push email service, which was a paradigm-changing technology at that time. The RIM 957, which launched in 2000, was a BlackBerry device with a large screen, a QWERTY keyboard, and the ability to access email on the go, which was an important feature for business customers at a time when email was being rapidly adopted for business communication. This device did not have mobile phone functionality. RIM introduced the first mobile phone, the BlackBerry 5810, in 2002, which can be considered in the smartphone category, although this device did not have a built-in microphone and speaker and required an external headset for phone calls. This device offered **Short Message Service** (**SMS**) functionality, which was used extensively by business customers. The first real smartphone was introduced by RIM in 2003 as the BlackBerry 7230, which had a built-in microphone and speaker. It also had a color display and provided a web browser.

BlackBerry devices were very easy to use with their QWERTY keyboard functionality. Launched in 2004, the BlackBerry 7100t offered a narrower keyboard with two letters on each key and predictive text software to assist users with typing. This device saw wide adoption with consumers. The BlackBerry Pearl 8100, introduced in 2006, had a camera, music player, and video player, and became the most successful device on the market. Over a period of 5 years from 2004 through 2009, BlackBerry users grew from 1 million to 25 million. BlackBerry subscribers peaked at 80 million in 2012. These devices were very popular. BlackBerry phones were used by celebrities and heads of states. The US government, including the Department of Defense, also had a large number of BlackBerry users. The decline of RIM started with the launch of the BlackBerry Storm in 2008. After the launch of the Apple iPhone in 2007, a large touchscreen had become the clear choice for mobile user interfaces. The BlackBerry Storm had an unstable user interface as a result of the integration of the touchscreen into their product. BlackBerry OS was not designed for touchscreens. BlackBerry's SureType technology for its QWERTY keyboards was unique in the industry and was appreciated by BlackBerry users. The failure of the Storm appears to be due to not leveraging this unique competitive strength properly. Their second big mistake was that BlackBerry did not encourage third-party app developers to develop apps for BlackBerry OS. This was a very big drawback for BlackBerry in the face of competition from Apple and Google, who had massive armies of app developers who created solutions for iOS and Android OS. This is particularly ironic given that the first Google-made mobile phones looked like BlackBerry clones and BlackBerry had the capability to download apps on their mobile phones much earlier than Apple and Google.

BlackBerry kept the popular BlackBerry Messenger tied to their own hardware. The BlackBerry Messenger service offered an unlimited, instantaneous communication service to its users and generated a revenue of $3 billion in 2007. We know, through Facebook's acquisition of WhatsApp for $19 billion, that an application that can be offered on multiple platforms can become very successful. WhatsApp has over 2 billion users in 2020. BlackBerry stopped manufacturing mobile phones in 2016.

Let's next look at Nokia next.

## Nokia

In the late 1990s and early 2000s, Nokia was considered the world's dominant mobile phone maker with a highly valuable brand. Nokia launched the first compact mobile phone, the Mobira Cityman 900, in 1987. The Nokia 9000 Communicator, developed in 1996, had the features of a smartphone, including telephone, email, and internet connectivity. Steadily gaining market share since the mid-1990s, Nokia reached the milestone of a 50% market share in the mobile phone sector in 2007. However, in less than 6 years, Nokia's market share had dropped below 5% by 2013. There are several reasons for this dramatic collapse of a market leader with a highly recognized brand name. Let's consider them now.

Nokia had an effective leadership team responsible for the decisions that lead to the company's early successes. As mentioned earlier, Nokia had developed a smartphone in 1996. Nokia was the first mover in the smartphone space with the Symbian operating system. The first phones with Symbian were launched in 2002. Nokia did not adapt to a touchscreen-driven user interface quickly. Apple's launch of the iPhone in 2007 clearly changed the consumer preference toward a simple, touchscreen-driven user interface. Symbian could not be utilized to develop a similar user experience and Nokia could not adapt to such change fast enough. Nokia moved to the Windows Mobile operating system in 2011, but it was too late. Nokia's development process for mobile phones was more hardware-focused and the company failed to recognize that software was an equally critical component to the success of a product.

In 2007, when Nokia had a 50% market share, almost all its revenue and profits were generated by the non-smartphone segment. The company's investment in this period was more to sustain growth in its non-smartphone market segments, and investment in innovation and R&D into newer technologies slowed down significantly during this time period. In the early part of the 2000s, when Nokia experienced rapid growth in market share, managing the supply chain became critically important. The effort put into maintaining their supply chain overshadowed other priorities in the company.

Nokia implemented a matrix structure for the organization in the mid-2000s in order to improve the agility of the company in the changing and competitive landscape of the mobile phone business. However, it can be said that this reorganization was not effectively implemented. It resulted in the departure of key executive members from the company. The mid-level management teams were not experienced in working in this structure. Hence, this reorganization had the negative effect of slowing down the decision-making process, along with a lack of innovation and a negative effect on morale. Microsoft acquired Nokia's mobile phone business in 2013 for $7.9 billion.

Mobile phones have become a key component in driving digital transformation. Mobile phones and the technologies they offer now enable numerous use cases for both business and private individuals, from secure emails, messaging, information access, and camera-enabled applications, to social media, banking, online shopping, and many more. As mentioned earlier, all three of these companies – Motorola, RIM, and Nokia – had a leading market position and the necessary technological elements that are found in mobile phones today. However, these companies could not transform their business models to changing industry landscapes and in some cases, their organizational structures could not adapt either.

In the next section, we will look at a selection of failed transformations and the primary causes of these.

# Failed transformations

In this and the subsequent sections, we will take an in-depth look into some failed IDT projects and examine the primary reasons why they failed. Let's first look at the public sector.

## Public sector failures

The public sector has experienced a number of significant digital transformation failures. Some failures look very much like private sector failures. However, most public sector failures demonstrate the challenges that are particularly prevalent in the public sector, which we discussed in detail in *Chapter 6, Transforming the Public Sector*. As we discussed in that chapter, the public sector tends to accumulate a great deal of technical debt and generally has a shortage of qualified technical resources. These challenges, combined with the complexities of public contracting, tend to result in both a reliance on more traditional development methodologies and the outsourcing of transformation projects to systems integrators. To further complicate public sector projects, they are also subject to political considerations that may impact budgets, schedules, and project objectives, especially at the federal and state levels.

In this section, we will discuss two high-profile government implementation failures: HealthCare.gov, which we mentioned in *Chapter 1, Introducing Digital Transformation*, as the genesis of the government digital services movement; and the California DMV system.

## HealthCare.gov

As we discussed in *Chapter 1, Introducing Digital Transformation*, the failed launch of HealthCare.gov was the impetus for the digital services movement in the US federal government. Therefore, it's worthwhile for us to look at why the launch of HealthCare.gov failed. There were many challenges in the initial implementation of HealthCare.gov. We'll discuss just a few of the major problems.

Probably the single greatest factor in the failure of HealthCare.gov, the federal government's Affordable Care Act healthcare exchange, was that even though CGI Federal was selected as the contractor for the project in December 2011, the Department of **Health and Human Services (HHS)** did not provide the final specifications to the contractor until just months before the system was due to be online. The general consensus is that the Obama administration did not want to publish the specifications before the presidential election. However, the fact that the specs weren't delivered until months after the election points to the inability of HHS to develop and agree on specifications internally. Regardless, the result was a rushed effort to design and code a solution, which in turn resulted in a poorly conceived architecture, sloppy coding, patchy testing, and the presence of security flaws.

The selection of CGI Federal itself was an artifact of antiquated federal procurement processes that lock out new vendors who would have be able to use agile practices in favor of large, legacy vendors using legacy methodologies such as *waterfall*, a methodology particularly ill-suited for a project where the requirements were not known until a year after the project began. These processes resulted in what should have been a relatively small project becoming a large investment with a contract value of $93.7 million over the course of 5 years, likely an order of magnitude greater in both cost and complexity than a similar solution developed for a private-sector customer.

Finally, to round out the major issues confronting HealthCare.gov, **Centers for Medicare and Medicaid Services (CMS)** significantly underestimated the number of users who would visit the site, resulting in poor performance of the parts of the solution that were functional.

Even as the issues with the system became clear to the CMS team, they were not raised to the oversight committee. Frank Baitman, the CIO of HHS, later testified before Congress that he had no authority over the program and was not aware of the issues before the system went live.

In the end, not only did the rescue of HealthCare.gov start the US government's digital services movement, but Mr. Baitman's testimony before Congress started a discussion that ultimately resulted in the passage of the **Federal IT Acquisition Reform Act (FITARA)**, which increased federal CIO authorities.

## California DMV

If you happen to live in California or have heard from Californians about the state's **Department of Motor Vehicles (DMV)** being a nightmare, it is because the California DMV has tried to modernize their technology and failed not once, but twice. Between 1988 and 1994, the DMV spent $44 million on a failed modernization led by Tandem Corporation and Ernst & Young. At the time the project was cancelled, the DMV's director believed that another $157 million would be required to save the project.

While the California legislature never received a full explanation from the DMV, the legislative analyst who investigated the project indicated that agency staff didn't understand the technology, that the size of the project was underestimated, and that project management and oversight were inconsistent. Reading between the lines from the position of being 25 years in the future, we can see a project with a poorly defined scope and whose requirements were being managed by stakeholders who did not understand the technology being deployed.

While the DMV stated in 1994 that they would look for a lower-cost, off-the-shelf solution, that apparently never happened. In 2006, the DMV started a new modernization project, awarding a $208 million, 6-year contract to Hewlett-Packard. Seven years and $134 million later, the DMV canceled the project citing lack of progress on the project. A lack of good project management, or at least an unwillingness to share bad news, seems to have been the culprit in this case as well, as the project was *yellow* right up until the day it was cancelled, never having reached the *red* status that indicates a project is in serious trouble.

The result of these failures is seen in long waits at DMV offices, incorrect voter registrations, and issues implementing the Real ID law. The DMV also suffered major IT outages in 2016 and 2018 and at least 34 minor outages over the 20-month period from January 2017 to August 2018. The issues have been so serious that DMV performance was a major campaign issue in the 2018 California Governor's race. Soon after his election, Governor Gavin Newsome created a **DMV Reinvention Strike Team** and stated that any governor who can't fix the DMV should be recalled. It remains to be seen whether this governor will succeed in reversing 26 years of IT failure.

Next, we'll take a look at some private sector case studies, starting with an example that consumers are well versed in.

# Private sector failures

The private sector case studies that we'll examine will fall in the **Business-to-Consumer (B2C)** and **business-to-business (B2B)** categories. Let's begin with an example of a B2C case study.

## Blockbuster versus Netflix

Blockbuster was a market leader in the movie and video game rental sector. The company saw ups and downs as the market segment was disrupted by Netflix's DVD-by-mail subscription business in the early 2000s. In the early 2000s, John Antioco, CEO of Blockbuster at the time, recognized the disruption that Netflix, and to a lesser extent, Redbox, was bringing to the market. Antioco recognized two weaknesses in Blockbuster's model when compared to Netflix: their reliance on late fees, and their brick-and-mortar-only business model. Antioco proposed sweeping changes to the board, including a $200-million reduction in revenue through the elimination of late fees to compete with Netflix's flat-fee model, and a $200-million investment in Blockbuster Online, a digital platform to ensure Blockbuster's viability in an online world.

Unfortunately, while Antioco had gained approval from the board for his plan, he had not articulated his plan in a way that clearly conveyed the need for strategic change to the broader organization. As a result, one of the leaders on his staff, Jim Keyes, went around Antioco to the board and convinced them that his changes were too expensive. Keyes' actions, coupled with the efforts of activist investor Carl Icahn, resulted in the board losing confidence in Antioco. Antioco was fired and replaced by Keyes, who immediately reversed all of Antioco's changes. Blockbuster was bankrupt by 2010, within just 5 years.

# Three causes of failure

While the causes of failed transformations appear very diverse, they generally fall into three major groups:

- A misalignment between the vision and expectations for transformation, and the results that are actually achievable
- Economic failure
- Technical failure

Let's look at them one by one.

## Misaligned transformation visions and expectations

Many digital transformations, whether for an entire organization, within a division or department, or for a single project, fail because different parts of the organization or project team have different visions of the objectives and outcomes of the transformation. Misalignments may show up as a mismatch between expectations and results, as disagreements between the business and IT departments, or between the transformation process and the organization's culture.

In many cases, misalignment is due to lack of a clear strategy for the project, unit, or organization. Many organizations start their transformations without performing their alignment groundwork first. A strategic direction must be developed first. Only then can decision-making processes, project governance and business processes, and the actual transformation follow.

Many organizations develop a clear strategy for their transformation and then, in the rush to start their transformation, fail to take the time to document and streamline their business processes. Well-understood, documented, and optimized business processes are an important enabler of transformation, whether the business process improvement is the goal of the transformation or an enabler for the delivery of new or transformed products or services. Process transformation is as important as cultural change for a successful digital transformation, ensuring that the entire organization is driving toward the same transformation outcomes.

Many organizations take the time required to develop their digital transformation strategy and to develop and implement all the enabling processes, only to fail to communicate the strategic vision to the organization as a whole. As discussed in the earlier chapters of this book, employee engagement and culture are crucial to a successful digital transformation. If employees do not understand the strategy or vision of the organization, they cannot support the transformation. This misalignment can happen at any level of the organization, from the C-suite not articulating the corporate vision, to a project manager not sharing the project's goals and objectives. Regardless of the level at which the misalignment occurs, any misalignment that occurs can be fatal to organizational success.

The misalignments described so far can be fixed in a fairly straightforward manner, through improved communication and the completion of all necessary groundwork to ensure the success of an organization's transformation. Other misalignments are more challenging to resolve. These involve individuals or groups with conflicting agendas. There are generally three situations where agendas come into conflict:

- Individuals at a senior level
- Departments
- Staff groups

While in theory, the development of a digital transformation strategy should ensure the alignment of all the senior leaders in an organization, that is not always the case, especially in organizations that are highly political or where the most senior leader in the organization does not resolve conflicts. In these cases, while all leaders may support the transformation in public, they may act to undermine the transformation in private. This may be because they see the transformation as threatening to their position in the organization or because they disagree with the strategic direction.

Just as individual senior leaders may feel threatened by a digital transformation, at a division or department level, digital transformations almost always elevate parts of an organization while reducing the size or importance of other parts. If staff in the impacted departments are not engaged to understand the vision, why it is important to the organization, and how they will be part of the transformed system, those departments may actively or passively disrupt the organization's digital transformation.

Finally, if staff in the broader organization are not fully engaged in understanding the vision for transformation and the value of digital transformation to the organization, then individuals (or even groups in a unionized workplace) may actively resist the transformation. Staff must understand why the transformation is important to the organization as well as to them as an individual and, ideally, have input into appropriate aspects of the transformation in order to be fully engaged and effective participants in the transformation process.

To illustrate the problem of misalignment and how it manifests in organizations, we will now take a brief look at several examples of digital transformations that failed due to the lack of a shared strategic vision.

## Ford Motor Company

In 2014, Mark Fields, CEO of Ford, announced a new division called Ford Smart Mobility to build digitally enabled cars and to move Ford into the *personal mobility* business, putting innovation at the center of the company. The division was headquartered in Silicon Valley, thousands of miles away from Ford's Dearborn, Michigan headquarters.

While Ford's objective was for the division's technology to be at the center of every vehicle it produced, Ford Smart Mobility operated as a standalone organization and was not integrated with the rest of Ford. Consequently, the division was seen by staff in Dearborn as a separate entity with no connection to other business units. Ford spent a great deal of money in an attempt to reach the objectives for the division, but its capabilities were not integrated into products and the lack of executive focus and funding for the core business negatively impacted the quality of Ford's vehicles.

A significant drop in share price and the resignation of Mark Fields in 2017 have been directly tied to the failure of Ford Smart Mobility. Mark Fields wanted to drive digital innovation at all levels of Ford, rather than continuing to silo digital innovation in the Smart Mobility business unit. His goal was to leverage advances in connectivity, mobility, autonomous vehicles, data, and analytics to enhance the experience of Ford vehicle owners.

## British Broadcasting Corporation

In 2008, the **British Broadcasting Corporation (BBC)** launched the $150 million **Digital Media Initiative (DMI)** with the goal of streamlining broadcasting operations by moving to a fully digital, tapeless workflow. Siemens and Deloitte were contracted to complete the initiative. Siemens was hired for the project without the competitive process that is usually followed by government agencies, resulting in a lack of clarity about the project's deliverables while an attempt to transfer all project risk to Siemens resulted in an arm's-length relationship and a lack of awareness on the BBC's part about Siemens' lack of progress. After cost overruns, the BBC fired Siemens and brought the project in house to complete it, an effort that ultimately resulted in failure.

When the project was brought in house, it was already 18 months behind schedule, causing staff stress and resulting in the continuation of releases that did not meet expectations and led to a loss of stakeholder confidence. Possibly the most important indicator of impending failure was that both the Siemens team and the BBC project team focused on technology to the exclusion of organizational and process change management. As a result, features that were delivered by the project team were not adopted by the BBC. The project was suspended in 2013 and the BBC's chief technology officer was placed on leave and eventually terminated.

In the next section, we will discuss projects that failed for economic reasons.

## Economic failure

The failure of the transformation can be due to economic reasons. An ill-executed transformation initiative can run out of money before delivering the projected returns. Let's look at what metrics are typically used by a company undergoing digital transformation to track the outcomes of that transformation. The major ones are as follows:

- Digital revenue growth/new revenues
- Productivity and cash flow
- Overall **Profit and Loss (P&L)**
- Customer experience/engagement, and new customer segments (a measurable goal for this would be profitability per customer)
- Category leadership/thought leadership/patents (intangible)

In order to have checks and balances in place, it is important to have a continuous loop of validation and improvement. This is needed to quantitatively track the progress during the implementation and deployment cycles of the transformation. *Figure 9.1* shows the details of this process:

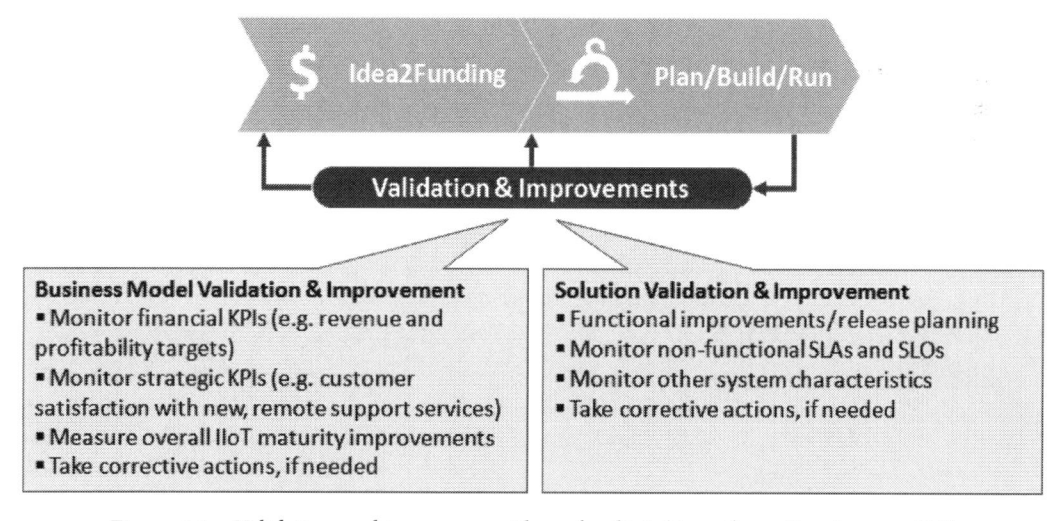

Figure 9.1 – Validation and improvement loop for digital transformation (source: IIC)

The investment decisions taken regarding transformation should be evaluated against the opportunity costs. We have seen earlier in this chapter, in the cases of Motorola, RIM, and Nokia, that the cost of missed opportunities is usually fairly high. Hence, the cost of *do-nothing* does not imply no net expense; rather, in many cases it may be an existential threat to the company. Banks have spent a lot of money on building ATMs and digital banking apps. It may be hard to calculate the impact of doing nothing in such cases. Likewise, companies investing in building digital platforms are driving the future value of the company to its stakeholders, compared to companies who invest in incremental improvement of their traditional business models.

Next, we'll look at the failures that are driven by various technical factors.

## Technical failures

According to the **Industrial Internet Consortium** (**IIC**), IDT focuses on leveraging operational context and new knowledge to enable new business outcomes. In the past, due to a lack of relevant digital technologies, such tasks had to rely on experts' assumptions and delayed or incomplete information. Hence, digital technologies play a critical role as an enabler of transformation. However, the choice of such technology and an alignment with the transformation objectives is key to preventing failures.

In the following example, let's look at the recent trends in the automotive sector where digital technology fell short.

### Battery-powered electric vehicles versus hydrogen fuel cell electric vehicles

At the present point in the transformation of the energy we use to power our automobiles away from fossil fuels and toward the use of renewable and clean energy sources, there are two options available:

- **Battery-Powered Electric Vehicle (BEV)**
- **Fuel Cell-Powered Electric Vehicle (FCEV)**

BEVs, such as those made by Tesla, use the energy stored in lithium-ion batteries to drive electric motors for the propulsion of automobiles. FCEVs such as the Toyota Mirai use the electricity generated by combining hydrogen stored in the fuel tank of a car with oxygen from the air to power the car.

The research and development of hydrogen FCEVs has been ongoing for the past several decades. The electrical systems in the Apollo space capsules and lunar modules were powered by fuel cells. However, the adoption of hydrogen FCEVs by consumers has fallen significantly behind that of BEVs.

FCEV technology has many advantages. This technology is currently in use in more than 23,000 fuel cell-powered forklift trucks used in warehouses and distribution centers across the US. Hydrogen is the most abundant element in the universe. Hydrogen has been in use in industrial processes for several decades and the transportation mechanisms for hydrogen have already been fully adopted. Refueling an FCEV takes a few minutes, just like gasoline vehicles. This is a big plus compared to charging BEVs, which takes a lot longer. The range of FCEV cars that are sold commercially by major OEMs such as Toyota and Honda is more than 300 miles. Despite all of these advantages, the adoption of FCEV has been stagnating as compared to BEVs (see `https://afdc.energy.gov/vehicles/fuel_cell.html`).

One of the primary reasons for this lack of adoption is the availability of hydrogen refueling-station infrastructure. Across all of the US, there are only 39 hydrogen refueling stations. 35 of these stations are located in California. Over 280 million Americans have no access to fuel cell cars or refueling stations.

Around 2.2 million plug-in BEVs were sold in 2019. There are now 10 automakers that each sell more than 100,000 BEVs per year and there are now hundreds of new BEV models available from these OEMs. BEVs are preferred by consumers for a combination of reasons. The cost of ownership of BEVs is approaching parity with comparable internal combustion engine-powered vehicles. With the driving range of BEVs approaching 300 miles, these vehicles are preferred by consumers because of superior driving performance, a quieter ride, lower operating costs, and no emissions. In March 2020, there were more than 25,000 electric vehicle charging stations offering 78,500 charging outlets across the US. Battery technology has been improving and it is projected that with newer metal-ion chemistry and advancements in newer materials, the storage capacity of batteries will increase to more than 1,000 miles per charge. The wide availability of charging stations and longer-lasting batteries will further drive BEV adoption.

Next, let's look at Nike.

## Nike

In 2010, Nike started **Nike Digital Sport** (**NDS**) as a new business unit. The goal of NDS was to power digital initiatives and build the necessary technological capabilities that would allow Nike users to track their own activities and performance. This data shared with Nike would provide key insights about their customers. However, in 2014, Nike announced that the NDS workforce was being cut by about 75%. The FuelBand fitness product was being sunset. Nike claimed that it could not find the appropriately skilled engineers to help monetize the data generated by the FuelBand. In our opinion, Nike lacked a proper digital platform to harness the data and analytics obtained by the FuelBand at that time.

In sharp contrast, during 2020, Nike capitalized on the COVID-19 crisis and improved its digital business. The Nike women's apparel division, showed about 200% growth, as women quit formal dresses and jeans in favor of active wear such as yoga pants for exercising and comfortable clothes for working from home. Nike is a good example of digital technologies applied to B2C scenario.

Let's look at GE next.

## GE's build-versus-buy dilemma

GE was first planning to build its own data centers to deal with the scale and industry compliance required for handling industrial data in domains such as aviation and healthcare. Initially, GE wanted to pursue a multi-cloud strategy and be able to run GE's Predix over AWS, Azure, and other major public cloud platforms. It used Pivotal Cloud Foundry as the **Platform as a Service** (**PaaS**) on which to create a layer of abstraction from the public cloud provider. This strategy enabled both AWS- and Azure-based offerings and gave GE's end-customer companies the choice of aligning GE's Predix with their selected cloud vendors. However, for GE, the cost of maintaining their offering on two clouds was a big overhead, which distracted the company from making the solution feature-rich quickly.

GE also faced the dilemma of opting for organic growth versus acquisitions of software and technology companies. GE started with a strategy of **IIoT**-platform leadership using its Predix Platform versus selling applications for the ease of adoption by its customers. Eventually, GE had to pivot from leading with its Predix Platform for IIoT to selling killer applications such as **Application Platform Management** (**APM**) and Brilliant Factory. During this period, GE acquired the following:

- Wurldtech (for cybersecurity).
- Meridium for APM (for industrial asset monitoring).
- ServiceMax (for field service management).

- Many other smaller acquisitions (Wise.io, Bit Stew, and so on).
- Investments in start-ups: **Industrial Internet Incubator (I3)** was created with Frost Data Capital and investments were made in start-ups such as MAANA for AI and FogHorn for Edge computing (see `https://www.ge.com/news/reports/industrial-internet-incubator-backed-by-ge-and-2`).

These acquisitions jump-started GE's software product lines and brought pure software customers in, but added to GE's challenges in technological integration. Another industrial giant, Siemens, who also embarked on its own IDT in a similar time frame, had a somewhat different approach. GE and Siemens are examples of digital transformation in B2B scenarios.

In the following table, we compare and contrast the approaches taken by these two digital industrial giants:

|    | Attribute | General Electric | Siemens |
|----|-----------|------------------|---------|
| 1  | Founded when | 1892 | 1847 |
| 2  | Revenues (2019) | $95 billion | $99 billion |
| 3  | Employees | 205,000 | 385,000 |
| 4  | IIoT platform | Predix (2013) | Mindsphere (2016) |
| 5  | Industrial specialty | Turbines | Automation |
| 6  | Software foundation (starting point) | Cloud Foundry | SAP |
| 7  | Digital unit/venture | GE Digital (2015) | Next47 (2016) |
| 8  | Digital investment | Over $1 Billion | Over $1 Billion |
| 9  | Country of HQ | USA | Germany |
| 10 | Acquisitions | ServiceMax ($915m, later divested) | Mendix ($700m) |
| 11 | Smart buildings | Current by GE (divested) | Acquired Enlighted (2018) |
| 12 | Software engineers | 22,000 software and IT engineers in 2016 | 17,500 software engineers in 2016 |

Interestingly, GE and Siemens had competed for the Alstom deal in 2014, thereby driving the cost of the acquisition higher for GE. GE's acquisition of Lufkin for $3.3 billion in 2013 would have been profitable if crude oil prices stayed over $100/barrel. However, the price fell below $50 soon after. These factors, along with GE's approximately $5 billion investment by 2016 in GE Digital with the target of achieving $2/share in profits by 2018, put a lot of pressure on GE and its IDT journey. One of GE's main investor groups, Trianz, had speculated that there would be 50% greater demand for gas-powered electricity over the next two decades. With the rapid growth of renewable sources of energy such as wind and solar power, this was another blow to GE Power, which had a large customer base of big utility companies using its gas generators.

Siemens has taken a more disciplined and sustainable approach to IDT and has been more successful so far. They reported 15.6 billion euros in digital revenue in 2018. This segment of revenue included software and automation. On a relative scale, after all the divestiture by GE, the estimated GE Digital revenues are now around $1 billion. However, some of GE's lines of business later built solutions directly on Microsoft Azure and Amazon AWS instead of on top of GE's Predix (which in turn can run over AWS or Azure). Siemens MindSphere first partnered with SAP, then started using AWS in 2017, and then started supporting Azure in 2018 as well. Unlike GE's Predix, Siemens never went down the route of considering building its own data centers. Siemens also acquired Mentor Graphics, a company in the electronic design automation space, in 2016 for $4.5 billion.

Overall, we can say that compared to GE, Siemens has been a lot more successful in its initiative to become a digital industrial company, due to a combination of factors. Other industrial companies such as ABB, Schneider Electric, Honeywell, Bosch, and Hitachi are also pursuing their own IDT paths just like GE and Siemens.

The IDT journey can also lead to cybersecurity challenges.

## Cybersecurity challenges

As companies move forward with initiatives to drive new digital revenues, the physical world is becoming increasingly connected to the digital world. Just like the connected "smart" thermostats in our homes increases the attack surfaces of our homes, the servitization of the physical products also comes at the cost of increased cybersecurity concerns. GE's purchase of Wurldtech, a cybersecurity company, was driven by this factor.

According to a recent survey of 1,500 global executives, cyber attacks and related threats remain one of the major risk management concerns in 2020. As digital transformation spawns a number of new digital initiatives, cyber-physical systems could become more vulnerable unless they have gone through rigorous security review. Overall, the role of security and cyber-resilience in IDT has become critical. During the product life cycle, early assessment of cybersecurity and heavy involvement in the design process is key. The **Chief Information Security Officers (CISOs)** of relevant companies are increasingly investing in this area. DevSecOps is the new buzzword. It is the practice of incorporating security principles within the DevOps process.

In the preceding section, we looked at several examples of failures of IDT initiatives due to reasons such as misaligned vision, along with economic and technological factors.

## Summary

In this chapter, we learned about the leading indicators of failure in IDT projects, as well as looking at case studies for examples of failed initiatives. We compared large IDT initiatives and critically analyzed their success and failures. Finally, we looked at the growing importance of cybersecurity, which could derail transformations if ignored.

In *Chapter 10, Measuring the Value of Transformation*, we will learn about ways to consider the benefits of IDT in terms of new digital revenues, productivity and efficiency gains, and societal benefits.

## Questions

Here are a few questions to check your understanding of this chapter:

1. What are some examples of digital industrial companies?
2. What are some of the leading indicators of failure in an IDT?
3. Give examples of technical causes of failure in IDT projects?
4. What is the role of cybersecurity in IDT?
5. Can transformations fail due to economic reasons?

# 10
# Measuring the Value of Transformation

In the previous chapter, we learned about the pitfalls of industrial digital transformation. We looked at the leading indicators of failure of transformation. We compared some large industrial companies to deep dive into the success and failure of digital transformations.

In this chapter, we will learn about developing the business case for investment in industrial digital transformations. We will also discuss how to evaluate investment outcomes. This chapter will cover the following:

- Developing the business case for transformation
- Productivity and efficiency gains
- New digital revenues
- Social good

# Developing the business case for transformation

Before we start our transformation journey, we will need funding for our project. In most organizations, that requires a business case. Even in the rare organization where a business case is not required to obtain funding, it is a good practice to develop a business case to ensure that the organization is fully aligned with the objectives of the transformation and that the transformation will provide value to the organization. This is important whether the transformation will involve one small project or an entire Fortune 500 company.

In this section, we will briefly explore the process of developing a business case and provide you with the tools necessary to create a business case for your digital transformation. In a traditional product or project development environment, the first activity would be to build the business case. However, one of the common challenges with digital transformation is that the entire agile approach of digital transformation does not lend itself well to creating a well-defined business case.

As we have learned throughout this book, starting in *Chapter 2, Transforming the Culture of an Organization*, the early part of a digital transformation will involve starting small and experimenting to prove viability, solve the hardest problems, and ultimately narrow the cone of uncertainty before embarking on the bulk of product development. For this reason, we recommend that organizations develop innovation or transformation funds that can be used to fund the initial exploration phase of projects and prove feasibility. After that, it will be easier for product teams to develop realistic business cases for digital transformation projects.

In Agile methodology, spikes (see `https://www.scaledagileframework.com/spikes/`) are often used to explore new and risky problems. These are time-bound cycles, used to try out the feasibility of a new technology or approach before they are used in mainstream development cycles.

For example, say our goal is to incorporate **Augmented Reality** (**AR**) into a solution dealing with the field maintenance of physical assets. Since it is a new bleeding-edge technology, within the development team, one or two software developers or architects could be assigned to conduct Spike work, to test the feasibility for the team. After the Spike work, it will be easier to estimate effort and cost for future solutions that may involve AR; or, in some cases, the team may decide that the new technology is not worth the risk at that stage. Spikes can be used during your proof of concept to prove the feasibility of your solution and can also be used later in the development cycle to respond to unexpected problems and identify solutions without impeding the overall progress of product development.

Once the product team has demonstrated feasibility, there are many approaches to developing a business case. A common approach for technology projects involves a seven-step process:

1. Define the problem.
2. Define the expected benefits.
3. Estimate the cost of the project.
4. Identify and assess risks.
5. Recommend a preferred solution.
6. Describe the implementation approach.
7. Calculate the **Return on Investment (ROI)**.

We will briefly discuss each of the seven steps of business case development for a digital transformation project.

> **Important note**
> Keep in mind as we go through the steps that digital transformation projects don't always fit neatly into the traditional business case framework, and you should be prepared to make adjustments for your specific project.

## Defining the problem

The first step in any business case is to define the problem. Since we recommend that digital transformation projects include a proof-of-concept phase prior to business case development, this step should be complete by the time you are ready to write the business case. However, let's look at this step anyway. Throughout this section, when we refer to the problem, the same principles apply to new business opportunities. A product company launching a product as a service would be an example of such a business opportunity, with the goal of generating new digital revenue.

There are two fundamental goals that are met by defining the problem. The first is to quantify the nature of the problem; that is, to describe it in a way that will allow funders to understand the problem that you want to solve and that will allow the project team to define their work. The second goal is to bound the problem. One of the classic problems that development teams encounter is the inherent desire of engineers to make things better. If the problem is not well bounded, the development team will continue to deliver new features well past the point where the features are worth the investment. Understanding who your end users are and what they need from your product will guide you in bounding the problem.

To look at a specific example of a poorly bounded problem, a Fortune Top 50 company developed a new and innovative printing technology that had the potential to revolutionize the commercial printing market by increasing the speed of color printing by an order of magnitude without reducing quality. The manufacturer worked on this product for 7 years and spent over $1 billion on the product but could not deliver the product to market. The engineering team continued to add advanced features that would be important to only a few customers. Ultimately, a new leader was hired who forced the product teams to stop development and deliver the product to market, where it was received to great acclaim. However, the extremely rich feature set resulted in the product being too expensive to manufacture and it lost money. The engineering team was unable to cost reduce the product and it was discontinued, leaving the manufacturer with a large loss and customers unhappy that
a product they loved was no longer available.

Some questions that you should consider when developing your problem definition are these:

- Why does the problem exist? Are you able to identify the cause of the problem?
- Who or what is impacted by the problem? Employees, customers, business processes?
- What are the consequences of the problem? Is the problem impacting productivity or employee or customer satisfaction? Is it limiting market penetration?
- What will change when the problem is solved? How will your products, services, or processes be different?
- When is a solution needed? Are there statutory or market deadlines? Or is there a limited window of opportunity?

Once you have considered these factors, develop a short problem statement. The problem statement should be no more than a few sentences long and easily understood by everyone involved in the project.

# Defining the expected benefits

At this point, you will not only have defined the problem, but you will have completed your proof of concept, which will give you a greater sense of the value of the product you are developing. As we have discussed in earlier chapters, digital transformation efforts frequently deliver new products and services to customers. However, they can be equally valuable when focused on increasing the enterprise's efficiency and effectiveness.

Some potential benefits to consider are these:

- **Market opportunities**: Does this project deliver a new product to market or improve an existing product with new features, better quality or service, or lower cost? Will this project open up new lines of business to your organization?
- **Improved internal processes**: Does the project automate or streamline workflows or improve collaboration?
- **Better decision making**: Does the project provide better or faster analytics tools?

At this point, you should have identified a reasonable number of benefits from the project. The first two to five benefits will likely provide the vast majority of benefits. Your analysis can include a few more, but after about 10 benefits, the value of each benefit is likely to be so small as to be irrelevant to your business case.

# Estimating the cost of the project

While the proof of concept for your project will have allowed you to solve the project's hardest problems and narrow the cone of uncertainty regarding project cost dramatically, any cost analysis for the project will still be an estimate. It will be easiest to estimate your project cost if you have some historical data about the productivity of your development teams. If you have past productivity metrics in the form of velocity or other metrics on the speed and cost of feature development, you can estimate the number of features or any appropriate productivity metric you track and apply your historical cost per feature to estimate the product development cost.

Your productivity metrics should include the cost of developing, testing, and releasing features, either on a per-feature basis or as a fixed cost for the estimated duration of the project. Other costs to consider include the following:

- Infrastructure for development, testing, and deployment
- The cost of purchased hardware or software components
- Support costs
- For products, marketing costs and sales commissions

Once you have estimated the cost of the project, your next step is to evaluate the project's risks.

## Identifying and assessing risks

In *Chapter 9, Pitfalls to Avoid in the Digital Transformation Journey*, we discussed the most common causes of failure of digital transformation projects. These reflect the risks inherent in digital transformation projects. These risks include the following:

- Alignment risks can be the result of a lack of clear understanding among all the stakeholders about the project purpose and scope (the problem statement) or a misunderstanding of market conditions.

- Financial risk can be the result of a wide range of errors, including product development overruns, excessive operating costs, and poor pricing strategy.

- Technical risk can result from the inability of the project team to deliver all the features required for a successful product, failure to meet regulatory requirements, and the obsolescence of tools and features provided by suppliers.

For each risk that your team identifies, you should develop a risk mitigation plan and include those activities in your project plan.

## Recommending a solution

In a traditional project, the solution recommendation may include an extensive alternatives analysis and recommendation. For a digital transformation project, your proof of concept will likely have narrowed the technical solutions to one or, at most, two solutions. Therefore, this section of your business case should describe the following:

- The proof of concept, including the technical solution that was selected and the options considered or tested and discarded, along with the technical reasons why those options were discarded
- A summary of the costs, benefits, and risks of the proposed solution that were identified in the earlier sections of your business case

The solution recommendation is, along with the ROI that we will calculate in step seven, the core of, your funding request and should provide a compelling case to move your project from a proof of concept to a fully committed development program.

## Describing the implementation approach

The purpose of describing the implementation approach in your business plan is to help the project stakeholders understand how you will accomplish the business results that you intend to achieve. This part of the business plan does not involve developing a complete implementation plan and schedule. In this section, you will describe the processes and tools that you will use to deliver results and a rough delivery schedule. Some questions to consider in this section include the following:

- Will you complete the project in-house or will you outsource some or all of the development?
- If you're delivering a product that involves hardware, will you manufacture that yourself or hire a contract manufacturer?
- If you're delivering a service, where will it be hosted and how will it scale?
- What development methodology will you use?
- What tools and standards will you use? Think about your **Computer-Aided Design (CAD)** system, test suites, development languages, source code repository, and other critical tools.
- Approximately how long will the project phases take and when do you expect to deliver your completed product?

Your description of your implementation approach should build confidence in your sponsors and stakeholders that you are prepared to deliver a product.

## Calculating the ROI

While we all acknowledge that it is difficult to estimate how long a digital transformation project will take or to fully understand the project's benefits, stakeholders will not fund projects without some sense that the project will be a good investment. This fact, once again, points to the importance of the proof of concept that you completed before you started to develop your business case.

The proof of concept will have narrowed down the cone of uncertainty, allowing you to better estimate the costs that you described in section three of your business case as well as the schedule that you estimated in section six. In addition, your success in solving the project's technical challenges as part of the proof of concept will have helped you better understand the benefits the project can achieve, which you described in section two of your business case. Even though everything may still seem uncertain, by this point you are ready to calculate an ROI for your project and obtain funding.

In the next section, we will discuss the process of calculating your project's ROI.

# Productivity and efficiency gains

The ROI, during an industrial digital transformation, can be in the form of business productivity and process efficiency gains, in addition to new digital revenue. Let's take the example of airline baggage handling.

## The airline industry

Prior to the COVID-19 pandemic, Delta Air Lines carried about 180 million passengers annually along with about 120 million checked airline bags. In 2016, Delta decided to invest $50 million to modernize its baggage handling solution and use **Radio-Frequency Identification** (**RFID**) enabled baggage tags (see `https://news.delta.com/iata-follows-deltas-lead-rfid-bag-tag-mandate`). This would improve the efficiency in the system, reducing any adverse impact of mishandling baggage. The intended outcomes of this RFID initiative are as follows:

- Reduced instances of bags left behind, misrouting at a connecting airport, or delayed arrival at the destination
- Reduced instances of theft of bags or pilferage and physical damage to baggage
- Improved airline passenger experience with baggage
- Improved compliance with **International Air Transport Association** (**IATA**) Resolution 753 (see `https://www.iata.org/en/programs/ops-infra/baggage/baggage-tracking/`)

The cost of mishandled airline baggage to the aviation industry was around $2.5 billion in 2019, according to the company **Société Internationale de Télécommunications Aéronautiques** (**SITA**). The preceding case is a good example, where a transformative initiative at Delta is targeted at improvements to its operating margin, as well as strengthening its airline customer experience, to improve its overall competitive positioning. In the longer term, Delta can offer its digital platform for baggage handling to its partner airlines for new digital revenue streams.

Let's look at another airline scenario this time involving aircraft. While the average commercial aircraft can last for up to 30 years, let's assume the life of a jet engine is 25 years. If the airline was fully responsible for the maintenance and servicing of the engine, then it would need spare engines as well as parts. It is important to note that a given aircraft often offers a choice for the make of the engine. Hence, the decision of the airframe does not necessarily dictate the make of the jet engine. The additional challenge for the airline is that the need for servicing an aircraft engine can arise at an airport that is not its major airport or hub location. If the spare engine or the part is not locally present, then it has to be flown in, at the cost of downtime of the aircraft. The cost of a canceled flight for such an aircraft can be as much as $40,000. A canceled or delayed flight can also have a cascading impact on other flights. As a result, airlines often transfer their risk of operational downtime to the **Original Equipment Manufacturer** (**OEM**) and buy long-term service contracts. Let's say that the annual service contract is about 20% of the cost of an engine, or $5 million per year. The **Service Level Agreement** (**SLA**) tied to such a maintenance contract allows the airline to focus on flying the passengers and ensure that the OEM is responsible for the operational risk of downtime. This leads to productivity gains for the airline.

From the OEM's perspective, in a business-as-usual scenario, it earns $5 million per jet engine and is responsible for its uptime and servicing. Suppose that based on the large fleet of engines that it maintains, the expected cost of maintenance is $3.5 million per year. This equates to about (1.5/5.0) or a 30% gross margin on the service contract. Now, as part of the industrial digital transformation initiative, this OEM invests in a digital platform. This platform uses the sensor data from the aircraft while it is flying (summary data) as well as using more detailed data after it lands. The functionality of this platform includes the following:

- Ensuring that the aircraft engine is safe to fly for the next flight
- Capturing any leading indicators of when to plan the next inspection or maintenance
- Helping to identify what kind of maintenance would be needed
- Ensuring that an engine is using fuel optimally

All of the above are *high-value problems*, due to the sheer cost of the engine and the criticality of the engine to the aircraft. Let's assume that by using this digital platform, the cost of maintenance reduces to $2.5 million per year. That is a $1m-per-year improvement, on average, on the margin of the service contract per engine, due to this transformation initiative. It assumes that the cost of this digital platform is spread across the entire fleet of engines being maintained by this OEM. In this case, the margin on the service contract improves from 30% to 50%. Let's assume the average annual cost of using the digital platform is $0.75 million; then, it represents an ROI of $0.25 million/$0.75 million, or 33.3%, in this specific initiative in a stable state. This is a simplified calculation of ROI but it demonstrates the components of costs and benefits.

Now let's look at it from the airline's perspective. When the airline sees a streamlined process for maintenance and the majority of its unplanned aircraft downtime events are changed to planned maintenance activity, improving overall aircraft utilization and airline passenger satisfaction, it may look for similar capabilities for all of its operations.

The same digital platform can then be sold to the airline customer to let them do predictive maintenance on similar/related equipment that they maintain on their own. Such equipment could be airline baggage and cargo handling equipment, **Ground Power Units (GPUs)**, de-icing machines, and so on. Such equipment could be from different manufacturers. The engine provider can then provide this as a digital platform service with applications built for various types of critical physical assets and charge a subscription fee to generate new digital revenue. They can also sell apps for the *operational efficiency* of the assets to the airlines.

In GE's digital industrial business model, GE Aviation and different lines of business used GE's Predix Platform and applications built on top of that to improve the service business. Other applications, such as Brilliant Factory, were sold to manufacturers to provide smart factory applications, thereby generating digital revenue. In the previous section, we looked at possible ways to quantify the ROI from offerings around a digital platform that is an outcome of industrial digital transformation.

Gartner recommends using a limited number of **Key Performance Indicators (KPIs)** to track the progress of digital transformation initiatives. These KPIs should be limited to ones that are easy to correlate to the business outcome and are leading indicators of progress. For example, the on-time departure of flights with aircrafts using GE jet engines would be a leading indicator, and the customer satisfaction of passengers with the airline would be a lagging indicator. Such KPIs should be actionable and easily explainable to business leaders (see `https://www.gartner.com/smarterwithgartner/how-to-measure-digital-transformation-progress/`).

In the next section, we will look at new digital revenue through industrial digital transformation.

# Digital revenue

This section will focus on new digital revenue from transformation, which helps to improve the-top line revenue of the company. Let's begin with an example from the energy industry.

## Electricity value chain

Let's look at the electricity value chain here. Utility companies use gas or coal generators to generate electricity. In order to meet the fluctuating demand from a hot summer day for cooling and from a cold winter day for heating, often utility companies have to engage in energy trading. Northern California encountered a serious electricity shortfall due to excess heat in August 2020, leading to significant rolling power outages. This is primarily driven by the fact that electricity cannot be stored at large scale by utility companies. Due to the variations in energy supply and demand on a daily and even hourly basis, energy prices fluctuate over a wide range. On average, the US residential customer pays about 13 cents per **kilowatt hour** (**kWh**). However, it can be less than 10 cents in Washington state or more than 30 cents in Hawaii.

As the consumer demand or the load changes, utility companies have to manage the supply side for the equilibrium; otherwise, it would result in load-shedding when demand exceeds supply. The load can change due to weather changes, industrial activities, and the use of renewable sources such as rooftop solar panels. The supply, or the generation, side has to deal with capital costs and variables such as fuel costs and human costs. The utility companies estimate a certain sustainable peak energy generation from their installed capacity and forecast the load. If there will be a gap between load and supply, they have to proactively buy energy from the open markets and often pay a premium price for that. Likewise, the utility company can sell its excess capacity to others.

A new avenue for digital revenue is an application family that can be referred to with the generic name **Electricity Economic Optimizer** (**EEO**). EEO will be based on an electricity value chain digital platform. This would be a good example of industrial digital transformation in the electricity value chain. This EEO application would be a digital offering by the OEM of the generators, who would have the necessary domain knowledge in the digital industrial world of electricity generation, transmission, and distribution. The main capabilities of EEO will be these:

- Forecast the load using weather predictions, historical consumption data, and macro and micro-economic factors.
- Estimate the supply using the installed generation capacity, historical uptime, any planned maintenance activities, and any external factors such as weather and fuel prices.

- Provide a decision tree of how much energy to buy ahead of the shortfall and when to buy it.

- Provide advisory on a fair price to bid for electricity based on historical pricing and market conditions.

- Provide advisory on when to reduce generation or decide to sell excess capacity in the energy trading market.

In this example, the ROI of the transformation would be measured by the provider of EEO as the new subscription revenue compared to the cost of developing and maintaining this application and the underlying digital platform. The utility company would measure the ROI as the productivity and efficiency improvements to its operating model.

Large digital industrial companies such as Siemens, GE, and ABB have clearly realized that often digital capability is an enabler of its industrial equipment sales and acts as the differentiator. The industrial product along with the associated digital services, creates a stronger relationship with its customer. In some cases, there may not be standalone digital revenue, but the bigger product sale or service contract was enabled by the digital capability. Industrial digital transformation can also drive non-linear revenue models and increase the multiplier on earnings to improve stock valuations. Companies with digital platforms and digital revenues usually attract a higher multiplier for valuation purposes. For example, Carvana (stock: CVNA), which started in 2012, has a market valuation of over $32 billion (as of August 2020), which is a good example of how a digital platform-based company, for the used-car industry, is valued. Ford (stock: F) is valued at $28 billion, as a point of comparison. In a nutshell, traditional industrial companies are trying to unleash the potential exponential growth possible from the digital platform-driven part of their business. See *Figure 10.1* for a graphical representation of this transformation:

**Exponential Growth Potential of Transformation**

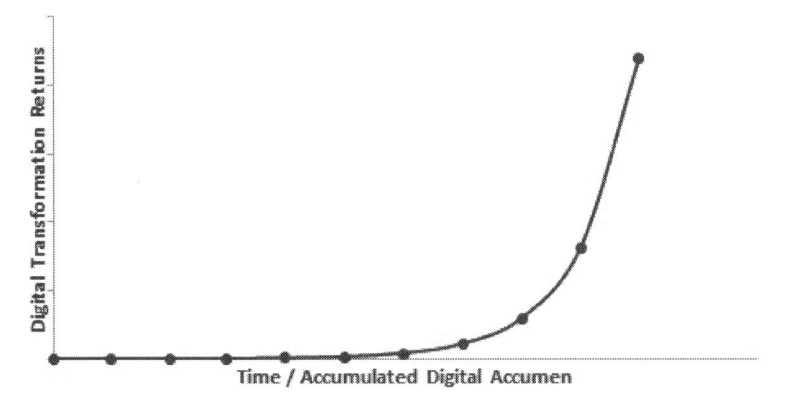

Figure 10.1 – Exponential growth potential of transformation

The next section looks at digital airports. Airports are often owned and operated by cities or counties but work closely with airlines, retail stores, ground transportation, and car rental companies, which are often privately owned.

## Digital airports

As we have seen already in this book, many public sector organizations have been undergoing a digital transformation over the last decade. For the most part, public sector organizations have moved existing services online and any incremental fees have been small, such as fees for accepting credit cards. These digital services have been designed to improve the public's experience interacting with the organization, not to generate new revenue. In fact, many public sector organizations are not legally able to create new revenue streams. One notable exception is airports.

Airports have a great deal of freedom in offering new services and setting new fees, primarily in their role in managing the operations of their facilities. In some cases, digitizing processes indirectly impacts airport revenue. For example, introducing automated gates at security checkpoints can reduce the amount of time passengers wait in line, providing them with more time to shop and eat after clearing security. This additional revenue for airport vendors translates into additional fees for the airport. In other cases, the airport is able to gain new revenue directly from the newly digitized process, either directly as the supplier of services or indirectly by levying a fee on the ultimate supplier of services to airport users.

An example of an airport generating new revenue from digital technology is **San Francisco Airport's (SFO's)** collection of fees for rideshare pickup. The pickup fees charged to taxis and town cars were a major source of revenue for SFO. The introduction and subsequent popularity of ridesharing services put a tremendous dent in that revenue. At the same time, rideshare drivers were in violation of SFO's rules and risked receiving a ticket whenever they picked up at the airport. As part of agreements with major ridesharing vendors Uber, Lyft, and Sidecar to allow them to legally pick up passengers at the airport, SFO built a tracking system that works with the GPS embedded in ridesharing apps to identify when a ride is requested within SFO's geofence. SFO has also made this application available to other airports, for a licensing fee, adding an additional revenue stream by productizing their internally developed application. The use of this application has resulted in several million dollars a year of incremental revenue for the airport from airport fees and licensing.

**Los Angeles World Airports (LAWA)**, which operates the **Los Angeles International Airport (LAX)**, provides a web presence focused on helping airport visitors navigate the airport and identify where they'd like to go for a meal or to pick up last-minute items before a flight. The implementation of this platform has provided the airport with the ability to drive additional revenue by offering food to go in partnership with Breeze, a new company founded by entrepeneur Anabell Lawee to deliver pre-ordered food directly to passengers at airports. LAX is the first Breeze customer. Passengers can order food through LAWA's website, through the the Breeze app, or text their order. The food is prepared in *ghost kitchens*, existing food preparation facilities at the airport that do not have a retail presence. The use of digital technology allows the airport to lower the overhead of food preparation by using kitchens outside of prime terminal space and, also, to collect a larger share of revenue than they can from restaurants operating in the terminal.

In the next section, we will discuss Airbnb, a company that brought the relatively small market of home-sharing into the mainstream and into direct competition with hotels.

# Airbnb Experiences

Airbnb had brought in Catherine Powell, a 15-year Disney executive, as head of Airbnb Experiences. Airbnb's goal was to diversify its revenue stream beyond home-sharing. The connection was simple: Disney is known for creating memorable *experiences* for its guests. Airbnb Trips started in 2016 and in 2018 was changed to Airbnb Experiences. In the first three quarters of 2018, it generated about $15 million in new revenue. The new digital revenue quickly rose to over $1 billion in the second quarter of 2019. In early 2020, Airbnb had reached about 40,000 experiences from around 1,000 cities globally.

In a July-August, 1998 Harvard Business Review article, the term *experience economy* was first used. It took a while for this concept to mature. Airbnb branded Experiences with the tagline *Meet the World from Home* during the Covid-19 crisis (see `https://www.airbnb.com/s/experiences/online`).

The investment in Experiences allowed Airbnb to easily pivot to focus on at-home experiences in early 2020, when the travel industry came to a grinding halt. The revenue from Experiences is a partial replacement for the rapid decline in home-sharing revenue. In this scenario, the *digital transformation* has been a means to survive in the travel industry. For Airbnb, the ROI is not only quantitative, it is qualitative; it is a means to ride out a crisis.

Let's now look at the societal benefits of digital transformation.

# Social good

The third type of benefit from digital transformation is social good. Social good is something that benefits a significant number of people. For example, the United States Environmental Protection Agency's mission to ensure clean air, water, and land is a social good. Social good is the basis for much of the work performed by governments and philanthropic organizations.

In 1970, Milton Friedman, one of the most famous economists of the 20th century, put forth the theory that the role of a CEO and, therefore, a corporation, was to maximize corporate value without regard for any effects on individuals or society. This theory was widely embraced and the effects of corporations maximizing profits without regard to their impact on others, known as externalities, resulted in substantial negative impacts, such as environmental pollution. However, in recent years, most private sector organizations have recognized the impacts of negative externalities and embraced their role as providers of social good. They have learned the value of doing well by doing good. For example, Dell Technologies' mission statement is to *create technologies that drive human progress*, and among the company's 2030 goals are six goals focused on sustainability along with other goals to increase inclusion and educational attainment. Intel has set the goal of 100% water reuse from its semiconductor operations (see `https://www.intel.com/content/www/us/en/environment/water-restoration.html`). This ties to the United Nations' sixth sustainability goal, of clean water and sanitation as described in *Chapter 1, Introducing Digital Transformation*.

Digital transformation has allowed both private and public sector organizations to create social good. Arguably, any digital transformation in the public and not-for-profit sectors is intended to be a social good by those delivering the transformation. Even those transformations that make public sector and not-for-profit entities more effective, allowing such organizations to deliver more programs and services with the same funding, can be considered a social good. That said, in the remainder of this section, we will focus on digital transformations in both the public and private sectors that directly make services more accessible to residents or improve overall quality of life. For more examples of digital transformations that delivered social good, refer back to the examples in *Chapter 6, Transforming the Public Sector*.

## The United Nations

Perhaps the most far-reaching not-for-profit organization is the United Nations. In *Chapter 1, Introducing Digital Transformation*, we discussed the United Nations' 17 sustainability development goals. Progress toward most of the goals can be accelerated through digital transformation and some of these goals, such as sustainable cities and zero hunger, are of such magnitude that a new approach through digital transformation will be required to achieve them. As we discuss examples in this section, we will share how they align with the United Nations' framework.

## Kenya

In 2008, Kenya launched an initiative to transform the country into an industrialized nation with a prosperous middle class by 2030. In 2011, the government launched the Huduma Kenya effort to accelerate the country's transformation, empower citizens, and reduce corruption. When Huduma Kenya was created, virtually all public services in Kenya were delivered face to face.

The experience of interacting with the government involved traveling long distances to the Kenyan capital of Nairobi to one government service center and long waits in lines to interact with staff handling manual processes. The large number of manual processes with poor controls resulted in a high level of corruption as well. Furthermore, the trip to Nairobi was expensive for citizens, which meant that individuals often had to sell assets such as livestock to pay for transportation to Nairobi, and process inefficiency meant that often the transaction could not be completed in one day. In those cases, citizens would have to sell more assets to return to Nairobi the next day.

The goal of Huduma Kenya was to decentralize services so that citizens could obtain the services they needed without leaving their towns and villages and do so at a price the government and citizens could afford. Huduma Kenya created Huduma Channels, a suite of new government services. The first service created 52 branch offices, called Huduma Centers, across the country. To enable this, manual processes were automated and delivered as a service to staff at local offices, who were equipped with laptops to process transactions. All data was maintained securely in the cloud. In addition, Huduma Channels provided several other capabilities, including these:

- *Huduma Life App*: A mobile application that allows residents to access many government services directly from their smartphone
- *Huduma Contact Center*: A single number that uses digital technologies to route and manage calls for all government agencies
- *Huduma Card*: A prepaid card that allows citizens to make digital payments for public and private sector services

A government study demonstrated that Huduma Kenya has saved Kenyans millions of dollars in transportation costs and lost earnings and reduced corruption by 96%. Huduma Kenya was so successful at improving the lives of Kenyans that the program earned the United Nations Public Service Award for Improving Delivery of Public Services.

Huduma Kenya's programs support several United Nations sustainability goals, including goal 1, no poverty, and goal 9, industry, innovation, and infrastructure. When covering these United Nations sustainability goals in *Chapter 1, Introducing Digital Transformation*, we stated that these are opportunities to solve high-value problems for social good, using digital transformation.

## Microsoft – technology for social impact

While corporations can include social good in their own transformations by becoming more sustainable organizations or delivering products and services that are safer or more accessible to people with disabilities, some private sector entities establish partnerships to assist nonprofits and governments with their digital transformations. One such project is Microsoft's **Technology for Social Impact** (**TSI**) group, which works with nonprofits to enable their digital transformations. A few examples of how TSI has supported nonprofit organizations follow:

- In the Philippines, **Gawad Kalinga** (**GK**) collaborated with Microsoft to create an online platform that can be used to manage the deployment of volunteers and aid during a natural disaster. When disasters have passed, the same platform is used by GK to help individuals obtain sustainable livelihoods, speeding the recovery of their community.

- The Thai Social Innovation Foundation helps match people with disabilities with jobs. Before working with TSI, their processes were entirely paper-based, limiting the number of people they could place in jobs. TSI helped digitize the foundation's workflows and documents, enabling the foundation to increase its impact by an order of magnitude.

- The Cambodian **Child Protection Unit** (**CPU**) worked with TSI to move their data to the cloud so that police officers could access information and collaborate in the field, enabling them to find more missing children faster.

Microsoft is only one example. Many companies are applying their digital transformation expertise to assist nonprofits to achieve their missions more efficiently and effectively. Microsoft's TSI aligns with the United Nations' sustainability goals through the creation of a partnership to achieve sustainability, goal 17. The projects delivered by the partnerships address a variety of goals by reducing poverty (goal 1), decreasing inequality (goal 10), and providing decent work and economic growth (goal 8), among others.

## COVID-19 response

During the early stages of the COVID-19 pandemic, private sector companies retooled and repurposed digital technologies to deliver **Personal Protective Equipment (PPE)** and medical devices that were in short supply.

In April of 2020, Ford Motor Company reopened its shuttered Rawsonville, Michigan plant and redeployed one thousand employees from truck manufacturing to ventilator manufacturing, producing the **General Electric (GE)** Airon Model A-E ventilator as a subcontractor to GE Healthcare, with the goal of producing 30,000 ventilators a month.

Automotive manufacturers around the world, whose operations are well suited to complex precision manufacturing activities, redirected their resources to build respirators and ventilators, including GM, Tesla, and Fiat Chrysler. In the UK, Rolls Royce and McLaren joined the Ventilator Challenge, a consortium of large companies that produced thousands of ventilators. Companies that operate on a design and manufacturing timeline that usually takes years to design and ramp up manufacturing retooled in a matter of weeks with the use of digital technologies including CAD and rapid prototyping.

Companies around the globe repurposed their production facilities to the pandemic response work that best suited their capabilities. Companies of all sizes, from Ford to Formlabs, with manufacturing and prototyping capabilities began producing face shields and swabs for COVID-19. Clothing brands including Hanes, Eddie Bauer, and Gap made face masks, surgical masks, gowns, and other PPE. Alcoholic beverage manufacturers, from small wineries to global brands such as Pernod Ricard, produced hand sanitizer.

The sudden transformation of the operations of many thousands of companies, both large and small, required extensive use of digital technologies. Perhaps the most well-publicized technology supporting the digital transformation engendered by COVID-19 was 3D printing. Virtually every manufacturer, university lab, and home hobbyist with a rapid prototyping lab repurposed their 3D printing capabilities to manufacture face shields. In addition, major manufacturing operations reprogrammed and retooled complex computerized manufacturing systems to perform different operations on different parts, something that would have been impossible with traditional fixed manufacturing processes.

In perhaps the most challenging transformation of the pandemic, sophisticated global supply chains were redesigned and redirected to deliver different raw materials to different locations. When air transportation interrupted supply chains, manufacturers found new suppliers for raw materials and subcomponents who also repurposed their production activities.

These efforts resulted in a change of direction in manufacturing and distribution not seen since the world redirected production during World War II in service of social good. While the global response to COVID-19 could be aligned to any number of United Nations sustainability goals, it most clearly supports goal 3, good health and wellbeing, as the world searches for solutions to combat and eliminate the threat of COVID-19.

In this section, we have explored examples of digital transformation that deliver social good in the public sector, private sector, and nonprofits and considered how all of them align with the global goals of the United Nations.

# Summary

In this chapter, we learned how to measure the value of transformation. We learned how to build a business case for your digital transformation and about the three types of business value that can be gained from industrial digital transformation: productivity and efficiency gains, new digital revenue, and social good. This chapter has provided us with the tools needed to obtain funding and get ready to start on our transformation.

In the next chapter, we will put everything we have learned so far together and create a blueprint for success. We will discuss how to ensure the success of a digital transformation, provide a playbook that can be followed, and sustain a digital transformation.

# Questions

Here are a few questions to test your understanding of the chapter:

1. What are the seven steps of developing a business case for digital transformation?
2. Why is it important to complete a proof of concept before building your business case?
3. Describe the three types of benefits that can come from a digital transformation project.
4. What are the key factors in an ROI analysis?
5. Give some examples of the societal benefits of digital transformation.

# 11
# The Blueprint for Success

In the previous chapter, we learned how to measure the value of digital transformation. We learned about creating a business case for a transformation. We also learned the three types of value that can be gained from digital transformation: productivity and efficiency gains, new revenue streams, and social good.

In this chapter, we will learn about best practices to ensure success in industrial digital transformation and how to sustain it in the long term. We will cover innovation models and templates that you will find useful for your own transformations. This chapter will cover the following:

- How to ensure success of a digital transformation
- The transformation playbook
- The business model canvas
- How to sustain the pace of transformation
- Digital transformation at home

# How to ensure success in digital transformation

We have reached the final chapter of the book and it is time for us to put everything we have learned together to execute a successful digital transformation. In this section, we will discuss the critical success factors for ensuring that your digital transformation achieves your goals. We will discuss the following eight factors that will be critical to achieving a successful transformation for your entire organization or for a single project:

- Know what you are trying to accomplish
- Complete the right proof of concept
- Obtain organizational support and resources
- Select initial teams and projects wisely
- Align your culture and hone your team's skills
- Do what you said you would
- Measure your progress
- Scale cautiously

Next, we will look at each success factor in more detail.

## Know what you are trying to accomplish

Before you begin your digital transformation, it is important to have a clear understanding of the objectives of the transformation. Is your goal to deliver one product that is critical to the success of your organization, or is it to transform the way your entire organization buys and builds products? It is critical that you are clear on the scope of your effort before you begin your transformation. This clarity will help you scope all of your future planning and execution efforts. It will also help you to ensure that you communicate your goals effectively and align expectations throughout the organization. Our discussion in *Chapter 1, Introducing Digital Transformation*, that reviewed some of the typical objectives may be helpful in defining your objectives.

## Complete the right proof of concept

Often, project teams are tempted to complete a proof of concept that demonstrates the user interface or delivers an entire use case. But that's not the point of your proof of concept. The goal of your proof of concept is to use early development sprints to demonstrate that you can solve the hardest problems that you expect to encounter while developing the product. Whether you need to invent a new battery technology or perfect authentication, choose a proof of concept that will demonstrate that you have solved the hardest problems and are ready to build a product. In *Chapter 2, Transforming the Culture in an Organization, Figures 2.3-2.5* and the accompanying text discuss the early phases of the project and how to reduce risk through experimentation. Once you have solved the most challenging technical problems, you can define your business case as described in *Chapter 10, Measuring the Value of Transformation*. If you discover that the most challenging problems aren't solvable–either there is no feasible solution or the solution is cost prohibitive, now is the time to cancel the project. Remember that failing fast and learning from failure is as important as success.

## Obtain organizational support and resources

Once you have determined the scope of your digital transformation, you will be ready to obtain support and resources. You must build support throughout the organization to enable digital transformation. Whether you are the CEO, a middle manager, or an individual contributor, you need to obtain the support of the leaders who will fund and staff your transformation. You will also need the support of the staff who will execute the digital transformation. As we have learned throughout this book, including in *Chapter 2, Transforming the Culture in an Organization*, specifically in the *Skills and capabilities for digital transformation* section, successful digital transformations require the active support of everyone involved in the effort.

## Select initial teams and projects wisely

For your digital transformation to be successful, it is important to select a group of people who are interested in and excited about your digital transformation, rather than skeptical or hostile about it. It is likely that you will have enough organizational skepticism and resistance outside the core digital transformation project team. Don't make it harder on yourself by trying to recruit a team that feels like the transformation is a punishment or otherwise doesn't believe in the effort. We often refer to this as forming a *coalition of the willing*. Likewise, even if your goal is to transform your entire enterprise, unless there is a crisis that gives you a mandate or burning platform to attack your organization's biggest and hardest problem, don't start there. Start with a small, manageable project that you can confidently deliver even if some things go wrong.

## Align your culture and hone your team's skills

As we discussed in *Chapter 2, Transforming the Culture in an Organization*, employees must learn new skills and ways of working to successfully execute a digital transformation. Cultural alignment and skill development are listed here together and discussed together in *Chapter 2, Transforming the Culture in an Organization*, because they are intertwined. Successfully aligning the culture to your digital transformation will require the development of both new technical skills and new ways of working individually and as a team.

It is important to identify each team and individual who will be involved in the transformation project as well as their role and what new skills they will need to be successful participants in the transformation effort. You will need to create a training plan for each individual. When developing employee training plans, it is important to include both technical skills and soft skills. It's also important to make sure that soft skills training is provided to intact teams to bring the most value to the organization. Refer to *Chapter 2, Transforming the Culture in an Organization*, for ideas about the kind of training that will be required to complete your transformation.

## Do what you said you would

Doing what you said you would is a simple idea but can be difficult, especially for technologists who become enamored with solving problems and adding features. Deliver the product that you scoped and committed to, not something with more features or fewer features and not a completely different product that the development team identified along the way. There are occasions where a change of direction is truly called for, such as when a development team at a government agency discovered that they were building a solution that industry didn't want. They shifted gears and built the solution that industry would use. In those cases, you should agree to a change of direction with your funders. Otherwise, staying the course enables you and your transformation effort to build credibility by meeting expectations.

## Measure your progress

It is important that you not only deliver the right product, but that you also deliver the product right—that is, that you deliver a high-quality product on schedule. In order to ensure that you do that, it is important to measure your team's performance against your plan. While digital products are often delivered by agile teams with no pre-defined feature delivery plan, development teams are expected to deliver timely results and to meet internal and external deadlines. At the beginning of the project, your team should select a set of metrics that you will use to track your performance. These can include quality metrics, such as successful regression tests, and performance metrics, such as the velocity of feature delivery. The specific metrics should be driven by your business needs. What is important is that you have a set of metrics that will allow you to track progress and identify delivery or quality issues early.

## Scale cautiously

Scaling is the point where many transformation efforts fail. Regardless of the planned scope of your transformation effort, you should use caution when moving from one project or team to a larger group of projects and teams. You'll need to have a carefully prepared scaling plan and follow all the guidance in this chapter just as you did for your initial product to ensure that your transformation doesn't stall or collapse under its own weight. *Chapter 2, Transforming the Culture in an Organization*, provides a number of strategies that will help you scale your transformation effectively.

Now that we have identified the critical success factors for your transformation, in the next section, we will share a number of playbooks that you can use to facilitate success for any type of transformation, from a small product to a moonshot.

# The transformation playbook

One of the approaches that organizations take to help them implement and institutionalize their digital transformation is to create a playbook or a series of playbooks that provide strategies and approaches for teams to follow when they execute their transformation. In this section, we will share several playbooks that you can use or adapt to your work, as well as providing some guidance to help you create your own playbooks for your organization.

Playbooks serve a number of purposes in enabling your digital transformation journey:

- Playbooks educate teams, clients, and partners about what you're doing and how a digital transformation is different than how you've worked in the past.
- They formalize new ways of working and set standards that define new practices.

- A playbook professionalizes the digital transformation effort and allows the team to set their direction, whether that team is a Fortune 500 corporation or a single product group.
- Playbooks reduce political confrontations by setting policies rather than forcing individuals to defend practices when there is disagreement.

We recommend that all organizations start with a playbook. If you've already started your transformation without a playbook, consider whether you should add one now. If your teams are struggling with setting standards and priorities, conflict, or repeatedly explaining the same concepts to end users, it might be time to create or adopt a playbook.

## Transforming products and processes using existing technologies

The most common digital transformations involve redesigning existing processes or products, such as digitizing workflows or moving service delivery from in person to online. These transformations tend to involve existing teams, processes, products, and services. The playbooks we will discuss in this section will be more focused on preparing an organization for change than the playbooks we will discuss later in this chapter. Later playbooks will be focused on new products and technologies.

There are many digital transformation playbooks that have been made publicly available, primarily by government agencies. We will discuss some of those playbooks in this section, as well as how to develop your own transformation playbook.

There are playbooks available for product transformations and for many activities that enable transformations. Let's look at some examples:

- Refer to the **United States Digital Services (USDS)** playbook (`https://playbook.cio.gov/`) for basic digital transformation plays.
- The United States Department of Veterans Affairs Digital Services Handbook (`https://18f.gsa.gov/partnership-principles/`) will help you learn key plays that will assist you in effectively delivering new products.
- Leverage the gov.uk service manual (`https://www.gov.uk/service-manual`) to gather ideas for everything from service standards to creating your key performance indicators.

If you're in the public sector, you may need some help with government procurement processes. In that case, you may want to look at the plays in the TechFar (`https://playbook.cio.gov/techfar/`) playbook to help you understand the flexibility in the procurement process that you can use to speed up your project. Or, if you need help understanding how to better partner with the business unit that you're working with to develop new products and processes, you may want to review the 18F partnership principles (`https://18f.gsa.gov/partnership-principles/`).

Generally, private sector organizations don't make their playbooks available for public consumption, as they are part of their competitive advantage. This is what makes the public sector playbooks such valuable references regardless of where you work. However, some private sector organizations are beginning to share specific playbooks publicly. Here are some examples of private sector playbooks:

- Data collaborative company Brighthive published a series of responsible data use playbooks (`https://playbooks.brighthive.io/`).

- GE published two versions of their Data Transformation Playbook. Download the short version here: `https://www.ge.com/digital/sites/default/files/download_assets/2019-Digital-Transformation-Playbook-GE.pdf`. The long version can be downloaded here: `http://media.salon-energie.com/Presentation/ge_digital_industrial_transformation_playbook_whitepaper_761202.pdf`.

- Landing AI published this playbook on driving transformation through AI adoption. Download the playbook here: `https://landing.ai/wp-content/uploads/2020/05/LandingAI_Transformation_Playbook_11-19.pdf`.

- McKinsey Digital has shared a blueprint for the digital transformation of automotive industry suppliers that can be downloaded from this page: `https://www.mckinsey.com/business-functions/mckinsey-digital/our-insights/a-blueprint-for-successful-digital-transformations-for-automotive-suppliers`.

- RingCentral published this playbook with a focus on enabling remote work: `https://remote-playbook.com/`.

- In *Chapter 8, Artificial Intelligence in Digital Transformation*, we discussed the need for increased awareness of cybersecurity during the transformation journey. Download the best practices for developing a cybersecurity playbook here: `https://www.infosecurityeurope.com/__novadocuments/414937`.

Once you have reviewed a variety of playbooks, you may choose to adopt an existing playbook for your transformation, or you may decide to create your own playbook. If you decide to create your own playbook, it can include whatever you believe is important to ensure the success of your transformation. With that idea in mind, here are some of the things that you may want to include in your playbook:

- **The value proposition for your digital transformation**: A simple statement that explains why the transformation is happening. This reminds everyone of the value of the transformation.
- **Roles**: Define the roles of team members, users, and stakeholders in the development process. This ensures that everyone understands the commitment they are making to the success of the project.
- **Prioritization**: Set criteria for project prioritization. If the transformation includes multiple projects, this will help customers and stakeholders understand how you select the projects you work on.
- **Guiding principles**: List your design principles to ensure that everyone in the organization understands them. This will aid decision making throughout the project.
- **Project planning**: Define the project planning process and approaches, such as the use of user stories. This will ensure that everyone stays aligned throughout the project.
- **Project management**: Explain how projects run. This should include all the major steps of the project. More detail, such as your development methodologies or how products are tested and released, can be included if there are specific areas of conflict or confusion. Metrics can also be included if performance measurement has been an area of concern on past projects.
- **Post release roles**: Define ownership and responsibilities for the project team, product owner, and other stakeholders after release.
- **Technical standards**: Define any technical standards or constraints. For example, maybe all tools will be open source or a particular testing tool will be used. This ensures that everyone knows the tools that will be used and any constraints they need to abide by.
- **Compliance**: Identify any legal requirements that are of particular concern to your organization. This ensures that everyone is on the same page from the beginning, avoiding potential fines or other regulatory issues.

Whatever you put in your playbook, it is important that the playbook is short and to the point. The most important role of a playbook is to communicate with the stakeholders of your digital transformation. To accomplish that, the playbook needs to be attractive and easy to read. *Figure 11.1* shows an excerpt from the USDS playbook:

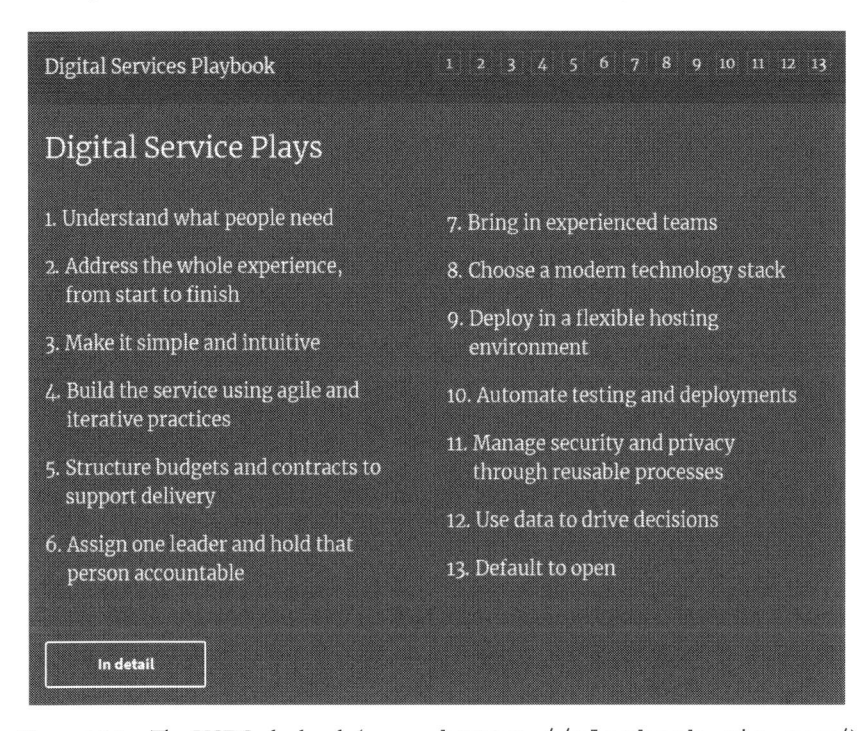

Figure 11.1 – The USDS playbook (source: `https://playbook.cio.gov/`)

This playbook lists the 13 USDS plays in short, declarative, and attention-grabbing sentences and provides links to the individual plays where readers can learn more. If we click through to a specific play, we will find a simple two- or three-sentence description of the play, a short checklist of items that will help us to execute that play, and some key questions that will help us think about the play more deeply. This is a great structure for a playbook because it is visually interesting and easy to consume.

Now that you have seen a number of playbooks, you are ready to get started. You can adopt one of the playbooks that we have reviewed in this section, search the web for a publicly available playbook that is a better fit for your team, or create one of your own. Remember that the goal of your playbook is to guide your team's work and communicate with the broader stakeholder community. Regardless of whether you create your own playbook, modify one that is available to you, or adopt one as is, make sure that it will help you accomplish your goals and objectives.

## Business model canvas

While your playbook should guide your team through many projects with limited changes, you may find that you also need a tool that will help you concisely frame each individual project to ensure that everyone on the team fully understands the project objectives and expectations. If you would like to create a visual representation of the entire project, you may find the business model canvas, introduced by Alexander Osterwalder in 2005, to be a useful tool:

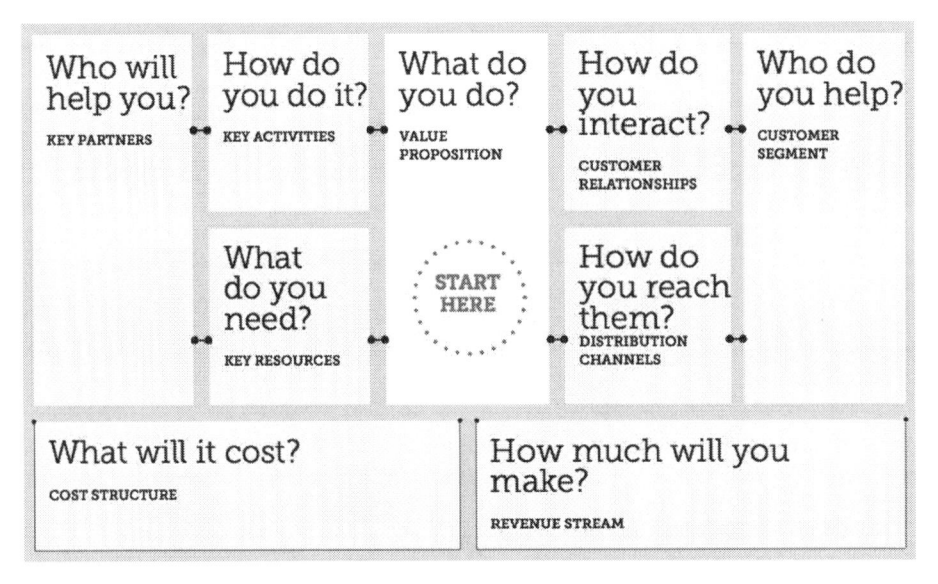

Figure 11.2 – Business model canvas template (Source: `http://diytoolkit.org/tools/business-model-canvas/`, License: CC BY-SA-NC)

A variation of the business model canvas, called the digital transformation canvas, was developed by Ricardo Ivison Mata and is shown in *Figure 11.3*. It showcases the use of the digital transformation canvas for planning out a personal health initiative. Such one-page visuals are quite popular for summarizing transformation goals and the journey:

| 1) Business Driven Product / Service Description | 3) Key Stakeholders | 4) Data Objects in Scope | 5) Data Objects Current Available format | 8) Business Value Drivers |
|---|---|---|---|---|
| Pro-Health app is a mobile app + devices to provide:<br>• Life Policy quotations for desired life/health products<br>• A benchmark of how much can be saved if some health related metrics improve<br>• Set up a suggested plan to improve health supported by devices connected to the app<br>• Motivate and close the purchase once prospect customers have achieved target milestones | • Chief Actuarial<br>• Chief Operations Officer<br>• Marketing Director<br>• Operations Manager<br>• Compliance Officer<br>• CIO / IT Delivery Head | Prospect Customer Personal Data: age, date of birth, etc.<br><br>Prospect customer biometrics: weight, blood pressure and sugar<br><br>Products suit for prospect customer<br><br>Health Measurements and milestones | - Health measurements (Biometrics) Data: Not available<br>- Policy and quotation forms: paper-based | Increase Revenue |
|  | 7) Partnerships |  | 6) Machine Readable DO transformation technologies | 9) Implementation Model |
|  | - Devices for bio-metrics: IoT for health connectivity<br>- Health coaches<br>- App Usability. |  | - Devices connected to provide health measurements (IoT)<br>- Digital forms and electronic signature | - Mobile Application with connected devices (body measure, IoT bracelet |
| 2) Business Value Proposition |||| 10) KPI's |
| Our **Pro-Health app** help prospect customers **who want to get** more affordable life and health insurance **by** improving their overall health status through an easy to use app and devices to set up a tailored program targeted to accomplish key health metrics goals, **unlike** traditional approaches who focus only on prospect customer risks. |||| - 10% in increased premium<br>- 4% persistency<br>- 5% improvement in opportunity to closed ratio. |

Figure 11.3 – Digital transformation canvas for planning personal health transformation (source: `https://medium.com/@ricardoivison/the-digital-transformation-canvas-a56b29ed219d`)

Now that we understand playbooks and the business model canvas tools that help transform existing processes and products, we will examine models that will help us develop new products.

# Digital transformations to embrace new opportunities

Let's look at a model of innovation for transformation to identify and embrace new technology and business opportunities. This model can be simply stated as the 70:20:10 percent rule and is illustrated in *Figure 11.4*. Note that while the percentages used here are 70, 20, and 10, depending upon the company and situation, it could be different: 75:15:10 or 80:10:10, or any ratio appropriate for your organization. We are providing directional guidance only; you can use this as a template and tweak it further:

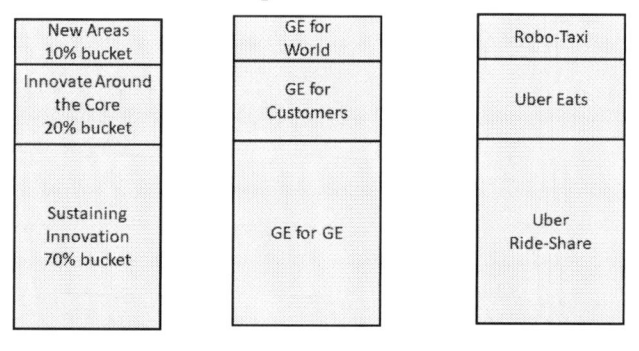

| New Areas 10% bucket | GE for World | Robo-Taxi |
|---|---|---|
| Innovate Around the Core 20% bucket | GE for Customers | Uber Eats |
| Sustaining Innovation 70% bucket | GE for GE | Uber Ride-Share |

Figure 11.4 – Industrial digital transformation innovation paradigms

According to this simple model in *Figure 11.4*, the three buckets are as follows:

- **Sustaining Innovation bucket**: This bucket refers to incremental innovation around the core of the business for its existing processes, products, and services. This is where most traditional businesses spend the bulk of their resources. For example, **General Electric** (**GE**) has been adding sensors to its industrial products and using AI and analytics on the data from these assets. Building an Industrial IoT platform for internal use by the different **lines of business** (**LOBs**), to improve the efficiency and profit margin, would be the incremental innovation around the core of the business. Likewise, smart manufacturing capabilities and overall industrial product enhancements, leveraging the insights from this platform, would also fall in this bucket. The company defined it as *GE for GE*, or in this case, the Industrial Internet platform and applications built by GE Digital (first GE) for use by its LOBs (second GE). Typically, the CIO and the CTOs of the LOBs are tasked with this activity, in coordination with the business leaders. They in turn may leverage GE Digital or external partners to accelerate the adoption of new digital technologies.

- **Innovation Around the Core**: This bucket often refers to the exploration of new digital revenues adjacent to the main business. Back to the GE example: the servitization of the industrial assets or product-as-a-service offerings to its current industrial customer base would fall in this bucket. This is the *GE for Customers* bucket, where customers refer to existing industrial asset customers. In GE's case, it creates a differentiation for their industrial products over competitors' products. No doubt Siemens, ABB, Honeywell, and others are all trying to do the same. Typically, this stage often requires the CDO organization to accelerate the pace of change. In this phase, often the CDO's department brings in external digital talent who have experience building digital platforms. Uber Eats and Airbnb's Experiences would fall in this category based on our viewpoint, as they are innovations around the core business. A company offering a combination of ride-share, room-share, food-delivery, and destination experiences as a single all-inclusive package for the entire family could be an example of this category.

- **Exploring New Paradigms**: This bucket is often the most innovative and therefore highest-risk area of innovation, especially for established companies. New acquisitions and investments by the venture arm of large companies are common in this category. We will often hear these activities described as moonshot opportunities. This is where ambitious and ground-breaking projects are undertaken with the goal of building new business lines with new and preferably high-margin digital revenue. See *Figure 11.5*. In the case of GE this was the idea behind *GE for World*:

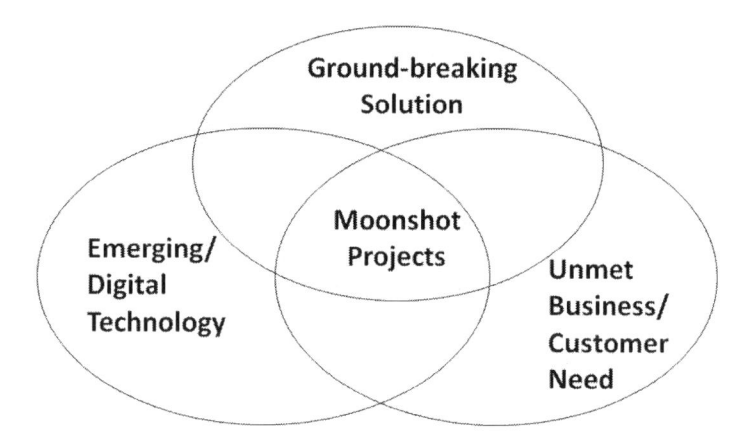

Figure 11.5 – Moonshot projects

GE's Predix platform and the applications built on top of it could be sold to new customer segments such as automotive manufacturing, **consumer packaged goods** (**CPG**), chemical industries, commercial buildings, and cities, thereby making GE a software-as-a-service provider, bringing the physical and digital worlds together. The digital platform/software-as-a-service business is typically much higher-margin than the industrial products business and draws a much higher multiplier for the stock market valuation of the company. Businesses in this category may include autonomous driving platforms for use as robo-taxis, or autonomous ride-share with no human driver, in the case of companies such as Uber, Lyft, Tesla, and Waymo. An amusing idea for a *moonshot* opportunity for Airbnb is to explore space hotels (see `https://www.space.com/40207-space-hotel-launch-2021-aurora-station.html`).

## Innovation model applied to the public sector

Does the innovation model of 70:20:10 apply to the public sector? Public sector organizations are never driven by profits and rarely pursue new revenue. They also tend to be risk-averse. While these conditions may limit innovation, as discussed in *Chapter 6, Transforming the Public Sector*, they do not preclude innovation completely. An example of a public sector vertical where this model applies is airports. Public sector airports have three main sources of revenue or funding, namely aeronautical (directly related to airline operations and passenger fees), non-aeronautical (retail- and ground transportation-related revenue), and tax dollars. Let's explore some of the innovative projects at the **San Francisco Airport** (**SFO**) under the leadership of its CIO Ian Law.

Let's explore some of the innovative projects at the **San Francisco Airport (SFO)** under the leadership of its CIO Ian Law:

- Dynamic gate allotment: Airlines are allocated gates dynamically based on the volume of passenger traffic and connections rather than there being fixed gates for specific airlines.

- Guided navigation in the airport: Passengers can use their smartphones for guided navigation, such as for navigating to a departure gate.

- Noise abatement: IoT sensors are used to detect aircraft engines that are not shut off after parking at the gate and are causing noise pollution.

- Virtual TSA lines: Passengers are able to be in a virtual queue at the security checkpoint until they are close to screening, to reduce physical contact while waiting in long lines.

- Digital square footage: The revenue from retail store sales in airports is traditionally tied to physical square footage, but in this age, the digital footprint of a retail store can be used to increase revenue. For instance, revenue can be generated through the ordering via a smartphone app of coffee or food for pickup from a kiosk nearest to a given gate. This topic was covered by Ian Law in his article titled *Airports: Managing the Digital Square Foot*.

- Virtual queuing for taxis: A similar case to that of virtual queuing for TSA lines.

- Ride-share management: Revenue sharing with companies such as Uber and Lyft; see the patent details here: `http://patft.uspto.gov/netacgi/nph-Parser?Sect1=PTO2&Sect2=HITOFF&p=1&u=%2Fnetahtml%2FPTO%2Fsearch-bool.html&r=1&f=G&l=50&col=AND&d=PTXT&s1=10,535,021&OS=10,535,021&RS=10,535,021`.

When we evaluate this list from the perspective of the 70:20:10 innovation model, we would put the first four items in the 70% bucket (as core aeronautical activities), the next two items would go in the 20% bucket (as non-aeronautical revenue from retail and ground transportation), and the last item would go in the 10% bucket – it is a groundbreaking means of generating revenue from ride-share companies as well as a patented technology that allows the future monetization of this digital transformation solution with other private airports both in the US or abroad. This ride-share management initiative fits the description of a successful moonshot project coming from the public sector.

We will explore moonshot opportunities further in the next section.

## Moonshot digital transformations

Moonshot projects are opportunities for companies to step outside their comfort zones and sometimes even consider disrupting their own successful products and services before a traditional or non-traditional competitor can disrupt them. See *Figure 11.5* for a visualization of moonshot projects. Sometimes, moonshot projects may involve leveraging the diverse new skills acquired by a corporate merger.

## Exploratory (moonshot) project template

Digital transformation projects can be taken up within large corporations as exploratory projects. Projects that have not gone through extensive risk-benefit analyses can be taken up in this structure. This model has been successfully adopted by many large companies. In 2010, Google created a subsidiary known as X Development Company, located about 1.5 miles from its main campus in Mountain View, California that is engaged in research and development activities that fall under a category known as *moonshot* projects. This company considers hundreds of ideas each year and a few are turned into fully resourced projects. An example of a fully invested X moonshot is the autonomous car project that has successfully transitioned into a new company known as Waymo and is now a subsidiary of Google parent company Alphabet.

## Business case

In 2012, when GE started the industrial internet journey, they discussed *The Power of 1 percent* (see `https://www.ge.com/news/reports/the-industrial-internet-is-already-changing-our`). According to this table, 1% more fuel efficiency in aviation can save $30 billion over 15 years. The corresponding number in savings due to 1% fuel savings in power generation is $66 billion. Such huge business outcomes from investments in the industrial internet seem like moonshot projects. However, in this case, GE could present those projections as they have a dominant market position in power generation and aviation. One-third of the world's electricity is generated on GE's equipment and 70% of the world's commercial aircraft run jet engines manufactured by GE and its joint ventures. We used this example to show that market leadership provides companies opportunities to strive for ground-breaking solutions with massive global outcomes. Due to the large market share of GE in certain industry sectors, the company came out with the slogan in September 2020, *building a world that works*. However, such large-scale endeavors also come with a need for a high level of investment and significant risk as they are susceptible to changes in market dynamics. In this case, the growth of renewable sources of energy such as solar and wind turbines that do not require *fuel* disrupted GE's ambitious plans. Likewise, the COVID-19 pandemic starting in the spring of 2020 has reduced the size of the global aviation industry drastically, at least for several years. The business case for moonshot projects needs to consider the experiences of others and account for checkpoints at different levels.

In the context of moonshot projects, you will hear the term *unicorn*, which often refers to a start-up that is valued at over $1 billion. This term was coined by venture capitalist Aileen Lee in 2013. When established companies want to create a new digital business, they often use unicorn companies as a benchmark (see `https://www.cbinsights.com/research-unicorn-companies`). The established companies are often willing to make risky investments or big bets to generate order-of-magnitude increases in business value delivered to their customers. This is often referred to as 10X value (see `https://singularityhub.com/2017/04/03/how-to-make-an-exponential-business-model-to-10x-growth/`). In other words, every $1 invested in moonshot projects is intended to generate $10 in revenue. In that case, to build a $1 billion valuation, $100 million worth of investment would be needed. If the goal of a moonshot project is to create a unicorn, the business case needs to provide a strong rationale for a $100 million investment. As a result, companies such as Google evaluate many ideas and projects in the early stages and go through detailed vetting processes to see which ones show promise to become the next unicorn. GE used to call such a vetting process fail-fast. In other words, run quick experiments, and either fail, learn from failure, and pivot, or if the initial pilot is successful, improve and iterate to the next level.

## Moonshot project team

This team needs to have a combination of people, some with mindsets that drive invention and others that are innovative. In this case, invention is defined as the creation of a new machine, product, or process that did not exist before. On the other hand, innovation is defined as transforming a product, process, or idea into a new solution that adds value.

This team needs to have domain experts with the depth of knowledge and breadth of experience that is needed to overcome a variety of challenges, such as resource constraints, technical hurdles, and uncertainties, when charting new territory. It is likely that due to organizational dynamics and sometimes competing targets, such a diverse group of trained experts would not be collaborative enough to learn from each other, share their knowledge with others, or, when needed, share the workloads of other team members to overcome unexpected challenges.

Team leaders play a very important role in leading moonshot project teams. It would be ideal to find a team leader who has domain expertise and is task-oriented as well as relationship-oriented to create a collaborative environment for expert team members.

It is also important to consider training team members to enhance their collaboration skills, as discussed in *Chapter 2, Transforming the Culture in an Organization*. Skills that allow teams to resolve conflicts productively and encourage people to appreciate the point of view of others are very important in this context. Building a sense of community in the team through informal events can be effective.

It is important to define the roles of team members and ensure that these roles are well understood by the entire team. When roles are well defined, team members will be more inclined to be collaborative where the approach to solving a problem is not well defined and tasks require creativity.

Let's next look at a systematic approach to a moonshot project.

# Innovation process steps for a moonshot project

Innovation processes in a moonshot project always start with the definition of a problem statement. The six stages of this process are shown in *Figure 11.6*:

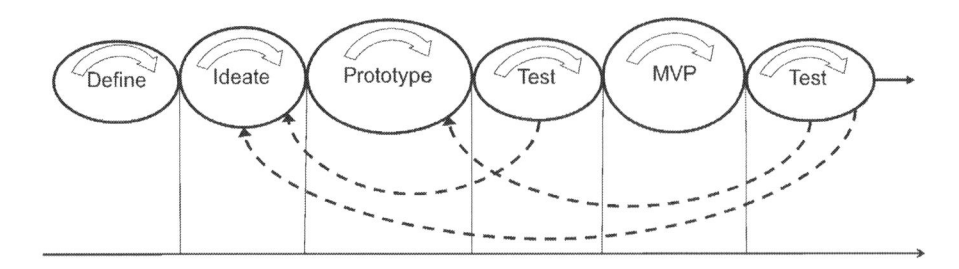

Figure 11.6 – Process stages

The process stages in *Figure 11.6*, fit well with the agile development paradigm discussed in *Chapter 2, Transforming the Culture in an Organization*.

## Define the problem statement

In the definition phase, information is gathered on improvements that can be achieved through digital transformation. This information can include proposed options for business process modifications, possible process improvements, or customer-driven modifications. This information is then analyzed by the moonshot project team to define the problem statement.

## Ideation

This is the phase where the project team generates various ideas and solutions for the problem statements that were developed in the definition phase. This process can start with an event where all the team members come together to achieve alignment on all available information and knowledge about the problem to be solved. It might be useful to include relevant stakeholders in this activity, including project sponsors, designers, engineers, and marketing and sales staff. If the problem is very large and complex, it would be better to break up the problem into manageable segments for this process. Ideation can be accomplished through a variety of techniques, such as brainstorming or sketching. Brainstorming is an ideation technique that is very popular with designers. It promotes out-of-the-box thinking to solve problems using creative, strategic, and sometimes indirect approaches. It allows team members to not just use their own ideas but build on the ideas of others as well.

An ideation process allows project team members to ask questions and combine different perspectives and generate a variety of innovative solutions that go beyond the obvious.

## Prototype development

The ideation phase will help generate the best possible solution that can be used to build a prototype. The prototype will provide various stakeholders with the ability to understand what a product would look like. A variety of prototypes can be generated at this stage. The options can include functional prototypes, user experience prototypes, or working prototypes of subsystems. Prototypes allow early validation of the best possible solution and enable teams to obtain feedback on proposed transformation solutions.

## Extensive test stages

testing stages after the prototype and MVP phases are the most important parts of this process. They provide key decision points for the project progressing to the next stage or being canceled. The testing process is designed to test the hypotheses, validate product requirements, and obtain user feedback on the intended product.

Moonshot projects require a great deal of experimentation. It is very important to rapidly build prototypes early in the process and conduct extensive testing to gain insight into the problem. Multiple iterations of rapid prototyping and test cycles will provide wide-ranging insights about different potential solutions and whether they will work or scale. This approach allows us to quickly expose complications with potential solutions and provide learning that will enable the team to reach objective decisions to either graduate to the next stage or terminate the project.

Test planning after the prototype stage should include obtaining feedback from various stakeholders along with normal and extreme users.

## The minimum viable product stage

As the name implies, the **Minimum Viable Product** (**MVP**) is built with the minimum number of functional features needed for it to be made available to users. Since an MVP is a basic working model, it can help validate product design and feasibility. The selection of the minimum number of features in an MVP is context-dependent and is determined with the help of various stakeholders, including marketing and sales functions, collaborating with the project team. Building an MVP generates the maximum amount of information about the likelihood of successful development and customers adopting the final product with a sustainable expenditure of resources (talent, money, and time).

### How to graduate or cancel the project

Exploratory or moonshot projects are designed to address complex problems with unconventional solutions, possibly based on advanced technology. Since talented people, money, and time are scarce resources, it is critically important to determine when to cancel a project or idea in this process. There are two critical testing phases: 1) after the prototype is built, and 2) after the MVP has been built. The project team should have a provision for an evaluation team that can conduct rapid evaluation at either of these two testing phases to assess the viability of the project based on the test results, as well as having the potential to realize the best possible solution for the problem. The evaluation team can recommend graduating the project for the next level of development, pivoting back to the ideation phase, or canceling the project. Canceling the project at the prototype or MVP stage allows the organization to retain its learning and at the same time quickly free up the moonshot project team to go to the next challenge.

In this section, we learned how to go through a structured process to decide whether to persist (graduate) or pivot (cancel) a project.

## Some lessons from X Development for moonshot projects

X Development is a subsidiary of Alphabet, Inc. It was founded by Google in 2010 as a research and development facility that works on moonshot projects. Here are some of the basic tenets that the company embraces:

- Shoot for technical solutions that are 10 times better and not 10% incremental improvements: `https://www.wired.com/2013/02/moonshots-matter-heres-how-to-make-them-happen/`.

- Astro Tellar, leader of X Development, recommends for moonshot projects a balance of unchecked optimism to fuel a vision with a harness of enthusiastic skepticism to breathe reality into those visions: `https://www.cmu.edu/news/stories/archives/2016/october/astro-teller-frontiers.html`.

- The best evaluators for a project are like player-coaches. They create, they manage, and then they return to creating: `https://www.theatlantic.com/magazine/archive/2017/11/x-google-moonshot-factory/540648/`.

- Do the hardest thing first: `https://www.inc.com/business-insider/alphabet-google-x-moonshot-labs-how-people-work-productivity-monkey-first.html`.

Now that we've looked at moonshot projects, let's now look at how to sustain and scale innovation over time.

# Sustaining the pace of transformation

Now that we have reviewed the critical success factors for a transformation and have looked at examples of playbooks, we're ready to talk about sustaining and scaling digital transformation. When we talk about scaling a transformation, we need to go back to the ideas at the beginning of this chapter and ensure that we are clear on the goals for the transformation. There are a number of potential goals for your transformation. Three of the most common ones are these:

- Delivery of a single product or process
- Creation of a digital center of excellence
- Transformation of the entire enterprise

Next, we will review each goal in more detail.

## Delivery of a single product or process

If the goal of your transformation was to deliver a single product, then once you have delivered that product or process, there is no need to sustain your transformation. However, few organizations have any interest in a one-off transformation. Even if a transformation was sold that way, once the product is complete, most organizations will see the value in continuing on the transformation journey. Those organizations will need to choose whether to create a center of excellence or embark on a broader transformation, which we will discuss in the following sections.

## Creation of a digital center of excellence

Many organizations decide that rather than trying to scale their digital transformation throughout the organization, they will create a digital center of excellence. This is often an outgrowth of an innovation lab. Digital centers of excellence don't face the scaling problems that we will discuss in the next section. However, they have their own set of challenges when trying to sustain a digital transformation.

When a digital transformation is implemented as a center of excellence, it is often seen as a silo where some of the engineers have the opportunity to work on exciting projects while the rest of the organization focuses on keeping the lights on. This can breed resentment within the rest of the organization. It can also result in a highly cohesive but insular digital transformation team that, over time, loses touch with the needs of the business and, because the team is static, does not grow and change through the infusion of new skills and ideas.

The leaders of the center of excellence must focus on building relationships with the rest of the organization to ensure that the center of excellence continues to work on the right projects and stays relevant. They must also develop rotation programs that will ensure that new staff join the organization on a regular basis from other parts of the organization and from outside the organization. Finally, product owners and other business and technical experts from outside the center of excellence must be embedded in the center of excellence for each project or the center of excellence staff must embed in the business. This ensures a shared understanding of the business needs, dramatically increasing the likelihood of project success.

An example of a successful model for a center of excellence is the **United States Digital Service** (**USDS**). USDS staff are limited to 4-year terms to ensure a constant flow of new blood into the organizations. In addition, USDS does not complete projects independently; USDS staff are embedded in the departments and agencies they support, becoming part of their project teams rather than operating independently.

## Transformation of the entire enterprise

Certainly, the most ambitious model for digital transformation is scaling at the enterprise level. Scaling a digital transformation to an entire enterprise is extremely challenging and there are few examples of organizations succeeding at this effort. However, even if it is your intention to ultimately scale your transformation to the entire enterprise, this is not the logical next step after the first project's success.

Following the success of an organization's first digital transformation efforts, there will be a great deal of excitement and energy around the transformation. Most likely, other teams within the organization that have seen the success of the first digital transformation will be interested in transforming their teams as well. The excitement following the first successful transformation project is an opportunity to extend the coalition of the willing that was discussed in the first section of this chapter.

In *Chapter 2, Transforming the Culture in an Organization*, we discussed Geoffrey Moore's technology adoption model. The principles of that model can be used to describe the adoption of digital transformation in an organization. The initial digital transformation project team are the innovators in Moore's model. Senior leaders, managers, and project team members who express an interest in becoming part of the digital transformation effort can be seen as early adopters. These teams are fairly easy to bring on board and can be used to spread the ideas and practices of digital transformation throughout the organization. If there are enough early adopters and the necessary cultural changes and development opportunities (also described in *Chapter 2, Transforming the Culture in an Organization*) are implemented across the organization, the transformation can grow organically until it crosses the chasm and is adopted by the majority of the organization. This transformation model requires senior leadership to support the transformation by communicating its importance, embracing the new culture required for the transformation, and providing the resources to train staff in the new way of working. The model requires management to reward team members for working in new ways. Finally, staff must embrace the new culture and skills and be part of the transformation.

A more structured approach to scaling digital transformation is the digital factory model. In this model, the transformation is rolled out across the organization in a structured fashion. In this model, senior leadership authorizes a number of digital factories, generally providing one to support each business unit. The factories rely on the initial digital transformation teams and centers of excellence to provide subject matter expertise in new technologies and methodologies, while the individual factories deliver new digital products to their business units. This model does not rely on the coalition of the willing. However, the structured environment created by the digital factory does not eliminate the need to create a new digital culture and provide staff with the hard and soft skills necessary to operate differently and deliver different products.

As mentioned at the beginning of this section, scaling a digital transformation across a large organization is difficult. In *Chapter 9, Pitfalls to Avoid in the Digital Transformation Journey*, we discussed a number of examples of transformations that failed to scale, including those at both ABB and GE Digital, where the CDO role was created and then eliminated. There are, however, examples of organizations that have scaled their digital transformations, often in unexpected places. We'll look at a few of those next.

## AB InBev

AB InBev has successfully transformed their organization, starting at their breweries and extending all the way to their retailers and customers. AB InBev started with the *Beer Garage*, an innovation lab that experimented with the use of artificial intelligence, machine learning, and IoT to do everything from increasing efficiency and quality at their breweries to monitoring sentiment on social media.

Moving beyond the lab, new capabilities have been deployed to their breweries and the field. The breweries have been transformed into *connected breweries* that leverage IoT to monitor the quality, temperature, and production quantity of each batch of beer. The AB InBev team also created a mobile app that allows stores to request products online and uses machine learning to suggest additional products to order. Retailers no longer need to wait for the sales staff to arrive on-site to place orders. This allows sales staff can focus on higher-value conversations with their retailers when they are on site.

## Unilever

In 2010, Unilever, one of the largest CPG companies in the world, found itself operating in a declining market. It responded to the shift in market dynamics by moving away from packaged foods and toward health and beauty products. This meant that Unilever had to learn how to be agile at scale, beginning their digital transformation journey.

First, Unilever took control of their customer base, shifting from purchasing customer information from market-research firms to gathering their own anonymized data from product registrations, store loyalty programs, and other sources to build a database of over 900 million customer records. They used this massive database to analyze their customers and markets and drive product selection and marketing plans.

Next, in 2018, Unilever's new CEO, Alan Jope, explicitly described Unilever's new strategy to digitize all aspects of their business and leverage data to increase their effectiveness as a company. With the foundation of big data, Unilever has been able to make better decisions faster, reduce costs, and sell more products. As an example, Unilever's database allowed them to target advertisements for Baby Dove in India and achieve the same brand awareness as they would have with traditional methods at one-fifth of the cost.

Unilever also set up digital hubs around the world. These small teams were comprised of analysts who studied and segmented customers based on past behavior while also leveraging artificial intelligence to predict upcoming trends. These teams combined what they learned about past and predicted behavior to build targeted content for consumers.

Understanding customers is important, but it is equally important to be able to deliver products to those customers. Once the company understood its customers better, it found that its supply chain management and master data management were becoming bottlenecks. To resolve this problem, the company implemented robotic process automation to streamline and automate supply chain and data management processes, speeding products to consumers faster.

These final examples demonstrate that, while it is not easy, digital transformation can scale to encompass all of an organization's activities, enabling it to be more nimble and achieve better results.

# Digital transformation at home

As we wrap up the book, some of you may be thinking that you're not in the position to lead a digital transformation in your workplace. Digital transformation can be a grassroots effort, though, and you may have more ability to start a digital transformation project at work than you believe. Regardless of whether you can lead a transformation at work, the technology exists to complete your own personal transformation projects.

In *Chapter 6, Transforming the Public Sector*, we discussed the Village Green and provided links to instructions to build your own Village Green. There are many other citizen science projects that you can engage in that will allow you to gain experience using the digital technologies that we have discussed in this book. You can find these projects in many places, including the US Government citizen science site (`https://www.citizenscience.gov/#`), National Geographic (`https://www.nationalgeographic.org/idea/citizen-science-projects/`), and NASA (`https://science.nasa.gov/citizenscience`).

In addition to engaging in organized citizen science, you can create your own digital transformation. The most common individual digital transformation is the digital transformation of the home. While we aren't quite living in the Jetsons' world of flying cars and robot housekeepers, there are many exciting technologies that you can implement to transform your home. *Figure 11.7* shows some typical smart home being controlled by a mobile app:

Figure 11.7 – Typical smart home and mobile app
This Photo by Unknown Author is licensed under CC BY-SA-NC

We'll use the home of one of our authors as an example. While by no means a fully smart home, the author has used digital transformation to reduce operating costs and increase convenience through the addition of digital technologies. Our author has implemented the following digital technologies, all of which are readily available in the marketplace. While some of these technologies require a substantial investment, the more expensive ones can be leased, and some can be purchased for as little as $150:

- **Solar panels**: The author has installed enough solar panels to replace nearly 100% of the electricity used by their Silicon Valley home, with a year-end *true-up* bill of $15 in the most recent year.

- **Battery backup**: The author has two backup battery packs that not only store power generated during the day for use at night but also manage power usage to optimize cost, sending power to the grid at peak energy use times and drawing power from the grid during times when rates are lowest. The batteries are connected to the internet and will fully charge and conserve power when the possibility of a power outage is high. The solar array and the battery system are managed through a combined mobile app that allows the author to set rate schedules and backup thresholds and monitor power generation and battery status. Of course, the batteries serve as a seamless backup during a power failure as well. On a recent Saturday morning, the author was unaware of a power outage until a neighbor knocked on the door to ask if their power was out. The power was out and the battery backup was performing as expected.

- **Electric vehicle (EV)**: The author also has an EV that charges on a schedule, taking advantage of stored battery power or low energy rates, depending on household power usage. The EV has completely eliminated the author's gasoline bill and time spent at gas stations. In addition, the vehicle receives new features over the air on a regular basis, ensuring that the car gets better over time, something not possible with traditional vehicles.

- **Smart thermostat**: The author has a smart thermostat that can be programmed and then learns from changes made by members of the household and adjusts its program. It also connects to a mobile device and can automatically adjust temperatures based on when the author leaves and arrives home. Temperature can also be adjusted remotely, such as when leaving or returning from a trip.

- **Cameras**: The author has cameras strategically placed to keep an eye on pets when the house is not occupied by people. These cameras recognize and can alert the author to motion inside the home or at a door. The cameras also integrate with mobile devices and can be managed on a schedule or set to turn on when the device leaves the house and turn off when the device enters the home.
- **Alarm system**: While not exactly a new feature in homes, most newer alarm systems, including the author's, are entirely wireless and can be installed in an existing home without running cables. Alarm systems now integrate with mobile devices and can be both set and disarmed remotely.

While our author's home has an extensive collection of household digital technologies, there are many more advanced technologies that you can install in your home, some with as little effort as screwing in a lightbulb. These include the following:

- Smart lights
- Smart doorbells
- Robotic vacuums
- Indoor air quality monitors
- Indoor air purifiers
- Smart watering systems
- Water use monitoring systems
- Water recycling systems

While the smart home technology landscape is still evolving, many of these technologies can be integrated together and controlled by a single system, such as a mobile device or a smart speaker. Upgrading your home to a smart home can be a great opportunity for you to tinker with new technologies as well as making your home more comfortable and efficient, even if you won't have a robot housekeeper any time soon.

## Summary

In this chapter, we learned about the critical success factors for ensuring the success of a digital transformation. We also learned about digital playbooks and how they can provide implementation guideposts for organizations that are transforming. Finally, we learned about methods for and challenges in sustaining and scaling digital transformations.

In this book, we have explored industrial digital transformation from concept to implementation. The first three chapters of the book focused on understanding the basics of digital transformation. We learned what digital transformation is, why culture is important to a successful transformation, and the emerging technologies that enable digital transformation. In the second section of the book, we learned about transformation in a variety of industries as well as the public sector. We also explored the transformation ecosystem and delved into the importance of artificial intelligence to industrial digital transformation. In the final section, we focused on your digital transformation journey. We identified pitfalls to avoid in your transformation journey and provided you with tools to plan your transformation and measure your success.

Thank you for reading this book and joining us on the journey to understand the importance of industrial digital transformation. We wish you success in your own digital transformation journey.

## Questions

Here are a few questions to test your understanding of the chapter:

1. What factors are critical to the success of a digital transformation?
2. Why are playbooks important to the success of a digital transformation?
3. Explain the 70:20:10 percent rule for innovation models.
4. What is a moonshot project?
5. What are some models for sustaining a digital transformation?
6. What are the challenges in maintaining a center of excellence?
7. What is a software factory?

# Other Books You May Enjoy

If you enjoyed this book, you may be interested in these other books by Packt:

**Hands-On Industrial Internet of Things**

Giacomo Veneri and Antonio Capasso

ISBN: 978-1-78953-722-2

- Explore industrial processes, devices, and protocols
- Design and implement the I-IoT network flow
- Gather and transfer industrial data in a secure way
- Get to grips with popular cloud-based platforms
- Understand diagnostic analytics to answer critical workforce questions
- Discover the Edge device and understand Edge and Fog computing
- Implement equipment and process management to achieve business-specific goals

**IoT and Edge Computing for Architects**

Perry Lea

ISBN: 978-1-83921-480-6

- Understand the role and scope of architecting a successful IoT deployment
- Scan the landscape of IoT technologies, from sensors to the cloud and more
- See the trade-offs in choices of protocols and communications in IoT deployments
- Become familiar with the terminology needed to work in the IoT space
- Broaden your skills in the multiple engineering domains necessary for the IoT architect
- Implement best practices to ensure reliability, scalability, and security in your IoT infrastructure

# Leave a review - let other readers know what you think

Please share your thoughts on this book with others by leaving a review on the site that you bought it from. If you purchased the book from Amazon, please leave us an honest review on this book's Amazon page. This is vital so that other potential readers can see and use your unbiased opinion to make purchasing decisions, we can understand what our customers think about our products, and our authors can see your feedback on the title that they have worked with Packt to create. It will only take a few minutes of your time, but is valuable to other potential customers, our authors, and Packt. Thank you!

# Index

## A

AB InBev  393
access to new technology
    challenge  218-220
access to new technology
    challenge, solutions
  challenge-based procurements  221
  contests and hackathons  222
  multi-award vehicles  221
  technology innovation labs  220
Advanced Driver Assistance
    Systems (ADAS)  100, 290
Advanced Driver-Assistance
    Systems (ADASes)  146
Affordable Care Act (ACA)  21
agile development
  as foundation, for digital
      transformation  52-54
  versus traditional development  56, 57
agile development, phases
  continuous improvement phase  55
  development phase  55
  discovery phase  55
agile manifesto
  reference link  53
  values  54

Airbnb Experiences
  reference link  364
Aircraft inspection
  by drones  305
air force software factories
  capabilities  234
alarm system  397
Amazon Web Services (AWS)  316
American Institute of Aeronautics
    and Astronautics (AIAA)
  URL  279
American Telephone and
    Telegraph (AT&T)  40
Application Platform Management
    (APM)  346
Application Programming
    Interface (API)  105, 137
application security testing
  Dynamic Application Security
      Testing (DAST)  324
  Interactive Application Security
      Testing (IAST)  324
  Runtime Application
      Self-Protection (RASP)  324
  Static Application Security
      Testing (SAST)  324

tools 324
approaches, business case
  benefits, defining 355
  implementation approach,
    describing 357
  problem, defining 353, 354
  project cost, estimating 355
  risks, assessing 356
  risks, identifying 356
  ROI, calculating 357
  solution, recommending 356
Arizona State University (ASU) 81
Artificial Intelligence (AI)
  about 294
  for cybersecurity 325, 326
  for dynamic optimization, of
    warehouse operations 307, 308
  for predictive maintenance 300-302
  in aviation 317, 318
  in factories 300
  in healthcare 305
  in image recognition, for quality
    of inspection 304, 305
  in inspection 303, 304
  in medical domain image
    recognition 305, 306
  in quality assurance 303, 304
  organization change,
    influenced by 318-321
  security considerations, for industrial
    digital transformation 322
  versus deep learning 294
  versus Machine Learning (ML) 294
Artificial Intelligence (AI), in Airbnb
  evaluating, whether guest
    can be trusted 319
  experiences, ranking 320

message sentient 320
Artificial Intelligence (AI), in public sector
  about 314
  computer vision 316
  crime sprees, detecting 315
  gunshots, detecting 314
  law enforcement 316
Artificial Neural Networks (ANNs) 294
Asset Performance Management
  (APM) 164
Augmented Reality (AR) 352
Automated Imaging Association
  (AIA) 300
Automated Material Handling
  Systems (AMHS) 180
Autonomous Mobile Robots (AMRs) 308
autonomous shuttle 255
Autonomous Vehicle Computing
  Consortium
  URL 279

# B

Baker Hughes (BHGE) Company 162
BakerHughesC3.ai
  URL 162
Base Transceiver Stations (BTSes) 332
battery backup 396
Battery-Powered Electric Vehicle (BEV)
  about 344
  URL 345
BHC3 Suite capabilities
  for oil and gas sector 163
Bluetooth Low-Energy (BLE) 99
Boeing's Analytx Platform 124, 125
buildings

transforming  205
business case
  developing, for transformation  352
business drivers, industrial
    digital transformation
  identifying  18, 19
  identifying, in commercial sector  19, 20
  identifying, in public sector  21-24
Business Intelligence (BI)  322
business model
  reinventing  145-148
business model canvas, creating
  about  380, 381
  digital transformations, using  381
  exploratory (moonshot)
    project template  385
  industrial digital transformation
    innovation paradigms  381-383
  innovation model, applying
    to public sector  383
  moonshot digital transformations  385
business model, changes
  cash-cow products and offerings
    cannibalization  152-154
  cash-cow products and offerings
    cannibalization, avoiding  152, 154
business outcomes and shareholder
    value, quantifying
  about  44
  digital revenues  44
  productivity gains  45
  social responsibility  45
business process improvements
  about  134, 135
  customer-driven process
    re-engineering  139-141

  data-driven process
    improvement  137, 138
  transformation, using  136, 137
business-to-business (B2B)  339
Business-to-Client (B2C)  130
business-to-consumer (B2C)  339

## C

cameras  397
Car Connectivity Consortium (CCC)
  URL  279
causes, failed transformations
  about  339
  economic failure  343, 344
  misaligned transformation visions
    and expectations  340, 341
  technical failures  344
Centers for Medicare and Medicaid
    Services (CMS)  337
chemical industry
  digitization, for inspection and
    maintenance  173, 174
  digitization, of process control  170-173
  monitoring, for demand predictability
    and optimized delivery  175-177
  transforming  170
Chevron  155
Chief Digital Officer (CDO)
  as leader, of digital transformation  75
  emergence  72
  in public sector  75
  rise  72
chief financial officer (CFO)  210
Chief Information Officer (CIO)
  about  68
  versus Chief Digital Officer
    (CDO)  73-75

Chief Information Security
    Officers (CISOs) 349
chief innovation officer 76
Chief Technology Officer (CTO) 71
citizen experience
  transforming 230
CliftonStrengths
  URL 89
cloud computing 105
cloud computing models
  hybrid cloud 106
  multicloud 107
  private cloud 106
  public cloud 106
Cloud Controls Matrix (CCM) 323
Cloud Foundry Foundation 279
Cloud Security Alliance (CSA) 323
Code-Division Multiple
    Access (CDMA) 99
community-based organizations
    (CBOs) 271
Computed Tomography (CT) 306
Computer-Aided Design (CAD) 357
computer-integrated manufacturing
    (CIM) 180
computing 104
Configurable Logic Blocks (CLBs) 313
consortiums
  about 279-281
  role, in industrial digital
    transformations 279
Convolution Neural Network (CNN) 299
cooperative federalism 247
Coronavirus Aid, Relief, and
    Economic Security (CARES)
  URL 260
coronavirus control
  in New Zealand 262, 263

COVID-19 HPC Consortium
  URL 279
Custom Fleet 137, 143
CyberOptics
  URL 184
cybersecurity
  Artificial Intelligence (AI), using 325

# D

data assets
  about 309
  business case study 309, 310
  monetization 309
  monetization, for high-value
    business scenarios 308
Decentralized Citizen-Owned Data
    Ecosystems (DECODE)
  URL 255
Deep Belief Network (DBN) 299
Deep Boltzmann Machine (DBM) 299
deep learning
  about 294
  versus Artificial Intelligence (AI) 294
  versus Machine Learning (ML) 294
deep learning
  in radiology 306
deep learning algorithms
  about 299
  Convolution Neural Network
    (CNN) 299
  Deep Belief Network (DBN) 299
  Deep Boltzmann Machine (DBM) 299
  Deep Neural Network (DNN) 299
  Long Short-Term Memory
    Network (LSTM) 299
  Recurrent Neural Network (RNN) 299
deep learning (DL) 196

Deep Neural Network (DNN) 299
deep reinforcement learning (DRL)
    for factory scheduling 182, 183
DELFI cognitive 155
Department of Defense (DoD) 234
Department of Motor Vehicles
    (DMV) 338
design thinking 66-70
development, security, and operations
    (DevSecOps) 323-325
digital capabilities
  need for 94, 95
digital competency 72
digital connectivity 253
digital revenue
  about 361
  Airbnb Experiences 364
  digital airports 363
  electricity value chain 361, 362
digital services, capabilities
  about 59
  adoption, of open source
      code and tools 64
  agile 60
  API-first development 62
  cloud 62
  cyber-physical security 63
  DevOps 63
  DevSecOps 63
  Lean practices 65
  open source code repository 64
  shared services 61
  user-centered design 60
Digital Supply Chain (DSC) 156
digital talent
  about 78-80
  capabilities model 80
  scorecard 80

digital transformation
  about 71
  agile development 52-54
  capabilities 82
  case studies, from consumer
      industries 125
  cultural pre-requisites 52
  in consumer products 95, 96
  in manufacturing 95
  in public sector 96
  in response, to public emergencies 96
  pace, sustaining 391
  skills 82
  sustaining 78, 81
  top-down, versus bottoms-up 77
digital transformation, examples
  Nest 129, 130
  Peloton 126, 127
  ridesharing 127, 128
digital transformation failures
  about 331
  Motorola 332, 333
  Nokia 335, 336
  Research-In-Motion
      BlackBerry 334, 335
digital transformation, goals
  at home 395-397
  digital center of excellence,
      creating 391, 392
  entire enterprise, transforming 392, 393
  single product or process, delivering 391
digital transformation,
    leadership principles
  about 83
  customer focus 84
  informed risk-taking 83
  learning organization 84
  partnering 85

digital transformation playbooks
  about 375, 376
  products and processes,
    transforming 376-379
digital transformation, societal benefits
  about 365
  COVID-19 pandemic, response 368, 369
  in Kenya 366
  Microsoft's Technology for
    Social Impact (TSI) 367
Digital Twin Consortium (DTC) 280
DISC
  URL 89
disruptive innovation 65, 66
distributed computing 104, 105
DMV Reinvention Strike Team 338
driver-assistive truck platooning
  (DATP) 270
drones
  using, in conservation industry 115
  using, in defense operations 114
  using, in emergency response 114
  using, in healthcare industry 115
  using, in infrastructure
    inspections 114, 115
  using, in insurance industry 115
  using, in live entertainment 115
  using, in sporting events 116
Dynamic Application Security
  Testing (DAST) 324

# E

ecosystems
  role, in industrial digital
    transformations 279
Edge AI and Vision Alliance 285

Electricity Economic Optimizer
  (EEO) 361
electric vehicle (EV) 396
emerging platforms, AI
  big data 111, 112
  image recognition 111
  virtual agents 110
emerging platforms, robotics
  about 112
  drones 114
  industrial robotics 112, 113
  medical robots 113, 114
emerging technologies
  3D printing 118-120
  digital platforms 123, 124
  digital thread 122, 123
  digital twins 120
  identifying 97
  identifying, ways 97, 98
  industry landscape 98
  maintenance types 120
  supply chain 122, 123
emerging technologies, AI
  about 109
  deep learning platforms 110
  machine learning platforms 109, 110
emerging technologies, AR
    and VR landscape
  about 116, 117
  applications, in manufacturing 117
  medical applications 117
emerging technologies, maintenance types
  about 120
  condition-based maintenance 121
  predictive maintenance 121
  preventive maintenance 121
Enhanced Dynamic Global
  Execution (EDGE) 70

Index  407

Enneagram
  URL  89
ensemble learning algorithms
  about  298
  averaging  298
  boosting  299
  bootstrap aggregating (Bagging)  298
  reference link  299
  stacking  299
  voting  298
Enterprise Ethereum Alliance  280
Enterprise Resource Planning (ERP)  300
environmental protection
  about  247
  story maps, examples  248
  story maps, using  247
  Village Green project  248, 249
European Union Agency for
    Cybersecurity (ENISA)  323
Exhaust Gas Temperature (EGT)  317
Experienced Architecture Leadership
    Program (EALP)  82
Exploration and Production (E&P)  155
exploratory (moonshot) project template
  about  385
  business case  386
  innovation process steps  388
  project team  387
Export Administration
    Regulations (EAR)  267

# F

facility monitoring  205
failed transformations
  about  336
  causes  339
  cybersecurity challenges  348

  private-sector failures  339
  public sector failures  336
Failure Mode and Effect
    Analysis (FMEA)  304
Federal Aviation Administration
    (FAA)  69
Federal IT Acquisition Reform
    Act (FITARA)  338
field-programmable gate arrays (FPGAs)
  about  185
  using, in edge solutions  313
Food and Drug Administration
    (FDA)  269
front opening unified pod (FOUP)  179
Fuel Cell-Powered Electric
    Vehicle (FCEV)  345

# G

General Electric (GE)  33, 35, 368
Global Navigation Satellite
    System (GNSS)  99
Global Positioning System (GPS)  95
Global Shipping Business
    Network (GSBN)
  URL  267
Global Technology Systems (GTSes)  153
government culture challenge
  about  222
  compliance culture and
    misaligned incentives  223
  inappropriate decisions and
    decision-makers  224
  organizational fatigue  224
  risk aversion  223
government operations
  about  232
  in Nebraska state  232, 233

government services
  expectation, by citizens 231
  role 231
Government Technology and
    Services (GTS)
  URL 280
gross domestic product (GDP) 170
Ground Power Units (GPUs) 360

# H

Health and Human Services
    (HHS) 21, 337
HealthCare.gov 21
Heating, Ventilation, and Air
    Conditioning (HVAC) 325
Hexaco
  URL 89
hiring challenges
  about 225, 226
  responding to 226
hiring challenges, solutions
  preferences, setting 227
  special hiring authorities 228
  streamlined hiring, for
      high-demand positions 227
  training 227
Home Area Network (HAN) 130
Human Capital Management (HCM) 215

# I

IATA Res 753 282
IBM Watson Expert 306
independent digital services office 76
industrial companies, challenges
  about 157-159
  overcoming 160

overcoming, by partnership 162-164
overcoming, with business model
    change by Tesla 160
overcoming, with digital technology 161
Industrial Control Systems (ICSes) 325
industrial digital transformation
  about 16, 17
  AI 28
  analytics 27
  business drivers, identifying 18
  challenges, in public sector 218
  data aggregation 27
  evolution 30, 32
  failure indicators 328
  impact, on business 42, 43
  optimization and simulation 29
  partnerships 270
  partnerships and alliances 283
  phases 45, 46
  playbooks 375
  revolution 36, 40
  revolution, Industry 4.0 40-42
  sensing 26
  statistical analysis 27
  success factors 372-375
  technology drivers, identifying
      for transformation 24-30
  transformation opportunities,
      and crises 32-36
  visualization and dashboards 29
industrial digital transformation,
    failure indicators
  about 328-330
  lack of strategy development 328
Industrial Digital Transformation
    (IDT) failures 328
industrial digital transformation, phases
  about 46-48

concept  46
customer trials and compliance
    and regulatory testing  47
design  47
manufacturing  47
prototype and validation  47
industrial digital transformation projects
    autonomous vehicles  269, 270
    exploring  266
    farm folk  268, 269
    shipping industry  267, 268
Industrial Internet Consortium
    (IIC)  280, 322
Industrial Internet Incubator (I3)  347
Industrial Internet of Things (IIoT)  154
industrial manufacturing
    design prototyping, of mechanical
        parts  200, 201
    disrupting  198
    flexible manufacturing  198-200
    techniques, for preventing
        downtime  201, 202
    value beyond product  202-204
industrial sector, state
    about  154
    oil and gas industry  155
    semiconductor industry  156
industrial worker safety
    promoting  210, 211
Inertial Measurement Units (IMUs)  116
Infrastructure as a Service (IaaS)  105
InnerSense
    URL  184
innovation process steps,
        moonshot project
    about  388
    canceling  390
    extensive test stages  389

graduating  390
ideation  388
Minimum Viable Product (MVP)  389
problem statement, defining  388
prototype development  389
Intelligent Passenger Security
    System (IPSS)  316
Intensive Care Unit (ICU)  33
Interactive Application Security
    Testing (IAST)  324
International Air Transport
    Association (IATA)  280, 358
International Data Corporation (IDC)  74
International Electrotechnical
    Commission (IEC)  283, 284
International Traffic in Arms
    Regulations (ITAR)  267
Internet of Things (IoT)
    about  95-99, 177
    applications  184
    computing  104
    sensing technologies  102-104
Inverse Reinforcement
    Learning (IRL)  297
IoT computing
    cloud computing  105
    contextual applications  107, 108
    distributed computing  104, 105
    situational awareness
        applications  107, 108
IoT connectivity
    5G technology  101
    about  99
    bluetooth  99
    cellular  100
    Low Power Wide Area Network
        (LPWAN)  100
    Wi-Fi  100, 101

Zigbee  101
IoT sensors
  case study  184
iterative model
  reference link  53
IT Service Management (ITSM)  90

## J

Janadhan-Aadhaar-Mobile (JAM)  259
Jedec  284
Joint Center for Energy Storage
    Research (JCESR)  280
Joint Venture (JV)  162

## K

Kanban
  URL  227
Kelley Blue Book
  URL  160
Key Performance Indicators
    (KPIs)  303, 360
K-Nearest Neighbors (K-NN)  109

## L

Lean Startup  57, 58
Light Detection and Ranging (LIDAR)  17
Line of Business (LoB)  73
Linux Foundation  280
Long Short-Term Memory
    Network (LSTM)  299
Long-Term Evolution (LTE)  278
Los Angeles International
    Airport (LAX)  364
Los Angeles World Airports (LAWA)  363
Low Power Wide Area Network
    (LPWAN)  100

## M

Machine Learning (ML)
  about  294, 310
  Micro-Electromechanical System
    (MEMS) sensors framework  311
  micro-electromechanical system
    sensors framework  311, 313
  versus Artificial Intelligence (AI)  294
  versus deep learning  294
maintenance, repair, and
    overhauls (MRO)  318
manufacturing ecosystem
  digitization, for risk management  210
  role of digitization  208, 209
  transforming  207
Manufacturing Execution
    System (MES)  199
Massachusetts Institute of
    Technology (MIT)  193
Massive Open Online Courses
    (MOOCs)  318
Master of Global Management (MGM)  81
Material Control System (MCS)  181
Mean Time to Failure (MTTF)  301
Mergers and Acquisitions (M&As)  35
Microcontrollers (MCU)  311
Micro-Electromechanical System
    (MEMS)  102, 311
Microsoft Azure Marketplace
  URL  123
Minimum Viable Product
    (MVP)  55-59, 389

# Index 411

misaligned transformation
visions and expectations
about 340, 341
British Broadcasting
Corporation (BBC) 342
Ford Motor Company 342
ML algorithms
categories 296
deep learning algorithms 299
ensemble learning algorithms 298
reference link 296
RL algorithms 297, 298
selecting 295
Mobility-as-a-Service (MaaS) 269
Model Predictive Control (MPC)
reference link 172
Myers-Brigg Type Indicator
URL 89

# N

National Institute of Standards and
Technology (NIST) 266, 322
URL 189
Natural Language Processing (NLP) 319
Nest 129, 130
Nike Digital Sport (NDS) 346

# O

Obamacare 21
Omnitracs 99
online learning 245-247
On-Road Integrated Optimization
Navigation (ORION) 69
On-Time Delivery (OTD) 298
Open Data Center Alliance 280
Open Fog Consortium 281

Open Meter
architecture 251
Open Platform Communications
Foundation 281
OpenPOWER Foundation 281
Open Subsurface Data Universe
(OSDU) 155
OpenWeave
URL 130
Operations Technology (OT)
about 161, 277
URL 329
Oracle Cloud Marketplace
URL 123
Original Equipment Manufacturer
(OEM) 359
Overall Equipment Effectiveness
(OEE) 303
Overall Line Efficiency (OLE) 303
Over-the-Air (OTA) updates 20, 125, 160

# P

particulate matter (PM2.5) 103
partner programs
about 277
Independent Software
Vendor partners 278
resellers 278
technology partners 277
telecommunication partners 278
partner programs, semiconductor
company ecosystems
about 289
ARM AI Partner program 290
ARM Partner programs 289
automotive 290
caution 291

infrastructure 290
mobile technologies 290
security 290
STMicroelectronics (ST)
    Partner Program 289
partnerships and alliances
  about 283
  Edge AI and Vision Alliance 285
  International Electrotechnical
      Commission (IEC) 283, 284
  Jedec 284
  Semiconductor Equipment and
      Materials International (SEMI) 284
partnerships, for industrial
    digital transformation
  about 270
  partner programs 277
  public-private partnerships 271
PCBWay
  URL 200
Peloton 126, 127
Personal Protective Equipment (PPE) 368
Platform as a Service (PaaS) 346
point anomalies 186
policy and governance echo
    chamber concept 71
printed circuit board (PCB) 200
private-sector failures
  about 339
  Blockbuster, versus Netflix 339
Product Lifecycle Management
    (PLM) 199
Profit & Loss (P&L) responsibilities 73
Programmable Logic Controllers
    (PLCs) 199, 300
Proportional, Integral, and
    Derivative (PID) 171
public-private partnerships

about 271
billboard 274
Columbus Smart City Project 276, 277
examples 272-274
Partnership for Next-Generation
    Vehicles (PNGV) 275, 276
preparing for 272
structuring 272
public safety
  ensuring, by temperature and
      crowd detection 235, 236
public sector challenges, industrial
    digital transformation
  about 218
  access, to new technology 218, 219
  budgets and technical debt 228, 229
  digital divide 229, 230
  government culture 222
  hiring challenges 225
public sector failures
  about 336
  California DMV 338
  HealthCare.gov 337

# R

Radio-Frequency Identification
    (RFID) 358
Random Under Sampling (RUS) 193
Receiver Operating Characteristics
    (ROC) curve 302
Recurrent Neural Network (RNN) 299
Reinforcement Learning (RL)
    algorithms 295-298
Remaining Useful Life (RUL) 301
Remote Operation Control
    Centers (ROCCs) 177
reorganization

Index  413

versus strategic transformation  76
Request for Proposal (RFP)  21
Research-In-Motion (RIM)  334
resident services
　about  242
　non-emergency reporting (311)
　　applications  242, 243
　online permitting and remote
　　inspections  243, 244
Return on Investment (RoI)
　about  353
　airline baggage, handling  358, 360
　business productivity  358
　process efficiency gains  358
reverse-mentoring programs  81
revolutions per minute (RPM)  126
ridesharing  127, 128
Robotic Process Automation (RPA)  319
Runtime Application
　　Self-Protection (RASP)  324

## S

SalesForce AppExchange
　URL  123
San Francisco Airport's (SFO's)  363
semiconductor company ecosystems
　about  285
　nucleo ecosystem  287, 288
　partner programs  289
　STM32Cube ecosystem  288
　STMicroelectronics ecosystem  286
Semiconductor Equipment and
　　Materials International (SEMI)
　about  284
　URL  179, 281
semiconductor industry
　Automated Material Handling

　　Systems (AMHS)  180-182
　big data, and digitization for
　　yield management  192
　big data, for yield
　　troubleshooting  194-196
　digital twin  190, 191
　digitization  178, 179
　digitization, for process control  188
　digitization, for process monitoring
　　and control  183
　digitization, of inline
　　inspection  196, 197
　lights-out manufacturing  178, 179
　ML, for yield prediction  192, 193
　process control  190, 191
　standards, significance  179, 180
　transforming  177
　virtual metrology  189
sensing technologies  102-104
sensor data
　about  184
　for predictive maintenance  188
Service Level Agreement (SLA)  359
shape anomalies  186
shipping industry form, examples
　bill of landing  267
　certificate of origin  267
　commercial invoice  267
　Destination Control Statement  267
　inspection certificate  267
　Shipper's Export Declaration (SED)  267
Short Message Service (SMS)  334
smart buildings  206, 255
smart cities mission
　about  252
　in China  260, 262
　in India  260
smart homes  253, 254

smart metering  250
smart thermostat  396
Société Internationale de
    Télécommunications
    Aéronautiques (SITA)  358
soft skills, for delivering digital
    transformation
  about  85
  coaching and employee development  88
  diversity  88
  effective feedback  87
  emotional intelligence  86
  equity  88
  inclusion  88
  integrity  88
  meeting management  87
  personal accountability  87
  personality and work styles  89
  trust  88
Software as a Service (SaaS)  106
solar panels  396
Spikes
  reference link  352
sport utility vehicle (SUV)  200
Static Application Security
    Testing (SAST)  324
Station Controller  181
statistical process control (SPC)  27
STM32Cube ecosystem  288
STM32 Open Development
    Environment (STM32 ODE)  286
STMicroelectronics (ST)
    Partner Program  289
Stock Keeping Units (SKUs)  307
Storage as a Service (STaaS)  27
strategic transformation
  versus reorganization  76

Substitution, Augmentation, Modification,
    and Redefinition (SAMR)  244
Supervisory Control and Data
    Acquisition (SCADA)  325
supply chain management
  concerns  207, 208
Support Vector Machines (SVMs)  326
Sustainability Development
    Goals (SDGs)  41
System Integrator (SI)  277
System on Chip (SoC) circuits  289

# T

Target Wake Time  101
technical failures
  about  344
  battery-powered electric vehicles,
      versus hydrogen fuel cell
      electric vehicles  344, 345
  GE's build-versus-buy dilemma  346-348
  Nike  346
technical skills, for delivering
    digital transformation
  about  89
  conferences and off-site training  90
  cross-training  90
  degree programs  90
  formal education  90
  in-house training classes  90
telegestore system  250
telemedicines  237, 238
testbeds
  URL  282
the Industrial Internet
    Consortium (IIC)  344
third-party logistic providers (3PLs)  208
Time on Wing (ToW)  203, 304

time series
  anomaly detection  185-188
time to market (TTM)  200
Total Productive Maintenance (TPM)  304
Toyota Production System (TPS)  304
TradeLens
  URL  268
traffic management  240, 241
transformation, on national
    and global scale
  about  255
  airports  256, 257
  Digital India  258, 259
transformations, across government
  about  231, 232
  education  244
  environmental protection  247
  government operations  232
  healthcare  236, 237
  military  234
  public safety  234
  resident services  242
  social services  239, 240
  transportation  240
  utilities  250
Travel Security Administration (TSA)
  URL  34

## U

ultra-wideband (UWB)  205
Unilever  394
United Parcel Service (UPS)  69
United States Digital Service
    (USDS)  21, 392

US Advanced Battery
    Consortium (USABC)
  URL  281
US Environmental Protection
    Agency (EPA)  23

## V

Very Large-Scale Integration (VLSI)  94
virtual metrology  189
Volatile Organic Compound
    (VOC)  103 , 205

## W

waterfall model
  reference link  53
worker safety solution
  designing  212-215
World Wide Web Consortium (W3C)  281

## Z

Zigbee  101